Virgil Fox
(The Dish)

An Irreverent Biography of the Great American Organist

by Richard Torrence *&* Marshall Yaeger
Based on a memoir by Ted Alan Worth

Contributions by
William Armstrong, M.D., Marilyn Brennan *(photo editor)*,
Louise Clary, Andrew Crow, Carlo Curley, Steven Frank,
Robert Fry, Albert Fuller, Robert Hebble, David Lewis,
Douglas Marshall, Richard Morris, T. Ernest Nichols,
Michael Stauch, Frederick Swann,
Charles Swisher, and Floyd Watson

Designed by
Len Levasseur

Published by
Circles International

Commissioned by
The Virgil Fox Society

Virgil Fox
(The Dish)

An Irreverent Biography of the
Great American Organist

Copyright © 2001
by Richard Torrence & Marshall Yaeger

Circles International • One Lincoln Plaza 32P
New York, New York 10023 • 1/(212) 875-1941
www.organarts.com

Manufactured in the United States of America

THIRD PRINTING

The photo on the cover of this book (by Truman Moore) was used in advertising on the subways of New York by the renowned music publicist Alix B. Williamson to promote the first of four "Fanfare for Organ" concerts performed by Virgil Fox at New York's Philharmonic Hall, Lincoln Center for the Performing Arts during the 1969-70 season. Next to the photo was copy that included a recipe for "Chicken à la King of Instruments." The photo became part of an extraordinary press kit prepared by the publicist to promote Virgil Fox concerts throughout the country. (The photo was supposed to be used in the food sections of local newspapers.)

Virgil Fox had imported the overhead chandelier from Italy ("In a box the size of a Volkswagen," he used to say); but Richard Torrence had to lend him the chafing dish for the photo, since—despite numerous place settings he had collected in Europe—there were almost no pots and pans in his kitchen with which to cook. The Italian faience dishes and candelabra were his, however, as was the Georg Jensen sterling silver serving spoon. Virgil Fox never cooked, but he loved to entertain with the many sets of dishes he had purchased during his travels.

Overleaf and back cover photos by Don Jacobsen.

A great man is he who
never loses the heart of a child.
Mencius
c. 370-300 BCE

You can take the boy out of Princeton,
but you can't take Princeton out of the boy.
Anon.

I have something marvelous to share.
If you come across, I'll come across!
Virgil Fox
May 3, 1912 - October 25, 1980

Contents

Virgil Fox at Cannon Beach, Oregon (early 1970s) — (photo by Rodgers W. Jenkins)

Prelude

Marshall Yaeger

The idea for this book about the most successful American organist in the history of the instrument might be credited to me. It came about when my partner, Richard Torrence, and I visited Ted Alan Worth (who had been the late Virgil Fox's confidant, protégé, and artistic heir) in San Francisco in the late 1980s. Richard had been Virgil Fox's manager from 1962 to 1979, and I had written most of Virgil's—and Ted's—flyers, pressbooks, and record liner notes during the 20-year duration of "Richard Torrence Management" and its successors.

Teddy, who had always appreciated my literary talents (especially after I wrote so many glowing tributes to his enormous talent—for which he paid me, of course—but which were nevertheless all true!) suggested that I should write Virgil's definitive biography, "warts and all." I knew I lacked the most rudimentary knowledge and musicality required even to dream of such an undertaking; and so I suggested that Ted write the first draft of such a book, and I would take it from there. I even gave him my first Macintosh computer (vintage 1984) with which to do it!

Alas, Ted never learned to use a computer; but he spent at least an hour every morning (usually, while watching I Love Lucy *reruns) for several years completing a 375-page manuscript in longhand, which he gave to his best friend, Richard, shortly before dying of cancer in 1998. When I saw the completed manuscript and realized the amount of work required just to read it—not to mention typing it up!—I dumped the entire project into Richard's able hands and wished him the best. Much later, after considerable work had been done, Richard brought me back into the project, mainly as the editor. The original foolscap manuscript now resides in the archives of the Virgil Fox Society for anyone curious enough to check the original against Richard's and my "improvements."*

Ted did exactly as I had instructed him to do: "Write as automatically as you can; and don't bother with spelling, punctuation, or style—we'll take care of all that when the time comes."

His result was a single, pen-written paragraph, 375 pages long.

Richard typed up the first two-thirds of the manuscript, editing out hundreds of "wonderfuls" and "verys" as he went along; and Dennis Block kindly volunteered to type up the last third, unedited. I thought I had removed all the remaining "wonderfuls" by the time I finished editing until I tallied up the final number that remained and discovered 97 still present, plus 37 "splendids" (which was only one of my several solutions to Ted's overuse of "wonderful").

Try as I might, I couldn't refrain from altering all but ten of the Worth/Torrence sentences, all of which occurred in the last section of the book—and all of which I reproduce here in their entirety (for the curious) in the order in which they appeared, for they tell their own story:

> Why not? His face would radiate with joy. He had always been our support and leader. Francesco Ruffatti had arrived there to supervise the finishing of the reed stops. He was overjoyed to see Francesco, and delighted to meet Keith. Ladd knew the Poulenc well. Rubin was CEO and President of one of Austin's most prestigious banks, and Jimmy was Vice President. This portion of the service was inspiring and touching. The afternoon of November 9, 1980 was sunny and warm. These men carried the casket down the main aisle of the Cathedral as I played Mulet's "Thou Art the Rock."

The severity of the editing process indicated by the number of all the other sentences in this book was no harsher than Richard or I would have been with our own first drafts. (I often rewrite sentences 10 or 15 times before I'm satisfied; and I insisted that Ted not rewrite a thing.) Throughout, I tried to revise everything as if Ted were doing it, stating his opinions or reflecting his impressions, especially when they differed from my own.

Editing Ted's manuscript about Virgil was an emotional experience for me (as well as for Richard) that was unlike any other writing task I ever completed. I laughed and cried and ended up awestruck at the depth of character these two men demonstrated with considerable flash throughout their extraordinary lives, "warts and all." Above all, Ted's compassion and sincere affection for so many odd characters whom we both knew affected me deeply. I would never let stand an expression like "this dear friend," or "that dear soul" in my own writing; but I let pass all such examples of Ted's extraordinary regard for the tenderest qualities that can attach to human beings.

Ted didn't write much about his lover of more than 30 years, Reid Betten (who died of stomach cancer nearly two years before Ted). Therefore, let me just say, here, that Reid was ever cheerful, ever lovable, ever moody, ever quiet, ever polite, excessively handsome, and not unknown to me—how shall I put it?—in the biblical sense, which caused a silent and permanent tension between Ted and me from the time Ted found out until the day Ted died, 30 years later.

At one point, the two men lived next door to Richard and me in Virgil's Englewood carriage house for a year. I've always believed that that brief affair (which was almost certainly little more than a permanent embarrassment to Reid) when added to the fact of my unforgivable betrayal of Ted's friendship, may have abetted Ted's decision to move back to Philadelphia, and thence to San Francisco, where Ted and Reid sold Rodgers and Ruffatti organs. This move came right at the zenith of Ted's career, by which time he had become one of the highest paid concert organists in the world, after Virgil.

From then on, things declined as Ted changed professions from touring artist to resident salesman—mainly, we all believed, to keep Reid close to him, either out of loneliness, fear, or (I believe) simple mutual adoration.

Ted and Reid maintained their distinguished business for many years. It was called "Organ Arts," which was a name I suggested, and, in Ted's honor, is the name we chose for this publication's website. Their company always seemed to give away its profits in order to provide customers with more complete and glorious instruments. This noble and generous practice finally drove the company into utter collapse.

By that time, Ted and Reid had become so distraught by their catastrophic finances that they decided to commit a double suicide. They actually went so far as to distribute a rather notable collection of pornographic magazines and videotapes to various waste receptacles throughout the Castro district where they lived—

which must have reflected a grave decision, indeed! However, they found that they just couldn't tolerate the smell of a Bronco's exhaust in their crowded garage long enough to stop themselves from breathing. In a tearful, sorry state, they went to bed instead. Ted telephoned Richard in New York the next morning, trying to make light of their futile attempt to end it all. (When dawn arose, they had both rushed out to retrieve their lost cache of smut, but someone had beaten them to it.) Richard put them in immediate touch with a California lawyer who solved their dilemma through bankruptcy protection.

In the end, then, just like Virgil, Ted proved himself to be a colossal, godlike talent who was reduced to human dimensions by love.

And there you have (1) the constant theme of this book, which is the influence love can have on geniuses, as it had on Ted and on his idol, the greatest organist who ever lived, Virgil Keel Fox; and (2) the dish.

1. Enter Ted

I first fell in love with the organ when I was 14. I had moved to San Francisco from Chicago to live for a year with my maternal grandmother—whom I adored, while my parents wound up affairs in the Midwest before moving themselves. I later joined my parents, sister, and brother to live in Menlo Park, which is in the San Francisco Peninsula, just south of the city.

One muggy Sunday afternoon in San Francisco I was particularly bored, and "Nana" suggested I take the California Street cable car up to the great stone Episcopal cathedral (then only half completed) that dominated the top of Nob Hill.

The minute I stepped through the side entrance doors to take in the size and height of the building—with but a moment to gaze at the monumental "conic" blue stained glass windows at the crossing—a great cascade of sound stopped me cold.

There was an organ recital in progress!

I was amazed! After the initial shock, I walked over to one of the great cathedral pillars to catch my breath and generally take it all in.

I had always loved classical music, and had sometimes dreamed of a career as a concert pianist. I was fortunate to have studied with a couple of fine church organists in Chicago, who taught piano to some of the interested choirboys. I didn't like the drudgery of practice, however, and didn't progress rapidly because of it. The experience in Grace Cathedral that Sunday afternoon changed everything.

How auspicious that an impressionable youth should have been in that glorious place at just that moment!

The concert was a recital of the music of Brahms, Schumann, Mendelssohn, and Liszt.

I had never paid much attention to the organ when I was a young choirboy. The instrument led the hymns, of course; and it sometimes got exciting during Stainer's "Crucifixion" or Gounod's "Unfold, Ye Portals"; but it never really attracted me. This concert was a revelation that would have lasting effects on my entire life.

That afternoon's performer was the Resident Organist and Master of Choristers, Richard Purvis. He was internationally known, and he was playing one of the most extraordinary and famous

Æolian-Skinner pipe organs in America. He was also performing some of the greatest masterpieces of Romantic organ literature; but I didn't understand, yet, what he was doing. I was simply entranced.

The concert ended with the great "Fantasia and Fugue on '*Ad nos, ad salutarem undam*,'" by Franz Liszt.

After the final chorale played on the full organ concluded, and the final chord reverberated down the nave of the cathedral, a new convert had been made for the organ. I knew that if this experience was as life transforming as it felt, this determined boy had set out to become an organist!

I can't remember whether it was after that first concert or the following Sunday after the services that I introduced myself to Richard Purvis and explained my determination to be an organist. Mr. Purvis was almost abrupt with me, saying that I would have to audition for him first on the piano before we even discussed moving on to the organ.

Following my audition, Mr. Purvis told me that I would have to study the piano (especially technique), the Bach "Inventions," and so forth with him for several months. Only then could I proceed to study the organ.

Mr. Purvis was right, of course; for an organ student has to prepare properly on one keyboard before progressing to multiple keyboards—to say nothing of adding both feet! Mr. Purvis also suggested that I join the Grace Cathedral choir.

I jumped at the chance.

In the wondrous months that followed, a new world opened to me. I lived for every rehearsal and service, especially Thursday nights and Sundays when we were in the Great Choir (the area of the church between the crossing and the altar) and heard the sounds of that wonderful organ in the hands of Richard Purvis.

Mr. Purvis was a magnetic and powerful person. He ran the choir—indeed the whole cathedral—in an autocratic, strict fashion. He brooked interference with no one, and led the choir like an army drill sergeant. You had to address him as "Sir." He, in turn, referred even to an 8- or 9-year old probation chorister as "Mr. Kelly," or just "Mister."

He could be harsh, and sometimes cruel ("You are all idiots! Who ever told you that you could sing?"); but the boys in the choir adored him because he got the right results; and we were all proud of those results.

His extreme musicality and vitality shone through his sternness, however. When he got the sound effect he wanted, a look of love and approval would come over his face, completely erasing the terrible scowls and frequent rages into which he flew when someone sang the wrong note or committed some other grievous sin.

When he began to teach me the organ, although I practiced diligently, I would sometimes make a foolish error at my lesson and he would say, "Mr. Worth, perhaps your mother should let you be a plumber; then you could still play with pipes! You surely can't play the organ!"

They were harsh words, but Mr. Purvis had an uncanny sense of what would make people mad enough to work hard for him and give him what he wanted. He knew the people who needed strong words (which I guess included me), and those who needed gentler prodding. It always worked.

I made wonderful friends in those early days at the Cathedral. We all shared the same interest in music, especially the music of Grace Cathedral and all the remarkable sounds that poured out of the splendid organ when Mr. Purvis sat down to play.

He was a great player who could improvise superbly on any given theme. It was a real treat to hear him. He was a brilliant colorist who could evoke magical sounds from that instrument that remain uniquely his, even to this day.

A few of us would be at the cathedral almost every waking moment: after school, on Sundays, and on Saturdays, when Mr. Purvis would practice or give lessons. We seized on any excuse to hear the organ and be near his magnetic personality.

Mr. Purvis was also one of the two civic organists at the California Palace of the Legion of Honor, where the two organists alternated every other Saturday and Sunday afternoon, playing on a venerable old E.M. Skinner pipe organ. We never missed any of those concerts by Mr. Purvis. Once, after he had seen me all week long at the cathedral, either for choir rehearsals, services, or generally haunting the place—and still not missing one of the Legion of Honor concerts—he said, loudly and in front of people, "Mr. Worth, must you follow me wherever I go?"

Undaunted by his rejections, I worked ever harder at the organ, devouring every book or periodical I could read on the organ or organists; and anything related to organ or to the great cathedrals, churches, and concert halls that housed those wondrous musical machines. As I recall, I was almost rabidly interested and in love with the organ—and I idolized my teacher.

I was fortunate to be able not just to study with him formally, but to watch Mr. Purvis at choir rehearsals, at cathedral services (where I was sometimes asked to turn pages, which was a signal honor), and generally whenever the organ motor was running.

We students learned much by osmosis—like a sponge—watching a master perform before our eyes: how he made this sound or that; how he achieved astonishing crescendos and de-crescendos; how he made playing a mechanical instrument seem as pliable as conducting a symphony orchestra, to say nothing of familiarizing us with the entire gamut of masterpieces written for the King of Instruments.

It was a heavenly world for me, and I was definitely in the right place at the right time. Many of us were becoming musical snobs (in addition to being "sacristy rats") for we were convinced that any music not performed in the cathedral on its organ was surely not worthy of our attention. Except for the San Francisco Symphony (then conducted by Pierre Monteux), which we were encouraged to attend, nothing could compare with Grace Cathedral's music. We didn't realize at the time that our presumptuous judgment wasn't entirely true

2. Enter Virgil

My idyllic life continued for some time, until one afternoon, after choir rehearsal, Mr. Purvis announced to a few of us who were fascinated with the organ that a famous organist named Virgil Fox, who was Organist of the Riverside Church in New York, was coming to town to give a concert in a week or so. Mr. Purvis thought it would be a good idea for us to hear him.

My first thoughts were that I'd never heard of Virgil Fox (actually, I didn't know of any other famous organist at the time), and the Riverside Church was not Episcopal—how could its organist be any good? To make matters worse, the concert would not take place in the cathedral but in the local Calvary Presbyterian Church, where I was sure the organ and building would be inferior.

Nevertheless, a fellow chorister and I went to the concert, holding our noses high in the air.

The first thing that struck me when we arrived was that Calvary Presbyterian Church was jammed to capacity! We actually had to stand, along with many others.

I was amazed. Except for Christmas or Easter—or some special great event—Grace Cathedral was rarely filled. It was certainly never well attended for an organ recital! The normal attendance was only a few hundred people—the same as the weekend concerts at the Legion of Honor.

Calvary Church turned out to be a wonderful, large Victorian building in the elegant Pacific Heights area of San Francisco. The organ was located high above the choir, and the organ façade dominated the entire front of the sanctuary.

You could see the organ console situated in the middle of the choir area. I thought such a placement was a splendid idea. Grace Cathedral's console wasn't visible to anyone who wasn't seated in a small section of the Great Choir. (Later they got a new, movable console that could be positioned so that everyone could see the player during a concert.)

I remember our excitement: with a packed house and a visible console, we felt something extraordinary was about to happen.

Then I noticed that I couldn't see the music rack on the organ console, or any music in evidence. What was going on?

The minister of the church appeared and made some welcoming announcements, including one about applause for this evening's concert being permitted. Indeed, applause was invited!

How *tacky*, I thought. Grace Cathedral would *never* permit applause! (Happily, that policy was to change within a few years).

The minister then asked the audience to welcome Virgil Fox. A small, bespectacled, but amazingly energetic, youthful, and spirited man strode to the console. He sat down, began to push buttons, adjust stops, and generally look over the console. Aristocratic in manner, he definitely took his time. I couldn't wait for him to begin.

I noticed, again, that there was no music rack, and no sign of music. How could this organist possibly begin without his music? And where was the page-turner?

At last, Mr. Fox finished fooling around with the stops, and seemed poised to begin. Then he turned, swung off the bench, and stood up to face the audience.

Aha, I thought. Now he's going to call for his music and the page-turner!

A wonderfully resonant, almost stentorian voice came forth that was astonishingly clear, even without a microphone. Virgil Fox began to speak about the first work on the program (the "Concerto Number IV in F Major" by George Frederick Handel—complete, in four movements). His remarks were entertaining and informative; and he delivered them with great authority.

(Photo by Bruno of Hollywood, early 1950s)

Then he began to play—from memory.

From the first chord, I knew that this man was a true master. The rhythmic and dynamic way he attacked the manual and pedal keyboards captivated me immediately. A kaleidoscope of Baroque effects emanated from the instrument, alternating with rich orchestral sounds as he skipped from solo organ portions to the orchestra's portions. (The original concerto was written for organ, strings, and woodwinds.)

Toward the end of the first movement, he inserted a decidedly un-Handelian cadenza. It started building in volume, went down to a whisper, then built into a powerful crescendo, culminating in a display of pedal technique on the full resources of the instrument. It took my breath away.

I was especially susceptible, as all young devotees of the King of Instruments are who prefer to hear the instrument played as loud as possible.

Before the last chord of the first movement, the audience burst into a wild ovation; and a star-struck, youthful organ student had a new idol.

Of all of Virgil Fox's students, Carlo Curley is one of the most widely acclaimed popular concert organists today. Now based in London, he was the first classical organist to play a solo organ recital in the White House, and currently appears constantly in recitals and on radio and television. He has made over 30 recordings, as well as the first commercially-available video of a classical organ performance, "Organ Imperial," for Decca International. His book, In The Pipeline *may be ordered from HarperCollins.*

Carlo Curley

I first experienced Virgil Fox in-the-flesh and in concert with no less than the Atlanta Symphony, albeit without Robert Shaw conducting (he was waving his arms abroad). No matter, as I would happily discover that Virgil would be merrily leading the orchestra no matter who was perched on the podium!

As I sat wedged into my seat, the veil was truly rent. As this "devil" performed, my eyes became exophthalmic, my ears grew numb. There was no denying that all my youthful senses were stimulated as never before! Here was a true master, of whose talents I had been disparagingly misled for so long. Any of Virgil's real or imagined artistic infidelities were swept aside in an instant as he gave the Jongen and Handel concerti incredibly moving readings that will remain with me until the moment of my departure from this mortal coil—and probably beyond. Each movement was undoubtedly jealously coveted and meticulously prepared. His soaring sense of rhythm and line; his devotion to making the virtually inaudible passages as moving as the ragingly triple-fortissimo ones; his delicate, daring flirtatiousness with the stops; his shockingly impressive technique—all these things, especially when topped'n'tailed by the man's sheer chutzpah, combined to render me virtually senseless. I do not exaggerate when I say that I left the hall in a daze, mightily confused. That night I yearned for sleep in any quantity, but lay wide-awake until the dawn as though in the throes of a severe, Starbucks-induced high.

To hell with the staid organ purists of my school days. His was a sonic and visual five-star feast served up with extraordinary abandon, yet very much under control, going miles beyond anything I had ever heard or dreamed imaginable. Virgil's performance provided, for the ludicrously low price of a single admission, a far headier elixir than the finest vino collapso. Everything I had gleaned from the naughty nay-sayers had been obviously based on envy and gross misunderstanding. Their views were as transparent as a department store window. I wanted to play as he played. I had to meet this maître. I wanted desperately to work with him. Carlo Curley's dreams were suddenly made real.

3. Meat and Potatoes

A page-turner never did appear, of course. Virgil Fox always performed from memory—a feat that few concert organists attempt, even today. The Handel concerto closed with what I had always thought was a rather dull fugue; but in the hands and feet of this wizard, it was a total joy—thrilling beyond measure.

We were then treated to a wonderful little gem of William Boyce, "Ye Sweet Retreat." It turned out to be a transcription that Virgil Fox had made of a piano arrangement by Harold Bauer. It was tender, lilting, and highly orchestral.

The melody began in the pedal, and alternated between the manuals and pedal throughout. It ended on the softest registers of the instrument with a lush re-harmonization of the opening tune. It was gorgeous.

Then the monumental "Toccata in F" of Johann Sebastian Bach. I heard, for the first time, the speech that Virgil Fox often delivered when introducing a work of Bach's: "It is a far cry from the street songs of any era to the towering counterpoint of Sebastian Bach," as he launched into a general description of what was about to occur and what to look for in the music. With the opening pedal point—thunderingly deep 32-foot stops that shook the building—the canons started as if far in the distance, and began to get louder and more intense with each measure until almost the full organ was on. Suddenly, as every stop was clearly on, the powerful pedal solo began—played completely from memory at a speed I'd never dreamed possible.

With three chords, he began the canons again in the key of C. I was mesmerized, and could barely remain still because it was so rhythmically sound and alive. (This feeling is like what young people experience when first exposed to rock'n'roll: they just can't stop moving to the beat. That visceral experience is the most effective way to win the audience's fancy; and this man had that talent in spades.)

Again, at the close of the "F Major Toccata," there was shouting acclaim and a standing ovation. The artist was clearly delighted with his performance, and with the ovation he richly deserved. I noticed that he was perspiring as he left the console and stepped off the platform, presumably to wipe his brow and to rest. He had given an athletic performance that was also moving, musically.

When he re-appeared, he told the audience that, so far, we had only sampled the appetizers and the soup. As with any fine meal, it was now time for the meat and potatoes!

The main course was to going be a filling one because he had programmed the "Sonata on the 94th Psalm" by the twenty-four year old student and protégé of Franz Liszt, Julius Reubke.

Virgil Fox explained that this overwhelming Romantic masterpiece, one of the major works for organ from that era, was one of the only pieces written by a musical genius that died young. I had never heard of Reubke; but by now, although only forty-five minutes had passed since the concert began, I was ready to believe every word that Virgil Fox uttered!

Reubke's sonata is built on paraphrases on the 94th Psalm. After explaining what to look for in the work, Virgil Fox intoned the opening phrase, "O Lord, to whom vengeance belongeth, show thyself." Following these foreboding words, he began to play the opening, dark measures. The incredible technical (but, more importantly, musical) and orchestral fireworks display that made the next twenty-five minutes speed by boggled my mind! Hands flew, feet flew, and the stops plunged in and out.

Orchestral sounds melded in and out as if blending, as any great conductor would make them do, with an entire orchestra. This man was doing it by himself, and the audience loved it! They responded with a roar of approval that I had never heard, even at the San Francisco Opera House (where the symphony played) or at any solo concert that I had ever attended. I had certainly never heard such acclaim in Grace Cathedral.

During the intermission, one could sense real joy and excitement all around. I couldn't speak.

When we returned to our seats, Virgil Fox treated us to lighter fare. First was an elegant scherzo of Louis Vierne that sounded like the fountains of Versailles. Although it was technically forbidding, he tossed it off as if it were nothing! Then a fine arrangement of the "Londonderry Air," which everybody loves. I thought, how could he put something so ordinary on a program filled with masterpieces? I later learned from the great man that somewhere in every program there must be a melody that everyone recognizes.

The printed part of the program ended with a "stem winder" (in Virgil Fox's words): a toccata by the 19th Century French organist, Henri Mulet, called "Thou, Peter, Art the Rock; and the Gates of Hell shall not prevail against thee." With that piece, Virgil Fox brought down the house. The audience leapt to their feet and demanded more. After three encores (Henry Purcell's "Trumpet Tune and Air," the "Fugue à la Gigue" of Bach, and the "B Minor Toccata" of Eugene Gigout) my mind was dancing with delight and love for this man and his inspiring performance.

There was more.

He began to play an etude for pedals alone by a composer I had never heard of, Wilhelm Middelschulte. He simply announced it *"Perpetuum Mobile* for Pedals Alone." It started out light, delicate, and soft, but soon the feet were flying and I noticed that Virgil Fox was actually playing "thirds" (pedal notes that were two notes, or a third, apart) with his right foot while the left played single notes. All the while his hands continuously manipulated the stops and couplers (in order to connect the keyboards with the pedalboard), adding stops gradually, one by one.

The volume built. Then the left foot started playing thirds. I thought, how is it possible? By this time, the volume and tempo were increasing, and the two feet were a blur. The organ roared! Then the pedals stated the original theme "wide open" (as Virgil would later describe it). Suddenly both feet played crunching chords: three notes with the right foot and two with the left. Then, for the first and last time in the three-minute piece, the right hand, on a manual keyboard, made a glissando and struck the final chord.

I couldn't believe my ears or eyes, although the ovation was deafening all around. Only later did I learn that this piece was the hallmark that Virgil Fox used to close almost every concert. He had arranged the piece himself, and thus had made it his "vehicle." Few organists in the world could copy his virtuosity, although he eventually published his edition of the music for any that dared to try.

Pandemonium raged, and Virgil Fox was repeatedly called back. He motioned for silence, and asked the audience to turn in their hymnals to "The Church's One Foundation." He proceeded to instruct us how to sing this hymn. We were to take deep breaths, filling our lungs with air—as we were supposed to "compete" with him and the organ.

He wouldn't make the competition easy for us, either, for he intended to use "every ounce of wind this organ has in it," and expected us to do the same.

There would be an interlude between the first and second verses; a second between the second and third (lowering the key "for those who always feel hymns are too high"); still another interlude between the third and fourth verses, raising the key higher than in the first verse ("for every brave soprano and tenor"); and finally the last verse in unison, much slower than the first ("with a great Amen going up the scale, not the usual same-note Amen").

He dared the audience to outdo the volume of the full organ; and then he proceeded to play the introduction of this great Protestant hymn with such authority, excitement, and majesty that when the audience began to sing, a roar came out of them that I had never heard come out of any congregation.

The interludes were thrilling, and only seemed to excite the immense crowd to even further determination. By the time the final Amen had sounded, I felt I had witnessed and partaken in a musical miracle. Never before had I heard a sound so thrilling as an entire congregation singing their hearts out, inspired and led by a complete master of his art.

4. My New Ambition

I don't remember how I got home that evening. I was in a daze then and for several weeks after; and I could think of nothing but the magnetic genius that had entered my life and the incredible concert that I was fortunate enough to attend.

My life to that point had been relatively happy, although I didn't have many friends in my first year of high school. (Not too many high school students are interested in churches and pipe organs!) There weren't many musically oriented students to whom I could relate; but the cathedral and Mr. Purvis were godsends to me; and my entire life revolved around the church. I had made a few good friends at the cathedral, where I felt some people cared and were kind to me, and were genuinely interested.

After I experienced the concert by Virgil Fox, however, my life took on a purpose. Now I felt that I, too, must become a concert organist, not just study to become a church organist. I should be someone who did things, who could play the organ like Virgil Fox.

I began to practice much more diligently, and tried to do everything Mr. Purvis instructed me to do at my lessons. He was kind enough to give me free lessons, but he still insisted on sticking to the basics on the piano, and then practicing simply on the organ using chorales, pedal exercises, and simple repertoire. The experience was valuable. Without this background, my dreams would never have been possible.

My dear grandmother was pleased with these developments because she felt she didn't have to worry about me. She was pleased with my new ambition.

My grandmother's sister, Elsa, and her husband, Ludwig Emge, were also influences on me at that time. Uncle Lou was a distinguished gynecologist at Children's Hospital. He had taught at Stanford University and the University of California Medical School, and our whole family was proud of him. Aunt Elsa was a grand woman, and she was interested in music. She had studied piano in Europe; and while living in Chicago, was a pupil of the famous Fannie Blumfield Zeisler. I spent many afternoons listening to Aunt Elsa play the piano.

The Emge's were people of considerable wealth. They were formal, and almost stiff in their bearing, possibly because of their own strict upbringing. They were, however, kind to my dear Nana and me, and we spent a lot of time with them.

I remember seeing my uncle many times at San Francisco's Palace of the Legion of Honor, where he attended the organ recitals. He supported my interest in the organ, and shared 78-RPM recordings with me of many of the great works for organ. (Long-playing records were just about to be introduced.)

One afternoon he played a recording of a work of Mozart: the great "Fantasy in F Minor," K. 608.

What a sound—what energy—what a piece! I wondered how there could have been another performer with the same energy and fire of my idol, Virgil Fox.

It turned out that I was listening to a Virgil Fox recording. It was part of an album he had made at the John Hays Hammond Museum organ in Gloucester, Massachusetts. (That organ and the Hammond Castle in which it was installed would become important forces in Virgil's life, years later.) I listened to that album every time I visited Aunt Elsa and Uncle Lou. They finally gave it to me. It contained the Mozart (written originally for a mechanical clock), the "Sonata I" of Mendelssohn, Bach's "Fugue à la Gigue," and the "Prelude and Fugue in G Minor" of Marcel Dupré. I was determined to learn every one of these pieces, from memory, although, at the time, they were far beyond my abilities.

I got a lot of encouragement from my grandmother and from Aunt Elsa and Uncle Lou. My aunt and uncle even went so far as to promise to help with my musical education when the time came—if I promised to work very hard. My parents, too, were enthusiastic, although at first they only learned about my new ambition through letters and telephone calls. I suppose they all thought that this new idea, to make the organ my life, would be a short lived "phase" that would pass as soon as I discovered how much work I'd have to do. Nevertheless, I did the

Signed: "For T. Alan Worth. Cordially, E. Power Biggs"

work, thanks to nearly daily injections of inspiration from Mr. Purvis, either at the organ, while singing in the choir, or while listening to him teach others or rehearse by himself. Things slowly began to sink in.

Around this time, I became acquainted with the radio programs of E. Power Biggs from the Busch-Reisinger Museum of Germanic Culture at Harvard University. I enjoyed the programs because he played so much early music; but hearing Richard Purvis—and then the great Virgil Fox—had spoiled me. E. Power Biggs was famous; but in my mind, the colorful playing of Purvis and the rhythmic drive and virtuosity of Fox made Biggs dull by comparison. From the beginning, I inclined towards the more dramatic and colorful approach.

5. Virgil Takes Charge

About a year after I first heard Virgil Fox in that concert at Calvary Church, Mr. Purvis announced that the American Guild of Organists would have its Biennial National Convention in San Francisco that coming June, and the cathedral would be the scene of quite a few activities.

What a thrill it would be for me to see and hear all these famous people. I wondered whether Virgil Fox would play at Grace Cathedral. "Indeed not!" Purvis said. "Virgil will play where he belongs, at the Civic Auditorium!"

I thought that was strange, for I wanted to hear the greatest organist on what was for me the greatest organ.

June finally came, and Nob Hill seemed inundated with organists from all over the country. I was not yet a member of the American

Guild of Organists (the "AGO"), and so I could only get in to hear the programs that took place at the cathedral. I did get to hear one famous virtuoso organist by the name of Richard Ellsasser. He played at the Fairmont Hotel on a Hammond organ, and I was not too impressed with the sound of this small, early type of electronic instrument. In fact, I was horrified! I do remember, however, that Ellsasser dressed elegantly, looked good, performed rapidly (probably because of the ugly sound), and played the "Flight of the Bumble Bee" with his feet. He was no match for Virgil Fox, however. I was certain of that!

Mr. Purvis and Searle Wright from St. Paul's Chapel of Columbia University in New York performed splendidly in the cathedral. The legendary organ builder, G. Donald Harrison of the Æolian-Skinner Organ Company of Boston—who built the cathedral organ—was there. Not long before, he had rebuilt the lovely two-manual Æolian organ in the Chapel of Grace. There were concerts scheduled on that organ as well, of music of the Baroque period, just then coming into vogue.

One of Mr. Purvis's students at that time was a young Catholic organist by the name of E. Paul Fitz Gerald. (We could never determine whether it was supposed to be "Fitzgerald" or "Fitz Gerald"; but Paul always included the extra space.).

Another student was a wonderful friend, whom we all adored, named Dora Shively. I saw them often, as they also haunted the cathedral and went to Mr. Purvis's Legion of Honor concerts. They were both a little older than I was, and they were kind to include me in their group. I think they were slightly amused by such an opinionated, young student.

Paul was active in the AGO, and had recently been elected Dean of the San Francisco Chapter. Paul knew how much I adored Virgil Fox, and promised to get me into his concert at the Civic Auditorium. (Just before that time, my parents had finally moved to Menlo Park, which required me to change high schools and curtail my activities at the cathedral somewhat. I had to commute, and that meant taking the train to and from the City and Menlo Park, which is about 18 or 20 miles south of San Francisco. My parents were not pleased with this commuting, but they consented, since it meant so much to me.)

A few days before the Virgil Fox concert, Paul said that Mr. Fox was rehearsing at the Civic Auditorium that evening, and asked if I would like to go to hear him rehearse—and maybe even meet him. I was thrilled at the opportunity, and so we appeared at the Civic Auditorium, a great barn of a place seating 8,000 or so for concerts, at about 7:00 p.m. The big old Austin organ console was in the center of the empty stage, looking impressive with the organ pipes behind it. I could hardly wait until the great man appeared.

However, wait we did. 8 o'clock. 9 o'clock. I was getting worried because my mother would be furious if I wasn't home by 10 o'clock. Finally, at about 9 o'clock, that wonderful voice boomed out of the darkness, "Paulie, Honey! How are you? I'm sorry I'm late but dinner went on too long. And who is this little cherub you have with you?"

I was then introduced to Virgil Fox, who promptly had to know everything about me. Paul explained that I was a young organ student and new fan of his, and had come with him to the rehearsal. Virgil was delighted to have us both there but said, "Young man, does your mother know where you are? It's going to be awfully late when I'm done rehearsing." Before I knew it, he had arranged that I stay with Dora Shively and her parents, and was talking to my mother on the telephone.

"Mrs. Worth, this is Virgil Fox. I have your son here with Paul Fitz Gerald, and I want them to stay for my rehearsal. Teddy can stay with his friends, the Shivelys tonight. Will that be all right?"

My mother was surprised but pleased, and said it would be fine. At least she knew where I was, and with whom.

I'll never forget that first meeting: how Virgil took charge, his kindness, and his genuine interest in a young and adoring fan. His concern for my worried parents was typical of his thoughtfulness and his interest in people's parents and their "roots."

Then he proceeded to change his clothes in preparation for his rehearsal. I was to learn there, and on countless later occasions, that Virgil Fox didn't care who was around when he changed his trousers! If there were women present, he would try to hide behind the console; but he usually went about his business without false modesty.

So, there he was in bold striped boxer shorts, rummaging through a small suitcase for a pair of wrinkled practice pants and some wonderfully shiny patent leather shoes. Thus attired, he began another practice session—which I witnessed that night for the first time.

Whenever Virgil would begin a practice session, and before a performance, he would clean all the keyboards himself. Paul and I were dispatched to the restroom to bring several sopping wet paper towels and several dry ones. After Virgil wrung them out to just the right water content, he began vigorously to scrub the keys, all the while reciting a dissertation about how filthy the keys were and how he "would not have it!" He explained how even his own fingers would leave a residue of sweat that would anger him later, and how he liked the feel of clean, smooth keys.

6. The Big Honk

To see Virgil rehearse that evening at close range was a revelation! He left no detail to chance. He began by setting up pistons to get exactly the sounds he wanted, playing bits and pieces of this piece and that to try out certain sounds. He even asked us, "Kids, what do you think?" Imagine!

The "bits and pieces" were electrifying, and again I fell under the spell of this wizard. My admiration didn't go unnoticed; and Virgil delighted in my enthusiasm, doubling his efforts to impress me.

The organ tuner arrived with some lighting people and stage-hands. The console had to be placed at just the right angle (always so that the audience could see his feet and right hand better—never in the usual organist's way of sitting with his or her back to the audience). "The people want to see more than just your rear end," he laughed.

The lighting was all wrong: he insisted on pink lights and "bastard amber, to make me look human, not like a cadaver or a ghost." There also had to be a "trooper" spotlight to follow him onstage and illuminate him properly during his speeches to the audience.

He presented an endless list of problems to the organ tuners. The tremulants (which create the mechanical vibrato that makes certain solo voice tones sing more beautifully) had to be adjusted—"all of them"—and he would supervise the work.

He never left these adjustments to chance, and had driven many a tuner across North America and Europe into a frenzy over the "trems." He would tell them, "the same vibrato that Kirsten Flagstad has on high F-Sharp in *Tristan and Isolde* is the effect I'm after."

I'm not sure how many organ tuners were familiar with Flagstad or *Tristan*, but they got a pretty good idea of what he wanted by the time they finished their adjustments, many hours later!

"Tune this, Honey; and touch up that; and what about these stops in the Echo Organ?" (a division high up in the ceiling of the Civic Auditorium, nearly a block from the main organ). "I'll need every single stop, and all of them must work perfectly!"

People ran in every direction. It astounded me to see how much extra work Virgil was doing for this concert. In later years, I learned that he put that kind of effort into every performance. It was partly his attention to detail that set him apart from other organists.

By now, it was nearly midnight, and Virgil seemed to come even more alive and get more energetic as the night wore on.

He then started to practice on the first part of the program he was scheduled to play. I particularly remember the opening work, the "Trumpet Voluntary" of Henry Purcell.

The opening trumpet tune makes use of the most commanding solo trumpet voice in the organ, and the auditorium organ had a big Tuba Magna stop that was really telling. Its home was on the fourth keyboard, and so Virgil drew the tuba stop to demonstrate its sonority—but there was no sound. Totally dead!

"What's wrong with the Big Honk?"

The tuners explained that the Tuba Magna had been disconnected at the request of the Civic Organist of the city, as it had once ciphered during a performance. (A cipher occurs when a piece of dirt gets into a pipe or the pouch beneath the pipe, causing the pipe—or sometimes a series of pipes—to blare forth by themselves until someone crawls into the organ to disconnect them. Ciphers are born performers. They love to "perform" in front of large audiences during the softest possible passages, and on the loudest pipes possible!)

"Hook that tuba up right away, dear man! If it ciphers, fix it! For there will be no concert without that stop!"

The offending stop was hooked up forthwith, and Virgil began to play the "Trumpet Voluntary." Although I loved and had heard this piece many times, Virgil's approach amazed me.

The first statement of the tune was on the Tuba Magna, accompanied by a smothered, full organ sound with no pedal. After the first statement, it was repeated on the full organ. The tempo was regal and majestic, yet always with that infectious, rhythmic, forward motion. How could anyone fail to be thrilled by such an approach? One could just picture Queen Elizabeth I in all her grandeur entering Westminster Abbey for a great state function.

It was getting late, and the next thing I knew it was about 3:00 a.m. Paul and I were getting really tired, but Virgil was wide-awake and full of energy. He had given his list of instructions to the organ tuners, and he expected them to begin tuning and repairing things.

He said, "Paulie, how late is that Manning's Cafeteria open?" It was open 24 hours, and Virgil announced that he needed some "sweets." And so we hailed a cab and went off to Manning's Cafeteria. I learned that night that Virgil loved cafeterias, and knew all the good ones in every city in which he had ever played. He particularly liked Manning's because it was open all night.

Virgil's voice was deep and resonant, and could be heard everywhere. He used this effect to his advantage, so that servers would have no doubt about when he wanted something and how he wanted it to be served. He liked cafeterias because he could see all the food, and could try out several possibilities. This evening, however, he had a large ("fresh squeezed") orange juice, peach pie, chocolate ice cream with chocolate sauce ("extra sauce, please!"), and tea with lemon wedges ("could I have three extra wedges, Honey?").

Chocolate, I was to learn, was his passion. He had no interest in vanilla. He certainly was not "vanilla" in nature. I had never heard of chocolate ice cream with peach pie, but he insisted I try it. He was right. I proclaimed it "sheer heaven."

Before we left the cafeteria that evening, he knew the names of several of the help, everyone in the place knew who he was, and he invited everyone to attend the concert.

Virgil made friends wherever he went. At first, people would be curious at this man with the big booming voice who wore a beret, usually caused a minor commotion, and more often than not made a lasting impression.

I soon realized that Virgil was a nocturnal person. He explained that he got more done because there was no one to bother him when he practiced late hours. Most people were asleep, except us, of course, who were fortunate to be a part of his late night rehearsals.

On the road, Virgil wouldn't get up until 3:00 p.m., and usually didn't retire until around 6:00 a.m.

In later years, his sleeping schedule became even more bizarre. I used to wonder how he ever got up on Sunday mornings to play for the services at the Riverside Church. Eventually I learned that he slept no more than three hours and then went to church.

Richard Torrence

*Virgil told me that his father, Miles Fox, had been an auction-
eer, and had a booming voice. He also owned the Princeton, Illinois
movie theatre; and his mother, Birdie E. Fox, ran the box office.*

*When Virgil started playing in public, his father would "pro-
mote" him with introductions to various people, and volubly sing
his praises. This embarrassed Virgil, and he wished his father
wouldn't speak so loudly, and always about him. After Miles died,
however, Virgil realized that he then had to promote himself. He
developed a style of self-promotion that to some people bordered on
that of a circus barker, but probably he was imitating his own
father.*

Bird, Virgil, Warren, and Miles Fox (1918)

The organ of the Civic Auditorium was built for the San
Francisco Exposition of 1915. It was one of the largest organs ever
built at the time, and most of the famous organists of the day played
on it. Camille Saint-Saëns had conducted a performance of his
famous "Organ Symphony" (*Symphony No. 3*) during the opening of
the Exposition. The organ was originally installed in a building built
for the Exposition called California Hall, about half the size of the

Civic Auditorium. After the Exposition, the organ was moved to the much larger Civic Auditorium, where it enjoyed great popularity. Edwin H. Lemare (who composed a piece called "Andantino in D-Flat," later to be sold for a pittance and renamed "Moonlight and Roses") was one of the city's regular organists that enjoyed great fame in the 1920s.

Following its halcyon days, the organ wasn't used often. By this time (mid-1950s), the instrument was definitely beginning to show its age—which didn't deter Virgil in the slightest, as he loved old instruments and had an uncanny way of making them sound in better shape and always more brilliant than they were.

The concert that took place during the AGO Convention was thrilling, and the audience that nearly filled the cavernous space was ecstatic. Another of the features of a Fox concert that had escaped me at the first one I attended was the crowd of adoring fans that surrounded him for autographs. These aficionados insisted on seeing Virgil in order to tell him personally how much they enjoyed his performance.

These after-concert greeting lines were extremely long. They comprised the young, the old, and many odd looking characters. I was amazed at how much time Virgil spent with each person. He called many of them by name: "Eileen! Honey! How are you?"

He would roar the name, embrace the old friend, and ask about the family. He recognized people he hadn't seen in decades, often recalling the exact year and month they met. He was amazing!

Throughout his career, Virgil received throngs of people after every concert. During his years at the Riverside Church in New York, he would receive visitors and devoted followers following the services.

Virgil had "total recall" of faces, and usually names; but more importantly, he was genuinely interested in each person he met. He was most interested in strange and outrageous characters and peculiar looking people, of which there were plenty; and he would have great fun at dinner afterwards describing these people and what they said.

I became even more inspired after the AGO Convention late-night rehearsal and first meeting, and the second concert that followed. I told Virgil how much I wanted to be a concert organist, and he said that it would take a lot of hard work and total dedication. I believed him; for although I had only witnessed one rehearsal, I saw the diligent pains he went to in order to make the concert memorable for everyone.

At the cafeteria after the first rehearsal evening, Virgil had told us how beautiful the new organ at the Riverside Church would be. We asked him about most of the other world-famous organs and organists. He knew almost all of them, but he had a real fondness for anything French. He loved the organs at Nôtre Dame and St. Sulpice in Paris. He spoke glowingly of Louis Vierne, Joseph Bonnet, and Marcel Dupré, with all of whom he had studied. He spoke French fluently; and everything about him made me want to emulate him. His life to me seemed vital and glamorous in almost every way.

I was delighted that he took such an interest in a mere schoolchild, and was more determined than ever to succeed. Virgil told me that if I wanted it badly enough I could attain anything I wanted in this world. As far as the organ as an instrument, he quoted the words of one of his first teachers, Wilhelm Middelschulte (then organist of Holy Name Catholic Cathedral in Chicago). "Dear Boy, the organ is the most mechanical instrument in the world. If you can conquer it—if you can make the instrument bend to your wishes, make musical phrases on it, and give those phrases *expression*—you will have accomplished something few have."

This concept was the main inspiration behind Virgil's approach to his art; and I therefore chose it as the model for my own.

---

7. My Audition

Dora, Paul, Richard Purvis, and many other friends encouraged me; and I began to make progress. What a wonderful experience and environment in which I could grow! Nevertheless, hearing and then meeting Virgil Fox was like throwing gasoline on a few sparks, turning them into an inferno of desire to achieve. I tried to do everything that Mr. Purvis demanded at my lessons; but in addition, I began to work on pieces that I heard Virgil play on the recordings my Uncle Lou had given to me. The first was the "Prelude and Fugue in G Minor" of Marcel Dupré—a work far too difficult for me to attempt at the time; but the fugue was so infectious and rhythmic that I was determined not only to learn it but to memorize it, no matter what.

Both Virgil Fox and Richard Purvis always stressed slow practice, with marked fingering and pedaling (that is, which finger goes on which note; and which heel or toe of which foot goes on which pedal note).

With diligence and determination, plus hours of rehearsal, I could finally play the Dupré work. I remember that after one lesson that didn't go well, I asked to play the work for Mr. Purvis. I thought I played it well; but he flew into a rage, and asked me who gave permission to learn that piece, and why I had been so foolish as to memorize it *all wrong!*

After that daunting experience, I didn't share any more of my extra-curricular pieces; but I did continue to memorize any pieces that I loved.

I'm sure Mr. Purvis knew what I was up to! He always acknowledged that Virgil Fox was a brilliant technician, but he didn't approve of his showmanship, or the way he "carried on—it is not dignified—and those speeches to the audience—cheap!"

Richard Purvis (1960s)

Those elements, however, where the very things that drew me (and thousands of others) to Virgil; and I was not about to be deterred. Nor did I care for criticism of Virgil Fox even if it came from Richard Purvis, to whom I owed so much.

About a year passed before Virgil came again on his yearly Western tour. This time he played in Oakland on a wonderful old Kimball organ at the First Presbyterian Church.

The instrument was in the front of the church, and the console could be rolled out front and center where everyone could see. The Organist and Director of Music at the time was Newton Pashley, a dear man who had a marvelous choir, played the organ quite well, and above all saw to it that most of the major organists of the world played at First Presbyterian from time to time. Of course, Virgil was invited to play as often as possible.

The concert there was hair-raisingly thrilling! Again, there was standing room, hymn singing, and standing ovations. The concerts were getting better every time!

In the greeting line after the concert, Virgil roared, "Teddy! Paulie! Dora! How are you, how good to see you, and are you practicing?"

I said yes. He hugged us and said he hoped to see us all again in a day, as his next concert was in Salinas (about 150 miles south of San Francisco, near Carmel).

My friend Dora (who was a talented musician) was the organist of St. Paul's Episcopal Church in Salinas; and the church had just installed a small but beautiful two-manual Æolian-Skinner organ on which Virgil was to give the dedication concert.

I couldn't hear any of Virgil's rehearsals, because we arrived in Salinas late in the afternoon the day of the concert. Virgil had already gone back to the local hotel to rest. The rector, who knew how much I thought of Virgil, had to pick him up at precisely 7:45 p.m. (the concert would start at 8:00 p.m.). He offered to take me with him when he went to pick up the "Great One."

Once I got to the hotel, he told me to go in, get Virgil, and bring him to the car. I was delighted to oblige! I asked the desk clerk what Virgil Fox's room number might be, and to please ring him to tell him we were waiting downstairs. The clerk couldn't telephone the room, however, as Mr. Fox had left strict instructions with the hotel telephone operator not to disturb him for *any reason*. I explained the urgency, and he finally gave me Virgil's room number. I went up to get him.

I knocked on the door to be greeted by an enthusiastic "Teddo! Honey! What a surprise, come in. I'll only be a moment."

He put on his tuxedo jacket, pulled out a handkerchief, and proceeded to dump large quantities of perfume all over it.

The bottle didn't look or smell like "Old Spice" to me, and so I asked what smelled so wonderful.

"Bonwit Teller Private Label." Virgil put some on my wrist.

"I love scent," he said, "so when I give a concert I want to play well and smell wonderful, too."

He then picked up a garment I had never seen before. It was a large, flowing black cape with a crimson lining. I was stunned!

He unfurled the cape and it flew into place on his shoulders. Then I walked him to the door and opened it for him, only to have the doorknob come off in my hand. I fumbled to get the knob back on; but by doing so, I only poked the shaft out the other end.

Virgil roared with laughter, told me to go to the telephone and tell the operator to send someone. Then he pounded on the door to rouse someone to put the knob back on from the other side.

All this excitement took about ten minutes. The operator took forever to answer, and I was mortified to think I would make this great man late for his concert. "Don't be silly, Child! They can't start without me!"

We finally arrived, and he performed another fantastic concert on the small jewel of an organ. As usual, he wowed the audience, and made the organ sound four times as big as it was. I could not help thinking "This man is a wizard, he plays like he's possessed!"

That evening, after he had greeted nearly everyone in the audience at a reception, he said, "I'm going to the hotel to bathe and change my clothes. Then we'll all go out to eat; but before we go, I want to go back into the church because I want Teddy to play for me!"

I was terrified, but at the same time honored. Virgil Fox actually wanted to hear me play! He told me to go into the church to familiarize myself with the organ for a moment. "And for heaven's sake," he said, "don't worry! Just play me a hymn or something simple that you know."

I went in, and with Dora's help, set up a few buttons. I already knew what I would play.

Virgil came in and asked, "So what'll it be? Do you want me to 'run' the organ for you?"

I said I would play the Dupré "G Minor Fugue," and that I could "run" the organ for myself.

"Really?" he said, with more than disbelief in his tone. "That will be fine. I'll just go out in the church and listen."

I began the fugue just as he did it on the record that I had nearly worn out listening to. I tried to match his extraordinary rhythm, and the fire he put into his performances.

The little organ responded well, and I completed the piece—not too badly, I thought. What a relief I hadn't fallen on my face!

There was total silence in the church. Suddenly Virgil appeared at the console. I had played the piece from memory, and I could see it surprised him.

"Play it again," he said—and not one more word.

I did as he asked, and again I thought it went well.

"The boy's a natural! I'm flabbergasted!"

I was never more thrilled in my life! He asked where in the world I had learned to take this approach. I explained that it all came from his record, and what I had observed him do at the previous two concerts I had attended.

He was obviously flattered, and he said, "Honey, let me give you a few pointers that would make it better," which he did immediately. "Now play it again to be sure you've got it."

I did so, and he seemed pleased.

When we left, I was filled with pride.

At dinner that night, Virgil asked me what my plans were after I graduated from high school, which was about a month away. I said that I had read somewhere that he had gone to the Peabody Conservatory in Baltimore. If my parents could afford it, I intended to go there myself.

Virgil said, "That's a wonderful compliment to me, Teddy, but I think you'll find the Peabody a very different place today than it was when I first entered. I think you should go to France and study with Dupré; and then you should go on to England and study at one of the famous cathedrals, because I can see you love all that boy choir sound as well. That's certainly the place to go."

He gave me good advice. Virgil always advised talented youngsters to study abroad, but particularly in France which he adored, and where he'd learned so much.

I said that I didn't think my parents could afford such an undertaking; but I'd get there, someday, somehow.

Although my heart was set on the Peabody, secretly I was determined to study with the master, Virgil Fox.

Virgil said that when I got to Baltimore in the fall I should call him and arrange to come to New York to see his fabulous new organ at the Riverside Church. He would welcome me.

Louise B. Clary was a former student of Virgil Fox, and is currently a church organist in Beloit, Wisconsin.

Louise B. Clary

One time, after a concert in Chicago, it was so cold backstage while Virgil was greeting people that he caught pneumonia! A doc-

tor told him always to put a coat on after a concert. Wearing an
overcoat over clothes soaked with perspiration was too awkward for
him to contemplate. Therefore, when a French organist friend sug-
gested a cape to him, Virgil ignored all the snide remarks people
made about his wearing a cape, and it became his trademark. His
mother made him his first cape, and over the years, she patched and
spruced it up many times. Later, he bought his capes in Europe. The
best one came from Spain.

8. Jesus Wept and Moses Slept!

Shortly after registering at the Peabody and finding a room in which to live—and before I had formed any opinion of the school—I decided to telephone Virgil to see if I could come up to New York for a few days before school began. I was dying to see him and his superb new instrument at the Riverside Church.

He said to come ahead; and so, the following Friday, I took the train to Mecca.

I remember being astounded at the sheer size of the old Penn Station; and I found Manhattan itself exciting beyond words.

I took a cab to the Riverside Church. (I didn't yet know anything about the subway system.) Up the West Side Highway we went on a magnificent autumn evening, lights just beginning to come on in all the great buildings, the beautiful greenery of Riverside Drive on my right, and the Hudson River to my left.

All of a sudden, the great tower of the Riverside Church loomed up, dominating the twilight, and making my heart pound with antic-ipation.

We arrived at the Claremont Street entrance, as Virgil had instructed, since the main doors on Riverside Drive were closed at 5:00 p.m. The Claremont Street entrance led to an enclosed medieval cloister framed by impressive stained glass windows. At the end of the room was a desk, and the church's central switchboard. The attendant asked whom I wished to see, and telephoned Virgil at the console to ask him if I had an appointment. I was directed to go up a staircase behind me that led to the narthex, and then into the great nave of the church.

The staircase and the narthex were both splendid: all carved stone and beautifully finished with elegant stained glass windows even in that utilitarian section. Little did I realize, then, how priceless those ancient windows were!

Two great doors led to the nave. When I opened them, I beheld one of the most magnificent sights in Christendom! The nave is over 90 feet high. The blue of the windows at that time of day became almost indigo in depth. The white carved stone reredos around the altar was fully illuminated. Huge wrought iron chandeliers with lighted candles flanked both sides of the nave down its complete length. At the top of every chandelier was a tasteful red "votive" light.

The choir area in front of the altar was illuminated as though the sun were shining on it. Many people were congregating in the choir area. Obviously, choir rehearsal was about to begin.

As I started up the center aisle, great trumpets of the Celestial division of the organ began a fanfare that gradually turned increasingly thunderous until I reached the center of the choir. Then every stop came on! It was the most staggering sound I had ever heard come out of any organ anywhere until that moment!

It was Virgil, improvising. When he finished, he came running to the center of the choir.

"Welcome, Teddo!"

He embraced me, and roared to the choir members that "This child plays louder and faster than I do! He's going to show you *now!*"

Whereupon he led me to the console.

What a sight! Five keyboards, hundreds of buttons and stops, expression pedals for miles! It was awesome, but the console was also the most elegant I had ever seen, with wonderful carving all around the top.

"Sit down, Kiddo. What'll you play? Don't be afraid. I'll run the organ for you, Honey!"

I had just learned the famous "Toccata from the *Fifth Symphony*" of Charles Marie Widor. (After the "Toccata and Fugue in D Minor" of Bach, the Widor is probably the most popular piece in the organ repertoire.) I had learned how to play the piece using the tutti button (that is, the "full" organ) and the crescendo pedal in a manner that allowed me to avoid having to set up a special combination action to select the stops.

I began with some piercing reeds in the Swell division, and plenty of foundation stops, including 32-foot stops in the Pedal division—all of which I drew by hand. I opened the crescendo pedal (which allows stops to come on or off as one opens or closes the pedal at will—I needed this effect so that I could create a de-crescendo midway in the toccata). I then put on the tutti button, which activated a "reversible" red coupler tablet. ("Reversibles" are controls that go on when you press them the first time, and off when you press them the second.)

"Are you sure you want all of that on, Kid? You're in for a real shock!"

I assured Virgil that I did, and that I thought I could run the piece alone; but I asked him to stand by, just in case.

From the start, I nearly flew off the bench at the blazing torrent of sound that poured forth from that organ!

How articulate and quick the action was! When the full pedal entered to introduce the theme, I nearly fainted! Never had I experienced the thrill of such raw power!

This kind of experience was euphoric for any organist who, like Virgil and me, could fall in love with sound.

I made it through to the end of the toccata; and after the final F major chords, Virgil and the whole choir roared with approval.

"The kid's not timid, I told you! He's a natural."

He then took me over to meet the Choir Director of the Riverside Church, W. Richard Weagly. Virgil introduced me as "the San Francisco boy I told you about." Richard extended his hand and said, "You make an awful lot of noise for such a little guy."

"Come along, Sweet Child," Virgil said. "Pay no attention to him, we're going to dinner."

I've no doubt, now, that my introduction to Riverside and its legendary organ was unique. Virgil had staged it all for my benefit, and I was bursting with pride to have experienced this man's touching expression of faith in my ability.

I wondered why Virgil decided to go to dinner just as the choir was about to begin rehearsing.

In those days, the Riverside Choir rehearsed two hours every Tuesday and Friday evening, and sometimes Sunday afternoons for an oratorio. Virgil only accompanied for the last half hour of the Friday evening rehearsal. The other portions were accompanied by Richard Weagly himself, playing and conducting from a small spinet piano that was rolled to the center of the chancel.

Virgil and I walked from the Riverside Church through the Columbia University campus to a restaurant called Butler Hall, situated on top of a building near the campus. On the way over, he pointed out the important institutions located nearby.

Directly across the street from the Claremont Street entrance stood the Gothic Union Theological Seminary. Within a block or two were the Juilliard School of Music (renamed the Manhattan School of Music when the Juilliard moved to Lincoln Center), Barnard College, Jewish Theological Seminary, and the sprawling Columbia University campus.

In addition, several blocks south of Butler Hall stood the immense Cathedral of St. John the Divine, the largest Gothic cathedral in the world.

Virgil loved this area, and I was impressed. What an exhilarating, creative atmosphere it was in which to live and work!

We arrived at the restaurant, and of course, Virgil seemed to know everyone from the manager to the bus boys. He called them by name, and greeted them in his outgoing manner. In other words, everyone knew we had arrived. I was dining with a celebrity, and I swelled with pride as friend after friend would stop at the table to ask where he had been on his latest tour, or about what was coming up at the Riverside Church.

Virgil was gracious and never annoyed by these interruptions. In fact, he thrived on them. The attention seemed to invigorate him.

He never failed to introduce everyone and explain what every person did, making all his acquaintances feel welcome and glad they had stopped to greet him. He attracted people like a magnet!

Robert Hebble is the renowned composer of choral and organ works whose music is known to almost every American organist and choir director.

Robert Hebble

Virgil was an impossible eater, slower than molasses, chewing his food practically to powder and then slipping the sorry remains out onto the rim of the plate. He always seemed to be leaving mini haystacks of pulverized food on his plate, driving everyone crazy who wanted to escape the restaurant while all the other chairs were being stacked on the free tables and the cleanup crew was mopping the floor with an ammonia detergent.

Finally, Virgil would waltz out with a white Holiday Inn towel over his head, brushing his teeth with a toothbrush as he walked.

During our enjoyable meal, Virgil was keen to learn how I was doing, and what were my first impressions of Baltimore and the Peabody Conservatory.

I had no opinion about the Peabody yet, other than that people had been nice to me, and things were going well.

Baltimore itself was another matter. I came from San Francisco, and had just experienced my first taste of Manhattan, which was much more to my liking than Baltimore. (Some friends I had met at school used to make fun of one of its sobriquets, which was "The Queen City of the Patapsco Bay Drainage Basin.")

I must admit to admiring the Mt. Vernon Square area where the Peabody was located, and where many students lived on St. Paul Street.

I lived in a school-approved rooming house (a typical Baltimore row house) run by an exotic character named Mayben Z. Wigfall (I referred to her as Maybu). Mrs. Wigfall had a constant habit of rubbing her breasts whenever she spoke to any of her boarders. She was kind, and always asked if we wanted a "sup o'beer."

One day, after I had just met her, I was talking to her when I looked behind her, down a long hallway, and saw a washing machine overflowing with soapsuds. The water was making its way down the hallway, and so I told her what I saw.

"Aw! You're just kiddin'," she said.

Then she looked over her shoulder and yelled, "Jesus wept and Moses slept! Get the mop!"

When I related this story to Virgil, he roared with laughter, not just at the situation, but also at the dear woman's name.

Virgil loved funny stories, and he loved unusual or amusing names as well. Mrs. Wigfall provided many more amusing anecdotes in the future, and Virgil always asked me about "Maybu."

During our first meal at Butler Hall, Virgil talked about a young protégé of his who was to have a big influence on my life. His name was Robert Hebble.

"Bob has just gone off to Paris to study with Nadia Boulanger," Virgil said, explaining that Bob had been his console assistant for some time. He was apparently a splendid pianist and organist who could improvise on any given theme at the drop of a hat; and he had gone to Paris to study at Virgil's insistence.

Bob had accompanied Virgil and Richard Weagly to Europe the previous summer, after which Virgil managed to convince Bob and his parents (as he tried to do with me) that he must go abroad to complete his education. He had already attended the Yale School of Music. Virgil sang his praises to me, and said he couldn't wait for us to meet.

Robert Hebble

It was the summer of 1954 when Virgil invited me to accompany him and Richard Weagly on my first trip to Paris. (French was my worst subject, and Virgil thought I might do better with the language learning it "au natural.") What I mainly recall from my first day in Paris, however, was walking down the Champs Elysée and seeing a body fall about 300 feet down from the Eiffel Tower.

That was my auspicious introduction to Europe!

Actually, my 30-year relationship with Virgil Fox began four years earlier. During half of my 30 years knowing him, I assisted at the console for virtually every rehearsal and worship service he played at the Riverside Church.

I'd stand to his right and turn pages or operate stops. He'd say, under his breath, "Get ready on the...," and I'd put my fingers on the designated stop. Then he'd say, "Now!" and I'd make the change.

Sometimes he'd ask me frantically to pull on a stop and I'd have to say, "It's on!" He'd cry out, "Then, take it off!" and we'd both start to howl.

When it came to paying me for my services at the console (which were to consist of my being with Virgil "every time" he "walked into the church"), the only deal he made with my parents and me was that he would give me a free education—"but it'll be worth $50,000!"

My mother was thrilled. I was thrilled. (I would have paid him for the privilege!) My father, who wanted me to take over his Buick dealership someday, wasn't thrilled.

What specifically got me in the door was my talent for harmony. Although Virgil was a supreme musician, his harmonic flow was, in a word, "basic." In other words, it was a bit cornball.

Enter me at age sixteen, cute and brimming over with colorful "$50 chords." Harmony had always been "my thing." Thus, I could really help him while he improvised during a service and he'd *ask me under his breath, "What chord should I play now?" When he'd play a crushing chord that I suggested for the occasion, he'd throw his head back in ecstasy, beam a twinkling smile and inquire, "Did you get any on you?"*

Virgil Fox at the Riverside Church console with Robert Hebble (1953)

9. Choir Practice

We finished our meal and headed back to the church. Virgil talked non-stop all the way. I took it in like a sponge. We entered the church through the Claremont Street entrance; and Virgil greeted the desk clerk and telephone operator in his usual, ebullient way. This time we stayed downstairs, walking along the hallways toward the front of the church. I was struck by the fact that even in the lower reaches of the church, everything was graced by the same finely finished carved stone, immaculately clean, and with beautiful lighting fixtures.

We passed a door marked "Choir Director, W. Richard Weagly." Virgil opened the door to show me a sumptuous suite, with a large Mason & Hamlin grand piano, a harpsichord, beautiful bookcases, a large seating area, and desks.

"This is where Weagly gives singing lessons. It's his palace."

We then proceeded up a circular staircase, and through a doorway hung with beautiful brocade drapes. There appeared the mammoth console. Virgil proceeded to turn on the organ (the choir was still rehearsing).

Richard Weagly, seated on a high stool, said, "It's about time! Now, is the greatest organist in the world ready to rehearse?"

Virgil paid no attention to Weagly. He proceeded to open the music that was programmed for the coming Sunday, and to start preparing the organ. "That one's in a bad mood! Never mind him. Honey, will you please turn the pages for me?"

The anthem was a new one, not familiar to Virgil, called "The Last Words of David" by Randall Thompson. It didn't look too easy to me.

Virgil was timid with the organ, while the choir, which knew the piece, was making wonderful sounds. "Could you try to play the right notes?" Weagly shouted over the choir.

Virgil looked straight at the music, not acknowledging the remark, and said to me, "Just wait until Sunday. He won't know what hit him!"

Virgil, I discovered, was not the greatest sight-reader in the world (nor am I); and this accompaniment was not easy. It was black with notes, and sounded strongly contemporary. He had not yet been able to make it "his."

He said in his low-pitched stage whisper, "When in doubt, play the extremes," which meant to play the top notes on the manuals and the lower ones on the pedals.

He got through the piece, and the rehearsal ended. The Riverside Choir was a friendly and enthusiastic group of almost a hundred singers. As they were leaving, many came over to greet Virgil. There were hoots, hollers, and laughter as the group was leaving the choir area.

Richard Weagly had gone downstairs without a word.

When everyone else left, Virgil took up the Randall Thompson anthem (it was a piano score, not even transcribed for organ) and proceeded to arrange it properly for the instrument and to work out the difficulties. After he had carefully prepared the work, he began selecting the various sounds and dynamics he would use. These choices were vastly different from the timid approach he used in the presence of Weagly and the choir. He then went through some of the hymns that would be sung on Sunday—and what thrilling sounds he got out of that wondrous machine, making it all look easy!

The prelude he planned for the morning service was to be the "First Sonata" of Mendelssohn.

What a revelation! I had heard this work many times, but under his hands, and on the Riverside organ, the work seemed entirely new. The last movement was played at a tempo twice as fast as I had ever heard; and it was thrilling, ending with every stop drawn. I was beside myself with joy and appreciation.

"A real stem-winder," Virgil roared.

"My God," he said, "it's after eleven o'clock, and there'll be hell to pay if I make any more racket on the organ. I have to play softly now, and only use the right side divisions."

He explained that immediately behind the Swell and Pedal divisions of the organ (which are divisions to the left side of an organist seated at the console) was an apartment building that housed teachers of the Union Theological Seminary. Some of their bedrooms were smack against that side of the church; and although a few feet of stone separated them, the big 32-foot stops, and the trumpets and mixtures of the Swell Organ, were plainly audible to the unfortunate tenants. (I'm sure they were especially aware of the 32-foot Contre Gambe in the Swell, which Virgil called the "32-foot Contraceptive" because its resonator was made of rubber Flexhaust!)

They had often been treated to late evening concerts; and Virgil told me he had to be careful with the volume levels after 10:30 p.m. He then proceeded to amaze me by playing the movement of a Bach trio sonata lightening fast on Baroque sounding flutes and mutations.

The trio sonatas were written for Bach's sons mainly to alert them to the various pitfalls of playing the organ.

The six sonatas are glorious music; but since they're ferociously difficult, too many organists had bored me with them. Virgil made them come alive; and with his infectious rhythm and enthusiasm, he made listeners love them.

"It makes one feel so naked—this wonderful counterpoint—one tune for the right hand, one for the left, and the pedal has a melody of its own—sheer genius! Of course, it helps if the player knows what he's doing!"

Virgil then answered scores of questions I had about the controls on this, the world's most brilliantly appointed console, which Virgil designed.

There was a reason for everything, and Virgil delighted in showing me every single device and gadget at his disposal. By this time, it was well past midnight. He said, "Come on, Teddo. It's time to get you to your hotel, and I want some ice cream."

We went back through the brocade drapes to a closet that housed a sink. Virgil proceeded to change from his practice pants into street trousers. I noticed many pairs of shoes and pants thrown in the closeted area as Virgil draped his pants over the sink.

"Oh, this is the 'Slop Salon,'" he said; and he proceeded to lead me around the passageway behind the great altar to another room opposite the console side.

"This is the 'Counting Room,' where they count the cash after the services." Virgil explained that he had also appropriated this area for his use, as his formal office was too far from the organ console (it was in the tower on the fourth floor). "I only use my office to take naps in, and sometimes to practice the piano."

I noticed file cabinets filled with his music library, and a large table underneath leaded glass windows that was strewn with letters—mostly unopened.

"These letters are never-ending! People would think I have nothing better to do than answer them! I have a lady that helps me wade through this twice a week or so."

I later learned that the letters were mostly from adoring fans. There were some crank letters, too, and people asking for loans, financial assistance, advice about which courses to take, or what to do about an old organ in a church.

Virgil adored fan mail; but as for what people should do with a worn out instrument, "I could tell them what to do with their old organ all right, but they'd never do it," he would bellow.

With that he raced back through the brocade curtains, crossed over to the console side, and pressed the button that would slowly dim the great circle of lights that illuminated the choir area.

He shouted, "Run for it, Kid," and we ran down the aisle as the giant nave slowly buried its Gothic treasures in darkness.

10. Red Blanket and the Biggest Pig

Out on Claremont Avenue, Virgil led me to his car, which was a brand new pink Cadillac convertible. If ever a car was made to suit an individual, this one was it.

"Isn't it a wonderful color? I love pink!"

With that statement, I got my first impression of the great Virgil Fox behind the wheel of a car.

Virgil drove a car exactly as he played an organ: fearlessly. He had no patience with lights, pedestrians, other drivers, or speed limits. He loved to lay on the horn—with a fiendish look on his face, baring his teeth—or drive down the New Jersey Turnpike at ninety miles an hour, eating fruit salad with a nail file out of a record plastic liner, and talking a mile a minute.

"The biggest pig gets there first!" was his motto, which he used often over the years to excuse his aggressive driving techniques.

Louise B. Clary

Virgil was the world's worst driver! I often had to grab the wheel when he would let go to turn and talk to someone in the back seat. When he'd take back the steering wheel, he'd say, "Thanks, Little One," (which was what he called me).

Once, driving from the Peabody to New York, we were stopped three times for various infractions. Each time he managed to talk his way out of a ticket!

Another time, when he failed to pick two of us up in his car, I said, "I'll bet he ran into an old friend and got to talking." When he finally showed up, he said, "Sorry, Girls! I ran into an old friend and got to talking."

Another time, on our way back to Baltimore, he said, "Little One, how would you like me to be your teacher?" That was how I found out he'd been made the new head of the organ department.

I began studying the organ during the Depression years at the Peabody Conservatory around the time that Virgil Fox was known as the "genius" (and the only music student in the school's history to complete a three-year scholarship course in a single year; he had to work 16 hours a day to do it).

As my teacher, he concentrated on interpretation. He'd pace behind me, saying, "Come on, Babe, thrill me!" or "Sing it out to me, Girl!" or "Come on, flirt with me!"

Once my mind went completely blank during a recital, but I kept going, doing what Virgil always said a player should do in such a situation, which was to keep improvising until the notes came back. I was so upset with myself that I left the concert hall and couldn't face my teacher again until he summoned me to his office to tell me how proud he was that I hadn't stopped when I hit the memory slip.

He told me I'd never be good as a concert organist because I didn't have the stamina; but that I could be a "damn good" church organist—which I've tried to be for 66 years as of this writing.

When we neared Central Park South, Virgil began looking for a parking place, invoking the phrase "C'mon, Red Blanket! Find me a place!"

"Red Blanket" was a spirit from "beyond the earth plane" with whom Virgil was acquainted—I had no idea how. Virgil simply explained that Red Blanket never failed to find him a parking place.

Sure enough, he spotted just the space he wanted directly across the street from where we were. He made a U-turn (which was strict-

Virgil Fox and Louise Clary

ly forbidden).

"Ho, ho! No one's looking," he said as he pulled into a parking spot suitable for a Volkswagen, but not (I thought) for this mile-long Cadillac! Undaunted, Virgil squeezed his machine into the space like a real pro.

When we got out of the car, he announced, "We're going to Rumplemeyer's, where they have the best ice cream and hot chocolate in New York. Believe me, Honey, I'm an expert on the subject!"

We ate delicious hot fudge sundaes, Virgil scraping every morsel of chocolate out of his dish, licking the spoon with relish, and demanding more sauce for us both. Most of the servers and the cashier seemed to know him well. He'd been an habitué for years; and Rumplemeyer's would become a mainstay for all of us in the years to come.

After this delicious second dessert, Virgil suggested that we walk down Fifth Avenue to look at shop windows. He pointed out the places of special interest, such as the Plaza, Pierre, and Sherry Netherlands hotels. We proceeded to walk past Tiffany's windows, where Virgil pointed out how important fine lighting was, making the delicate jewels sparkle intensely.

Then on we walked, past the Bonwit Teller windows to see the elegantly draped mannequins. I noticed a wonderful smell coming from the main entrance of that store and recognized the scent with which Virgil had drenched his handkerchief at the hotel in Salinas, California: Bonwit Teller "Private Label." During working hours, an automatic atomizer sprayed the scent above the customers as they entered the store.

I asked him whether it was a man's cologne (I only knew about Old Spice and English Leather at that time).

"Oh my no! It's for women! But what difference does that make, Child? A wonderful scent is a wonderful scent, and it doesn't matter which sex uses it. They certainly don't care in Paris!"

I vowed that I would purchase some the next day, providing it didn't turn out to be too expensive, as I wanted to emulate this great man in every way that I could—including smell. I settled for a small bottle of toilet water, since the cost of real perfume was prohibitively expensive for me at that point.

After checking out Bergdorf Goodman's windows, we walked east on 57th Street to look at the exquisite crystal chandeliers in Nesle's windows; the bathroom fixtures at Sherle Wagner; and, back on Fifth Avenue, the dishes and glassware at Richard Ginori.

Virgil loved beautiful things. He loved colors, especially blues and reds. Combinations of the two, such as shocking pink and fuschia, were his favorites. He was proud to show me this part of Manhattan, and to begin my education about the "finer things in life."

Following this first late night stroll past the "emporiums of the very rich," we would go again and again into this splendid area—but always at the same late hour, when every single store was shut.

Virgil walked me to my hotel and explained that he had to have dinner the following night with some business people; and so we couldn't meet on Saturday. But "would I be so kind" as to come early to church on Sunday to assist him at the console?

Kind! Bob was in Paris, and Virgil hadn't yet picked a replacement. I jumped at the chance, as you can imagine. After seeing me to the hotel door, Virgil embraced me in his natural, outgoing way and said, "Get a good night's rest, Kid. See ya Sunday at 9:30 sharp!"

Then off he went in a cloud of Bonwit Teller Private Label.

I could hardly sleep that night because of the many wonderful things I had seen and heard. I remember walking around as the typical tourist the following day, becoming properly smitten with Gotham. However, I was most excited anticipating seeing and hearing my first Sunday service at the Riverside Church.

11. Assisting at the Console

I arrived at the organ at around 9:15 a.m. Since no one was around yet, I descended on that beautiful console, beginning to memorize where the stops were and in which order. At about 9:30 a.m., Virgil appeared from behind the brocade drapes.

"Short night, Kid," he said. It must have been, for I hadn't been to bed much before 2:00 a.m. myself. Virgil had to drive to his home in Englewood, New Jersey after his Saturday night business meeting, and probably had not retired until 4:00 a.m.

It dawned on me that I had never seen Virgil until at least five in the afternoon; but this morning, except for a huskiness and even deeper than usual pitch to his voice, he seemed as bright as ever.

He wore a nice powder blue cassock, but he hadn't yet put on the white cotta with the large, slotted sleeves that organists wear. The whole choir wore blue and white vestments. When I admired the color, Virgil said that after we were finished with his organ rehearsal I must go down to the choir robing room and be fitted for the same. People could look down on the organ console from the overflow seating area in the "triforium," which went down both sides of the nave on the third floor level, and so I had to be properly attired.

Virgil proceeded to turn on the organ to rehearse some of the passages and mark the Randall Thompson anthem. He told me exactly where to stand to turn the pages, and instructed me with some of his console "lingo."

"Alter below" meant I was to push the reversible toe stud with my hand to activate or de-activate the 32-foot Bourdon, or the big 32-foot Open Wood, depending on the piece.

"Alter above" meant to turn "16-foot Manual Stops Silent" either on or off.

"Press Choir piston 14," he said.

I followed this instruction with great relish. Ordinarily, Virgil would cut off anyone's hand that would dare to touch a control while he was playing. When he played from memory during concerts or service preludes and postludes, he always operated everything himself. But when he played a church service, or accompanied an anthem or oratorio, he wanted to be able to act on spur of the moment inspirations; and since he might not have set up the organ's vast combination action for this or that effect, he required a competent console assistant.

He also liked to have someone nearby to tell him which verse of the hymn the congregation was singing, or simply to make amusing remarks during the service (which wasn't uncommon, but usually frowned on by the observant clergy).

Richard Torrence

I became Virgil's console assistant from 1962 until 1964, after our friend Sara Sindel had relinquished an enjoyable task that she diligently performed for a number of years.

It was great fun to stand next to Virgil at the console, and to peek over at the huge congregation. Once in a while, however, we got carried away by non-church related activities. One particular "black Sunday" comes to mind when Virgil had just completed the hymn before the sermon. To while away the time, he began reading the cover of that Sunday's printed program. He suddenly became seized with shaking, and motioned for me to read along. I didn't understand what was happening until I noticed that the long message on the front page referred quite innocently to an English poet whose name was sometimes corrupted by a certain group of people to signify a non-standard form of "penetration." The message began:

In my undergraduate years I had a friend who was a bewilderment to me and for whom I am sure I was a source of never-failing exasperation. He was a devotee of Browning. I can still recall strained half-hours when he would wax eloquent on the meaning and beauty of "Saul," "The Pope's Speech," "Paracelsus," "The Last Ride Together," and the pained expression of his face as his eloquence fell on dull and unresponsive ears. For I then knew nothing of Browning.

We couldn't keep ourselves from laughing audibly well into the sermon. After the service, one of the ministers scolded Virgil for our embarrassing behavior during Church. Virgil apologized lamely, offering no explanation.

I saved the program and have treasured it ever since.

Virgil reviewed the music some more, and then practiced slowly and softly some technical parts of the Mendelssohn "Sonata I" that was to be the prelude. He then said, "What would you like for a postlude?"

In San Francisco, I had heard him play the great French toccata, "Thou Art the Rock" by Henri Mulet. He said, "Perfect!" He lit into the first few measures, and set the controls for this piece.

I had noticed that Virgil listed the Mendelssohn sonata as the prelude in the printed program for Sunday morning, but had omitted any title next to the word "Postlude."

The postlude always interests organists, as it's usually a rousing work to keep the congregation in a positive frame of mind. It also serves to cover up conversation and commotion of people running for the door.

Virgil explained that he never listed the postlude because he wanted it to be a surprise. He also wanted the option of changing his mind at the last moment about which piece to play. He explained with a great deal of pride that well over half the congregation would often stay in the pews to listen to the entire postlude. That custom was definitely not normal in any churches I knew about; but there was nothing normal about this church, this organ, or this organist!

Virgil finished about 10:15 a.m., and told me to go put on some vestments. I peeked around the console and noticed that the church was already almost half full. I was amazed that the ushers who were leading in the faithful were wearing striped trousers and morning cutaways!

The Riverside Church was definitely like none I had ever seen. I mentioned to Virgil that there were many people out there. "We always have a full house," he said. "It'll be packed by 10:45."

He was right. When I returned at about 10:30 a.m., Virgil had gone out to put on his white cotta. I peeked around to see the entire nave filled and the back balconies almost the same. An impressive sight sparkled with the lights of magnificent stained glass windows and elegant chandeliers.

The sound of the tower bells was piped into the nave electronically. Although the Riverside Carillon was the largest in the world (74 bells included the largest tuned bell in the world), the tower itself was so high (at John D. Rockefeller Jr.'s insistence) that the bells could only barely be heard in the nave. Piping sound electronically into the church solved the problem.

Virgil swept through the drapes, and switched off the bell on his telephone (it had an amber light that blinked when the bell was off). This telephone was useful during services, for Virgil could call the control room to give the engineers instructions if certain lighting effects weren't synchronized exactly to his taste, or for emergencies. More importantly, Virgil often used the telephone for personal reasons, as the console was one of the few places people could reach him on a weekend, or when he was in town. Thus, it rang or flashed incessantly.

Virgil pressed a button that alerted the control room to fade out the carillon.

"We've had enough of that. We're ready to begin."

He told me to take a seat. He was going to play the Mendelssohn from memory, and he proceeded to inspire me and the vast congregation with a memorable performance of that masterpiece. At exactly 11:00 a.m., following the dazzling finale of the Mendelssohn, Virgil summoned me to stand to his right; and he began the introduction of the famous hymn, "Ye Holy Angels Bright."

He started with the smothered sound of the Gallery organ, buried high in the second balcony almost a city block away, with no pedal. Midway in the introduction, he began adding stops to the front organ, letting the pedal creep slowly in. By the end of the introduction, he made an enormous crescendo, bringing into play nearly the full resources of the great instrument—as if daring anyone to "top that!"

Hearing the roar of enthusiastic voices that came out of the congregation of the Riverside Church that Sunday morning from my special vantage point was an experience unlike any I'd had before. The sound of nearly three-thousand souls singing their hearts out thrilled me entirely.

Virgil modulated between verses of the hymn, taking the key down a third, or back up again to a higher key than before. I was in a frenzy of excitement as Virgil ran the organ up and down like a window shade! The modulations from one key to another were magical; and Virgil's registrations for each verse gave tremendous variety to the entire hymn.

People said that Thor Johnson (then conductor of the St. Louis Symphony Orchestra) used to come to the Riverside Church just to hear Virgil modulate from one verse to the other. Therefore, it's easy to understand why the congregation sang so well. Virgil led and inspired them; and they responded by giving their all.

People also used to say that Virgil "played a church service like a concert," while most other organists "played a concert like a church service." He certainly had no use for the type of organists who were characterized in silent films as "thin-lipped eccentrics sitting in foreboding organ lofts waiting for lost chords" (which was a line from one of Marshall Yaeger's pressbooks)!

Virgil gave the very best of his art whenever he sat down on an organ bench, whether it was for a church service, oratorio accompaniment, or solo concert. It never occurred to him that there should be a difference. Whether it was background music to move a preacher from the nave to the pulpit (usually played on the softest stops of the organ), or the mightiest of postludes, Virgil played everything with flare, musical line, and expression. The vast Riverside organ was an orchestra for him of nearly 200 "players." He used these players as a great painter would draw colors from a palette. Colors blazed in every musical sound that Sunday morning, as well as any time that Virgil presided over his organ at Riverside.

After the anthem (the Randall Thompson, which was thrilling!), Virgil sat down on a small, wooden chair, next to Richard Weagly. He told me to sit on the edge of the console platform.

Robert James McCracken, Senior Minister of the Riverside Church, gave the sermon. His preaching was memorable, and he was certainly never boring. In his gentle Scottish brogue, he seemed firmly able to lift the souls of the faithful to a higher sphere and leave them refreshed.

12. Holding Court

The Riverside Church was originally built by John D. Rockefeller Jr. for the great preacher, Harry Emerson Fosdick, still living then and often seen around the church as the Minister Emeritus. The original church had been called the Park Avenue Baptist Church. Rockefeller then decided to build a church worthy of the great Dr. Fosdick on the newly fashionable Riverside Drive.

In those days (the 1930s), it was fashionable to build churches with acoustics that only took into account the spoken word; and so the acoustics of the Riverside Church were certainly not ideal for music. When one considered the great size, height, and stone construction of the building, one would have expected the somewhat vast, rolling "cathedral-like" acoustical decays I was used to at Grace Cathedral. Riverside's ceiling, however, was not made out of stone. It was made of "Guastavino" bricks, which absorbed sound and only looked like stone. Many other materials used throughout the building were also sound absorbent.

I missed the elegant reverberation time I was accustomed to in Grace Cathedral when the organ played or the choir and congregation sang. But the audibility of Riverside's preachers was certainly enhanced; and the sermons were well worth listening to. Virgil always listened intently to every word, and would often discuss the content at meals following the services—although not for long; and only if the sermon had really inspired him.

I had been raised an Episcopalian; and the churchmanship at the Riverside Church at that time was completely Protestant and plain. It wasn't just a Baptist church, but was called "interdenominational and international" (whatever that meant—probably that the church wanted itself to be interracial).

Virgil used to say, "You Episcopalians prefer all that ecclesiastical drag; and all that incense and kneeling; and bowing, and scraping."

How right he was! He also explained that the rich Episcopalians liked the kind of "low" church ceremony that was practiced at St. Bartholomew's on Park Avenue—and at that time at St. Thomas Church on Fifth Avenue as well. In fact, most New York Christians didn't seem to care for the sort of rites that went on at "Smoky Mary's" (referring to The Church of St. Mary the Virgin, near Times Square, which was Anglo Catholic).

However, Riverside had the largest musical instrument in New York State. At that time, it was the seventh largest organ in the world. It also had a wonderful choir. True, the building had poor acoustics. Nevertheless, an organ with such awesome power still really "came off" well in the room. I could only imagine what it would have sounded like with acoustics to match the "look" of the place.

Virgil tried to make up for the lack of reverberation when he released massive chords on the full organ (when one would expect three or four seconds of reverberation) by a technique he made up called an "acoustical release." It was a kind of backward arpeggio, releasing the top notes first and ending with the pedal alone. He performed this trick quite rapidly and with great flourish, and he managed to create the illusion of some reverberation when, in fact, there was none!

In spite of the acoustical flaw, the service at the Riverside Church that Sunday, and nearly every service I attended thereafter, was an exciting and fulfilling experience.

While Virgil was playing the postlude ("Thou Art the Rock"), the greeting line was already forming. People were looking down at the console from high above on the triforium level of the nave. When Virgil finished the wonderful toccata, I beamed with delight. While he wiped the sweat from his brow (with the Bonwit Teller scented handkerchief) he said, "I've got to pee. Greet these folks from out of town. Many of them want to see the console, so you show and tell them all about it!"

I was honored! Soon, there were thirty-five or forty people gawking, mingling, and asking questions, which I answered as best I could.

I heard Virgil returning after refreshing himself in the bathroom below, exclaiming, "Bessie Woods! How are you, Honey, and how's your husband, Baldwin?"

He remembered nearly everyone in a line that sometimes included as many as two-hundred persons from all over the country, who had come to Riverside especially to hear Virgil.

His lines were often longer than the lines to greet the clergy—even those that included the head minister, Dr. McCracken, and other visiting dignitaries.

Virgil was patient and thoughtful with every person. He adored seeing people again, and loved to hear their kind words. I also loved to "hold court" at the console.

After greeting the last of his adoring fans, and then showering and dressing in a private room on the floor below (I thought Virgil must have been the cleanest person alive!), we set off again for Butler Hall to join Richard Weagly and several members of the choir, already midway through their lunch. After introducing me to everyone and telling them how beautifully the choir had performed, Virgil and I proceeded to order our lunch while he looked around, waving and greeting his many friends at other tables.

We had just finished ordering when an attractive young woman arrived at our table to join us. I was then introduced to Roberta Bailey, who was Virgil's concert manager. She was pleasant, if a bit quiet and aloof from the rest of the group; but she hung on every word Virgil uttered and clearly worshipped him.

After gorging ourselves on a wonderful meal, including two desserts, Virgil signed some autographs, bid goodbye to the help, and offered to drive me to my hotel (I had to return to Baltimore that afternoon). School was to begin the next day. Virgil hugged me goodbye, and told me he hoped I'd like the Peabody. He said, "Hit the bench and practice like the devil—because that's what it takes, Kiddo. Come back soon!"

13. Purists Infest the Peabody

Several months earlier, I had convinced my parents that the Peabody was the place to go. In September 1955, I arrived in Baltimore to begin my studies. I had hoped to study the organ with Paul Calloway, Organist of the Washington Cathedral; but he had recently announced his intention to leave the school, and wouldn't accept any more students.

I was lucky, in a way; for I was assigned to a wonderful teacher, Clarence Snyder, who was a friend of Richard Purvis's. Clarence was the organist of the duPont estate at Longwood Gardens in Kennett Square, Pennsylvania. In the Grand Ballroom of that magnificent estate stood the largest private residence organ in the world—about 150 ranks!

Clarence was kind, and he understood my fervent desire to become a concert organist. He was also a fan of Virgil's, which pleased me. I didn't realize at the time that not everyone was as enamored of Virgil or his style as I was. There were others who took different approaches to the organ, of course; and the new head of the Peabody organ department was one of those "others."

This man was a devotee of the school of organ players then known as "the purists." E. Power Biggs (who once upon a time played mostly "Romantic" organs) had become one of the main champions of early organ music. More significantly, he promoted the cause of performing on early, "Baroque" instruments.

This approach was a healthy development in the organ world, for it eliminated many sloppy performance habits among organ students, and it got organ builders out of the dull, drab mode into which too many of them had fallen.

There was liveliness and brilliance in these instruments, and in this new approach.

However, there was also a grave mischief going on in trying to eliminate what was truly good and beautiful in American organs! That expulsion is what many of the "purists" tried to do vigorously. Thus, we players were supposed to restrict our performances to mechanical action organs, much smaller instruments, and high-squeaking pitches more audible to tiny mammals than to human beings.

Any music written for the organ after the death of J. S. Bach was completely off the mark—except for a few contemporary composers' experiments, such as laying two-by-fours across a keyboard and a pedalboard with every organ stop drawn, then turning off the motor and letting the wind sag slowly.

Such experiments could produce agonizingly painful sounds; but they seemed to please the "conceptual musicians" greatly.

These ominous experiments suddenly became valid musical events in the 1960s. The music profession has suffered greatly because of them ever since. Fortunately, some signs of sanity began to appear in the 1990s.

Virgil, in this environment, by many of the other organ students and certainly by the head of organ departments, was considered a circus performer. In these people's opinions, everything he did was in bad taste. This judgment infuriated me. Such superior attitudes—over what?

When I heard many of these people play, I found them deadly dull, boring to anyone forced to listen, and none too accurate, either!

Virgil, on the other hand, blindfolded, and with only one hand and foot to play, could surpass every one of them!

My approach to the organ was similar to Virgil's (although I had a long way to go to be as good as he), and that artistic choice made me none too popular with the rest of the organ department.

There were some exceptions. Clarence Snyder was supportive, and some other organ students were enthusiastic and complimentary; but most of my friends came out of the instrument or voice departments—where they were taught to appreciate Romantic composers and follow a musical line.

I remember being told, when we studied organ keyboard harmony and improvisation, to pay no attention to any harmonic vocabulary beyond that of Buxtehude. In addition, we were to learn about how organs were built (which was a laudable idea), but only *true* organs, which meant tracker organs.

You can imagine my disgust, having grown up listening to the lush harmonies of Richard Purvis playing an "American Classic"— but decidedly Romantic—organ at Grace Cathedral. This new conservatism represented everything I hated. It was the complete opposite of what my idol, Virgil Fox, stood for.

I went straight to the director of the conservatory, Reginald Stewart—a very imposing man—and dared to complain. He was sympathetic, and he allowed me to take a piano harmony class where the atmosphere was much healthier.

I was excused from the organ building class, which didn't make me popular with the head of the organ department. I remember many times, when I was practicing at the fine E.M. Skinner organ in the concert hall, this man passing through and turning off the tremolos (a definite "no-no" in his book) while I was playing. I would defiantly put them right back on. He was not my teacher, thank God!

Virgil only hinted at how drastic a change had occurred at the Peabody Conservatory. Even the name had been changed. Apparently the State of Maryland was now underwriting the school, and so there seemed to be more interest in producing music teachers for the Maryland Public School system than teaching "applied music" for those of us who wanted performing careers.

We were advised to take the required courses for a bachelor's degree at Johns Hopkins University. This advice was undoubtedly sound, educationally; but Johns Hopkins was a long way away for me, and I hated those courses. I felt the teachers only wanted me to memorize useless facts in order to pass courses I didn't need; and I felt frustrated eating up valuable practice time I had to have in order to become a concert organist.

I must have been an impossible student for Clarence Snyder; but he and a few prominent local musicians—and some fine people in the administration office—were kind to encourage me and help me in meaningful ways.

Other than my lessons with Clarence Snyder, I felt that I got the most out of singing in the Peabody Chorus, which was conducted by Paul Calloway in his final year at the school.

He was a magnificent conductor, short in stature, and a kind and quiet person when one spoke to him. What a change when he stepped on the podium to conduct! He became Napoleon, and would brook no foolishness or poor musicianship. He would rant and rave, insult and scream. The volume of his voice was so great that it was hard to believe such a sound came out of a man so small. He made Richard Purvis seem mild by comparison!

I remember the fine results he achieved, however; for I had the privilege of attending many memorable performances that he conducted in Washington Cathedral with his choral society.

My dear friend, Rodney Hanson (the organist of the Pro-Cathedral in Baltimore, a pupil of both Calloway and Purvis, and a first rate musician) and George Woodhead (equally first rate; he worked in the administration of the Peabody, and was musical director of the English Lutheran Church in Baltimore) saw to it that I ate regularly and had a decent place to live. These men were angels in the way they cared and looked after me.

Carlo Curley

As life marches onward, the name and colorful reputation of the exceedingly singular Virgil Fox, even more than twenty years after his passing, continues to be as timeless and fresh as when I first experienced his recordings during the earliest days of my formative years at the North Carolina School of the Arts in Winston-Salem.

In those days, there were clearly-divided camps in the Organ Department with the conventional side (consisting of at least three-quarters of the students!) subscribing to a neo-Baroque, Orgelbewegung *tradition heartily espoused by some very correct professor or other. There was little doubt in any of their minds that the likes of E. Power Biggs, Helmut Walcha, and Dirk Flentrop could actually walk on water and heal the sick if decently inspired.*

The remaining pupils happily worshipped unapologetically at the shrine of a certain V. Fox. This reputed charlatan's "from-the-heart" virtuosic style and adoration of the American Symphonic Organ, coupled with a renowned joie de vivre *and a distilled hatred of "Purists," resulted in his disciples being considered laughable card-carrying members of the Grossly Unwashed.*

I'm ashamed to admit that while I was initially fascinated by his recorded efforts, I principally sided in those days with the former group, which I now put down to a piano upbringing, "running with the pack," and an overall general lack of experience.

My classmates who so adored Virgil's no-holds-barred performances were subjected to mountains of abuse, verbal and otherwise. For example, a preferred pastime was the wreaking of destruction on Fox recordings in the Library using a stylus as the convenient weapon-of-choice, inflicting irreparable scratches across the radius of all his titles.

Although the Peabody was a wonderful school, and the people I met were extremely kind; and many of them were talented young artists, the place could not compare to New York and the glamour and excitement surrounding Virgil—both the person and the artist. I had enrolled at the Peabody for an Artist Diploma in performance, which entailed keyboard harmony, improvisation, solfege, weekly organ lessons, a minor in voice (of all things—I croaked like a sick frog!), and the Peabody Chorus.

The chorus was mandatory for all students, and open by audition to non-students. In many ways, it was the most musically fulfilling of all the required courses.

In addition, to placate my dear mother who was adamant that I get at least a bachelor's degree, I took the required academic courses from the affiliated Johns Hopkins University.

To keep body and soul together, and supplement the small amount of money my parents sent me monthly, I had to take a church job—first at a Methodist church in the suburbs, where there was a new and quite good three-manual Möller organ, and an incompetent choir director.

Oh, how I would learn about *that* type!

Within six weeks, the church fired me "for playing too loud." This termination wasn't my first, nor was it my last. The real problem was more like "gross insubordination"; for I told the choir director he was a fool and should never be allowed near anything to do with music other than a record player.

Well, Richard Purvis would have said much worse!

Richard Torrence

And so might have Ted!—for he was famous for his cheeky comments.

My personal favorite occurred when a Rodgers organ salesman of whom Ted was not particularly fond called to say that he was arriving at the San Francisco Airport at such-and-such a time, flight number so-and-so. Hinting broadly that Ted should pick him up, he said: "What does the car look like?"

"It's yellow," Ted said, "and it has a light on top."

Another withering comment occurred following one of Fred Swann's concerts at Brick Presbyterian Church. According to Fred (who recently corroborated the story), things hadn't gone too well. Following the recital, Fred was explaining to the gathering throng how he could have butchered a piece as well known by him as Bach's "Prelude and Fugue in D Major" when Ted and Richard Morris entered the chancel. It seems that the console was in a state of total disrepair, almost to the point of being unplayable. The pedalboard was especially terrible, Fred said.

Ted stood by the console. He leaned over and surveyed the pedalboard. He said, "I see what you mean by the pedalboard, Fred. But how do you explain the manuals?"

No one who knew Ted well was ever surprised when he mixed his special sense of humor with the unvarnished truth.

I found a job at a small suburban, very high Episcopal Church (with lots of "bells and smells"), with a saintly man for a rector; an old, quirky Wurlitzer theatre pipe organ that couldn't play loud, and could barely make it through a service; and a nice group of amateur singers from within the parish to conduct; for I was both the choir director and the organist.

I found this arrangement more to my liking.

I soon realized that by attending all my classes, traveling back and forth to Johns Hopkins, and playing at the church, there was very little time to "practice like the devil," as Virgil had urged me to do. The academic classes at Johns Hopkins, although uninteresting, were not too hard to pass if one memorized a few facts. The French was not conversational, and it seemed to me of little use. Therefore, to the horror of my mother, I announced that I was no longer interested in the bachelor's degree if it was going to eat up my practice time. And that was final!

My parents' response was also final. They cut me off from all further financial assistance. I became poor from that time on; but with the church, the generosity of friends like Rodney Hanson and George Woodhead, and the friendship and camaraderie of a host of colleagues at the school, I didn't starve. I practiced, and I managed to have a great time at the school. My organ teacher, Clarence Snyder, was kind and understanding; but as the months passed, he sensed that I wasn't happy. Virgil was right. The school had changed greatly since he was a student there.

14. Wanamaker's

My next encounter with Virgil was by telephone in mid-December 1955, when I called him. He told me that I simply had to beg, borrow, or steal the money to get myself to Philadelphia a few days after Christmas. The AGO was having a mid-winter conclave, and he was going to play the much loved, gargantuan, six-manual organ in the Grand Court of the John Wanamaker department store. It was the largest playing organ in the world!

I scraped enough money together to make the trip to Philadelphia with my schoolmate and friend, Carl Freeman. We arrived at the neo-classic 30th Street Station (a magnificent building with vast open spaces, cathedral-like acoustics, and a beautiful angel standing at the entrance doors. What a place to have an organ, I fantasized!). After a short taxi ride, we arrived in front of the imposing emporium of John Wanamaker.

The concert was scheduled for 9:00 a.m., and the management delayed the regular opening of the store to paying customers until

10:30 a.m. This delay was made so that the organ could be heard to best advantage, unaccompanied by the noise of shuffling feet, crying babies, and ringing cash registers. It was a private concert for AGO members and friends, and a wonderful opportunity to hear the organ without the extraneous noises of a department store.

The Grand Court is a tremendous open space 12 or 13 stories high, surrounded by balconies on all four sides. In those days, there were enormous green velvet drapery hangings covering one whole side of the balconies that lamentably cut down the acoustic decay to almost nothing. On the opposite side of those ugly drapes was a magnificent white and gold organ case, towering a third of the way to the ceiling. Behind the case, almost to the top of the store, was the rest of the instrument—except for the Echo Organ, which was located high above the offending drapes on the other end of the Grand Court.

In the middle of the Grand Court was a large and wonderful eagle, poised to oversee all that transpired. The area around this statue was a popular place to meet friends when traveling to downtown Philadelphia. "Meet me at the eagle," was how you put it.

Several hundred people had already gathered. The concert was for a standing audience, for there could be no seats with so many sales counters in the way.

Virgil was announced. Everyone turned toward the middle of the court. Up nearly two stories, Virgil made his entrance from behind the console, which stood on a small, ornate balcony.

Virgil looked tiny from our vantage point on the main floor.

I believe that Virgil opened the program with the "Fanfare" from Wagner's *Parsifal*. I think he followed with a short and relatively light program, including the famous "Toccata" from the *Fifth Symphony* of Charles Marie Widor, the Bach "Arioso," "Giga" of Marco Enrico Bossi, and of course his own world famous arrangement of Bach's "Come, Sweet Death."

It was this unique instrument that Virgil had used to finish his legendary arrangement of the "CSD," as it was called, which he began while still at the Peabody. He needed the right orchestral organ to inspire him.

Virgil adored the Philadelphia Orchestra and its conductor at the time, Leopold Stokowski. He had heard the sumptuous Stokowski arrangement of the relatively simple harmonization that J.S. Bach made of the Chorale, "Komm, Süsser Tod" (Come, Sweet Death) in the *Musikalisches Gesangbuch*. The story of this piece thus centered on Philadelphia. It endeared Virgil to the city, and the city to Virgil.

He was asked to play one of the great evening concerts at the Wanamaker store in 1939, during an AGO Convention. When Rodman Wanamaker donated these concerts to the City of Philadelphia, they were free, and people came by the thousands. Virgil adored the Wanamaker organ because of its size, its unique symphonic sound, its enormous expressive capabilities, and its hundred-plus ranks of "string" stops—unlike any other organ in the world.

The Wanamaker organ was also linked with the greatest organ virtuosos of the time—Marcel Dupré, Marco Enrico Bossi, Charles Courboin, Sigfrid Karg-Elert, and Louis Vierne.

Many of these luminaries had made their American debut at Wanamaker's.

Virgil wanted to play something special for his first concert at this ultimate orchestral organ; and so, with the help of Bach, Stokowski, the Wanamaker organ's fabled String division, and his own special genius for molding all the above together—and at the urging of the organ tuner, Henry Baecker (they *are* helpful from time to time!)—his famous arrangement of "Come, Sweet Death" was born. It remained in his repertoire to the end of his life.

(I also played the piece at his memorial service—with the casket present—at the Crystal Cathedral in Garden Grove, California).

Hearing Virgil play the work on that organ during the mid-winter conclave was a moving experience for me. In all honesty, however, I was disappointed in the organ the first time I heard it. It seemed to me that an organ two to three times the size of the organs at Grace Cathedral and the Riverside Church should have packed more punch, and given me more of the "thrill" I was used to.

The problem was the drapes, which adversely affected the normally reverberant acoustics. (Now a "Lord & Taylor" store, the fabulous acoustics have been restored!)

I knew Virgil opened the organ "wide" several times; but it sounded like a great roar from miles away and had little impact on me. Still, Virgil brought down the house with his infectious drive and boundless enthusiasm; and he succeeded in rousing all those normally staid organists to cheering.

After the concert, we went to greet Virgil on the mezzanine level. After hugging me, he asked me to wait until most of the people had gone. He wanted to show me the console. At that point, we were in the women's shoe department, because you had to get to the console through a small aisle in the women's shoe stock room. This detour amused Virgil greatly. "Imagine, playing the largest organ in the world by having to walk through ladies shoes to get to the console!" he roared.

Once through the doorway and onto the balcony, there was an enormous six-manual console that contained hundreds of colored, tilting tablets to control the stops. By this time, the store was open for business, and I looked down at throngs of busy shoppers. Virgil hopped on the bench to demonstrate the innumerable controls.

There were eleven expression pedals that looked like the metal supports you put your shoes on at a shoeshine stand. These pedals controlled the expression of the various divisions of the organ. A crescendo pedal added and subtracted stops as you either opened or shut the pedal.

The crescendo pedal on the Wanamaker organ was placed midway in a row of expression pedals, instead of being the last pedal on the right, as it usually is on American organs.

Virgil began to operate the crescendo pedal. The organ went quickly from pianissimo to double forte.

Then he said, "Look at this, Teddy!" When the crescendo pedal was all the way open he simply raised the upper portion of his right foot to a point a little higher, where there was a lever that turned on the sforzando (which is another name for "tutti"). Then the monster really roared! Virgil touched the lever again, releasing the sforzando lever, and slowly ran the crescendo pedal down to the closed position and a shimmering pianissimo (or so I imagined, for the noise of the cash registers and shoppers drowned out most of the sound).

Virgil pointed out that it was possible to run this organ "up and down like a window shade—which you need to do, because not one button on this wonderful girl works!"

He began pressing one button after another that would ordinarily change the stops in rapid order to any sequence desired by the performer. Nothing happened—the action was totally dead. These buttons, located within easy reach, are part of the combination action that enables any organist on almost every contemporary organ in the world to set sounds and to manage quick registration changes of timbre and tone. It's this mixing of tone color and pitches that allows the organist to orchestrate (or "register") the sounds he wants, and makes the mixture of sounds "his own."

Dupré made Wanamaker's sound one way; Charles Courboin, the former Wanamaker organist, another; and Virgil had his own favorite mixture of sounds at Wanamaker's, as well as Riverside and every other organ he played throughout the world. Instant control was possible because of settable combination pistons or buttons—except on the Wanamaker organ!

At the console of the Wanamaker organ (1939)

Virgil explained that although the combination action here was surely the biggest ever imagined at the time, it had ceased to function several years before. "The powers that be aren't interested in coughing up the cash to pay for a new combination action," he said.

Therefore, Virgil had to play his concert with an assistant on each side, able to deal with 175 stops according to his shouted commands, and do the rest of the work himself using the crescendo pedal and the sforzando lever.

Of all the organs in the world that needed a large and reliable combination action, Wanamaker's was it! It astounded me how well Virgil played under such handicaps. It didn't seem to phase him.

A modern combination action has now been installed, and Lord & Taylor has invested considerable money into restoring the old store. An organization called "Friends of the Wanamaker Organ" is also restoring the great instrument so that future generations can enjoy music in the Grand Court's splendid acoustical setting.

---

15. Mary Vogt

"You could have a seated dinner for a dozen people in the back of this console," Virgil said to me. I believed him, for the console was immense. Then he introduced me to a tiny woman with sparkling eyes and red hair who had just stepped through the door from women's shoes. "This sweetheart is Mary Vogt, the organist of the Wanamaker Store, and the single reason this magnificent organ stands here. She's brought every famous organist in the world to play here: Dupré, Bossi, Vierne—*and me!* She's a pistol, and I adore her. Ted, you must come back here at noon to hear this little dynamo kick the you-know-what out of this baby."

Mary was nearly 70 at the time. The gigantic console dwarfed her. She hugged and kissed Virgil, and expressed her pleasure with the concert and such a large crowd, although they were mostly organists, whom she said she usually couldn't abide. "Most of the young ones are little snobby shits who want to hear squeaks and squawks and come here to laugh."

Virgil and I screamed with laughter, and Mary beamed! Virgil turned around on the bench, and launched into Elgar's "Pomp and Circumstance March #1," and toward the end of it, with all stops controlled by hand, crescendo pedal, and sforzando, the console telephone began to ring and the red telephone light flash. Neither Mary nor Virgil paid any attention until the march ended, whereupon Mary answered the telephone then said to us, "The lousy sons of bitches are calling to complain the organ's too loud!"

Mary then pleaded with Virgil to play the noonday concert. "How can I possibly play after the fabulous recital you just gave?"

Virgil said okay, and turned around on the bench. After softer melodic pieces and a scherzo, and another rip-roaring toccata, the offending telephone was continuously lighting and flashing. Mary said, "We'd better get the hell out of here before they lynch us. Besides, it's time for lunch, and I need a drink!"

We followed her; and for the next several hours she regaled us with wonderful stories about the famous organists connected with the Wanamaker organ. Virgil told me later how Mary began working in the sheet music department of the store when she was only 15 or 16 years old. She must have been a very attractive young woman in addition to her musical talent, for Rodman Wanamaker (son of the founder) took an instant shine to her.

Her rise to power in the music department of the store was rapid. She had a lot to do with running the concerts at both the Philadelphia and New York stores. The store in lower-Manhattan had an auditorium for concerts, and a large five-manual organ. Rodman Wanamaker loved music, and in particular the organ. Hence these two behemoths, in Philadelphia and New York.

The New York Wanamaker Store was closed in 1955. The organ had already been removed from the Auditorium. After that time, most of Wanamaker's musical energies enriched only the Philadelphia area.

Mary told us that Rodman had always envisioned another organ, the same size as the one in the Grand Court, installed at the opposite end so that they could "bark back and forth at one another." She told us of the wonderful collection of stringed instruments ("our Strads") that she had helped Rodman assemble; and of the legendary concerts of the combined Philadelphia and New York Philharmonic orchestras, Leopold Stokowski conducting, and with Charles Courboin at the organ, playing spectacular organ and orchestra arrangements of Bach's "Passacaglia and Fugue," as well as other works.

Rodman had once sent her to England to buy a great bell for the store. She returned with a monster so huge that it could only be installed on top of what became the Pennsylvania National Bank a few blocks away. The weight alone would not only have brought Wanamaker's ceiling crashing down over the Grand Court, but deafened its customers. What a wonderful sound that bell still makes to this day!

Mary Vogt was an institution in Philadelphia from the time Rodman made her Principal Organist of the Grand Court, playing at least two or three times a day (at noon and six in the afternoon, and at closing time every late business day). In addition, she was in charge of all special musical events, and of the famous Wanamaker Christmas pageants. She constantly complained about the management of the store in those years not taking care of the organ (although they paid for regular maintenance—just not a new combination action). She said that when she did play, the management complained she was "too loud, too high brow. They want show tunes and such. This isn't a theatre organ; but they're so damned dumb they don't know anything about it!"

She obviously adored Virgil, and he always treated her with great love and affection. In the many years I knew her she was always extremely kind to me. I had a standing invitation to visit her in the organ loft at the Grand Court, and always to play a piece or two.

Mary was a character, and she was always entertaining. She was so short that in order to put stops on and off, she had to roll up sheet music and swat at the tablets. Her system wasn't exactly accurate, but accuracy wasn't Mary's prime concern. Nor did the organ have to speak clearly. There were all those cash registers!

The store was always concerned about her welfare. As Virgil told it, Rodman had remembered Mary in his will, decreeing that she was to be the organist of the Grand Court as long as she lived. Virgil also claimed that when Rodman Wanamaker's wife died, Rodman was located at Mary's residence (where Virgil frequently stayed—it was a charming Philadelphia row house in the center of the city). She had previously been playing the tunes of Sigmund Romberg to him on the Grand Court organ until the early hours of the morning.

16. In My Glory

Virgil had invited me to spend some of the 1955-56 holidays in New York; but because of my church job, and since I was an impoverished student, I couldn't accept. I was overjoyed to have seen him in Philadelphia on the Wanamaker organ, and to have been included in the wonderful time with Mary Vogt, and I had to be content with that.

Virgil was concerned about my welfare, whether I liked the Peabody or not, and if I was practicing. The truth was that although

I was practicing, I hated the school. It wasn't because the Peabody wasn't excellent. In many ways it was.

Since my parents had refused to help me further, my financial situation was precarious, if not downright frenzied. Life at the school was not nearly as glamorous, exciting, or inspiring as a single hour spent with Virgil and his many friends. I spent the rest of the school year muddling through the courses, always practicing, but thinking of New York, the Riverside Church organ, and Virgil Fox.

Sometime during the summer of 1956, I telephoned Virgil to say hello, and he said, "Why don't you come to New York? I need some assistance. Bob's still in Paris."

I explained that I would come in a minute, but I had no job in New York, and no money.

"Oh, Teddo, we'll find you a job and a place to stay. You can work for me and pay for your lessons."

I immediately decided to go. The prospect of studying with this great man was too alluring to worry about where I would stay or what I would eat. I remember begging one of my colleagues to drive me to New York.

Virgil, true to his word, put me in touch with a woman at the Riverside Church, Edwina Hazzard, who helped me find a person who rented rooms to students. The next day I moved to a decent room in a dear woman's apartment on Riverside Drive. Her name was Irma Steves. Through an amazing coincidence, another friend of Virgil's told me of an organist/choir director job in New Rochelle, New York at the First Presbyterian Church. I auditioned for the job and eventually I got it. Therefore, I moved to New York, I had a job, I had a place to stay, and I had the greatest organist in the world as my friend and teacher.

At last I was in my glory, studying with, and observing a great artist on an almost daily (I should say nightly) basis, and privileged to hear and meet most of the illustrious organists and choir directors in New York.

The work I did for Virgil consisted mostly of looking after his music (he had a comprehensive library) and reading his correspondence, which was often amusing and interesting. I would also make sure that his organ preludes were listed in the Sunday programs at the Riverside Church.

I often had to drive him to the train station or the airport to go off on tour. I never minded this job, for it meant driving a luxurious

Cadillac convertible that made me feel like a king. Roberta Bailey, Virgil's manager usually drove him; but when she wasn't available, I would willingly fill in. In any case, I usually tagged along. Virgil liked company at all times.

The usual weekly schedule during Virgil's regular concert season had him playing the 11:00 a.m. morning service on Sundays, followed by a hearty lunch. He would return to the church and go immediately to his fourth floor office in the tower, where he kept a cot in the closet. He would nap (complete with pajamas) for about an hour and a half in the heavily draped room. Absolutely no one was allowed to disturb him.

Around 3:45 p.m., he would appear at the console to check on the combination action buttons, practice difficult spots in that afternoon's major oratorio, and run through the afternoon service preludes (usually a mini-recital), then practice another brilliant postlude.

After Virgil's usually hair-raising performance with Richard Weagly and the choir, the Great Man would greet hundreds of people, then shower, and preside over a dinner of adoring fans and colleagues. He ate either at Butler Hall or at Stouffer's at 666 Fifth Avenue (which he always called "the Sixes"). Then he would leave for Pennsylvania Station or Grand Central Station to catch an already moving train (it happened more than once!), thus literally disappearing in a cloud of steam.

He usually played concerts in two different cities during the week, either on Tuesday and Thursday (or Tuesday and Friday) evenings. He preferred Thursday evenings in order to return for Friday evening choir rehearsals at the church.

This exhausting schedule would be repeated every week during the fall, winter, and spring. Virgil never seemed to tire of it. Although the work was arduous, the audience's adulation always buoyed him up. When there was no concert audience, at least there was the congregation of the church or the Riverside Choir. Both groups were amply endowed with adoring fans and amusing characters.

When no listeners were around to hear his music, there was still the public. Virgil felt compelled to be "on stage" and noticed at all times. More often than not, during our late evening window shopping tours along Fifth Avenue, he would wear a Turkish towel, set turban-like, on his head. The sight of him attracted the desired attention. People pointed and stared in wonderment, which embarrassed me. Virgil roared with laughter.

"Never mind those fools! I've just taken a shower and I'm not going to catch my death from open pores!" He giggled fiendishly, like a small child.

Virgil occasionally went to the Automat near Carnegie Hall. (He loved the colorful kooks who often filled the place.) Virgil would always decide to go just at closing time (9:00 p.m.), and arrive at the door, with great delight, around 8:57 p.m. He would then proceed to order everything in sight. He loved cafeterias, and I must say the food was good. However, Virgil especially liked the fact that the Automat was cheap.

Virgil was well known in these eateries. Sometimes, when he arrived late, a minute before closing time, the management would glare and not want to seat him. Virgil, in his stentorian voice, would state the time and say, "Is the restaurant open, or is the restaurant *not* open," and sweep aside all opposition.

Signed: "For Ted—With high expectations and fond regards, Roberta [Bailey]"
(Photo by Bruno of Hollywood)

I can still picture him, sitting in the Automat, eating his third piece of blueberry pie with chocolate ice cream. Wearing his great fur-collared coat and a beret on his head, he's completely oblivious to the glowering chaos surrounding him.

All other tables have chairs on top of them, wet mops are swishing all around, and the lights are turning out, one by one. The commotion barely phases him.

"Just take your time. We're not moving 'til we're good and ready!"

Virgil takes his time, then finally sweeps grandly out of the restaurant. The rest of us sheepishly follow. Once out on the street, he roars with laughter, and says, "The *nerve* of them!"

Life was never dull around this man.

Virgil treated us all as if we were his children. He expected us to do as he wished.

For example, I could see how much his manager, Roberta, adored him. She hung onto every word. He treated her like his daughter, although she was supposed to be able to make the important decisions about his concert bookings and career. Even then, in the 1950s, he was the most popular concert organist around. Whenever the "other" one (E. Power Biggs) was mentioned, Virgil would say, referring to his nickname, "Poor old Jimmy! He's been dead from the neck up and the waist down for years!"

I remember one evening when Roberta lamented the fact that there were not enough concert dates for the coming season. Virgil was insisting on a higher fee than he had previously charged for a concert. He now wanted $750 per concert! Roberta replied that that was "suicide." Virgil answered, "Listen here, young lady! I'll make these decisions, and that's what they'll have to pay to get this one to play!"

It was the first sign of tension I noticed that concerned his career or his management. That tension would erupt from time to time.

---

17. The Palace in Englewood

I visited Virgil many times at his home in Englewood, New Jersey. He lived in quite a palace at 394 East Palisade Avenue. The imposing gray stone mansion was set back from the street on a wooded two acre estate. One could enter the house either through the front door, the rear door, or the door of the porte-cochere.

The small foyer opened onto a splendid hallway, that went up three steps. To the right was a beautiful oak paneled library. Directly ahead was the drawing room, which Virgil called his music room. On the left was a dining room painted mostly green with green and yellow murals on the walls. Off the dining room was the serving kitchen, which was adjacent to the larger kitchen and the pantry. Near the kitchens was "the sewing room," which was probably a servants' dining room before Virgil moved in.

On the left side of the hallway, as one entered the house from the foyer, was a grand staircase that led to the upstairs quarters. On the first landing was a lovely room over the porte-cochere. Up more stairs and to the right was a large suite that served as Virgil's bedroom. It was decorated in various shades of pink, and had an adjoining dressing room and bath. At the end of the central hall was another large bedroom, which shared his bath.

On the left at the top of the stairs—across from Virgil's bedroom—was the largest suite, occupied by Richard Weagly. It was superbly decorated in shades of blue, and had an enormous bathroom and closet. Next to Richard's bedroom was a sitting porch, then another suite (consisting of a bedroom and a bath) that was occupied by Richard's mother, Grace Weagly.

From the second floor, stairs went up to a third floor of less imposing size and stature. These rooms were supposed to be for servants; but Virgil used to put guests up there, saying, "We have no servants. We're the servants."

Virgil adored this 26-room mansion, and had lavished a lot of attention on it. It was decorated like its owner often was, in "Virgilian" hues of pink and lavender, plus large swatches of bolder color here and there for dramatic effect. The "music room" was the main room of the house; and just off this gracious and spacious room was a glassed in solarium with a vaulted ceiling that ran the whole length of the front of the house. Therefore, you could enter the solarium through one of the two arches of the music room that led into it, through the library, or from the outside. The solarium was furnished in a Southern California style, while the music room was filled with copies of period furniture and comfortable sofas.

Virgil's wonderful old ebony Mason & Hamlin grand piano sat in the living room. Framed prints of European organ cases and Italian Palladian prints hung on the walls. Italian glass, pictures in ornate frames, a Venetian mirror, a Malvina Hoffman statue of a nude male—quite lifelike and magnificent, dominated the long coffee table. A magnificent Savonnerie carpet in hues of violet, pink, and gray (usually rolled up to save it from wear and tear) lay on the music room floor. There was a wonderful tapestry on one wall (which was a gift from Lily Fogel, who descended from the Guggenheim family, and who was married to Henry Fogel, an Under Secretary to President Roosevelt's Secretary of the Treasury, Henry Morganthau Jr.) Over the fireplace was one of my favorite items: an oil painting of a French organ case surrounded by what looked like ethereal smoke—all painted impressionistically in hues of violet and pink. The title was *"Les Voix Celestes,"* named for the undulating organ stops we all loved. Angels seemed to be escaping from the organ case.

Virgil claimed that the painting wasn't good; but he loved it, and so did I.

The room was a hodge-podge of styles and colors; but it was nevertheless warm and inviting, especially when Virgil was in it.

When I first visited the house, there was no real organ in it, only a concert-model Hammond electric organ in the room above the porte-cochere. This instrument was seldom, if ever, played! Virgil claimed he bought the house because it had once had an organ in it; and it was true that there was an organ chamber in the basement, under

Virgil Fox's 26-room greystone Tudor house in Englewood, New Jersey

the music room. This chamber was too small for any organ Virgil might want; and when he finally got an organ in the house, he had to sacrifice large parts of his basement and his solarium.

I seldom visited the house during daylight hours, and so I rarely saw Grace Weagly, and would only see her son, Richard, at the church during the week.

Whenever Virgil and I went into the house, it was in the evening. Sometimes it was for a party with the choir. If it wasn't for the choir, then any gathering would soon become a small party after Richard and his mother had retired for the night.

Virgil was a nocturnal person in a house where Richard

Descending the staircase of the Englewood mansion wearing a Spanish Bullfighter's cape designed by Seseña of Madrid

and his mother kept more normal hours. Therefore, Virgil would keep his voice down in the kitchen and throughout the upstairs in order not to disturb them. I thought he was quite nice about it, since it was his house; but I soon learned that he simply didn't want to "rattle their cages," which could lead to an unpleasant harangue.

Richard seldom joined us at evening meals after the oratorios or concerts, preferring the company of the older women in the choir, or some of his voice students or friends in the music profession. He teased us for being Virgil's followers, calling us Virgil's "boys," or sometimes "sycophants." Although he usually said things with humor, there could often be a nasty tone to these remarks that disturbed me. Richard was usually nice to us when Virgil wasn't around; but he could be cool and abrasive when he was.

18. The Shortest Chapter: Virgil's Sex Life

Everyone who knew Virgil understood that he and Richard Weagly were lovers. Virgil was always open about his sexual preference, and made the subject a lively part of many discussions. He was matter-of-fact about the subject at a time when most gay musicians, even flamboyant ones like me, were terrified to peek out at the world from behind some frilly closet door.

Virgil was not effeminate. He had a deeply resonant voice and a wonderful open, friendly manner with anyone receptive to the sunshine of his smile and personality. He adored most women; and he got along with them extremely well, although he claimed never to have had sexual inclinations toward any of them.

Anyone who was gay knew exactly what Virgil was. For one thing, he belonged to the music world—and specifically, the organ world, which was dominated by gay men at that time. We often asked ourselves, why are so many male American organists gay?

I first learned about this phenomenon when I was a chorister in the Grace Cathedral choir. One day Richard Purvis called another choirboy and me who spent a lot of time around the cathedral into his office to warn us, "This cathedral is alive with homosexuals!" He told us to be very careful and report any advances made to us by visitors or the many people that "hung around" the cathedral.

That warning taught me the medical term for my own inclinations, which I accepted in a natural way; or, as they say, "like a duck takes to water"—that is, without the slightest remorse or trauma, even in those repressive days.

On the other hand, I lived in a world of people who, if they weren't gay themselves (as Richard Purvis was), were either extremely understanding, broad-minded, or at least tolerant. Thus, in many ways, I was lucky to be protected against intolerance by living in the rarefied atmosphere of the church and its music.

Then I met Virgil, who presented certainly the most influential role model I could possibly choose, and who was an openly gay man. He had "been" with Richard Weagly at that point more than 25 years, and professed to have an extremely happy, even lusty sex life with his "mate."

Virgil was deadly critical of promiscuity, and preached to everyone around him to stay out of bars—especially "gay bars, where God only knows what kinds of queers go there, or where they've been, or what awful things they've done!"

Almost as bad were "the alcohol and smoke!" which Virgil loathed; or "the drink"; and any form of tobacco ("that filthy weed!"). He was extremely Puritanical!

Virgil felt that one should find a lover and stay with that lover for life. He was quite proud of who he was, and never once did he feel the slightest bit second class. He projected a positive attitude for us all, and I shall always be grateful to him for making us feel normal about these things. A great many friends have had extreme problems and guilt about being gay—but not us!

Virgil did have an insatiable desire to know, however, what were the sexual predilections of anyone who entered his orbit. Thus, at some meal, or in the car, or while strolling with a new acquaintance, he would inevitably broach the subject. Bold as a brass monkey, he'd ask, "Have you ever had sexual relations with another male?"

If I was around I could feel it coming, and would nearly die with embarrassment (and often interest!) for the hapless victim.

I often felt that Richard Weagly was jealous of the many young men who surrounded Virgil. He shouldn't have worried (until some years later), for all that Virgil ever did was to demonstrate his love and affection by a hug or a kiss behind the ear.

Virgil called practically everyone "Honey," or "Sweet Child," or some other endearing name that wasn't exactly in the most masculine of styles—regardless of whether "Cherry Blossom" was straight or gay!

There was an incident when Dr. Tibbets, one of the most elderly and dignified ministers of the Riverside Church, walked by the organ console during a rehearsal and greeted Virgil, who replied "How good to see you, Honey!"

The good doctor wasn't amused. He said, "I'm not your Honey, and kindly never address me that way again!"

Virgil said, "I call everybody Honey; don't be upset!"

19. Artistic Differences

Both Richard Weagly and his mother Grace were envious of Virgil's career. They had lived with him for many years, during which the two men had made a truly wonderful team. Richard tended to the business of running the choir, chose excellent repertoire, attended church staff meetings, and handled the tedious details and clerical work that a church like Riverside required. Virgil took pride in the fact that he rarely attended staff meetings and only occasionally visited a meeting of the Music Committee—if any discussion might affect him. Such habits gave rise to jealousy and gossip among many of the church's employees. Virgil was the star of the music department, and he, and everyone else, knew it.

When the church first approached Virgil to be its organist, he insisted they hire Richard Weagly as well. Richard was a gifted and tasteful man, which he proved by creating one of the best choirs in New York. He was responsible for premiering and commissioning many contemporary English and American anthems and choral works—particularly ones by Ralph Vaughan Williams, who was Richard's friend for many years. The choral music in the services and oratorio performances at the church were always first rate. However, Richard was a perfectionist. He was overly cautious, and always worried about what the critics might say. He usually felt that Virgil's accompaniments to the hymns, anthems, and oratorios were too extroverted, too loud, and not in the "right style." Virgil paid little or no attention, or maybe offered a slight bit of restraint for fifteen minutes the following Sunday; but then he'd be off and running in his usual fashion.

So it went, as it always does for any gifted organist and most church congregations: the hymns are too slow, too fast, too loud, or too soft! People look upon organists as servants, to do as they're told to. Bach and Mozart suffered in this way, and so Virgil and all his gifted colleagues were—and continue to be—in good company.

Virgil insisted on being visible at concerts wherever humanly possible. This requirement was especially true at Riverside, where the new console had been placed on a movable platform so that it could be moved to the front and center of the chancel area where everyone could see exactly what the performer did on the organ. Virgil always said, "Rubenstein doesn't play behind a potted palm! Why should I?"

There was a serious problem at Riverside, however. Virgil was determined that at the opening concerts of the new organ his lovely console would be completely visible. Not many objected to this requirement in theory; but the antique carved stalls and choir pews at Riverside are extremely valuable and could easily be damaged. They were also not easily moved to be stored out of the way. Therefore, the music committee said, "No, they will not be moved!"

After a terrible row, they were moved for the dedicatory concerts—"but never again!"

Virgil had to be content with a large, heavy mirror installed behind the console just for the organ concerts. It was tilted so that nearly everyone in the church could see all five keyboards as Virgil manipulated the stops. The pedals were never visible, unfortunately, thus depriving the audience of viewing one of the most prodigious pedal techniques (and possibly the most spectacular) in history.

Virgil's pedal technique was uniquely his own. He always said, "Play on the pedals as you would walk." All his playing was extremely rhythmic, including that of the pedals; and he made great use of the toe (or "point" as he called it). The knees were not clamped tightly together, as some European methods recommended, but moved into various positions—whatever was comfortable. It all seemed effortless, and it all looked elegant.

For speed and accuracy, and most importantly, to be expressive of "the space between the notes" (which was how Virgil referred to the organ's unique manner of communicating rhythm despite its mechanical limitations), Virgil's technique was astonishing. He actually danced on the pedalboard!

T. Ernest Nichols, a former student of Virgil Fox, now resides in Muncie, Indiana.

T. Ernest Nichols

In 1948, Virgil Fox appeared at Vanderbilt University's Neely Chapel in Nashville. Although I was only ten years old, in military school, I was stunned by the playing. I immediately decided to learn from this great artist in person.

I moved to New York in 1960. By the end of the year, I was speaking with Virgil in one of his post-concert receiving lines at the Riverside Church and was astounded that he remembered me from twelve years before! He kept studying my face, then suddenly blurted out, "Military uniform. Nashville. Vanderbilt. Awful organ! Shades nailed shut!"

I stammered, "Yes! Yes!"

Around that time, I met Robert Hebble, who, in turn, introduced me to Ted Alan Worth, who recommended me for study with Fox. However, through Bob Hebble, I was able to observe Virgil's playing practically at his elbow for almost two years before beginning formal studies.

Just before my audition for Virgil, when the prospect of being rejected as a pupil made it difficult to keep down food or sleep for several days, Richard Torrence, his manager, gave me a pep talk that will remain with me always. I was petrified! However, Torrence said exactly the right thing: "Virgil respects you. He respects music. He is, above all, a musician. Just listen and learn. The things he will teach you can take you farther than an organ console."

They did!

Even Virgil's most ardent critics would say that he could not be equaled technically. The principal controversy about Virgil Fox was his "Romanticizing" of classical composers—along with the fact that most people don't like organ music.

Why should they? Most organ music is trite and without substance. Most instruments are second-rate and manned by dull players who feel that they have mastered the instrument by learning notes. It's not enough.

There was no doubt of Virgil Fox's technical prowess. Organists tend to be "glue fingered." Hence, the boring, droning sound generally associated with the instrument. Moreover, the release of a note is as important as its attack. Virgil Fox built his career mainly on those two facts: attack and release.

The Fox technique was simple: Keep your fingers on the keys ("not in, on!") and play the pedals "as you walk." Keep the knee above the ankle at all times. (In other words, don't play with your knees together.) Keep wrists down and play on the tips of curved fingers. Don't put your thumb on a black key. Play close to the front of the black keys whenever possible. Play sequenced passages with the same fingering—always. Do anything to avoid high wrists and turning the hand right to left—as in pushing the thumb towards the back of a black key. Don't stiffen your back to sit straight. (In fact, a little slouching keeps tension out of the forearms from the lowered wrists. If it was good enough for Horowitz and Fox, it's good enough for you!) Sit comfortably enough so that no matter how far you must reach for manuals, registration, or to play extensive pedal passages, you never have to turn your entire body. (You don't believe me? Play the last page of Bach's "In Dir Ist Freude," "Prelude and Fugue in D Major," or the last three pages of the "Final" from Vierne's Sixth Organ Symphony.) Arrange the height of the bench so that you have to lift your feet off the pedalboard to move them around. If the bench is too high, you'll have no balance. Play the pedals mostly with alternate toes (which gives clarity), but you must be able to use the heel without "stretching" the Achilles tendon. Oh, yes, push pistons with the flat of the thumb, never the end of a finger.

What most people do not realize about Virgil Fox is that he played the piano extremely well. He also insisted that his pupils work as diligently on the piano as the organ. It was a must. Virgil had hands like spiders, and he had worked out some kind of compromise with a playing system promoted by Wanda Landowska that was almost perfect for him. Virgil's system was loosely based on an "esoteric" piano technique fostered by the Polish pianist and pedagogue at Russia's St. Petersburg Conservatory, Teodor Leschetizky (1830-1915). Leschetizky taught Paderewski and Schnabel, among others.

The "actual" Leschetizky Method, as Virgil called it, mainly used the arched hand and flexible wrist. The result was a unique pianistic timbre for each player. The reason it was considered "esoteric" is that it was slightly modified for each player, the technique being a means to an end, as soprano, Amelita Galli-Curci, used to say. (She was a piano graduate of the Milano Conservatory, and used a phrasing and musical style similar to Virgil's. She became the legendary coloratura soprano after encouragement from the great Pietro Mascagni, who was a family friend.)

The Leschetizky Method is an adaptable system of playing that allows for maximum flexibility, power, and relaxation. Organists gain a remarkable technical consistency with the system. The pressure on the organ key involves the length of time the note sounds. The combination of acoustics and quality of sound gives the illusion of more or less sound.

Virgil taught that the player must press the key to the bottom of the key fall, also, because it allows each pipe to achieve full speech, and is the primary secret of the solid sound in Virgil's playing. Another secret was the release of each note. This enhances the rhythm and gives maximum clarity to, both, legato and marcato playing. He was accused of playing détaché; but, in reality, there was a phrasing that was included in those crisp, clean passages. Heifitz used the same phrasing as well as Galli-Curci and Wilhelm Backhaus.

"The Leschetizky Method is for the fingers, not the hand, not the arm, not the shoulder," Virgil would say. "Pianists are concerned with the areas other than the fingers because of pressures involved in timbre and volume exclusive to that instrument. But, even then, they must be used sparingly or tensions will develop in the upper arms and ultimately inhibit finger flexibility." One afternoon at the Riverside Church, Virgil caught me with my wrists up—actually, he could hear it in the playing—anyone can if they know what to listen for. He stopped me and got right in my ear, as if he were telling a secret, and said in a husky whisper, "Honey, you are not playing the Wanamaker String Organ. Get those wrists down!"

Virgil used to tell about escorting Artur Rubenstein around the recovery areas of Walter Reed Hospital during the Second World War. (Virgil was a musical therapist at Walter Reed during his service time in the military.) A soldier asked Rubenstein where the fingers should be when playing the piano. "On the keys, of course," came Rubenstein's terse reply. Virgil said the same if you asked him about playing the organ.

Virgil truly disliked Eighteenth Century Germanic-style instruments. He found them inflexible, too loud all the time, making everything sound alike, and limited in compass. He believed that anyone who claims they really enjoy playing tracker organs should ride to church on horseback, use oil lamps to read music, and hire adolescents to pump wind into their instruments. Think of what the New York Philharmonic would be like with a section of Sackbuts and Tenoroons! Or, how would Rubenstein and Horowitz have fared with the old pianoforte on which Beethoven composed the "Moonlight Sonata"?

I cannot extol the virtues of Virgil's technique enough! It worked for him for over 50 years. So far, it's kept me "in the business," as they say, for 52 years.

Virgil Fox was a great artist and musician. He was a technician without peer. Someone said that a genius is one who makes a science out of an art and an art out of a science. Virgil did that with every performance. He had the fortitude to persevere.

I can't imagine any organist—or pianist!—contributing finer or more sensible theories and practices.

In his library, studying a volume of his complete edition of
the Bach-Gesellschaft zu Leipzig *(the complete works of J.S. Bach)*

There's a wonderful story Virgil told about one of his first lessons with Marcel Dupré in Paris.

The great Dupré's students always played from editions that Dupré had edited himself. Thus, he had editions of the complete works of Bach, Handel, Mendelssohn, and Liszt, as well as his own famous and brilliant compositions. His editions weren't cheap, even in those days; and Virgil went to considerable expense to acquire the necessary volumes.

Dupré asked Virgil what he would play at his first lesson. Virgil replied "the Bach 'Prelude and Fugue in D Major.'"

The prelude opens with a D major scale and complicated pedal arpeggios. The fugue has a dazzling subject which, when Bach transfers it to the pedals, is a real *tour de force*. Virgil told us that he played the piece flawlessly throughout.

Dupré said, "Too fast, too detached!" (The French in those days were famous for a singing but often-lugubrious legato phrasing, even in a rhythmic Bach work.) "Where did you get that idea of pedaling? You must buy my editions of pedal scales with my markings for exactly how to pedal, the heel and toe, and so forth, and prepare them for me—just one or two scales before each lesson."

Virgil hadn't gone to the great Marcel Dupré to study pedal scales! He'd gone to study the great monuments of organ literature.

Infuriated, and hurt, Virgil purchased the Dupré edition of pedal scales, memorized the markings, and played them *all* in the style of Dupré at his next lesson.

Dupré's only comment was *"Bon!"*

Virgil said Dupré never asked to hear another scale; and Virgil said that he never again followed Dupré's markings!

Robert Hebble was present when the decision was made to replace the Riverside Church organ.

Robert Hebble

From the time I went to Riverside in 1950 with Virgil, the Hook and Hastings organ put in there in the 1930s had always behaved miserably during the week, but seemed fine and dandy on Sunday mornings. This odd phenomenon drove Virgil crazy, as he was always asking the Trustees at the church to buy a new organ.

Then, one fateful Easter in 1954, more than 4,000 people were crammed into the church (including President and Mrs. Eisenhower!—the guests of Mr. and Mrs. John D. Rockefeller Jr.) with loudspeakers blasting out on Riverside Drive to the overflow crowds.

As the choir finished a glorious anthem, three notes on what was then the loudest stop in the organ—the Solo Tuba—continued to play what was definitely not one of my famous "$50 chords." I was about to reach over to Virgil's left to shut off the organ motors when Virgil blocked my hand and said, "Don't touch a thing! This is the answer to a prayer!"

Dr. McCracken was unable to begin his sermon because of the raucous-sounding ciphers. Virgil started walking down the center of the chancel in full view of the congregation, down the steps, and over to the side door to the organ chambers where he turned on three floor levels of fluorescent lights. It wasn't pretty.

He climbed up two separate ladders while the whole congregation watched, disconnected the offending pipes at the very top level, then climbed back down.

At the end of the service, Mr. Rockefeller bolted through the curtained doorway behind the console.

"Virgil, what is it we need?" he asked.

"A new organ!"

About a year later, Virgil played the dedication concert of the new Æolian-Skinner organ!

Signed (across the bottom three manuals of the Riverside console):
"For Teddy Worth with the greatest anticipation. VF" (1956)

Richard Torrence

I remember finding the following letter from John D. Rockefeller Jr. while I was reorganizing Virgil's fourth floor office. I believe it said the following:

Dear Virgil:

My wife has spoken with you several times about how loudly you play the organ, yet you continue to ignore her warnings. What am I do to?

If I had a cook that I had instructed to make a soft boiled egg every morning for my breakfast, and she persisted in serving me a hard boiled egg, what would I do?

I hope that you will come to be a longstanding

member of the Riverside family.

Yours,
John D. Rockefeller Jr.

Virgil answered the letter simply:

Dear Mr. Rockefeller:

In your letter you speak of a servant-master
relationship.
Ours is not.

Sincerely,
Virgil Fox

*I knew that Virgil was upset when he wasn't asked to play for
Mr. Rockefeller's funeral. Both men rose in my esteem, however,
after I read this exchange of letters between Virgil and the man he
used to refer to as "John D. Rocks"—who chose not to fire Virgil
despite the obvious insubordination.*

---

20. Church Mice

Life around Riverside was always exciting. I loved being around
that stately building with all the eccentric characters that flourish
in a church like that.

There was Mrs. Coil, who ran the Riverside cafeteria, which produced good food at reasonable prices. Virgil adored her. She lavished
attention and chocolate desserts on him, and always took great care
of us. God help anyone who said anything offensive about the organist Virgil Fox within earshot of Mrs. Coil!

Students from Union Theological Seminary and the Juilliard School
of Music ate regularly at the Riverside cafeteria; and some of them
would make snide comments having heard their own less gifted teachers denigrate Virgil or his playing. Virgil claimed that if she ever heard
these remarks, "Coil would run them outta here with a butcher knife!"

Then there was Gertrude Fagan, whose office was in the narthex of the church. She was in charge of weddings, funerals, rehearsals, and guided tours (in that order). She was always reminding Virgil to be on time for wedding rehearsals. I had permission to practice on the organ whenever it was available, and I used that privilege to the fullest—and too often to the loudest! Gertrude was always asking me to play softer. When Virgil would return from a weeklong tour, she would tell him, "That kid nearly knocked the tower down while you were away. Too damned loud!"

Virgil would roar, "Fagan's going to murder you and make life miserable for me if you don't cut down the volume!"

I would always claim to be doing exactly what he did; and he would laugh and say, "You're the only person who plays louder than I do."

Many people worked at the switchboard and desk of the Claremont Street entrance. Virgil always had some new way to greet them, or some witty remark to share. Once, as we entered after dinner, he said to one young woman, who worked there, "I hear Aunt Jane is up in her tower, banging those bells." (He was referring to the rather staid male carillonneur of Riverside, James Lawson, of whom Virgil was genuinely fond.) Without blinking an eye she replied, "Virgil, people in glass houses...."

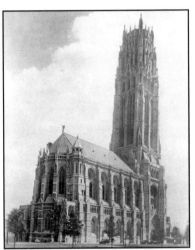

The Riverside Church, New York before a later six-story addition

Virgil screamed! He said, "I guess I've been told!"

A kind and long suffering night watchman, Johnny, would sometimes take 15 minutes to open the Claremont Street door for us after it was closed and locked for the night. He had to punch a clock throughout the church and tower at various hours, and so he was often occupied away from the door. Virgil, especially on cold or rainy nights, would say, "That damned Johnny's asleep in the tower again!"

Virgil had a key to the door (no one was supposed to have one), but he usually forgot to take it. Johnny was a dear, kind soul, who had to contend with late night telephone calls, and with the visitors whom Virgil would invite. He also had to contend with the occasional visits from people in their nightclothes, complaining about the organ playing too loud after midnight.

New York was then a Mecca for church music, organists, and fine organs. For example, Alec Wyton played at the Episcopal Cathedral of St. John the Divine. He had recently succeeded Norman Coke-Jephcott; and Virgil was friendly with both of those fine organists. I would often go to St. John's to hear the choir and the Æolian-Skinner organ. The cathedral was within walking distance of Riverside, and going into it was like entering another world, something like a medieval market place where people wandered around at will during services and musical events.

I love reverberation, but the 12 seconds of reverb that rolled around this largest Gothic cathedral in the world was often too much, even for me. The state trumpets above the west doors of the Cathedral were thrilling to hear. They were among the first (and loudest!) *en chamade* (horizontal) trumpets to be installed in an American church. They were so powerful, and potentially disturbing, that the church announced their use in printed programs.

Virgil said (probably apocryphally), "One woman who was unprepared got so frightened when she heard them that she had a heart attack!"

The trumpets are 600 feet away from the organ console, which is located above the Great Choir; and so it's a problem for the organist to blend their silvery blasts with the rest of the organ, due to the lag.

The Riverside Church area is called Morningside Heights; and it's located just west of, and overlooking, Harlem. Another superb place for music in the area was St. Paul's Chapel at Columbia University where Searle Wright was Organist and Director of Music.

Virgil and Richard Weagly were fond of Searle, and admired his compositions. One of their favorite oratorios was Searle's "The Green Blade Riseth." The two performed it almost every Easter at Riverside. The accompaniment to this work was well suited to Virgil's talents, and he delighted playing every note of it.

Searle was a first rate performer himself, and a fine conductor. Once each year the university paid him to conduct a concert with a full orchestra and his fine choir. They would perform contemporary oratorios, anthems, and festival hymn arrangements. Vaughan Williams, Holst, Howells, and Sowerby were among the fine contemporary composers represented. It was always a thrilling experience to attend those programs; for St. Paul's was also blessed with superb acoustics. (Never underestimate acoustics!)

Further downtown, on Fifth Avenue, John Huston (a close friend of Virgil's and Richard Weagly's) held forth at First Presbyterian Church in Greenwich Village. Robert Baker used to make wonderful music at Fifth Avenue Presbyterian Church; while William Self, Organist and Choirmaster at St. Thomas Church, tried making something else. (Attractive organists and male choir members would shudder whenever they heard Bill's famous greeting, "Hi, Fella!")

Vernon de Tar was at the Church of the Ascension, and head of the organ department at the Juilliard School of Music.

Vernon de Tar and Virgil were miles apart in their approaches; and the air would chill when they met on the street or at concerts. The Baroque movement had begun vigorously (although no one really knew how a Baroque organ used to be played), and Vernon was solidly in that camp. He and others advocated a cold, mechanical, and impersonal style of playing that Virgil came to loathe more and more with each passing year.

21. David McK.

Jack Ossewaarde was Organist at St. Bartholomew's Episcopal Church on Park Avenue. Leopold Stokowski had made the church famous, musically, while he was Organist and Choirmaster, just before he ascended into the musical firmament as the legendary conductor of the Philadelphia Orchestra.

Stokowski, whose music making Virgil adored, was followed by the brilliant David McK. Williams. Virgil and Richard Weagly revered David McK. When they used to work together at Brown Memorial Church in Baltimore (before they went to Riverside), they traveled to New York as often as possible to hear the Sunday afternoon oratorio performances at St. Bart's. Virgil told us that "every single seat was filled; and by the time those great afternoon performances were concluded, we felt like we'd been hit by a steam roller—it was that overwhelmingly beautiful and moving!" David had a great flair for the dramatic; and his use of the huge Æolian-Skinner organ at St. Bart's during hymns and oratorios was extremely orchestral and thrilling. (The acoustics were bad, however!)

David was completely patrician in appearance, and always wore a full-length cape when he was on church premises. In later years, he told me the reason was "to keep warm; the drafts, you know."

He would have had to look long and hard to find a draft in St. Bart's! The church was as well-heated in the winter as it was air-conditioned in the summer. Virgil used to laugh and say, "If St. Thomas Church on Fifth Avenue is for the millionaires, St. Bart's is for the billionaires!"

Virgil told me that David McK. used to improvise just before the opening hymn of the service. Once he described David's improvisation as little more than an excruciatingly dissonant, loud chord on the full organ that gradually altered and got softer until there was barely a whisper. The chord had become quite ordinary, giving the choir the right pitch with which to begin the hymn.

I would hate to think of any other organist playing that kind of a prank and continuing to be employed; but Virgil said, "It was sheer magic!"

Virgil explained that David had an assistant named Clifford. Before striking his horrendous chord, David said imperiously, "Clifford! Apply the Full Organ!" It was Clifford, then, who reduced the stops and volume of the organ gradually enough to create the proper effect.

Virgil told many stories about David. I think it's safe to say that as far as choir directors and church organists went, Virgil worshipped David more than he worshipped any other person. I think Virgil got many of his ideas about accompaniment and the orchestral use of the organ from David, and then made them uniquely his own.

"Of course, David didn't play much of the standard organ repertoire," Virgil said. "That man could mesmerize the choir and congregation by playing the great organ at services. He would conduct with great sweeping motions of his arm while doing incredible accompaniments."

David had an unusual and deliberate way of speaking. His voice was low and resonant; and his delivery was unusually slow while he fixed the listener with penetrating, dark eyes. Virgil said that when David was a young man he was the most attractive man he had ever seen.

Of course, Virgil said that about many men. For example, a great friend of David's was the organist-composer Hugh McAmis. Virgil often played McAmis's evocative piece, "Dreams," telling us that "Hugh was the most beautiful man I've ever seen!"

David said outrageous things to anyone who knew him, but always in a dignified manner. Once he was passing through the church offices when one of the secretaries inquired how he was doing.

David seemed preoccupied with something to do with his fingernail. She said, "Dr. Williams, what are you doing?" He replied, "I'm trying...to get this little piece...of shit...out from underneath...my fingernail!" Having sufficiently shocked his secretary, he went off to his own office, which Virgil said was opulent.

Virgil also loved to tell about David always feeling the return address printed on the back of an envelope he received in the mail. If the address weren't engraved, he'd throw the envelope in the wastebasket without bothering to open it. His secretary would later check all wastebaskets for important mail or checks.

David was demanding about punctuality at choir rehearsals. Any choir member who was late—even a minute or two—would arrive at the rehearsal room to find the door locked.

Virgil said, "It worked! They were never late again."

David was a legend in the world of church musicians. For example, he saw to it that services at St. Bart's began at the stroke of the appointed hour, whether or not the choir or the clergy were ready.

No one dared cross him, and he ruled the music of his "Park Avenue Palace" with an iron hand, which was gloved in lace.

Virgil did cross him once, however. The organ at St. Bart's at that time was the largest in any New York church. David invited Virgil to play a concert at St. Bart's shortly after World War II ended in Europe. Virgil was in the Army Air Force during the war, and he jumped at the chance. He had prepared the entire *Second Symphony* of Louis Vierne, but had only played a few movements of it before. This performance was to be his first of the entire work.

While Virgil was rehearsing for the concert, he said to David, "What will I say to the people on this momentous occasion? I have to tell them all about this wonderful symphony."

"Say nothing," said David. "We will have *no* speeches during concerts at St. Bartholomew's Church. People will come to hear you play, Dear Boy, not to hear you speak! If you announce you are going to give a lecture sometime, I shall be on the front row to hear you; but *not* during a concert, and *not* here!"

Virgil was determined, however, and he did speak about Vierne, the *Second Symphony*, and V-E Day.

David was livid and didn't speak to Virgil for weeks.

Many years later, David told me that he had changed his thinking on this subject when he saw thousands of people jammed into St. Mary's Cathedral in San Francisco to hear Virgil playing two concerts in a festival called "A Triumphant Blaze of Sound and Light."

I produced this festival of organ and environmental light shows in the cathedral, and played one of the concerts. Both Virgil and I spoke to the audience during our respective programs. David, who was in his late 80s at the time, told me afterwards that he now felt he had been wrong about speaking at concerts. He said that the audience had enjoyed the music more because of the informal talks; that the performers seemed more human; and that he, himself, enjoyed both our speeches.

Virgil spoke to audiences for many years before the St. Bart's concert, and he had no intention of not speaking there. He often told of the first time he ever thought about speaking to an audience. It was in Milledgeville, Georgia when he first started to concertize, and he feared that the audience at an organ inauguration would not be responsive. In those days, applause at church concerts was strictly forbidden, and the only way an artist knew whether he was "getting through" was to hear people's comments after the fact.

Virgil said, "I looked at their faces and I thought, I'm going to tell these Georgia crackers about this beautiful music, and what I'm doing on this wonderful organ!"

He would begin speaking while standing near the console. "A fugue has a *tune*," he would say, "and this is the tune of the 'A Minor Fugue' of Bach."

He would lean over the bench (sitting wasn't as effective) and play the tune. Then he would show how the second voice of the fugue entered.

"They loved it! Immediate gratification! I haven't stopped talking since!"

He never did stop for the rest of his life. However, he almost never talked at the Riverside Church or at formal concerts such as with orchestra. He always spoke at solo recitals when he was on tour, which was one of the main reasons why people loved to hear him play. He became an evangelist for the instrument and its literature; and many people who came to his concerts who were not fans of the organ, or didn't know what to expect, went away true believers after this dynamic man told them what to listen for. He then gave them something extraordinary to listen *to*.

Most music critics hate performers that speak to audiences, partly because music critics believe it's their job to elucidate the music. On the other hand, few music critics really know much about the organ and its literature. Therefore, some of Virgil's speeches did a better job educating audiences than most general music critics could.

Many organists, also, would titter and pooh-pooh Virgil's talking to an audience. The simple fact was, however, that he *had* an audience, and usually a large one. They did not!

Virgil used to say that seasoned symphony-goers know the Beethoven *Fifth Symphony*, the Tchaikovsky, Schumann, and Grieg piano concertos, and many Mozart and Haydn symphonies. "But what the hell do they know of Bach on the organ other than 'The Phantom of the Opera' [he was referring to the "Toccata and Fugue in D Minor"] or maybe the Saint-Saëns *Organ Symphony*?

"We have to help educate them in an entertaining, informative way; and that's why I speak."

Robert Fry worked for Virgil Fox's management for many years. It was his idea to appoint Marilyn Brennan to form the Virgil Fox Society.

Robert Fry

Virgil was a superb showman whose extroverted approach to music offended many conservative critics, especially when he talked too long, which was always. He reminded them too much of a revivalist preaching "The Gospel of Bach According to Fox."

His saving grace was sincerity. I once saw him practicing for a concert with his road managers watching. He launched into a verbal dissection of a Bach fugue, taking it apart and putting it back together with childlike wonder at the genius of its creator. His speech was no different from how he would speak to an audience, even though his roadies had heard the same kind of story dozens of times. For Virgil, every time was like the first time. He was always on; and his generosity in sharing his enthusiasm (if not his money) was boundless.

Richard Torrence

Community Concert circuit producers, for whom Ted and Virgil played hundreds of times on the Rodgers Touring Organ, used to tell me, "There are two kinds of artists: those who speak, and those who don't. The ones who speak are the most successful!"

22. The 1956 AGO Biennial

I n the summer of 1956, the American Guild of Organists held their biennial National Convention in New York. It was a grand occasion, because at that time New York had some of the best organs and choirs in the United States. Virgil's manager, Roberta Bailey, was the program chairman of the convention. She saw to it that fine performers were asked to perform. National conventions of the AGO drew one- to two-thousand organists and choir directors from a national membership of about 20,000; and everyone was anxious to travel to Manhattan for this great event.

I remember a virtuosic concert at St. John the Divine with Charlotte Garden, whom Virgil adored; and another, played by Ernest White at the memorable organ of St. Mary the Virgin.

E. Power Biggs played somewhere (I didn't attend); Catherine Crozier impressed everyone; Claire Coci played an Allen electronic instrument during a "Pops" concert of the New York Philharmonic at Lewisohn Stadium; and the legendary British organist, George Thalben-Ball (of Temple Church, London, who arranged "Jerusalem," the famous hymn by Sir Hubert Parry that was sung in *Chariots of Fire*) also played a solo recital on a big, blustery Casavant Frères instrument at Temple Emanu-El on Fifth Avenue.

I especially remember two of the concerts during the five-day convention. Pierre Cochereau, Titular Organist of Nôtre Dame in Paris, had been engaged to play a brand new Æolian-Skinner organ at St. Thomas Church on Fifth Avenue. The organ was a virtual monument to G. Donald Harrison, the head of the Æolian-Skinner firm of Boston. This instrument was a departure from the type of organs for which they had previously been famous. G. Donald opted for a classical style of voicing, a clearer and more severe—or brilliant—tone quality, and a European-style specification of stops.

Cochereau's concert was a triumph for both performer and instrument. Although St. Thomas Church is a magnificent Gothic church architecturally, the acoustics weren't reverberant (it has a Guastavino sound absorbent ceiling, like Riverside). That fact, together with an overcrowded, standing-room-only audience, didn't help the concert; but Cochereau overcame everything!

Tragedy preceded Cochereau's triumph, however, when we were told of the death of G. Donald Harrison. It had happened that afternoon.

Virgil adored G. Donald, although they differed on many issues and shared some disagreeable moments while the Riverside organ was being built. Virgil truly believed that G. Donald Harrison and the Æolian-Skinner Organ Company were *la crème de la crème* when it came to new instruments. In most ways, those organs were always his favorites. Pierre dedicated the program to G. Donald's memory, and played one of the most glorious improvisations I ever heard him concoct. I remember sitting with Richard Purvis. It was a sad and moving experience to be hearing the last of the great organs for which G. Donald Harrison was justifiably famous.

Signed: "Pierre Cochereau"

The second memorable occasion during that convention occurred at the Riverside Church, which presented a program for organ and choir. More than three thousand people jammed the nave and aisles of the church to hear Virgil play the prelude concert to the service (which was all Bach, and which included the "Prelude and Fugue in B Minor"). The performance was dedicated to G. Donald's memory.

The opening hymn was "O What Their Joy and Their Glory Must Be" (to the tune of *"O Quanta Qualia"*). The roar that came out of that congregation was hard to believe. Virgil opened the organ wide, and outdid himself on the interludes between verses. I sat with Richard

Purvis that evening, and shared his awe at the thrilling sound that came from the organ and the lusty singers. Tears streamed down my face.

It was only the beginning. The Riverside Choir sang the American première of Ralph Vaughan Williams' *Dona Nobis Pacem*. To hear this masterpiece performed magnificently was a unique privilege. The choir sang stunningly; but Virgil, who was all over the console like an octopus, outdid himself.

Some people claim that the organ is a poor substitute for an orchestra; and it's true that the "Dona Nobis" was originally scored for a full symphony orchestra. I have since heard the work many times with orchestral accompaniment; but anyone who heard Virgil accompany that oratorio would agree that it was more thrilling with the organ—providing Virgil played it.

I'll never forget the compelling, driving rhythm of the "Dirge for Two Veterans." The accompaniment begins softly, gradually building into a tremendous, pounding death march. It left me completely drained. The audience erupted in a tremendous ovation.

There was more. Virgil then played the American première of the *Suite, Opus 5* of the French composer, Maurice Duruflé. If ever there was a monument of impressionistic writing for the organ, this three-movement suite, with its closing "Toccata" (a *tour de force*), is it. The work is astonishing in every possible way. It requires every bit of color, nuance, and expression that a performer can give it; and it came out perfectly under Virgil's hands.

Although the work is fiendishly difficult, Virgil—as usual—made it seem effortless. The standing ovation from his peers obviously moved him deeply. When I went to greet him, he was dripping wet, tears of joy streaming down his face.

We had great fun during that memorable convention week. On one of the evenings, we were treated to a "pops" concert. It took place in the now-demolished Paramount Theatre in Times Square on its fabled Wurlitzer. During the concert, many classical organists who also loved and played the theatre organ made vignette appearances. Searle Wright played, and Richard Purvis performed a delicious rendition of "Tea for Two." Pierre Cochereau improvised in a jazzy fashion; and a dear friend of Virgil's, Roy Carlson, brought down the house with his rendition of the "Habañera" from Bizet's *Carmen*. He sang the piece in drag, in a flat falsetto voice, and with a rose in his mouth!

Roy was known to many people as the able and gifted organ-technician who maintained many organs in and around Boston—most notably Symphony Hall and the John Hays Hammond Museum in Gloucester.

Roy was a large man. Virgil said, "If he gets any larger he won't be able to get into the organ chambers!"

He did get larger; and in later years he had to hire trained assistants do the actual tuning and voicing while he held court at the console. People literally screamed with laughter watching Roy perform that night. Not the least of them was Virgil, who accompanied Roy in some of his numbers, then led the audience in a brief rendition of "Roll Out the Barrel."

I wish all organists could loosen up like they did that night, and stop taking themselves so seriously.

---

23. The Chicks Hatch Out

Shortly after the convention, an important and inspiring person came into my life. Robert Hebble arrived back from his year's study with Nadia Boulanger in Paris. I wasn't looking forward to his return, because he had been Virgil's console assistant before I had arrived, and I was afraid he would resent my presence. Virgil adored Bob, and referred to him as his "first born." He sang his praises to me constantly, which put me on edge about finally meeting him.

I needn't have bothered, for Bob was wonderful! In addition to being bright, attractive, and impeccably musical, he was entertaining; and he made me feel at home, like one of the family.

I was greatly relieved. We soon became inseparable, spending almost every waking hour together—and with Virgil in the evenings, when he was in town.

In addition to his friendship, Bob's talent overwhelmed me. To hear him improvise on the Riverside organ, or hear him accompany a singer of Broadway or pops tunes on the splendid Steinway in his tiny, elegantly decorated Washington Square apartment, was one of the great thrills of my life. Bob also taught me to appreciate beautiful things: paintings, furnishings, and all kinds of music for all kinds of instruments.

Bob spoke French. He and Virgil would often go on and on in French, teasing me, "If you want to know what we're saying about you, you must learn to speak the language!"

I think I fell in love with Bob, a little bit, in those days when he was becoming my true friend.

Therefore, life, at the time, was good to me. To be near Virgil, and to have Bob as such a close friend, was heavenly. However, some dark clouds began to hover.

Although I had a relatively good church job, it paid poorly. I couldn't avoid going into debt (which was a problem I never really solved throughout my life). In addition, I was so headstrong I couldn't stand to take suggestions from my music committee. Before long, they fired me; and I had to go to work as a clerk at the front desk of Columbia Presbyterian Hospital until someone could help me find another church job.

Richard Torrence

Ted got another job in a small office in the Empire State Building. It was a telemarketing operation that had something to do with radio jingles. For about a year, Bob Hebble worked there too (but not composing radio jingles!).

The jobs, which paid well, required frequent subway trips to visit Moe, Joe, or Vinnie (no one ever had a last name) at some bar or nightclub—never high class—in order to deliver sealed manila envelopes filled with what felt like bundles of cash. Ted later discovered that the envelopes did, indeed, contain as much as $10,000, sometimes much more.

For radio jingles?

I could no longer afford to go to restaurants nearly every day with Bob for lunch, then go with him later to join Virgil somewhere for dinner. Virgil understood the situation, and he came up with a solution that was typically "Virgil."

"Come on, Teddo," he'd say. "I'll pay anything over $3.00."

Moreover, he did. Otherwise, I would never have been able to keep up with them.

Bob was also generous, forever taking me out or feeding me in his apartment. (Bob's parents gave him a generous allowance, thank God!)

Bob and I had a wonderful time at Riverside, where we were constantly with Virgil. He called us his "chicks."

Weagly would often sneer, to our dismay; "There go Virgil's chicks! If they wore dresses they'd look just like girls!"

I would answer, "You ought to know about dresses, Richard, wearing that crimson, watered taffeta gown you call a 'vestment,' parading down the aisle every Sunday!"

Shortly after Christmas, that year, Virgil announced that he wasn't going to play the concert on the afternoon of Easter Day in the coming year. I was. "And you'd better get cracking, and it'd better be good!"

I was flabbergasted and overjoyed! I had never played a complete concert in my life, and now I was to have my first solo recital—going to make my concert debut!—in New York, on Easter Day, at the Riverside Church, on that gorgeous organ! I immediately asked Bob to write a piece for me (*gratis*, of course), and he was thrilled to do it.

Months of preparation followed, during which Virgil often coached me.

These coaching sessions were unusual. There would be a large group of people around the console, and Virgil would ask me to play for them. "This kid can knock the socks off the 'Bach D Major'" he'd say; and I would proceed to do just that—sometimes well, sometimes not so well. Afterwards, when we were alone, he would analyze my fingering or pedaling, and say, "Do it this way."

I doubt that in all the years I knew Virgil Fox that I ever had more than three formal lessons; but I was with him constantly; and I was able to observe exactly how he did everything. These unusual coaching sessions were numerous.

Evenings at Riverside were special in that there were interesting people or admirers constantly around Virgil. After dinner, a group of people would surround the console, and Virgil would play—or have Bob, some other "whiz kid," or me perform. After 11:30 p.m. or so (the "loud playing" curfew was supposed to have been 10:00 p.m.!), Virgil would dismiss the crowd—"Kids, you must go! I must work!"

Then the serious practice began, first on one or two simple, soft, but distinct stops. Virgil would begin to practice slow with rhythmic accents, then work on his repertoire until 4:00 a.m. Sometimes I would lay on top of the console just to observe, and he'd howl, "You crazy fool!" I learned so much in those evenings—through osmosis; and I'm so grateful for a privilege that few people ever have: to see an artist of Virgil's colossal gifts and stature create at such close range.

Many times Bob and I would go with Virgil on short concert tours that stayed close to New York. For example, we traveled to Connecticut, New Jersey, Pennsylvania, Ohio, and Massachusetts. These trips were great fun because Virgil drove. The non-stop conversation in the car covered every subject we could think of, from famous organs and organists all over the world to crazy, interesting, and dear people we were about to meet in the next city. Virgil never once turned on the car radio. It would have killed the conversation!

Virgil regaled us with many of his earliest childhood and family experiences, often interspersed with limericks. He knew thousands of limericks; and the more risqué the better he'd remember them! He would howl with delight at every off-color joke he could remember; and he had an endless repertoire in that department. However, when the language got particularly gross, and we'd really reached an all time low, he would admonish us with, "Kids, we've got to clean up this language! It's not right. I'm supposed to be setting an example here!"

After fifteen or twenty minutes of talking on a higher plane, he'd be right back at it again, and the car would rock with laughter—all of it going on, of course, at 80 to 90 m.p.h.

Virgil Fox

> A gay lad and lass from Rangoon
> Stayed up one night in their room.
> At a quarter-to-two, they were still wondering who
> Would do what, and with which, and to whom.

24. Futzing with the Organ

Virgil was always in a hurry, even when we were having great times. He had no use for speed limits, "road monitors," or drivers who dawdled in front of him.

When we would get to the city in which he was to play, we would go immediately to the hotel, inspect the room, always order extra blankets and pillows, often change rooms several times. He would establish contact with someone in charge of the event and head over to the church (which it usually was, concert halls with organs being rare). Upon meeting the right person, he would say "Lead me to the bench, Honey, I've got work to do!"

He usually went through this ritual just to "case out the joint," especially if he hadn't played there before. He would want to see whether the console was visible. If not, he would move heaven and earth to get the pulpits moved, the chairs or pews pulled out of the way, or, as a last resort, entreat them to rent, buy, or steal a large mirror so that the "Folks can see something!"

Many of these poor sponsors didn't understand why he had to be seen; but most did their best when possible, because Virgil felt so strongly about being seen. He was dead right!

The next request was to summon the organ tuner "immediately"; for even if the instrument were in good tune, Virgil would invariably find fault with the regulation of the tremulants.

The depth and speed of these adjustable mechanical devices, which produce vibrato effects, were of utmost importance to Virgil; and they *would* be adjusted to his liking! These adjustments were not easy tasks, for there can be several tremulants within one division of an organ. Thus, an instrument of several divisions could present real problems.

I can still hear Virgil saying, "No, no, Dear Boy, that sounds like a *goat* braying. You must think of the high F-Sharp that Flagstad holds in the 'Liebestod' of *Tristan and Isolde!*"

Too often the tuner would display little more than a blank stare, for he had no idea what Virgil was talking about. Virgil would then revert to a simpler method of trial and error that could go on for an hour or two; for some trems are cantankerous and don't want to hold at the level of depth or speed desired. These problems sometimes drove Virgil crazy; but he was always patient with the tuner, and eventually got things just the way he wanted them.

He would then try out the instrument to test the tuning and the various voices of the organ. If he heard or saw any acoustical impediment to the organ speaking into the room where it was to be heard (for example, thick drapes hanging in front of the chambers), he would shriek, "Get those filthy rags out of there! Move them or push them back! How can this poor organ speak through that hideous blanket?"

Some organ tuners were loath to touch a church's non-musical décor; and so on more than one occasion Virgil went himself into the chambers to tear down the offending "sound absorbers." He would reappear, looking triumphant. The ire of more than one church father was sometimes raised to fever pitch over these incidents.

Virgil was known all over the country by every reputable organ technician. If one of them worked once with him, they would never forget him. When Virgil arrived for return engagements in the same church, even many years later, the tuners knew what to expect. Some of them might claim, "The trems are just as you left them!" knowing they had been changed for this or that person, just to see if Virgil could tell the difference.

It took five seconds. "Oh my God, these are *awful!* Get in there and let's get at those *trems!*"

He would then discover obvious tuning and mechanical problems in the console, leave copious notes as to what he wanted, and leave for "some sustenance."

Carlo Curley

While Virgil had a pair of razor-sharp ears that could detect the ciphering of a single Dulciana note on the Echo organ buried in an attic with the swell-shades tightly shut, miles from the console, he could be an organ service person's nightmare.

Tales are legendary of his on-site demands for the meticulous tuning, regulation and even re-voicing of entire ranks; the covering of the Vox Humana pipes with blankets to "give them mystery," and the ceaseless and often tiresome regulation of tremulants.

A dear friend of mine was actually ordered by Virgil to serve as a "human tremolo" during a performance. A Holtkamp organ was installed onstage in a recital hall, and the Great division was not provided with a tremulant. Therefore, Virgil instructed my pal to go into the "belly of the beast" to find the schwimmer reservoir (where the air is stored); lie flat on his back during the entire second half of the recital (so that the audience wouldn't see him enter or depart); and, when a particular solo passage was played on the Great 8-foot flute, gently push the bottom of the flexible reservoir in and out with his hand to create the desired effect.

When working with Virgil in "matters organic," it seems that no effort was spared to achieve results.

Virgil changed the world of organ playing forever because he chose to stand proudly outside the accepted norms and traditions. He was neither trendy nor a follower; yet, he was an ultimate creator of trends and attracted thousands of followers. Any of us fortunate to have been bathed in the shining light of his prowess and personality are forever enriched in the most everlasting and positive way.

One other device that was of great importance to Virgil was the gradation of the crescendo pedal (which is actually a "shoe" located in the center of the console, above the keyboard pedals for the feet). This pedal (which, in this country, is the last pedal to the right of the expression pedals) puts on stops for the player, from the softest to the loudest, stop by stop, as the player presses the pedal. Crescendo pedals are often poorly wired, making the stops come on in "clumps." Sometimes the stops Virgil wanted didn't come on at all, or they came on in the wrong sequence. These problems often led to much soldering of wires before the concert, which was a job no technician wanted.

(With the advent of computer chips, it's often quite easy to change the arrangement of the crescendo pedals on a new organ. On older, non-computerized consoles, re-wiring the sequence was usually the only way.)

Virgil would have it no other way than the way he wanted. That was that!

Expression shoes operate large Venetian blind-type shutters in front of the chambers that house the expressive divisions of the instrument. Some larger organs have from two to six or more chambers that are expressive. These shoes were also of great importance to Virgil, and he insisted that they operate smoothly, without squeaks or groans. He also demanded that they not only open and close "all the way," but that they operate "like lightening" when put into operation.

When Virgil finally played a concert, most of the organs he played were in far better tune and working order than they had been in years. He exhausted the tuners and maintenance persons, however.

When inaugurating a new organ, Virgil was even more demanding. (He felt he was often forced to "make a silk purse out of a sow's ear.") He usually insisted that several factory personnel from the firm that built the organ be on hand to do his bidding. He tended to bewilder these people with demands; but when the concert ended they always had to admit that it was worth it; for their instrument would receive many extra accolades.

25. A Pretty Girl is Like a Melody

After taking his meal following the first practice, he would return to the church to practice until well into the morning hours, setting combination pistons, and deciding on the sounds he wanted for certain passages. Often he would say, "Kids, which sound do you like: combination A or combination B?" We would state our preference, and he would say, "Right, Kiddo, I agree." Sometimes I think he was just trying to keep us awake.

At about 3:00 a.m., Virgil would usually announce that he was finished for the evening. We'd all pile in the car in search of a late night snack—not so easy in a small town at that hour of the morning. Nevertheless, Virgil had an uncanny ability to locate an all-night café or truck stop.

He loved those places; and it was fun to watch the expressions on people's faces when confronted with Virgil Fox, all bundled up in a fur-lined coat, often with the Turkish towel he wore under a beret to protect him from the cold or drafts. His strange appearance and boisterous demands usually amazed the people who ran these eateries. Within moments, however, everyone within hearing distance knew who he was and why he was in town. He also learned the names of the servers, and sometimes asked to visit the kitchen to instruct the cook on how things should be prepared.

Most proprietors and help were amused and fascinated with their eccentric visitors. We were certainly a change from the norm; and Virgil always thought we brought "a little sunshine into their drab and dreary lives."

Once he found the all night café or diner, he would patronize it every night of our stay in the town; and would also remember the place every time he returned to that part of the country in later years.

One evening, in Elyria, Ohio, after a particularly hilarious evening at one of these eateries, we returned to our staid old hotel to retire to our rooms. Bob and I went to our room, dead tired. Virgil went to his room down the hallway, presumably to take another bath before retiring.

About ten minutes after we closed the door, there was a knock. We opened the door to see Virgil wearing a wicked grin on his face. He was still wearing his fur-lined coat with the great fur collar pulled around his head. He took a few steps back, turned, dropped the coat, and started to mince down the hallway, stark naked except for a long pink and fuschia silk scarf trailing behind him that was clenched between the cheeks of his buttocks.

The scarf (which he brought from his bedroom in Englewood, where it always rested at the foot of his pink satin bedspread) was at least 10 feet long. It was made of a tie-dyed, puckered silk. The sight of the great Virgil Fox, nude, with this scarf following him, making his way down the long hallway singing "A Pretty Girl Is Like a Melody," summoned forth great screams of laughter from both Bob and me.

Eventually Virgil erupted himself with gales of laughter, running to his room for cover.

We laughed for hours.

Virgil enjoyed this sort of clowning—the more shocking, the better. I'm sure he got an even bigger bang out of those silly pranks than we did.

The next day was usually Concert Day (unless we arrived two days early, which Virgil also loved to do). Virgil would be up by two in the afternoon, take a light lunch, and go to the church to practice from three until five, giving last minute suggestions to those in charge, and copious instructions to the organ tuner. We would return to the hotel, and Virgil would retire for about an hour, knowing we would make sure his tuxedo was pressed, and that instructions were left to deliver hot soup and crackers to his room at 7:05 p.m. promptly!

He was usually ready to depart for an 8:00 p.m. concert by 7:55. He never liked to be at a church or concert hall more than a minute or two before concert time; and he never worried about being late.

In those days, Virgil didn't want to be seen by any member of the audience until he made his formal entrance; and so he went to great lengths to find seldom-used entrances, pathways through basements, and so on. Often, when he discovered that there wouldn't be a bathroom near his entrance to a sanctuary or stage, he took a bottle with him just in case he needed to relieve himself before a concert. We would laugh, and he would wave us away, saying, "You brats! When you've got to go, you've got to go!"

The concerts were usually standing-room-only affairs; and Virgil gave the audience their money's worth many times over. The audiences adored how Virgil put their organ and his music on the map of their particular town for at least another year or two, until he could return for yet another transfusion.

After every concert, there would be the inevitable greeting line of old friends, new friends, and autograph seekers, waiting to be entertained by Virgil's howls of delight at seeing this person or that. Usually the church or presenter of the concert served coffee and pastries in the church hall, followed by dinner for Virgil and his friends at a restaurant or private home. Virgil would continue to entertain for hours.

When Bob was along, the two would often join on a piano, playing four hand versions of "Tea for Two" or "Night and Day." People ate it up—which was understandable, since the performances were quite good!

Accompanying Virgil on these small tours was an invaluable education for both Bob and me. Thus, we went with him every time we could, and we met many splendid people on our jaunts with our remarkable friend. Virgil always introduced us to anyone connected to the concerts as his "brilliant protégés." These people then became almost as attentive and kind to us as they were to Virgil. Many of them continued to be close friends for many years.

26. Tumult in the Praetorium

Easter Day of 1957, the day of my concert debut, was getting closer and closer; and I practiced like a fiend. Bob had composed a new work of rare beauty for the concert and me. He called it "Pastel," and filled it with passages of subtle color. It was almost Gershwin-esque, and dripped with orchestral sounds. Knowing of my love for rich harmonies, and with access to the wealth of tonal possibilities of the Riverside organ, Bob outdid himself for me. I delighted in every note of his impressionistic work.

In that piece, as well as in most of Bob's works, you needed "rubber fingers" to stretch from one crushing harmony to the next. In

"Pastel," there was also an exciting rhythmic scherzo in the middle section that required special skills.

None of it was easy to play; and memorizing it was "murderation" (as we used to say)—especially with only three weeks left until the concert.

I realized the importance to me of this recital, and began to get jittery at the nearness of the date. I told Virgil that I was getting frightened. He said, "Listen, Kid, that's only natural. I remember when I gave my first public performance in Cincinnati and had to play the Mendelssohn "First Sonata." My knees were knocking together so bad, it's a wonder they couldn't hear the noise in the back of that auditorium. I couldn't have said my own name! You'll do it, and you'll do it stunningly *or else!*"

He also said that I would play the prelude to the Maundy Thursday communion service at Riverside in order to accustom myself to playing to a large audience. Virgil usually played the "Crucifixion" (the third movement) of Marcel Dupré's *Passion Symphony* at the evening service. For my recital, I had planned to play the highly programmatic "Tumult in the Praetorium" from the *Passion Symphony* by the contemporary Belgian composer, Paul de Maleingreau. Virgil loved to hear me play the piece, and he said, "Play the 'Tumult' for the prelude that night."

I agreed; and on the night before Maundy Thursday, I performed most of my recital program for Virgil, Bob, and assorted friends.

I thought it went fairly well, and Virgil seemed pleased; but then he said, "Honey, that's terrific. However, when you play the 'Tumult' tomorrow, you can't play it that big. It'll scare the people half to death! You simply can't use the Celestial reeds!"

The Celestial division contained the most powerful reeds in the Riverside organ. It was located on the triforium level above the altar, and the pipes pointed directly at the congregation. We all adored this "crown" of the great instrument, and we used them as often as we could.

Maundy Thursday arrived. After I donned my vestments, Virgil led me to the console and said, "Good luck, and *no* Celestial reeds!" He then told me to wait two minutes for him to go into the congregation to listen. He proceeded (in his vestments) to walk down and seat himself in the first row of the congregation.

The church was packed as I began the work with the tumultuous passages that open the piece. (They depict the roaring mobs in the

Praetorium demanding Jesus' crucifixion). The work gradually grew louder and louder, culminating in full organ chords—when, out of sheer habit, I reached for the Celestial reeds!

They created the desired, shattering effect, of course. Then I thought, "Oh my God, I shouldn't have done that!" But again, when that section of the piece was repeated, toward the end of the work (which had grown even louder), I drew on the reeds again, and left them on for several more measures, which ended with an excruciatingly dissonant chord—during which I had a mental picture of Virgil flying over the console like a witch on a broom, to pluck out every last Celestial reed!

Fortunately, the work ends softly. During that soft and wonderful ending, Virgil made his way back to the console with a big smile on his face. "You little devil, you'll get us all fired! You used those damned Celestial reeds!"

He then proceeded to play the service; and it wasn't long into the first hymn when he decided to "solo out" the tune—and on what stops? The Celestial reeds, of course!

During the postlude, which was Alexandre Guilmant's "*Marche funebre et Chant seraphique*," he stomped on the full organ with the Celestial reeds. He shrieked at me over the full rage, saying, "You didn't think I'd let you play louder than me, did you?"

I knew I was forgiven.

I was getting anxious about the concert two days away, and was practicing as much as I could, both at Riverside and at my church, which was then St. Mary's Episcopal Church in Manhattanville. St. Mary's was only a few blocks from Riverside. It was a small parish with a terrible broken down organ—but it "played the notes." I also practiced at the church of a good friend of mine and Virgil's, T. Ernest Nichols, Emanuel Baptist Church in Brooklyn. Ernest was a true friend and a real character. He played extremely well himself, and was one of "our crowd" at Riverside. He was always encouraging, and I valued his criticisms and comments highly.

Ernest was a tall, handsome man from Clarksville, Tennessee who adored Virgil and his approach to the organ. Virgil would get Ernest to sing at parties every time he got a chance. Ernest's vocal repertoire ran the gamut from oratorio and grand opera to bawdy renditions of dated popular songs, such as "Alice Blue Gown." He could sing in an amazing falsetto voice, then make a tremendous portamento—in the middle of a phrase—to a deep alto tone, and deliberately end up as flat as possible. Everyone would be convulsed in laughter, with Virgil roaring the loudest. Ernest was a marvelous storyteller, and great fun to have around. He was popular with everyone.

27. Please God, Let It Be C Major!

By the time Easter Day arrived, I was excited. I couldn't remember how I got through the Easter services at St. Mary's. I remember walking to Riverside around noon on shaky legs, as the importance of this concert and my debut were pressing down on me. After an uneaten lunch with Bob, we went back to the church to set the combination buttons for my last practice. Men were still putting up the mirror behind the console so that the audience could see the organist. After it was properly placed, I went to work. Virgil had gone to lunch with some visiting friends, and said he wouldn't return until 4:30 p.m. (the concert was to begin an hour later).

The practice went well, but the mirror over my head made me even more nervous. However, I wouldn't consider not having it (nor did I have a choice).

Bob claimed that everything was perfect. He loved the way I played "Pastel," and was sure the concert would be thrilling. It was then four o'clock, and he said I should stop, rest, and put on my vestments. (In those days, even Virgil wore his blue cassock and organ surplice for concerts at the Riverside Church.)

By then, all sorts of insecurities were going through my head. Was I ready? What if I forgot? What if I let Virgil and my friends down? Would there be anyone there? After all, who was I?

At about 4:45 p.m., Virgil appeared in the choir room where I was waiting. He gave me a big hug and told me to say a prayer. He told me that before I went out through the drapes in the arch leading to the console, to put my hands up in the air and take several deep breaths, "And then do what God put you on this earth to do! I'm proud of you, and it will be great!"

Bob came running to tell me the church was well over half full, and many organists were present, including Alec Wyton from St. John the Divine and Ernest White from St. Mary the Virgin. Then I suddenly realized that I would be playing not only to a fine audience and these great New York organists; but that Virgil Fox, the greatest organist in the world, would also be in the audience! As I was standing behind those drapes—with trembling knees and clammy hands—I did exactly as Virgil had told me to do. As the great tower bells struck five o'clock, I made my way to the console to begin my career.

I remember setting the organ up for the first work on the program, which was Virgil's arrangement of Bach's "Now Thank We All Our God." I couldn't remember the key in which it was written! I thought, "Please God, let it be C Major!"

It was, and all went well through the next few pieces, including a Schübler chorale and the "Prelude and Fugue in D Major." I was actually enjoying myself, and was generally pleased with all that had gone before—until the Brahms chorale prelude, "My Faithful Heart Rejoices," which is a joyous piece that romps all over the keyboards.

Toward the end of the piece, I reached over with my right foot to press a toe piston to bring on the Pedal reeds. When I pressed the piston, all the Pedal stops fluttered in and out rapidly (due to Riverside's periodic combination action problems), making quite a noise. I faltered for a measure or two, and decided to go back and try again. Again the piston reacted in this strange way, and so I tried to go back a few measures again, but this time I got lost—and was frozen with fear. I was within two or three measures of the end of the work, and there we all were, hanging in mid air, so to speak. The silence was deafening. I was mortified, and for several seconds didn't know what to do. Therefore, I simply canceled the stops on the organ, and proceeded to the next work, which was the D-Flat Major "Sketch" of Robert Schumann.

The rest of the concert went quite well, but the tempos were definitely faster than I had planned. Afterwards, everybody was complimentary—even Richard Weagly was filled with praise. When I mentioned the terrible slip in the Brahms, he said, "It's a lot better than some of the improvising I've heard you-know-who do when he's had a memory slip!" I'm afraid that again I couldn't agree with Richard; but I was grateful to him and the sizable audience for receiving me so well.

Virgil was marvelous to me after the concert, and we all went out to a tasty dinner. A week or so later, Bob and I went off in the Cadillac with Virgil on a short tour to Pennsylvania. On the way there Virgil let fly with a tirade about the concert, the gist of which was that he didn't like anything about it! The Brahms was a horrible disaster the likes of which he had never before heard! Although he knew it had been my first public performance, he gave me absolute hell, and laid down the law that there would have to be practice that is more serious before I could ever hope to have a career.

I was shattered. I had thought that things had gone well except, of course, the unfortunate ending of the Brahms. Later, I asked Bob what he really thought, and he told me he thought it was a great first attempt, and to pay no attention to Virgil. He said that Virgil had seemed quite testy that evening anyway, and was acting like a "stewed witch." Nevertheless, his lecture affected me deeply, and I vowed to practice harder than ever. Virgil wanted to be proud of us, and was not prepared to put up with anything but the best that was in us. I'm happy to say that I never received a lecture like that again, or disappointed him that much—at least as far as my playing was concerned.

28. Counting Onions

After the euphoria of this exciting experience, I realized that one or two concerts wouldn't make for a career or a living, and so what was I to do? Virgil had been kind, but I knew I was becoming a burden on him, having to feed me half the time, and causing trouble because of loud and long practice at Riverside. During that past year, Virgil had had to consider a second organist at Riverside, to lighten his load at the church and free him to concertize more. Both Bob and I wanted the job, but he felt we were too young and inexperienced. In addition, he needed someone to calm the ruffled feathers around Riverside of those who didn't like his style of playing or the volume at which he played. Some people also resented his absence at the staff and other meetings that bored Virgil.

He knew and liked the then Associate Organist at Saint Bartholomew's Church, who had just completed a stint in the U.S. Army. His name was Frederick Swann; and from time to time, he had helped out at Riverside. Virgil said that he was a fine player with an excellent way with hymns and accompaniments, and that he wouldn't get Virgil into any more trouble. "He's just what the doctor ordered!"

When we first met Fred, Bob and I were wary (actually, green with envy!); but we liked him a lot. He was great fun, although we didn't get to see him that often in future days. Fred had his duties on "his weekends," which were the Sundays on which he played; and Virgil had his. Bob or I still assisted Virgil on "his" Sundays.

Frederick Swann succeeded Virgil Fox at the Riverside Church, then moved into further national prominence as the organist of the Crystal Cathedral in Garden Grove, California. He is currently the organist of the First Congregational Church in Los Angeles.

Frederick Swann

The famed organ architect William H. Barnes of Evanston, Illinois and his wife became sponsors of Virgil Fox in the early days of his career. It was in their home that I met him. They also took me to New York and to The Riverside Church in 1951. A year later, Virgil was most supportive when I moved to New York to attend Union Theological Seminary School of Sacred Music, allowing me practice privileges on the Riverside organ. This arrangement led to my becoming a regular substitute whenever he went on tour.

First Robert Hebble, and later Ted Alan Worth, appeared on the scene during that time, and we all became Virgil "groupies." Bob and Ted were closest to Virgil—almost his shadows. I was so much in awe of their talents that I mostly stayed quietly in the background.

Richard Weagly, Virgil's partner and the Riverside Choir director, had difficulty accepting the groupies; but Richard did take a special liking to me, and would almost always demand that I substitute for Virgil during his absences (which didn't help any of our relationships!). However, those were heady days, and we managed to coexist happily most of the time.

During the summer of 1957, Bob Hebble and I went to California. At last, I was able to show Bob the San Francisco I knew and loved. We had a grand time. While we were there, my friend, Paul Fitz Gerald, did a wonderful thing for me. Paul had become the Dean of the San Francisco Chapter of the AGO, and was determined that the Chapter would present me in a concert. He arranged for me to play a small recital for the program committee at the First Presbyterian Church in Oakland where Newton Pashley was the organist.

Newton was kind to allow my mini-recital, the outcome of which was a formal concert to be presented the following April by the San Francisco Chapter. I was thrilled, and so was Bob, for I played his "Pastel" at the mini-concert and would play it again in April. We decided the place to give the recital would be in San Francisco at Calvary Presbyterian Church—the very place I had first heard Virgil. It was a good omen for my San Francisco debut.

I had quit my job at the church and the hospital in New York in order to travel to San Francisco and prepare for the April, 1958 concert at Calvary Pres. After the concert, I decided to remain in San Francisco for a while. I got a job working as a clerk for the State of California. To be honest, I counted onions (using a heliotrope pencil) for one of the state agencies. It wasn't possible to make a decent wage as a church organist in those days, except, perhaps, at Grace Cathedral. Even there, I later learned, the salaries were a disgrace. I decided I would work at this job during the day in order to pay for food and rent, and practice at night to "feed my soul" and wait for my "big break."

It was Virgil's habit to vacation in Europe for one or two months every other year, and to drive across the country to California in alternate years. While in Europe, Virgil and Richard Weagly would attend the Salzburg Festival, then visit friends and famous organs in France, Germany, Italy, and England. Virgil adored Paris, the French people, and their language. Richard loved England, and usually left Paris early to attend the Three Choirs Festival. Virgil would join him in London before they returned to the United States.

In alternate years, when they motored to the West Coast, they would stop and visit many friends, taking in the national parks and some churches along the way, as Virgil renewed his acquaintance with a few of his favorite organs. They often stopped at the Mormon Tabernacle in Salt Lake City to visit Frank Asper and Alexander Schreiner, who were both old and good friends. Virgil always enjoyed the Tabernacle Æolian-Skinner, which was considered a "sister organ" to the Riverside organ.

29. Bird and Etna Hit the Road

One of the main reasons for the trip West was for Virgil to spend time with his mother, who had lived for a long time in Pasadena. On the way across the country, Virgil and Richard would usually stop in Princeton, Illinois (his hometown) to pick up his beloved Aunt Etna, and drive her out to Pasadena to spend a few weeks with his dear mama, Bird (Birdie E.) Fox.

What a kind, simple, and direct speaking woman Bird was. She was small, but she stood erect, and usually wore nice dresses with sensible white shoes. She was as quiet as Virgil was gregarious and noisy; and she knew how to speak her mind when provoked. When Virgil took too long at dinner, talking to this person or that; or they were going to be late for the theatre or a Hollywood Bowl concert, she would say, in a no-nonsense tone, "Come on, Virgil, cut out the conversation! We'll be late."

Virgil would move along, with no more delay.

Bird and Etna were full of life, and interesting characters. Virgil loved them both, and he and Richard Weagly spent great times with them while they were on the West Coast. On the summers that

Weagly and Virgil went to Europe, Bird would drive herself from California to Princeton, pick up Etna, and they would both motor to Englewood, staying there while Virgil and Richard were in Europe. These trips may not seem unusual; but both women were well along in years at the time; and they continued until they were both nearly ninety! Bird, like her son, was fearless behind the wheel; and the 6,000-mile round trip jour-

With "Aunt Etna," brother Warren, and the Key to the City, the "boy" returns triumphantly to Princeton! (1970)

ney seemed like nothing to her. She once said that the only part of the trip she didn't like was driving with Etna, who never shut up!

Robert Fry

> One summer, Bird Fox, then nearing 90, decided she couldn't stand the sight of a series of smudged radiator covers that ran the entire length of an enclosed solarium in her son's 26-room mansion. Being notably frugal herself, Mrs. Fox commandeered some brushes and paint and went to work.
>
> Virgil later told us, "That poor, sweet, white-haired old lady is upstairs resting, now; and she's totally exhausted! She actually painted three radiator covers! I told her, under no circumstances was she to paint more than two!"

David Jonathan Lewis (along with Floyd Watson) became one of Virgil's "roadies" in 1972, transporting the Rodgers Touring Organ and Heavy Organ light show around the country.

David Lewis

> Virgil drove into the driveway one day to find "Mama" way up on an extension ladder with Etna holding the bottom. They had locked their house keys inside and were planning how to climb up to the second floor window. I then understood the source of Virgil's dogged determination!

Once, when Virgil was in Los Angeles visiting his mother, he was invited to a Hollywood movie gala given by a music director (possibly Franz Waxman). Virgil came back, raving about the party, the movie stars present, and the lavish food they had to eat. "Why, the food was so exotic, there were elephant toes floating in the punch," Virgil exclaimed.

His wit and way of describing people, places, and events were unique; for the mental pictures he could conjure up were often exceptionally clever, though sometimes cruel. For example, on another trip to Southern California he was asked to consult with a wealthy man who was giving a large organ to a prominent church. Virgil agreed to meet the man at a local hotel, and tried in vain for several hours to convince this gentleman and his committee that the organ must be able to "play anything," which meant it should have lots of expression, a movable console so that a performer might be seen, and be built by Æolian-Skinner.

After the meeting, Virgil raved that he had "spent hours in a hotel lobby of bad breath and cigar smoke, talking to stones! They probably won't do anything I told them to do, because they didn't have to pay for my expertise."

He was right. They bought the opposite! The Baroque organ building movement was getting well entrenched by then. "They'll probably try to put some museum piece shriek-box in that church! Those poor people. These damned Baroquists, what are they trying to do? Kill the organ off completely?"

I have been fortunate in always having friends who were good to me. One such friend was Don Lindahl, a young man I had met who owned a hairdressing salon and was on his way to becoming a successful businessman in San Francisco. Don suggested that I share his large apartment, and the arrangement was perfect. As Don became increasingly successful, the apartment became increasingly sumptuous. Although I was only a clerk and lowly organist, I lived with him in swank surroundings for the next eighteen months. My bedroom was actually a large closet off the living room, connected to the building's fire escape. Nevertheless, it was perfect for me. Don loved the organ; and he always had a good time with my friends and me. I suppose in a way he was my first patron, introducing me to other people who would become my future patrons.

Virgil's next tour to the West Coast brought him to Seattle, Portland, and Los Angeles. He stopped in San Francisco for several days between cities. Together, we had several good meals and great late evenings, laughing and hearing about his latest triumphs. Before going to Los Angeles, he would perform in Paso Robles, which is about halfway between San Francisco and Los Angeles. This was to be a Community Concert played on a Hammond organ. Virgil was not looking forward to the trip or the organ! He decided to invite me along for moral support. I must confess I was curious to see what the great man would do with "a toy organ."

Virgil got permission to borrow Don Lindahl's new Thunderbird convertible. Thus, we decided to drive down the next day, play the concert, and get out as soon as possible to return to San Francisco.

The trip down, at 90 m.p.h., was an absolute hoot. I don't remember the concert except that Virgil played like a demon, with remarkable tempos and more virtuosity than usual.

"When you have to play a 'thing' like this, Kid, you've got to hit them with incredible speed; because God knows, there's not going to be another thrill! I learned this trick when I was in the Army, when the 'Hammond device' was all that was usually available."

I remember that the audience loved the concert, probably because Virgil acted as if he were playing the greatest organ in the world. He always seemed to perform well when faced with an organ he must have hated. He discovered a sound or effect he liked in order to make the "dismal dog" sound better than it ever would have under other hands.

30. From Onions to Organs

One day, for lunch, I left the State Building on my daily walk, which usually took me to Blum's on Polk Street. This day, I went down Golden Gate Avenue toward Market Street. When I reached Leavenworth Street, I noticed an organ retail store called "Leathurby's." I imagined that they sold "hideous Hammonds"; but as I passed by the display windows I noticed advertising for Conn electronic organs. I also noticed that, in the rear of the store, there was a three-keyboard instrument that didn't resemble any of the others strewn around the place. In those days, electronic instruments were often made for the home. They were used to play mostly popular music. Poorer churches also bought those organs; and new churches with barely enough money to build a roof over their heads had to resort to electronics also. California was full of such new churches; and the electronic organ was the best solution for most of their musical needs, although the instruments were usually uninspiring and unfulfilling.

Therefore, this three-manual instrument in the store intrigued me, for I had never seen such a large electronic organ before. I decided to go in and look.

As I entered, I was greeted by a jovial, large, red faced man with thick glasses, seated behind a desk opposite the object of my curiosity. His name was Phil Goss, and he showed me to the organ that interested me. It was called a Rodgers Organ, which was a name I had never heard before. He explained that Rodgers was a new company established by several engineers who worked for Tektronix, which was the celebrated company located near Portland, Oregon that built high quality oscilloscopes. He explained that Leathurby's was mainly a store that sold Conn organs of Elkhart, Indiana. At the time they were the Northern California distributor for Conn; but the owner, Clarence Leathurby, had been intrigued with the Rodgers Organ, and had purchased this instrument in hopes that it would be accepted by the classical organ community and the American Guild of Organists.

He invited me to try it out. I was astounded at the way it responded, and how well it sounded—it was far above any other electronic organ I had ever heard. The instrument had real power without the usual hideous distortion that most electronic organs produced whenever you played them louder than mezzo forte. It also had some convincing solo stops, and some beautiful soft celeste sounds. I was surprised and pleased, as was Phil Goss at my obvious delight. I must have played for an hour, and had to rush back to work, skipping lunch. I promised Phil I'd come back—soon.

I returned the next day, and Phil invited me to play as long as I wanted. He said he loved to hear the organ and me play it. I soon became a regular at the store, stopping by almost every day. One day I was playing when the front door of the store opened and a disheveled man entered. He slammed the door and flew past me into the back office, his gray hair askew, ashes flying off a cigarette dropping out of the corner of his mouth. No sooner had he disappeared into the back office than I heard him roar, "Goss! Get in here!"

I immediately stopped playing; and Phil—visibly shaking—lumbered toward the back office. I was just about to leave when Phil called me back to meet Clarence Leathurby, the owner of the store at 183 Golden Gate Avenue. With some trepidation, I went to the back office, and was kindly greeted by Mr. Leathurby, who said that Phil had told him about me. He invited me to use the store any time I wanted to practice. I was thrilled, as I had had to rely on several friends' churches for an instrument to use. I had no church job at the time, and many of the church instruments I used were odious sounding electronic organs, literally falling apart, although "they played the notes," as Virgil used to say.

Phil later explained that Mr. Leathurby belonged to a club nearby where he had lunch daily. Before and after lunch, he and his friends played dominos for high stakes. On the days that Mr. Leathurby lost, he would always appear fierce and grumpy, and usually slam the front door. When he won, he would beam, smile, and be his usual amiable self.

As the weeks went on, I became friendly with Phil, who told me hilarious tales of his life as a salesman for the Wurlitzer Theatre Pipe Organ Company—which used to be located near the Leathurby store. He had known all the great theatre organists, and it was a treat listening to his stories. He was a dear person, and a real character.

Many times, other organists would drop by to see Phil, usually playing a few tunes on the smaller organs. One of the organists was the famous George Wright, who played the theatre organ brilliantly and musically. In fact, most of the theatre organists I heard at Leathurby's seemed to have more musicality and inventiveness in their little fingers than many classical organists had in their whole careers. Phil always introduced me and had me play for them. They usually seemed genuinely impressed at both this new Rodgers organ and me.

Often Phil would ask me to answer the telephone, as he frequently sneaked across the street to have a "little nip" at the corner tavern. I later realized that these little trips "across the street" happened four or five times a day, and explained the redness of his nose and the tremble in his hands. I must say, though, that Phil never appeared the slightest bit intoxicated. He just seemed to be someone who needed to keep the alcohol level in his body constantly high.

One day Mr. Leathurby asked me to come into his office. He told me how much he liked my playing, and he wondered if I would like to come to work for him ("full time!") as a demonstrator of the Rodgers organ. I was astonished; and although I accepted the offer instantly, I explained to him that I was not a salesperson. I would be honored to help in any other way, however. He said he already had salespersons, and all I would have to do is play demonstrations for church committees and private buyers. The rest of my day could be devoted to practice.

What a godsend this opportunity was; and how wonderful Clarence Leathurby was to make this opportunity available to me! I shall never forget his kindness and encouragement—nor the kindness of all the people I had worked with at the state agency, many of whom attended my concerts in the Bay Area for years to come.

Ted's other duty at Leathurby's was (if and when he got around to it) balancing the company's checkbook. Most months he neglected this duty altogether, for no one had ever shown him how to balance a commercial account, much less his own checkbook—an example of which he had never even possessed up to that point.

Finally, he pleaded for my help. I was, after all, working for a stock brokerage (Francis I. DuPont & Co.) in the cashier's department.

I struggled with the problem for several nights. Finally, I declared the situation hopeless and advised the store to begin from scratch (meaning the most recent bank statement) and declare the past as irretrievably gone as last year's roses.

Leathurby's continued to flourish despite Ted's being relieved of all further bookkeeper's obligations.

31. A Third Chick Enters the Coop

I remember one memorable evening in June 1959 coming home (to Don Lindahl's apartment) to hear loud organ music on the stereo. It wasn't one of Virgil's records, but something by E. Power Biggs! I had most of Biggs' records, but they were not my favorites, and I seldom played them. As I entered the living room, I saw someone I'd never met sitting alone. He introduced himself as Richard Torrence. Don and a friend of Richard's had gone out together, and Richard decided to stay behind to listen to music. Richard was a handsome young man of small stature who seemed to have a good personality and a quick wit. I remember saying to him that I was glad he liked the organ, but his choice of players was certainly "suspect." He countered that E. Power Biggs was surely the greatest living organist; what was wrong with him?

"Oh, have I got news for you, Dear Boy" I thought, and promptly put on a recording of Virgil's. Though Richard didn't admit it at the time, I could tell he loved what he heard. At least he seemed more than intrigued.

Richard and I hit it off almost instantly. He told me that he and a friend, David McCaffery, had recently driven from Madison,

Wisconsin to San Francisco to seek their fortune. Both Richard and David had been discharged from the Army in April; and they arrived together in San Francisco in May to look for suitable employment. Richard was a graduate of the University of Wisconsin. With his obvious intellect and personality, he had no trouble finding a good entry-level position. I used to tell people he was a "junior broker" with the firm of Francis I. duPont & Co. In fact, I think he worked in the cashier's office.

I was immediately so fond of Richard that I insisted (with Don's approval) that he stay with us until he could find a suitable apartment.

Richard Torrence

Ted actually visited the apartment in which David McCaffery and I had stayed for about a month. It was in the seedy Tenderloin District of San Francisco, and it featured an elevator painted with aluminum paint.

Ted exclaimed that he couldn't possibly allow a friend to stay "in a building with an aluminum elevator!"

Our first month's rent was up, and so we both moved into Don Lindahl's apartment that very weekend, saving rent, and forever changing my life.

Richard had to sleep on the sofa in the living room. Since he needed to be at work at 6:30 a.m., it was difficult for him to endure our late social life every evening. After staying with us for a short while, he moved to Paul Fitz Gerald's apartment until he found his own place on Frederick Street, near Buena Vista Park. Richard and I soon became inseparable. We had similar interests. He especially loved the organ, as did I. He had a positive outlook and was always fun to be with. I must also admit that the fact that he was a great cook, and that he had a lovely Karmann Ghia car, were important considerations in our burgeoning friendship.

It took me only a few days to convert Richard into a Virgil Fox fan. Richard adored music of all kinds, and introduced me to many artists and composers with whom I was unfamiliar. We spent long evenings listening to records and talking, always enjoying a lot of good food. I dragged him to Grace Cathedral and to the Palace of the Legion of Honor to hear Richard Purvis, and to every interesting organ concert presented in the Bay Area. I also played for him at Grace Cathedral, but more often at Leathurby's on Golden Gate Avenue. I now had a key to the store, and I usually practiced there until midnight. Richard often came to hear me, dragging along some friends who kicked and screamed about having to listen to an organ!

Richard was taken with my playing, and always encouraged me, complimenting what was good and giving constructive criticism when my playing needed improvement. He had an excellent sense of what was first rate, and rejected most that was not. This kind of friend is what every artist needs and rarely finds. Richard soon became the best friend I ever had.

Through my friend, Don Lindahl, and some of his well connected social clients, I was able to get an audition with Arthur Fiedler to play with the San Francisco Symphony at the "Summer Pops" concerts in the Civic Auditorium where I'd first met Virgil with Paul Fitz Gerald. This appearance would have been a real coup for any organist; for the Pops Concerts usually featured brilliant young singers, violinists, pianists, and other instrumentalists—never organists.

It was a joy to audition for Arthur Fiedler. He put me at ease, and I know he liked what he heard because he hired me on the spot for the next Pops series in the summer of 1960.

My playing of the Henry Purcell "Trumpet Voluntary" especially intrigued him. He asked why I played it so slowly and grandly when his orchestra trumpeters played it at a much faster tempo. "Because I can," I said, referring to the much larger "lung" capacity of the organ. He liked that answer.

Maestro Fiedler asked what piece I would like to play, and I immediately said the *Symphonie Concertante* of Joseph Jongen. He said he had never heard of it, but if I liked it, we would do it together. I assured him that I thought it "the best piece for organ and full orchestra" (I had often heard Virgil say those very words). Actually, I had never heard the work performed with orchestra, but had heard Virgil play parts of it in solo concerts several times. In addition, I had heard Bob Hebble speak of it in glowing terms, having experienced the work at the opening of the Riverside organ, where he assisted Virgil during the organ and orchestra concert with the New York Philharmonic conducted by Dimitri Mitropoulos.

After learning the piece for the opening of the Riverside organ, Virgil transcribed the Jongen for solo organ—as if it weren't hard enough for an organist to begin with! Virgil was aware that his performances of the work would rarely be heard if he had to wait to be engaged by orchestras; so he proceeded to give legendary performances of all four movements as a solo work—something no one else has ever attempted, to my knowledge.

Fiedler asked for a copy of the score as soon as possible so that he could learn it during his busy schedule. Virgil was delighted that I had won this opportunity to play with Fiedler—and play the Jongen, which was very much his "personal property" in those days.

(Virgil and I didn't know until years later that Jongen, who was a 20th Century Belgian composer in the French impressionist style of Vincent d'Indy, was commissioned to compose the work for a concert—that never took place—at the John Wanamaker store in Philadelphia.)

It took a long time, but Virgil helped me get a conductor's score with the orchestra parts indicated. "Now get busy, Kid, and learn the notes. Then I'll show you what to do with them!"

David Lewis

Once, when Virgil played the Jongen with orchestra in Houston, the conductor, André Previn was out of town, and so the concertmaster took over. (He had been described to us as a "nasty queen" who had said that he hated the organ because it "absolutely ruins the sound of my strings!")

Virgil arrived for a 10:00 a.m. rehearsal (after staying up all night) looking disheveled, as usual, in his favorite paisley jacket with the back ripped open. (We often described Virgil as looking like a bag lady.) He announced, "My eyes feel like two pee holes in the snow! Let's get it over with!"

During the concert intermission the next night, the substitute maestro asked Virgil to draw an appropriate stop on the organ so that he could strike an "A" for the strings to tune up for the Jongen. By this time, Virgil had had it with this guy. Therefore, instead of drawing a standard 4-foot octave stop, he pulled out the 2 and 2/3-foot stop with the super coupler. This effect created a pitch an octave and a half above unison pitch. When the concertmaster put his finger on the "A," he got an "E" way up on the keyboard. Before he could figure out what happened, the strings of the orchestra had already begun a horrifying glissando trying to tune up, up, and away!

The audience broke into peels of laughter. After the concert, the maestro asked Virgil, "What kind of an organ is this where you play an "A" and you get an "E?"

Virgil turned on his heels, saying, "I simply don't know what you're talking about! I just play them. I don't know how they work!"

At the reception following the concert, Virgil introduced a bunch of us to the famous Ima Hogg—whose name he'd always made so much fun of. He said, "This is Floyd Watson. I'm not sure what he does; and this is Ken Van Grunsven, a strawberry farmer from Oregon."

Ken immediately replied, "And this is the great Dr. Virgil Fox, who wears a cape once worn by a bull fighter. And if you get close enough you can still smell the bullshit!"

32. The Patron That Wasn't

In the spring of 1960, Richard Torrence and I went to Los Angeles to hear Virgil perform at Hollywood High School on a modest three-manual Ernest M. Skinner organ. The first of two concerts was to be for the student body, and I was eager to hear what their reaction would be. (Most of them were more used to the music of the Everly Brothers and Elvis Presley.)

Virgil didn't play down to them in the slightest. Nevertheless, he held most of them spellbound for almost two hours—much to the amazement of the school officials, who sent the students home early, rewarding them for their attentiveness.

Virgil adored young people. He knew that in order for the instrument he loved to survive, young people would have to know what it was all about—and so he really showed them. He made it fun for them by telling them what they were going to hear and what to listen for. He dazzled them, had them cheering on their feet, and always left them wanting more.

Richard Torrence

This concert marked the first time I met the legendary Virgil Fox. Ted, another dear friend (Dudley Wiltse), and I flew to Los

*Angeles and stayed in a room for two people at the Hollywood
Roosevelt Hotel. (Since we were trying to save money, we pretend-
ed that only two people were sharing the room.)*

*What I didn't realize was that Ted and Virgil had become some-
what estranged after Ted moved out of New York. Apparently he
left a number of debts in his wake, one of which was to Virgil's dentist. I think Ted was determined to mend fences after two years
away from Virgil.*

*However, something awful had happened just before our trip.
Through the help of Donald Lindahl and others, Ted had located a
potential patron. This man, a prominent San Francisco doctor, seriously believed that Ted should get the European education that
Virgil and others believed he needed. When the doctor called Virgil
in New York to confirm the anticipated recommendation, Virgil
said the opposite of what everyone expected: he told the doctor that
Ted wasn't ready to study in Europe! ("He hasn't grown up
enough," were his words.)*

The doctor immediately withdrew his offer.

*Ted didn't write about this breach of friendship in his memoir.
Therefore, I'm including it. I believe, in a way, Virgil's action
destroyed the full potential of Ted's career before it got started.
Peeking over his master's shoulder at a console wasn't enough for
Ted. He needed a more formal and disciplined education in his
youth. He couldn't afford it, and Virgil didn't allow it.*

Ted always forgave people's cruelest offenses more readily than I.

It was during this trip that I first met Richard Simonton. Virgil
had often spoken of him. He was one of the original owners of
Muzak (which used to be the main provider of ubiquitous elevator
music). He was a tall, quiet, rich person who was fond of Virgil and
the organ. He had a lovely home in Toluca Lake, near Hollywood,
which had a movie theatre downstairs and a large, five-manual
Wurlitzer Pipe Organ in it. Upstairs, he was in the process of
installing a mostly Æolian-Skinner pipe organ in the living room. I
say "mostly" because the console wasn't Æolian-Skinner; and I suspect many other things were not. Nevertheless, most of the pipes
were from Æolian-Skinner.

Virgil was particularly anxious to see the progress of the organ
installation, because Simonton had already engaged him to inaugurate the organ during the National Convention of the AGO in Los

Angeles in the summer of 1962. There were to be two concerts for *la crème de la crème* of the Guild and various important friends of Simonton's. Virgil loved Los Angeles, Hollywood, Beverly Hills, Pasadena, Malibu, and anything having to do with movie stars, their homes, and people's glamorous life styles. He considered himself a star; and so did we.

The progress of the classical organ that we found upstairs wasn't encouraging. Nothing played, yet; so we had to be content with hearing Virgil romp on the Wurlitzer—which was great fun, and the instrument gave off quite an impressive sound. Richard Simonton was active in the theatre organ world, and many times had the great organists George Wright, Gaylord Carter, Jesse Crawford, and other people of that caliber play concerts for him. George and Gaylord, who were the top figures in the theatre organ world, were also good friends of Virgil's.

Richard Torrence and I were amazed that Richard Simonton, who owned these two immense organs, as well as one of Ravel's pianos (with a Welte Mignon player attachment hooked to it), couldn't play a note of music himself. However, he seemed to appreciate and support the artistry of others. Virgil and I met many similar people in our lives.

Virgil had always been convinced that Richard Simonton was going to be an important patron for him, and that he would provide the dream of his life: a large portable pipe organ with which he could tour the world. He wanted desperately to play not only in churches but also in concert halls where all the renowned artists appeared. "The church is fine, but too often they can't see you. There's usually no applause; and they can't charge for tickets, so the fees have to be too low. A touring pipe organ is the only answer!"

Virgil had often told us of the English organist, Reginald Foort, who had had a large, five-manual Möller theatre organ built for him that was carted all over the British Isles in several large vans. What Virgil probably didn't know then was how difficult it was to move that behemoth. When Foort would have an engagement at a theatre, the engagement had to be for several weeks or even months—not the kind of touring Virgil had in mind: one concert in one city, then another concert several hundred miles away in another city two days later. It's interesting to note that Foort's organ eventually stopped touring and was permanently located in the Pasadena Civic Auditorium.

Nevertheless, Virgil was convinced that Richard Simonton would see the wisdom in creating such an instrument for him, and provide the funds.

Two years after this 1960 visit, after the Los Angeles AGO convention, Virgil described his first concert on Simonton's classical four-manual organ during the 1962 convention. Nothing was ready! According to Virgil, the night before the concert, cables and pipes lay all over the place; half the stops didn't work; and the console was a mechanical horror that wouldn't behave at all. Virgil was beside himself. Had he not believed that Richard Simonton might one-day build a touring organ for him, Virgil surely would have canceled the concerts.

"The poor thing was simply not ready to be heard or played." Nevertheless, Virgil went ahead bravely, and everything turned out well. We had assumed that Virgil had a contract with Simonton for his regular fee for the concerts, but he didn't. A day or so after the concert, Simonton suggested that Virgil stop by a men's store in the Hollywood Roosevelt Hotel and charge a new overcoat to Simonton's account. That was Virgil's fee!

Ted Alan Worth at the console of the Grace Cathedral organ, signed on the back to Richard Torrence: "For Dick—A real friend and inspiration!!! Affectionately, Ted 1960" (Photo by Bill Marshall)

"Leave it to the rich," Virgil howled, "why the nerve of that greedy swine!" Nevertheless, Virgil remained friends with Dick Simonton, never giving up his dream of a movable pipe organ.

As nice as Simonton was, I must say that in all the years I knew him and visited his home, I was never offered so much as a glass of water. I also never heard a note from the classical organ upstairs. It was always in a state of repair—or mostly disrepair. The Wurlitzer always worked, however, and always sounded grand. I remarked to Virgil that we never met Richard's wife or family. Virgil said they were nice but belonged to some kind of Pentecostal sect and weren't interested in the organ. Finally I met one daughter, and she made a point of telling me that she hated the organ when the reeds were playing. That was enough of his family for me!

Once, years later, when I visited Richard Simonton, I entered his house through the garage and admired his new, burgundy Rolls Royce. I had never seen a Rolls of that color, and I remarked how beautiful it was. Richard said, "Oh, glad you like it, it's the only color they had." This remark typified his plain personality for me. Nevertheless, he remained a pleasant and good friend to Virgil until his death. He never gave Virgil the movable organ or a thin dime, as far as I know; but Virgil did have an expensive overcoat for his troubles.

33. My Pops Concert with Fiedler

By the spring of 1960, when Richard Torrence and I visited Virgil in Hollywood, I had learned the notes of the Jongen work, and Virgil gave me several valuable lessons during which he did, indeed, "show me what to do." Virgil was scheduled to play the work with the Detroit Symphony Orchestra. He was to play on the new Æolian-Skinner organ at the Ford Auditorium during the June 1960 National AGO Convention. He was adamant about my being there in order to hear how the whole thing went with orchestra. My engagement with Fiedler and the San Francisco Pops Orchestra was in August, and there was no way that I could afford the time or money to get to the convention, much to Virgil's consternation. His performance of the work during that convention was a sensation according to all reports (especially his).

My own concert was almost upon me, and was in some jeopardy since the orchestral parts had not yet arrived from Belgium. I had my first session with Maestro Fiedler about a week before the concert. It was held at the Leathurby organ store with a brilliant Bay Area organist, Garnell Copeland, at a second organ to play the orchestral parts from the conductor's score. Maestro Fiedler was worried about the arrival of the scores. Before we began the rehearsal, he told me that I had better think about playing a half-hour of organ solos in place of the Jongen in case the parts didn't arrive!

*Ted Alan Worth with Arthur Fiedler and the San Francisco Pops at
Civic Auditorium, Austin console (Photo by Bill Marshall, 1960)*

After the rehearsal he was so complimentary to both of us, and so fond of the work, that he announced that he would have the San Francisco Symphony pay to have the parts copied by hand from the conductor's score, and the cost be damned. He then asked if I would take him downtown shopping. Clarence Leathurby gave me the keys to his Cadillac convertible, and off I went to escort Arthur Fiedler on a shopping spree in Union Square. Fiedler was a person who put everyone at ease, and he was great fun to work with. He learned every note of the Jongen, which impressed me, for I knew he was unfamiliar with the piece before this concert.

I began my rehearsals on the Civic Auditorium's famous old Austin organ five days before the concert, and had my trials with the recalcitrant beast and the people who maintained it.

I've mentioned the stop in the Solo division called the Tuba Magna (which Virgil called the "Big Honk"), which seemed to double the volume of the organ when used. Although the stop had been connected for Virgil's concert, it had now been disconnected again.

Then there was a wonderful Echo division literally a city block away from the main organ, high in the ceiling of the auditorium. That, too, wasn't working. The combination action of the old console was temperamental, made worse by a family of mice that had taken up residence in the console and relieved themselves all over the stop

Virgil Fox with Arthur Fiedler in Boston Symphony Hall
(Photo by John Brook, 1950s)

action, pistons, and key contacts. Worse still, when I walked into the auditorium, the console was hidden behind a plaster statue of a Roman gladiator (being used for decoration at the Pops concerts). The organ maintenance crew informed me that the console couldn't be moved because the console cable was in bad shape and they didn't want to risk any more problems with the console. I was heartsick and furious! I went to a telephone and called Mr. Fiedler's hotel. Luckily, he was in. I told him of these problems. He told me to put the manager of the auditorium on the telephone, and—like magic—we got the manager to reconnect the Tuba Magna and the Echo Organ, and to have the console "front and center where the soloist belongs."

The music for the orchestra had arrived from Belgium; and the old Austin was in pretty good shape, except for the damage the mice had done in the console; and except for some amazing delays during the first orchestral rehearsal—during which the Maestro yelled that maybe he should have imported decent organ maintenance people from Belgium, too. Fortunately, the final rehearsal went well.

The concert itself was one of the biggest thrills of my life, with several thousand people cheering, and glowing reviews in the newspapers—for me, if not for the Jongen as a composition. After the concert, Richard Torrence and Don Lindahl gave me an enormous party at Donald's apartment, to which it seemed the whole audience had been invited. Arthur Fiedler came, and asked me to ride with him and his wife to my apartment in their limousine. During that ride, I witnessed a tremendous fight between them. He obviously had quite a temper, and I think he had had a few drinks. (Just before I went on stage to play the Jongen, he offered me a shot of brandy to "settle the nerves." I politely declined, for I would have fallen off the bench with one drop, I'm sure. Virgil would have fainted at the suggestion of "booze" at any time, much less before a performance!)

Mr. and Mrs. Fiedler were utterly delightful to everyone at the party—as if the fiery scene in the limousine had never taken place. The consumption of an entire bottle of brandy at the party that night didn't seem to phase him in the least, either.

34. The Substitute Pipe Organ

One day early in the summer of 1960, Mr. Leathurby asked me if I could use my influence with Virgil Fox to get him to try the Rodgers organ, and possibly even play a concert on one. I had been talking with Virgil on the telephone once or twice a month, and so he knew about Rodgers organs and about the generosity of Mr. Leathurby. When I asked him if he would consider playing the Rodgers, Virgil said, "Well, Kiddo, if you say this organ is so good and they're willing to pay my fee and promote the concert properly, we'll give it a try."

Virgil had often told us of his days in the Army Air Force when he had to practice and often perform on a Hammond organ; and so I knew of his trepidation about electronic organs. I remember the story Virgil told about his first appearance with the Philadelphia Orchestra with Eugene Ormandy, in the Academy of Music. At that time, the Philadelphia Academy of Music had no organ and the only electronic that was available then was the Hammond. During the rehearsal of the Bach "D Minor Concerto," Ormandy asked, "Virgil, where is the power of the great organ? We simply need more volume!" Virgil was crestfallen. He told Ormandy, "This is it. I've got the damned thing wide open!" (That occasion was one of the few times a conductor ever asked for more organ—conductors usually want less!)

Although Virgil was used to being frustrated at the electronic organ's limitations, I knew he wouldn't be with a Rodgers. The instrument was so superior to a Hammond (there was no comparison) that I knew that Virgil wouldn't be disappointed. I told Mr. Leathurby of Virgil's willingness, and warned him that the concert would have to be promoted in a first class manner. Richard Torrence and I had become friends with San Francisco's prominent concert impresario, Spencer Barefoot, who regularly presented artists such as Schwarzkopf, Rubenstein, and Heifitz. Clarence asked me to approach Spencer and say that he would gladly pay all expenses to make a Virgil Fox concert a big success.

All parties agreed, and the concert was scheduled for September 13th in the large auditorium of the Berkeley Community High School. The Rodgers Organ Company was so overjoyed that they sent a much larger and more comprehensive three-manual instrument to Berkeley for the great event. The acoustics in the Berkeley auditorium were good, and the way the technicians from the Leathurby Company and Rodgers factory placed the speakers, high above the stage in a chamber intended one day for a pipe organ, was a masterstroke. The organ sounded amazingly pipe-like. All its power was there without the distortion usually found in electronic instruments when played above a mezzo forte. I believed Virgil would be thrilled with the organ, the installation, and the audience.

Thanks to Spencer Barefoot and his expert promotion of the event, the hall was well on its way to being sold out. A few days before the concert the president of the Rodgers Organ Company came to San Francisco to see how the installation was progressing. This event was important for the young company, and the president wanted to make sure everything was done correctly. The president, whose name was Rodgers W. Jenkins, was one of the founders of the company. He was a studious engineer type, small in stature, with black, crewcut hair. He could not have been more pleasant and unassuming. My only negative impression was of his clothes, which were rumpled, and his tie, which was the widest, most unattractive one I had ever seen. I didn't think he looked like the president of anything.

Rodgers Jenkins, along with another brilliant engineer, Fred Tinker, had worked for the highly respected firm of Tektronics. They had always been interested in the organ, and soon found out that the owner of "Tek," Howard Vollum, was also a devotee of the instrument. In short, Jenkins' and Tinker's expertise, and Vollum's money, enabled them to begin their enterprise in a small section of the Tek plant. Their efforts flourished, and they produced their first instruments in 1958. Leathurby's, in San Francisco, was one of the first stores to represent them outside of Oregon.

When they decided to name the company, they realized they could hardly call it the "Tinker Organ Company"; and the "Jenkins Organ Company" sounded too British to them. They settled on "Rodgers," and this fine electronic builder was launched.

Rodgers Jenkins seemed quite pleased with the sound of the organ. In fact, he was pleased with everything. There was no ques-

tion that he knew how oscillators, keyers, amplifiers, and thousands of diodes worked— he had helped design the instrument. I wondered, though, if he really knew how an organ should sound. Actually, I think he was amazed at how well his instrument sounded in Berkeley.

I also wondered how this introverted, country bumpkin (whom I later learned was considerably more sophisticated than he dressed!) was going to react to the flamboyant personality that Virgil radiated 24 hours a day. Virgil and I arrived at the hall. The two were immediately introduced. Virgil warmly

Virgil with Rodgers W. Jenkins

grasp' Rodgers Jenkins' hand, inquiring how he was, and how one so young could put together anything so complicated. Rodgers seemed a little overwhelmed by Virgil, and responded in a likable but timid way. Virgil then said, "Well, let's get to it and hear what the thing sounds like."

Virgil put the organ through its paces, and within a few moments warmed to it considerably. "Honey, this is incredible! You've really created something quite extraordinary!"

Poor Rodgers was looking around for "Honey," not realizing that Virgil was addressing him. Virgil beckoned him to come closer to the console. Rodgers, by now a deep shade of red, came closer to accept more accolades from the master, and Virgil said, "Oh, never mind Dear Boy, I call everyone Honey!"

Berkeley was Virgil's introduction to the Rodgers organ, an instrument that would later have an enormous impact on many of our lives. Virgil was taken with the instrument, and I could tell that the upcoming concert was going to be superb. I thought to myself, "Wait until Rodgers Jenkins hears the concert. If he's thrilled now, wait until he hears what Virgil does to an audience!"

The concert had sold well. Virgil outdid himself. Rodgers Jenkins, Richard Torrence, and the audience were enraptured, and went wild with enthusiasm. Clarence Leathurby was thrilled, and the reviews in the newspapers were favorable to both Virgil and the fine new "substitute for a pipe organ." The Rodgers Organ Company, heretofore kind of a local, Oregon operation, was launched in the State of California.

I remember that Richard's parents, John and Louise Torrence, who were visiting San Francisco at the time, attended the concert. Virgil was wonderful to them, pleasing both Richard and his parents. It also pleased Virgil, as he "always liked to know the kind of roots you kids have." Virgil was immediately taken with Richard (of course, he also remembered him from Hollywood) and his outgoing personality. He commented several times about how much he approved of him, and how Richard "had the face of a cameo." These first few meetings made a deep and lasting impression on Virgil. Ultimately, they heightened his career and changed his life.

35. Bound for Europe

During Virgil's stay in the Bay Area this time, we went together to Grace Cathedral for a Sunday morning service. I was proud to be with Virgil on my own "stomping grounds." Virgil, of course, was familiar with the famous Æolian-Skinner at the cathedral, and loved to hear the choir sing and Richard Purvis improvise. This Sunday, however, he was not pleased with the hymn singing of the small congregation (which was nearly non-existent, except at Christmas and Easter). "Why, they just stand there like a bunch of cattle, and kind of move their lips. That's not what congregation singing is about. It's pathetic!" He voiced these feelings to Richard Purvis after the service, laced with kind words about the choir and the beautiful sounds he made on the organ. Richard responded, "They never sing. I don't care, this is an Episcopal Cathedral!"

Virgil was shocked, and quickly moved to the subject of Richard's compositions for organ and what new things he was composing. Richard said, "What difference does it make, you don't play any of my pieces."

That statement wasn't true. Richard had dedicated one of his works, the "*Dies Irae*," to Virgil. The piece wasn't one of his best, but Virgil had programmed many of Richard's works as preludes and postludes at the Riverside Church, and before that time, at Brown Memorial Church in Baltimore. He had also programmed Richard Purvis' famous, impressionistic "Communion" on his U.S. tours. However, Richard was in one of his abrasive moods that Sunday, and Virgil was in no mood for it. "I will play some of your music when you write some," he replied; and thus transpired a small contretemps with Richard that lasted for about another year.

"Why must Dick Purvis be so rude? He has so much talent; he writes so many beautiful melodies, and the harmonies are just wonderful. But, where's the development? He just changes the key and does the same thing again, adds a coda, and calls it a day. No! It won't do! On top of all that, you have to put with his bad manners and unkind remarks. Really!"

This encounter, and others between them, upset me, for I loved and respected both men. However, Virgil did have a point. Afterwards, he continued to rant about the hymn singing. "If that's what being an Episcopalian is about—no participation—I'm sure glad I'm not one of 'em! You've got to give something to get something out of a service; and they give nothing—for one reason: they have no leadership. Their hymn playing simply has no rhythm or drive. Don't you ever play hymns that way!"

This love hate relationship between Virgil and Richard did nothing to foster my fondest wish, which was for Virgil to give a concert at the cathedral. However, during Richard Purvis' twenty-five year tenure, few organists were ever asked to give a concert there. Virgil said, "Teddy, I'm certainly not holding my breath for an engagement there. Besides, I can't be seen by the audience!"

Shortly after the concert with Fiedler, my apartment mate, Don, with some of his wealthy patrons, decided that I should have the

European study that Virgil so strongly urged. They set up a scholar-ship fund for me to study in Europe for at least a year. I was elated, as was Virgil. They decided that I should go to the Royal College of Music in London during the winter, and the following summer try to study with someone in Paris: either Pierre Cochereau at Nôtre Dame, or possibly Maurice Duruflé, the composer and organist at St. Étienne du Mont.

Virgil was particularly pleased with the impending trip, because he had been scheduled to record the Jongen *Symphonie Concertante* with the Paris Opera Orchestra conducted by Georges Prêtre in the Palais de Chaillot that summer. It was decided that I would accom-pany Virgil to Paris in June 1961, be with him during the recording sessions as his assistant, and then go to London for a scholarship audition at the Royal College of Music. I would join him and Richard Weagly in Paris, tour Germany and Switzerland, go back to Paris with them, and then go to London for the beginning of the school year while they returned to New York.

During the next season, I continued to practice and work at Leathurby's. Richard Torrence and I became as thick as thieves, and spent most of our leisure time together.

The summer of 1961 arrived quickly, and I flew to New York a few days before our departure to Paris. I had time to say goodbye to all my friends, especially Bob Hebble, who was delighted at my good fortune. Virgil and I departed on a night flight via Pan American Airlines to Orly and Paris. It was my first flight with Virgil. We flew in the coach section of the plane. "I'm not paying those outrageous fares for a simple plane ride in first class," he would say. (However, if others were paying—such as a recording company or concert pre-senter—he would always ask for first class tickets.)

The flight was jammed, but Virgil didn't seem to mind. He was too busy telling me about Paris, and talking to the other passengers. He introduced himself to everyone nearby, asking, "Do you know who I am?" or, more importantly, "Do you own any of my records?" He disliked airline food even then, and told me not to eat too much as we would have a wonderful meal as soon as we reached Paris. It was a night flight; and after refueling in Goose Bay, Labrador, most of the passengers tried to get some rest—as did Virgil, who had placed his cape over his head and ears so that only his face was visi-ble. He looked like a nun, and I shrieked with laughter, and so did he. That didn't deter him, however; nor did the stares from the other passengers as they went back and forth to the lavatory. He produced the effect he always wanted: to be noticed, even while he was asleep. People rarely forgot his eccentric but lovable character, and he relished the attention.

I was so excited that I didn't sleep much; but the man next to me did, with a cape over his head and plugs in his ears. (Virgil learned to sleep with earplugs early in his career in noisy hotel rooms.) We arrived at Orly around six or seven in the morning. Since Virgil knew French well, he immediately began to exercise his considerable command of the language. His booming, rich voice savored every nuance of that beautiful language, and his vocabulary was formidable. His pronunciation, however, was "unique," according to French friends. (He had an unabashedly Midwestern American accent.) The important thing was that he made himself understood. He always chided me for not having learned to speak French, and said "You will have to learn it, and soon!"

36. Recording the Jongen

Our first taxi ride into the city was a treat. We were staying in a beautiful old hotel on the Right Bank of Paris, very near the Arc de Triomphe on Avenue Hoche, called the Hotel Royale Monceau. Virgil told the taxi driver our destination (in English). Within five or ten minutes, Virgil had determined that the driver was going in a roundabout way in order to run up the meter. A stream of French flew from his lips, telling the driver the best route, telling him he tried to cheat us, and that if he didn't take money off the fare, Virgil would report him to the authorities. "These damned French, they'll try to cheat every time. Not me they won't!" I was impressed!

During the rest of the journey, Virgil pointed out many notable sights as we approached the city. It was the dawn of a glorious summer day, and a perfect introduction to Paris. Virgil knew the city intimately, and loved it as much as he did Manhattan. As we crossed the Pont Royale, the travelogue and descriptions flew non-stop. I was dazzled both by Paris and by Virgil.

We arrived at the Hotel Royale Monceau (the cab driver had reduced the fare), and were at once surrounded by attendants ("slaves," as Virgil referred to them). I was apprehensive about the cost of the hotel, as I was on a restricted budget, and Capitol records wasn't paying for me to be Virgil's assistant or for my trip. Virgil told me not to worry. In his competent French, he told the receptionist of his own needs, then got me one of the servant's rooms on the top floor for almost nothing. My room didn't have a bath; but Virgil said, "Never mind, you can bathe in my room" (his bathroom was immense) and, "If you have to pee at night, just do it in the sink. They all do that!" After we got situated in our rooms, we slept most of the day.

In the early evening, Virgil took me to a nearby restaurant he knew for my first meal in Paris. We both settled on "charcuterie," which consisted of pork, roast, chops, and sausages. It tasted as great as the several desserts he ordered. The waiters fascinated me, for they were dressed as Turks with shoes that curled at the toes like a court jester's. The coffee they served had the consistency and odor of India ink. Virgil ordered tea. As always, he asked for as many extra wedges of lemon as he could get, which he squeezed and poked with the end of his fork. ("No wagon wheels! I want real wedges!")

After this memorable repast (and there would be many others), Virgil and I walked up and down the Champs-Elysées, pointing out this and that. It was dazzling to be in the City of Light, teeming with humanity from all over the globe. On our way back to the hotel we stopped at a café for some "*glacé*." It turned out to be the inevitable chocolate ice cream that Virgil adored. So did I; and this confection was topped with enormous globs of whipped cream. Normally I would have scooped up the cream in a single bite. However, I said, "This whipped cream is sour—gone bad, Virgil. Don't eat it."

He roared with laughter. "That's how they make it in Paris. Let that sour taste mix with the sweet of the ice cream. You'll love it!" He was right, and my European education expanded one more notch—of my belt.

The next day after yet another excellent, early evening meal with two or three desserts, we made our way to the Palais de Chaillot, where Virgil was to have his first practice session on the organ before the recording dates later in the week. We traveled by taxi, with Virgil giving a cook's tour and shouting instructions to the driver as to which route should be taken. The Chaillot is located on the Right Bank of the Seine, directly opposite the Eiffel Tower. Great colonnades of the Musée de l'Homme partially encircle the great plaza directly across from the tower, and a concert hall is beneath the plaza.

The main doors to the hall were locked, and so we entered by the stage door. I was immediately struck by the large size of the hall, and the hideous acoustics: dead as a doornail. Everything was padded. The walls and ceiling were covered with *cork!* Both Virgil and I were crestfallen after clapping and singing various notes to see if there was any "give" to the room. It was dismal.

Then Virgil exclaimed, "Where in the Hell is the organ?" The stage was completely bare: no console, no pipes, apparently no organ. Virgil, in one of his best stage whispers and "unique" French, said to the concierge, "Where is the great organ?" The man answered, "*Une minute!*" With the press of a button in his control room, a large metal fire retardant curtain began to rise, and the magnificent façade of the Chaillot organ began to appear.

This great Cavaillé-Coll organ had been built for another, earlier Parisian concert hall, the Trocadero. It was removed when the hall was demolished, and installed in the Palais de Chaillot. The Trocadero organ had been played by all the organ virtuosi of the day. The organ had been rebuilt and the façade redesigned for its new home at the Chaillot, with a new, modern-looking console—all the work of the firm of Victor Gonzalez. We were impressed with the modern and brilliant look of the façade; but the organ seemed miles from the audience. Then the concierge opened a door in the mid-section of the façade under the pipes, and climbed inside. At the press of another button, a giant, creaking noise started, and the organ began slowly to move toward us on a track embedded in the stage floor. Imagine several tons of a giant organ looming towards us, moving to front and center in regular concert position! Moments later, the unique console with its lighted pushbutton stop controls (which looked like square controls on an elevator) was pushed into position, plugged, and ready to go.

Virgil wasted no time climbing on the bench and letting fly with the first measures of the Jongen "Toccata." It was as if someone had thrown a lighted match on an instrument splashed with kerosene! The blaze and fury of what poured out of that instrument was electrifying. Virgil said he had never heard anything like that kind of furious intensity, and it took him an hour or two just to get used to the brilliance and brute power.

The acoustics, as I said, were nil. When Virgil would release snarling chords from the beast, they would instantly stop. Nothing held over, as in an anechoic chamber.

However, in addition to the great power and an enormous Pedal division, the organ had beautiful foundation stops and flutes. Some of the orchestral color reeds and soft celestes were not what Virgil wanted; but they would have to do. The tremulants, if they worked at all, were unacceptable. For example, the trem on the Vox Humana sounded awful, like a sick nanny goat.

The combination action presented more trouble. It seems that Marcel Dupré, when he inaugurated the organ in its new home two decades before, had set the general pistons for his concert, and no one had changed the generals that the *maître* had set—until now! Try as he might, Virgil simply couldn't budge them loose from Dupré's original settings!

Joseph Jongen (1873-1953)

The organ did have a crescendo pedal (with what seemed like hundreds of indicator lights that went from one end of the console to the other), and some of Dupré's combinations could be altered by hand as Virgil specified in performance. My work was cut out for me.

Fortunately, there was plenty of time to rehearse. The plan was to rehearse and record only one movement per day. When we discovered that the floor around the console was squeaky, I had to tip toe in my stocking feet from one side of the console to the other during recording sessions. Virgil whispered his commands a mile a minute.

The recording sessions were to take place in the mornings, which annoyed Virgil. I would bring him hot chocolate and pastry in the mornings to get him going; and by 9:00 a.m. ("Oh God, it's the middle of the night!") we would be on our way to the hall.

The recording sessions thrilled me. The orchestra was superb. Georges Prêtre loved the Jongen piece, and he milked it for everything it had.

Virgil was so used to using the solo version of the Jongen work, which he and Bob Hebble had arranged for his solo concert tours, that he had problems playing the piece with an actual orchestra. He had played the orchestral parts in his arrangement so often that it was difficult for him to leave them out. Thus, Prêtre, with his remarkable ear, would sometimes say, "Virgil, what is that? Where are those notes written in the organ part?"

We solved the problem by having Virgil render one keyboard "dead" with no stops sounding. He was then able to play the orchestra parts on the dead keyboard when he didn't want anyone to hear them. However there was another, more serious artistic dispute.

The "acoustical release" that Virgil often used to overcome overly dry acoustics—which were painfully present here—really irritated Prêtre. After a tremendous climax in some parts of the first and second movements, and especially in the "Toccata" at the end, Prêtre would bring down the baton to cut off all forces. Virgil's "acoustical release" would invariably continue the organ alone, although only for a split second. Virgil explained what he was trying to overcome, but Georges would say, "Come on, Virgil, cut off with me! They'll take care of the reverberation by adding it electronically in the mastering process."

Virgil tried his best, but in the final chord of the "Toccata," as one can hear on the recording, he hung on too long. He actually planned it that way. "No orchestra is going to drown out this organ in this piece," he screamed. Prêtre threw up his baton in seeming disgust. Then he started to laugh and came over to embrace Virgil warmly.

The recording was superbly done by all the artists; and this marvelous and colorful work for organ and full orchestra was at last recorded in still the finest version of the work ever made.

As we left the hall after the final recording session, I saw a chance to try out the organ myself with a fire curtain down that I thought might improve the acoustical setting for a solo instrument. I climbed on the bench and lit into the final movement of the Widor *Second Symphony*.

The blaze of raw power and fiery tone that poured from that instrument continued to amaze me. Virgil was astounded, and vowed to make another recording in the small space created with the fire curtain down. Alas, he never had the chance. No one will ever experience that particular thrill again, for the great organ of the Palais de Chaillot was eventually moved to a new concert hall in Lyon, France (where Pierre Cochereau told me the acoustics were far superior).

To celebrate the completion of the recording, Virgil splurged and took me and some of the Capitol Records people to lunch at the Relais Plaza in the sumptuous Plaza Athenée Hotel, where Virgil used to say that he had met King Farouk in his early student days in Paris.

37. Gravely Crestfallen

While in Paris, Virgil took me to see many of the great organs. One vivid recollection was the first time I saw the superb instrument at St. Sulpice, and saw and heard Marcel Dupré. One Sunday morning I decided to venture out to the church by myself. Virgil was asleep, and probably wouldn't wake until late afternoon. I remember being determined to see the magnificent façade of the organ, with its eight classic columns and figures in the rear of the church, before I saw the rest of the interior. This effort required me to search for a back entrance to the church and find someone to direct me. Although I spoke only a smattering of French, a kindly priest outside was able to help me get into a sacristy behind the altar. When the door opened, I held my breath as I beheld my first gaze of the majestic organ façade in its entire splendor!

I remember being struck by how dark the church was, and how dark the wood in the façade seemed to be—almost black. There weren't more than fifteen worshippers attending, and it was only ten minutes before the organ mass was to begin. Someone told me that Marcel Dupré would be the organist. He was the most famous French organist of that time.

I took my place in one of the pews in the nave. There were seats in the organ gallery for those who wanted to watch the great master perform from above. Since this visit was my first, I preferred to hear the organ from downstairs. The atmosphere was dark and gloomy, and I remember seeing a dear old lady sitting in quiet reverence, saying the rosary across the aisle from me. All of a sudden, the most horrendous dissonant roar came from the great Cavaillé-Coll beast in the gallery! It was awesome, and it came so suddenly that I must have jumped in the pew!

I instinctively looked at the dear woman across the aisle. She was completely unruffled by the thunderous prelude to the service. She must have been used to it. I remember thinking at the time that if I tried that at home, I'd be fired immediately after the service!

The improvisation continued as a long and increasingly beautiful diminuendo, which introduced the Gregorian themes for that particular Sunday. The remainder of the service was lovely; but dull, I thought. I looked forward to the postlude, which I hoped would be a rip-roaring toccata. Instead, Dupré improvised a rather strict fugue on the rich foundation stops of the organ. It sounded almost like Brahms. Dupré must have been in his late seventies or early eighties by that time. I thought it a marvel to be able to improvise a fugue like that at any age!

That summer, Virgil's dear friend, Pierre Cochereau, invited him to play the prelude to the High Mass one Sunday. The organ at Nôtre Dame was Virgil's favorite organ in Paris, and one of his favorite instruments anywhere in the world. He loved the power, fury, grandeur, and richness of this great Cavaillé-Coll instrument.

Pierre had added some new and extremely loud *en chamade* reeds to the organ, and a new, more English-American type of draw knob console, with an extensive combination action. Purists were outraged about all this modernization, for it seemed like a mortal sin to desecrate this shrine with modern contraptions. Nevertheless, Pierre had the power and will to accomplish these innovations. He as much as told his detractors to go to Hell. Virgil agreed completely with all the additions and the modernization. He said that the old console was hard to control, and that his hands would ache after a few hours of playing on it. The cathedral retained the old console in a quasi-museum, where anyone interested could visit.

Virgil was thrilled to be able to perform at Nôtre Dame. In those days, there were no regular Sunday vespers concerts that later drew thousands of people every week. When there were formal concerts at Nôtre Dame, usually the titular organist played. Virgil invited everyone he knew in Paris to be with him in the organ loft for the prelude to the mass—including many Americans who were visiting Europe that summer. Virgil had played the Nôtre Dame organ on countless occasions at night, of course, but never for a real audience. Therefore, he decided to play the entire *Suite, Opus 5* of Maurice Duruflé. The three-movement work, with its dark, brooding, and tonally expansive "Prélude," the enchanting, impressionistic "Sicilienne," and the rip-roaring "Toccata" were just the ticket for the occasion.

Virgil was given all the rehearsal time he needed. He wallowed in the beauty of that rich instrument, playing most of his favorite works of Widor, Vierne, and Mulet during the rehearsals. He decided to ask Maurice Duruflé, and his wife, Madeleine, to come to one of his rehearsals so that he could have a coaching session with the composer on the "Suite." Virgil was interested in the way that the "*Maître*" approached his masterpiece—although I should note here that Virgil thought his very attractive wife, Madeleine Duruflé–Chevalier, played the organ better than her husband did. Time proved him right; for after her American debut in Philadelphia's Academy of Music as part of the 1964 National Convention of the AGO, she became—and long remained—one of the most sought after virtuoso organists in the world.

Virgil had already made some minor changes to his own interpretation of the work. For example, he heeded Duruflé's suggestions about cutting certain parts of the "Toccata," which the composer felt went on too long. He actually suggested that Virgil omit the entire "Toccata." He considered it "unworthy." (In fact, he told Virgil he hated it!)

Such liberties were unthinkable to Virgil, who always begged Duruflé to write an extended work for organ and orchestra. (Virgil even offered to pay for such an undertaking—which was quite out of character for him in those days!) Virgil believed that Duruflé was one of the few contemporary composers who could make a meaningful contribution to the scant repertoire for organ and full orchestra. Unfortunately, the work was never composed.

Richard Torrence

Virgil took me, once, to meet Maurice and Marie-Madeleine Duruflé in their charming Paris apartment overlooking the Church of Saint-Étienne du Mont (where Duruflé was organist). They later took us out to dinner at what seemed like a delicatessen—but I never ate so well!

Virgil again appealed to Duruflé to write an organ concerto. Duruflé protested that it took him too many years to write anything. (He was famous for being brilliant and creative, but not prolific.) Virgil was disappointed, of course; but the evening was lovely. The couple obviously loved being with Virgil, and they were highly amused by his unique French pronunciation.

On the Sunday morning that Virgil was to play at Nôtre Dame, Virgil's friends whom he had invited to climb up the spiral stairs to the organ gallery besieged the little red door in the tower. When the gallery was jammed to near capacity, Pierre Cochereau ran to Virgil and said, "There are many too many people up here! I'm afraid the gallery will fall down and we'll all plunge to our deaths! Where did these people come from? Who invited them? No more may squeeze in!" Virgil paid no attention. He was delighted at seeing the throng and by all the commotion, and he began a thrilling performance of the Duruflé "Suite."

Pierre Cochereau, of course, played the remainder of the service. Almost all of it was improvised. Virgil was enchanted by everything Pierre did. For the final "*sortie*," or postlude, Pierre improvised a toccata so staggering it made the Duruflé "Toccata" sound like a child's piece. "He did everything but play with his nose!" said Virgil. "He just had to show me up! He was jealous of all these people that had come to hear me."

Virgil may have been right, but this incident never affected their true friendship, or each other's admiration for the other man's genius.

By this time in late July, it was time for me to leave for London. All the plans had been changed. After Paris, Virgil was to head for Vienna and Salzburg, where he and Richard Weagly would meet. They would then go on to Switzerland, Italy, and back to France, and meet me in London before returning to the United States. They wanted to introduce me to many of their friends in England, and to see that I was properly situated in what would be my home for the next academic year.

Alas, none of it was to be. Soon after I arrived in London, I learned that part of the money to back my year's study wouldn't be available for at least three months. Although I had watched my pennies and won a partial scholarship to the Royal College of Organists, it would not be possible for me to realize my dream of studying abroad. I was heartbroken, depressed, and alone. I had no idea where Virgil and Richard Weagly were at the time that I received this disastrous news; but there wasn't much they could do about it anyway.

For the next two weeks, however, I attended every church service and cathedral concert in order to see and hear every great organ and organist I could. My only relief was being able to speak to my dear friend, Richard Torrence, in San Francisco, who tried valiantly to relieve my depression over this sad state of affairs.

A gravely crestfallen youth boarded the train for Southampton on a rainy day that August. My spirits were somewhat lifted when I saw the great liner, "Queen Mary," which was to bear this "failure" home to America—and to only God could know what fate! I did have a pleasant voyage; and the other passengers were fun; but it would have been more fun with Richard, Bob, or dear Virgil along.

Although I was in Second, or cabin, class, I was aware that a Very Important Person and his wife were traveling in First. Therefore, I took every opportunity to sneak up to the first class deck to get a closer look.

It was Leopold Stokowski and his new wife, Gloria Vanderbilt. I was thrilled to see this giant of a musician up close. He was much shorter in person than I had realized when seeing him on a podium with the Philadelphia Orchestra, or on the movie screen in *Fantasia*, where he was made to look larger than life. Virgil had told me many stories about him, and about how much he delighted in all of his interpretations. Stokowski had been an organist in London in his earlier days, before coming to New York and St. Bartholomew's.

It was fun, of course, to see this titan of a musician at such close range at the very height of his career; but I didn't meet him on that trip. (Years later, as I shall tell, I not only had lunch with him and Richard Torrence on Manhattan's Upper West Side, but also played the organ for him in Carnegie Hall!)

---

38. The Vatican Organist

Bob Hebble met me at the pier in New York in the fall of 1961, doing all he could to console me. I had already decided to go home to San Francisco and try to eke out a living. Richard Torrence was ever my true and best friend; and for a long while, he saw to it that I had a place to stay and plenty of good food to eat—plus 24-hour entertainment!

After Virgil and Richard Weagly returned from abroad, there were many phone calls of concern—sometimes even hostility—for Virgil was determined that I study abroad. To him, Europe was the only place to go! I wasn't so sure; for even through I was dazzled by all I heard and saw in Paris (and electrified by the service playing of the highest order in the Anglican tradition at King's College in Cambridge, Westminster Abbey, St. Paul's Cathedral, and the Temple Church), I still never heard anything like the organ playing and color sense of my two American teachers: Richard Purvis and Virgil Fox!

In the fall and winter of 1961, a major event took place in San Francisco at Grace Cathedral. With Herculean effort, and almost solely by himself, Paul Fitz Gerald, our good friend, produced concerts by the first organist of the Vatican's St. Peter's Basilica, Fernando Germani. In a series of 14 marathon concerts, Germani played the complete organ works of Johann Sebastian Bach! A concert with orchestra kicked off the series, in which I played the continuo parts on the Grace Cathedral organ. Germani was the evening's soloist, of course.

It was a mammoth undertaking, and a huge success. Paul involved the Italian and German consulates, as well as an impressive list of San Francisco's most prominent socialites. Albert Schweitzer and Marcel Dupré were Honorary Chairmen. Almost all the concerts were packed. What a wonderful opportunity to hear all the organ works of Bach!

Richard and I were heavily involved as volunteers, for this kind of an event rarely makes money. I was appointed page-turner for Maestro Germani, and Richard was to house and feed him (actually, to feed all of us). It was before churches started charging admission, and Paul and I were poor in those days.

Germani was great fun to be with, and was a charming and delightful raconteur. His stories about the ecclesiastical "snakes" in the Vatican with whom he was apparently in perpetual conflict (and from whom John XXIII, himself, was a constant defender) were especially fascinating. He was also portly, and always hungry. I remember once at breakfast, Richard had prepared a feast for all of us consisting of eggs with heavy cream and cheese, bacon, and enough English muffins for an army. Fernando seemed rather peeved when we all sat down. He said, "I suppose you've eaten already." I think he would have eaten it all himself if he could.

Germani had a reputation as a major virtuoso here and abroad in the 1940s and 1950s. This series was an enormous undertaking for him. He had played the complete works of Bach a few times in Europe; but this was the first time in the United States. The opening solo concert was a glittering affair with a packed house. Even Virgil showed up (he was on tour), and was given a seat of honor in the

Great Choir opposite the console, where he could see everything and be seen. As Germani's page-turner and console assistant, I had a wonderful view of Virgil where I could see his reactions.

Fernando used several different German editions of Bach, all of them in various states of disarray and decay. There were more than three hundred works! He asked me to use the programs from his last Italian performance of the series to tell him what to play next—although the programs that Paul produced were superior, by far, and in English.

At his first concert, as at all of them, Fernando would begin and end with a well-known large work. He usually didn't need his glasses for the first and last works on the programs because he had memorized them. The opening "Prelude and Fugue in A Minor" was therefore quite grand. (As Fernando got excited and instructed me to add more organ, I did so with great relish!) There was an ovation at the end of the fugue; and although it was a vast departure from the way Virgil did it, I thought it was thrilling.

Then, on went the glasses; and the sight-reading and the boredom set in. Fernando seemed suddenly nervous and in a hurry as he played a dozen lengthy chorale preludes, preceding each with the chorale on which it was based. All the while, he kept chattering to me, every once in a while saying, "Get the next chorale ready!"

I could see Virgil looking around from time to time; but he was generally well behaved. Then came one of the trio sonatas. These works of Bach are extremely difficult to play, for they make the ultimate technical demands on a player. By this time, Fernando had become agitated. With his head and face as close to the music as possible, he began playing a frantic first movement.

The trio sonatas are dance-like works, full of independent melodies, and should have sparkled with rhythmic clarity and splendor. What came out was anything but clear and splendid! There was a lugubrious 16-foot Bourdon in the pedal, and some nondescript flutes in the manuals. Fernando flailed away, and the music sounded like a great hodgepodge. I caught the expression on Virgil's face, which was incredulous, and I didn't dare look at him again or would have started laughing uncontrollably! The trio sonata worsened. I tried altering the registration for Fernando, but the music remained the same dark and murky glop.

In fact, the whole concert was mostly tedious (not every work of Bach is a masterpiece!). Nevertheless, Fernando saved the day with the first and last piece on the program. Unfortunately, whatever came between was pure sight-reading, which, although an admirable skill, wasn't always accurate.

One time, Fernando began one of the concerts with a big, well-known chorale prelude. He was just about to play the chorale preceding the prelude, when he hit the first chord. Every single note was wrong! He immediately stopped and said to me, "*Mama Mia!* This is only the beginning!"

The works he knew well he usually played quite well. He had a prodigious technique, especially in the pedal (Leo Sowerby had written the fiendish "Pageant" for him). Nevertheless, I felt his musicianship lacked what Virgil used to refer to as "the all important spaces between the notes."

---

39. Caméo

Virgil called me not long after he arrived back in New York. He was distressed because his manager, Roberta Bailey, had moved from New York to Worcester, Massachusetts after she married Richard Johnson, who was a lovely man we all liked.

The wedding had taken place some years before (while I was in New York after leaving the Peabody), and it was quite an affair. The entire Riverside choir sang; Virgil played the prelude and the service, and the incomparable Pierre Cochereau (whom Roberta also managed at the time) performed one of his fabulous improvisations. I understand that Roberta looked lovely, and the reception afterwards was splendid. I was not among the guests, however, because Virgil decreed that I could not attend. Someone had to baby-sit for Roberta's sister's children, and Virgil appointed me. (I was not amused!)

Roberta, of course, intended to keep her impressive organ management running from Worcester. By the time Virgil called me in San Francisco, her "stable" (I've always thought that word was an awful choice to describe a collection of artists!) also included the famous German organist and conductor, Karl Richter, and Richard Westenberg. Even at the onset of her plans to marry and relocate her management near Boston, alarms went off in Virgil's head. He wanted any manager responsible for him to be able to devote at least twenty-three hours of undivided attention per day to his career!

It was now six months after I had returned in defeat from England. I could bear life in San Francisco no longer. I had practically no money, only a little bit of unemployment insurance. There were no attainable well-paying church jobs in San Francisco; and I missed Virgil and Riverside. Richard Torrence arranged for me to get an inexpensive, first class railroad ticket from San Francisco to New York; and I informed Virgil that I would be there in five days via train. He was delighted.

When I arrived back in New York in November 1961, finances were still tight (although manageable, since the State of California had just extended the term of unemployment insurance for an additional three months because of high unemployment in the state). Paul Fitz Gerald, who by that time was also living in New York, helping Virgil promote a Bach concert series at the Riverside Church, arranged for me to move in with him into a large room of an enormous apartment in the "Wyoming," at 54th Street and Broadway.

The apartment in the Wyoming (in which several famous musical personalities lived at the time) was owned by a curious, ancient, and dear woman by the name of Mrs. Schnapper. (Her first name was Mary, but no one called her that.) She had many young, male tenants inhabiting various rooms of the dark and vast establishment. These tenants were all "relatives" (actually, "nephews"). It seemed that the formerly grand Wyoming did not want to be perceived of as a rooming house; and so the building's management frowned on anyone renting rooms to unrelated men. The management must have known what was going on, however, for "Schnaps" had been renting out for years. No one could have had so many scores of blood-related "nephews" dropping in and out from month to month.

Virgil loved to call me late at night from the Riverside console. One time he asked me if that "dear boy" he met in June 1961 in San Francisco, and at the concert in Berkeley ("You know, the sweet child that has the face of a cameo?"), would be interested in helping him out.

"He can handle you; and if he can do that, he certainly won't have any trouble with me!"

I roared with laughter, and said I would certainly inquire. I was afraid that Richard, who lived with his friend, Marshall Yaeger, in a charming apartment on Telegraph Hill, would never consider such a move.

However, after speaking with Richard, and perhaps making it sound more glamorous than I believed it was, Richard thought the plan might work. Virgil played a concert in San Francisco in May 1962; and the two of them spent several days discussing working together. Finally, Richard agreed to go to New York for a six-month trial to see if he could "stand it."

Richard had to accept a new nickname, however. Virgil said, "There are too many Richards and Dicks around the Riverside Church! Your name will be Caméo."

We all shrieked; but Virgil used the name for years, much to our delight.

Ted Alan Worth, Virgil, and Richard Torrence (1962)

After Richard arrived, Virgil expected Richard to accept out-of-state unemployment insurance as part of his compensation for working for him. Virgil supplemented the meager amount of insurance with an extra $100 per month, thereby getting a full-time secretary on the cheap—which delighted Virgil's sense of frugality.

Richard Torrence

For the record, Virgil's fee had been $500 per concert during the 1961-62 season, and he had insisted that Roberta Bailey raise it to $750. She resisted, as Ted reported, calling it "suicide." In fact, the $500 stated fee had often (too often, in Virgil's opinion) been discounted to as low as $350; and the $750 fee during the following season would be discounted to $500, when necessary.

Virgil had just learned that Capital Records, with whom he had made eight recordings, was abandoning the classical music business. Virgil needed a new record company, and he felt that a "personal representative" working in New York could find one more effectively than could his manager, who lived in Massachusetts.

Roberta and I never had a problem with each other. I assume she decided to tolerate me, never considering that I might become a threat to her business relationship with Virgil. By the autumn of 1962, however, I started looking for a recording company for Virgil. I first went to Wilma Cozart Fine. She ran Mercury Records, which had made some splendid recordings of Marcel Dupré at St. Sulpice, and which was known for its excellent sound. The company's recording engineer was Robert Fine, who was married to Wilma.

In those days, I was terrified to telephone anyone as important as Mrs. Fine for an appointment. (I have since reformed!) I eventually screwed up my courage and went to see her. We spoke briefly about recording Virgil, and I was thrilled when she said no! I was able to bolt out of her office and tell Virgil accurately that at least one record company didn't want him!

Around that time, I was living in a servant's room in a large apartment on West 88th Street. One of my four roommates was a photographer who had done some work for Command Records. He recommended that I speak to Robert Fine of Fine Recordings (who was Wilma Cozart Fine's husband), and by this time I had become a bit more aggressive. Mr. Fine took me to meet Enoch Light, a major big band leader who now headed Command Records. We made a deal for a three-year contract with Virgil, specifying two recordings per year.

The first record was to be on the new Æolian-Skinner at Philharmonic Hall, Lincoln Center. Novice that I was, I accepted the Command contract without legal advice, and made an excellent deal for the record company—which wasn't so good for Virgil. Still, Virgil was pleased to have a "record deal," which, by that time, wasn't so easy to come by. Ultimately we made all six recordings for Command: Philharmonic Hall, an all-Bach album at Riverside, an album on the Wanamaker organ in Philadelphia, a Christmas album at St. Paul the Apostle in New York, and two great recordings at Symphony Hall, Boston.

Some of these albums are still in the bins. All of them should be, for they are splendid!

Virgil's calling me "Caméo" somewhat embarrassed me, especially when his explanation wasn't always truthful. The fact was, he chose the name shortly after he learned that Ed Sullivan's assistant was called "Carmen," and because he claimed that I had the chiseled features of a cameo. He did, of course, have to differentiate me from Richard Weagly, Richard Johnson, and anyone else named Richard who wandered into his life.

John Grady, who was a sometime student of Virgil's and the Organist of St. Patrick's Cathedral in New York, invited us to an impressive dinner in a townhouse on Beekman Place. Virgil explained to one of the more distinguished of the Catholic priests attending that although my name was really Richard, he called me Caméo, which was an ancient Greek name.

"I've been a scholar of ancient Greek for many years, and I never heard of it," the white-haired priest said.

Virgil spun around to me and whispered loudly, "Caught!"

We all roared.

40. Schnapper Releases

I arranged for Richard to have a room for two months at the Schnapper establishment. Although I was sharing a large, divided room with Paul Fitz Gerald to save money, Richard got a recently vacated tiny room complete with its own bathroom. It had been a house cleaner's room; and it was ideal for one small person. Richard found the place fascinating, and fit right in.

It was always dark in the hallways. The only lights were 25-watt lamps, strategically placed. Every shade was drawn; and so you couldn't tell the day from the night without sticking your head out the window to look.

Mr. Schnapper had lost all his money in business in Cuba. Neither he nor Mrs. Schnapper ever went out, which explained why

Mrs. Schnapper frequently declared Broadway to be the most beautiful street in New York. It must have been some time since she had last ventured forth! She ran the apartment with the help of a house cleaner named Agnes. Both Mrs. Schnapper and Agnes were particularly fond of Richard, Paul, and me. Paul was a church musician at several Roman Catholic parishes, and Richard and I were associated with the Riverside Church through Virgil. That was all that Mary Schnapper and Agnes needed to know to consider us choice tenants.

Mrs. Schnapper, like her house cleaner Agnes, was a strict Roman Catholic. She was always talking about her parish church, St. Malachi's, often called "the Actors' Church." (I'm sure that Mrs. Schnapper hadn't seen the inside of any church in several years.) She claimed she was "eighty-six and a half" years old, and she looked it. Her appearance and mode of dress were always the same. She was tiny and frail, almost translucent, with the thinnest wrists I'd ever seen. Her blue-white skin was without a wrinkle (there wasn't enough to wrinkle!); and she always wore a "waffle iron" pattern, red-polyester smock over her dressing gown. Like Dresden porcelain, she gave the impression that if she were to move too abruptly she might crack, and a limb or two might fall off.

On top of her distinctive, blue-white face, with sparkling, kindly blue eyes, she wore a jet-black wig. Wisps of white hair stuck out at several points. On top of that confection was the kind of Dickensian cap that used to be worn by housewives in earlier centuries; although hers was made out of the same dreadful polyester waffle iron fabric as her smock, and in the same color.

She would often careen around one of the many hallways, touching the walls with her hands as she walked; and one had to be careful not to knock her over. The apartment had a telephone for the exclusive use of her "nephews." It was a pay phone with a loud ring. Virgil made liberal use of it. If I left him at the church at the ungodly hour of 3:00 a.m., when I got back to the apartment the telephone would ring and wake everyone up. Virgil, of course, thought that everyone should be awake when he was. Often Mrs. Schnapper was, and was always delighted to talk to him about her "boys." Virgil was highly amused by her. He delighted screwing up his face and lips and roaring her name, "Sshhnnnapper!" then exploding with laughter.

One evening I heard the telephone ring at a late hour. I ran for it, because it could only be "VF" calling. As I rounded the corner of the hallway, I spotted Mrs. Schnapper coming out of a bathroom directly opposite the telephone. As I approached, she seemed flustered. I noticed she had a hot water bottle in her hand. I picked up the telephone in a rush (it *was* Virgil) and began to speak. Mrs. Schnapper had turned around to go back into the bathroom. It was then that I noticed the hot water bottle had a hose attached to it that was going up the back of her dressing gown. The hose had been caught on the doorknob of the bathroom door. She was completely flustered; and so she turned around again, and...

Released.

The poor woman had been in the midst of self-administering an enema! I told Virgil I would have to call him the next day, and fled to my room, leaving poor Mrs. Schnapper mortified! When I related the tale to Virgil the next day, I think he screamed with laughter for a full ten minutes. He often retold the story, and asked me to retell it the last time I saw him in Palm Beach. When I got to the words "She released," he produced a wonderful roar of laughter with his head thrown back and his mouth wide open. How he loved funny stories!

41. A First Class Manager

As Virgil's secretary, Richard took over the office on the fourth floor of the tower of the Riverside Church. Virgil seldom used the office except for his Sunday afternoon naps between lunch and rehearsal for the afternoon oratorio. The office was spacious and nicely furnished with the quasi-Elizabethan style furniture that graced the offices of the higher staff members of the church. Bookcases containing Virgil's complete *Bach-Gesellschaft* (the complete works of Bach published in Germany beginning exactly one century after he died) lined one wall. Two high, leaded, Gothic windows overlooked the Hudson River. The room was pleasant, private, and spacious—perhaps 15 feet high. There was also a Bechstein grand piano in the office, but it was an early import—I imagine with inadequately dried wood for the central heating common in America—and therefore always out of tune. Richard had the office humming in no time, and it soon became the center of all operations for Virgil and his career.

Richard had taken on a difficult job. There used to be a joke around the Riverside Church (based, perhaps, on the release of several tawdry "slush" albums for Capitol Records that Virgil recorded—beautifully—mainly for the money), that "Virgil Fox tends to cheapen himself. Roberta Bailey finishes the job." This accusation was unfair to Roberta, because Virgil was so headstrong and demanding. He would do what he would do.

Virgil and Richard got along extremely well. Virgil learned quickly that "Caméo always gets his way" (which he usually did); and so it was pointless to argue with him. One only ran into a brick wall of persuasive charm and argument (or, according to Marshall Yaeger, who lived with him before and after this period, a somber "Gardol Screen"). Richard was popular with the entire staff of the church, and the entire "Fox crowd" began to visit Caméo, the undisputed ruler of the newly established "Richard Torrence Management."

Virgil could not have picked a better artist's representative. Richard adored Virgil and his great genius. He was creative with Virgil's press materials; and he began working on changing Virgil's image, his outlook, and his long-term goals.

He succeeded Roberta Bailey as Virgil's manager in June 1963. It wasn't an easy decision for anyone involved, but Richard had to force the issue in order to be able to afford to continue working in New York. He insisted on raising Virgil's fee again (to $900), which both delighted and frightened Virgil. Virgil relished the thought of higher fees, but he feared that churches and AGO chapters that had been loyal to him throughout his career could not or would not agree to pay more than a few hundred dollars per appearance.

At that time, the fees for concert organists were appallingly low. (Relatively speaking, they're not that much better today!) In the late 1950s and early 1960s, Virgil's popularity was already great; but he worked and practiced for a pittance, both at Riverside and for his concerts. When I first went to New York the combined salary for the Director of Music of the Riverside Church (Richard Weagly) and the Organist (Virgil Fox) was $10,000 per year ($5,000 for each)! This paltry sum may eventually have been doubled; but even that amount was nowhere near enough for artists of their caliber.

Low wages have always been the miserable plight of the church musician. I believe that St. Bartholomew's Church on Park Avenue was the only place in Manhattan that paid more for their organist-choir director. "David McK. Williams got $25,000 at St. Bart's, and that was years ago," Virgil would declare. So it took a lot of courage on Virgil's part to allow Caméo to raise his fees each year. Virgil was therefore delighted when it turned out that almost no one balked at the new fees. Suddenly there were more bookings than ever! I think people started to realize Virgil's true value once they realized how much they would have to pay for it.

It was evident from the beginning that Richard's style of management, and the way he handled himself and everything about his office, was first class. Virgil couldn't bear to think of him ever going back to San Francisco. News in the organ world travels fast and, of course, Virgil had told everyone on his tours about "My new man, Caméo—there's no one like him—he's a miracle!" Suddenly, other instrumentalists, singers, and organists began to call or visit Riverside's fourth floor to see if some of the "Torrence magic" might wear off on them; or whether Richard might consider other artists. Richard had to refuse any potential clients at that time, for he had his hands full managing Virgil's personal affairs and concert career.

42. Wiggles

Virgil was habitually late for everything (except church services and his own concerts); and so getting to a train or plane was always a harrowing experience. Virgil drove with a determined—even fiendish—expression on his face, a leaden foot on the accelerator, and one hand ready to activate the horn (which he used liberally).

More than once, Richard and I put him on a moving train, tossing luggage and cape amidst loud and fond farewells—and last minute instructions. He thrived on the hustle and commotion because it never failed to draw attention to him and his entourage.

Upon arriving at an airport, there was often a great commotion and a loud pleading to "Hold that plane!"—(even if the gate had already closed). "I've *got* to get on that plane!" One time, he actually threw a brief case loaded with music under the wheels of a moving aircraft! It was a small plane in a tiny airport, and so he managed to get on. However, the airline personnel were infuriated, and there was even mention of criminal sanctions until Virgil expressed an adequate amount of contrition.

We were sometimes mortified at the snickering that went on around us, for we knew we must have been a bizarre sight! Virgil would loudly exclaim, "Pay no attention to them, Chicks. They're fools!" and roar with laughter.

One time I had to meet his train at the old, cavernous Penn Station in New York. The great train roared in and disgorged all of its passengers—but no Virgil! I thought he'd finally done it—missed the train. I was ready to head back uptown, when out of a cloud of steam came a wearied Virgil, dragging his luggage and cape. He exhaustedly proclaimed, "This old rattletrap made sleep impossible!" He then proceeded to speak about his "triumphs" and his "legions of fans" on the tour he was returning from. "Let's go to Rumplemeyer's for some ice cream," he exclaimed, his weariness having vanished from his face.

Life around the Riverside Church continued as it was; but the bonus of Richard now acting as VF's manager spiced things up considerably. Bob Hebble and I were constant visitors to the office; and we took most of our lunches and dinners together. Dinners and late nights when Virgil was in town were *de rigeur*.

Virgil was immensely popular with most of the people who went to, and who worked at, the church; but he did have his detractors. Some of them were quite powerful. Richard often got an earful from them. Many people on the staff continued to resent the fact that Virgil never attended the regular meetings. How could he? He was usually away. Even if he could attend, meetings were generally held at ten in the morning, an unspeakably impossible hour for Virgil.

"Never!"

If some people didn't resent Virgil's flamboyance, they envied his immense popularity; or they deprecated his pink (or white Eldorado) Cadillac prominently parked in Riverside's recently-completed, luxurious, underground garage; or they made fun of his large, stone mansion in Englewood.

One person who delighted in all this gossip and backbiting was Virgil's lover for 33 years, W. Richard Weagly (whom we sometimes called "Wiggles"). He had every reason to be jealous of Virgil's achievements and popularity; and although he occasionally defended Virgil's reputation, he tolerated and sometimes even initiated negative comments about Virgil. As VF put it, "He loves to stir shit!"

I think Weagly was actually quite fond of Richard Torrence, Bob, and me; but when we were around the church, he liked to make derogatory remarks about Virgil, the organ, and "all you organ queens!"

The real problem seemed to be that Richard Weagly was such a prude that Virgil's all-male dinners, coupled with his flamboyance, were beginning to sow some ugly seeds of destruction in their relationship.

Virgil was a night person, "Loud and vulgar!" as Richard Weagly put it.

"Oh, he's a great organist, I suppose; but he has no taste. Can't you boys get him to calm down, and be a little more reserved in his approach to the music?"

This advice was heresy to me. I always countered Weagly directly. I stopped him cold whenever he went on like that.

Frederick Swann had already been appointed the other organist of the church. As a musician, Fred was a great favorite of Weagly's. He would always do things tactfully and exactly the way Richard wanted them done. Fred took over more and more of the regular duties—especially the oratorios of Handel, Haydn, Mozart, and Bach. The Baroque movement was "in" with a vengeance; and Weagly would have none of Virgil's approach to Bach and Handel!

I remember the 1962 Thanksgiving dinner in Englewood, when "the chicks" (that is, Bob Hebble, Richard Torrence, and I) were all seated around the table. Weagly gave one of his exhausted sighs. Virgil asked, "What's wrong?"

Weagly said, "I just don't know how I'm going to gather the strength!" He was talking about preparing an upcoming performance of the St. Matthew Passion, which he was to conduct with a small orchestra and Fred playing the organ.

No sooner had these words come from his mouth, than I said, "Oh! Another dreary performance of Bach at the Riverside Church!"

Virgil exclaimed, "Teddy, how awful!"—(but with a gleam in his eyes, and his hands clasped over his mouth to conceal his obvious glee).

Weagly left the table in tears, and ran upstairs to his room.

Richard Torrence, Bob, Virgil, and I roared with laughter! Virgil insisted, however, that I go upstairs, apologize to Weagly, and beg him to rejoin us for Thanksgiving dinner.

I did, but "Wiggles" refused to come down.

43. Long Stemmed Rhodes

In the late summer of 1962, I had been invited to play one of the noonday concerts on the Æolian-Skinner organ at Trinity Church, Wall Street. I had not been feeling well during the rehearsals. The day of the performance was unbearably warm and humid; and the church was not yet air-conditioned. I couldn't finish the end of the concert (the last movement of the Vierne *Sixth Symphony* was just too much to contemplate), and I felt faint. Richard Torrence took me to a doctor I knew who told me I had walking pneumonia. He said I would be fine after three weeks of bed rest.

Virgil and his dear mother would not hear of my staying at Mrs. Schnapper's; and so I was "tucked away" on the third floor of the Fox mansion in Englewood, where everyone looked after me. I was disappointed, for Virgil was scheduled to play a concert at that time at the Methodist campgrounds at Ocean Grove, New Jersey. The organ, which was in an enormous auditorium, was an old orchestral instrument built by Robert Hope-Jones, the innovative genius that helped develop the Wurlitzer Theatre Organ.

Virgil recounted his "triumph" in Ocean Grove when he returned. "Of course, the place was packed!" he said.

"But it had a dirt floor!" he screamed.

Although Richard and Bob told me that much of the organ was in hideous disrepair (it has since been considerably enlarged and refurbished), they both said that Virgil performed and acted as if it had been one of the most perfect organs of the world.

Virgil discovered that the instrument had a unique feature. There was one stop, which, when depressed, caused a garish flag made of electric lights to "wave" across the façade of the organ. Virgil pressed it, and, to his delight, caused the audience to stand up! There were many standing ovations that night!

The summertime was always active and great fun for Virgil on the East Coast, for he was in great demand at the beach communities in and around Manhattan. There was also the "Summer Series" at Riverside, which Virgil always inaugurated. Many of the world's great virtuosos, and the finest gifted young organists, were given an opportunity to perform on this distinguished series. Among the best concerts I remember were the young John Weaver and the beautiful

Cherry Rhodes (whom Virgil always called "Long Stemmed Rhodes"). Both of these greatly gifted, good friends have gone on to brilliant careers. Virgil always fostered and encouraged talent, especially when it was as rare as these two possessed.

I remember one time when Virgil was on his way to a summer concert in the Midwest. It was customary for him to wear a white dinner jacket at summer concerts. Caméo and I despaired that Virgil had only one ancient, and by this time yellow "white jacket," and begged him to replace it.

"Now Chicks," he said, "this jacket is magnificent and will do perfectly well! When Mama puts flour all over it, it turns white again!"

While we were rushing through La Guardia Airport, late as usual, Virgil asked me to carry this ancient rag, which he had gotten fresh from the cleaners in a clear plastic bag. Richard and I decided to make an end of this disgraceful garment; and so I gently lifted the plastic and began dragging the thing across the floor, occasionally stepped on it, grinding my shoe over it when I could, and proclaiming, "Oh, Virgil, I'm so sorry! Look what I've done! I have ruined your jacket!"

"That's alright, Honey. I'll get it cleaned again, and put flour on it."

I said, "Oh no, it goes!" and began to fold the hangar all around it, ripping off one of the sleeves; then I threw it into a nearby trash can.

Virgil screamed, "You brat! How dare you do that to that wonderful coat!"

By now he was laughing, and admitting it was about time he got a new white dinner jacket. When pushed hard enough, he could have a delicious sense of humor about himself.

Virgil, at that time, was definitely no fashion plate! He had a penchant for wearing some bizarre outfits and color combinations; and he held onto almost every old jacket and suit he ever owned. At the time he purchased these clothes, they may have been expensive and in vogue; but many of them—including that disgraceful, flour-stained dinner jacket—were worn out and out of style. Although he had innate good taste in most things (for example, he adored the scores of good-looking shoes and hundreds of attractive ties he owned), his love for terrible old clothes was a characteristic Caméo was determined to change.

Virgil's love of strange clothes came, we think, from his considerable collection of extremely rich (and eccentric) older women. One of the most influential of them was Nan Erickson, whose husband had founded the advertising agency, McCann-Erickson. She gave Virgil many of her late husband's old jackets, including the memorable, old, mink coat that Virgil modeled so outrageously for Bob and me in the hotel corridor in Elyria, Ohio.

There was also Anne Archbold, who befriended Virgil during his service days in the armed forces when he was responsible for the music at Walter Reed Hospital in Washington, D.C. Virgil lived in her palatial home (he always referred to it as a "palace") during most of World War II, sleeping between "silk sheets."

Anne (whose father had founded Standard Oil with John D. Rockefeller Sr.) adored Virgil. He would play for her at any time she requested on an Æolian pipe organ in her vast music room. The two of them collaborated on many parties given for sick and wounded service members; and Virgil was constantly rounding up all types of talented musicians to entertain at her soirées.

Virgil told many stories about this remarkable woman. Although she lived like a queen, at times she could be penurious. She never threw out old things if she thought they were good, no matter how worn. He said that if she spied even a speck of dust on her piano she would yell for Donald, one of the servants, to "polish the piano!" We all thought that Virgil had picked up her most eccentric traits—especially if they amused him.

In later years, Ms. Archbold would invite Virgil down for a winter visit at her estate in Nassau. She would usually sponsor him in a concert at the Anglican Cathedral on those visits, which Virgil especially liked since it made his trips tax-deductible. Virgil remained a close friend with her until she died. Of all the rich people Virgil had known—and he specialized in knowing rich and fascinating women—Anne Archbold was the only one who left him money. He got $10,000.

Virgil also had befriended the famous sculptor, Malvina Hoffman. She lived in a fascinating house on "Sniffen Court" in Manhattan; and she adored Virgil's playing. She had been commissioned to create a series of 101 life-size figures for the "Hall of Man" at the Museum of Natural History in Chicago. Virgil had always admired one of them called "Nordic Man: God's Gift to Women"; and so, when Malvina had smaller castings made, she sold one to Virgil.

Virgil always kept that bronze statue prominently displayed on his living room coffee table. It was one of his favorite treasures and the only important piece of art he owned.

Richard Torrence

Virgil told me that Malvina (whom he and I visited) had sold the statue to him for $1,500. After he gave her a couple of small checks, she said, "That's enough." Essentially, she had made the statue a gift to Virgil.

Virgil loved to tell that Malvina had confided in him that the model for "Nordic Man" was actually an Italian who lived in Brooklyn. Virgil was especially interested to note that Malvina had made one of Nordic Man's testicles lower than the other. He was fascinated by her attention to this "anatomically correct" detail, which convinced him that more than modeling had been going on.

Virgil played for Malvina's funeral at the Church of the Incarnation on Madison Avenue. He was dismayed by the Baroque butchering of the fine old organ that some New York enthusiasts had wrought. However, when it came time for the pallbearers to lift the casket and carry it out of the church, Virgil devised a postlude that seemed to lift the casket way beyond the stretch of the pallbearers. In this remarkable way, Virgil's inspired playing seemed actually to transport Malvina on her way to heaven!

44. I Get Work!

Soon the unemployment benefits that supported both Richard and me in 1962 came to a shrieking halt. We had almost gotten used to going to the unemployment office to pick up our checks and deliver some form of written confirmation that we were still trying our darndest to locate an honest job. Fortunately for us, the Manhattan unemployment office for out-of-state applicants (from which both Richard and I drew our California benefits) was only a block away from Schnapper's rooming house. It was miles away in ambience, however. Richard had been assigned to the same, odious-looking clerk as had I. Since he had fat, ugly hands with tough-looking, unkempt nails, we always referred to him as "the beast with the cloven hooves."

In the knick of time, an opportunity opened for me in the form of a good church job in one of the suburbs of Philadelphia known as Frankford. Virgil urged me to take the job, and gave me a glowing recommendation to the church's rector, The Rev. Mr. Albert Fischer. I already had several good friends in Philadelphia, and so the job appealed to me. I made an appointment with Mr. Fischer, and I took the train to Philadelphia.

Frankford had once been a posh suburb of Philadelphia, with many lovely homes and green open spaces. The greenery had disappeared, however; and in its place, along Frankford Avenue, was an unfortunate surplus of seedy stores and hash houses. Adding insult to injury, the Frankford Elevated, which was an extension of the city subway system, ran above Frankford Avenue like a giant, elongated umbrella.

St. Mark's Episcopal Church, Frankford sits in the middle of the town. (One always has to be careful to add "comma Frankford" to the name, because there's another elegant church in downtown Philadelphia called "St. Mark's"—to which the Wanamaker family helped give a charming organ.) Like a Gothic structure from England, the Frankford church is plopped right down on the Avenue. In fact, the elevated train runs right in front of the church, only 15 feet from the stained glass windows at the altar end.

When I entered the handsome edifice, the sight was magnificent! There were wonderful examples of stained glass, magnificently carved pews, and a carved stone altar and reredos that soared from floor to ceiling, and was filled with angels and saints, each in an individual niche. It was like a miniature St. Thomas Church, Fifth Avenue. (It was actually designed by the same architects—Cram and Goodhue.) Unlike St. Thomas, however, the Frankford church was blessed with very good acoustics. Best of all, it had a new, three-manual Æolian-Skinner organ. The instrument sounded fine in the room, and much larger than its 45-ranks.

I fell immediately in love with the place, and probably would have relocated there for nothing in order to make music in such wonderful surroundings. Mr. Fischer was an imposing clergyman, but he made me feel immediately at ease. He seemed impressed with my playing; and he said, "When can you start?"

I was thrilled! Here was a splendid building and organ, and a man who maintained everything beautifully. Furthermore, the job almost paid a living wage!

Virgil and the New York crowd were pleased; and so I left with my music and belongings for the "City of Brotherly Love." Not only were Mr. Fischer and his lovely wife, Betty, wonderful to me, but they even invited me to stay with them until I could find accommodations.

One day, Mr. Fischer announced that he had recently conducted a funeral for the last remaining parent of one of his parishioners. Now there was a young man living alone in a large house who loved the organ—especially the one at St. Mark's. Albert Fischer spoke to Walter Lee Mellbourne about me, and they agreed that I could be a paying boarder in his house. God must have been with me in that September of 1962, for He delivered a wonderful job along with a longtime friend and patron!

Walter had been an only child, and his parents had been frugal. Walter was a high school teacher when his parents died, leaving him a tidy sum and plenty of valuable real estate—including the family's home, which was a large row house at 4748 Penn Street. Walter had always been quiet and kept to himself, but things were going to change radically in the next few years for dear Walter. I think he enjoyed all the excitement, and that it truly broadened his perspective and made his life happier. He turned out to be a wonderful friend who was generous and supportive in every way.

I enjoyed the job immensely, and spent hours every day at that splendid organ. The choir at St. Mark's was not the greatest, but they tried hard. I managed to hire a few paid singers, which helped us out a great deal. One of these singers was a large, rotund tenor by the name of David Page.

I had gone to one of the Sunday evening oratorios at what we facetiously called the "Sansom Street Opera House" (it was the First Baptist Church in downtown Philadelphia). Earl Ness, the Organist and Choirmaster there, produced astonishingly good programs nearly every Sunday evening. On this particular Sunday, he conducted the Berlioz *Requiem*. I went there with another member of my choir, William Marsh. Bill was always knowledgeable and helpful to me, and he was one of the most professional singers with whom I ever had the pleasure of working.

Bill and I were sitting in the church, thrilled with the entire presentation. We both noticed a large man in the choir who seemed to take up two or three seats. Whether the choir stood or sat, it didn't seem to matter, as it appeared that the large man never moved. It was as if he were suspended in place. He also had a certain hauteur, seemingly "above it all" in both spirit and flesh. Bill and I poked each other, highly amused by this character.

The "Sanctus" movement was next. It turned out that the large man was the soloist. What poured out of his mouth sounded divine! I couldn't believe his superb control, tone, and absolute musicality. I will never forget that evening!

David Page became a good friend. He was great fun to be around, full of marvelous stories and cheer. He "made" the Christmas Eve services at St. Mark's with his unique rendition of "O Holy Night," Max Reger's "Slumber Song," and Gustav Holst's "In the Bleak Midwinter." Tears flowed when he finished these works. I'm sure it was David's size, and maybe bad luck, that kept him from becoming another Pavarotti or Domingo; for he certainly had the talent and a glorious vocal instrument!

Walter Mellbourne became increasingly involved with church activities; and after a good deal of coaxing, we talked him into sponsoring a series of organ concerts at St. Mark's. We decided to do the concerts properly, with printed programs and good advertising to a large mailing list (which is the key to any successful concert or concert series).

Of course, one must deliver the merchandise! Virgil Fox was the right artist to start things off with a bang.

---

45. Lincoln Center

Virgil packed the church, and he played like a demon. He adored the organ and the building. The only drawback was that the organ console was neither movable nor visible. We did our best with mirrors, and that suggested a project for us for the future (which I'm sorry to say we never completed).

Virgil, Richard Torrence, and a whole crew of friends from New York descended on Frankford and stayed with us at 4748 Penn Street. Walter had hired a cook and housekeeper by the name of Livinia; and she prepared exactly the kind of food that Virgil loved: roasts, lots of vegetables, potatoes, and a piecrust to kill! Walter was never the same after this first visit by the Great One. He became a dedicated, life-long fan of Virgil's.

Virgil stimulated enormous interest in the St. Mark's series. Suddenly we had a fine thing going. These were the days before admission was normally charged at church concerts (it seemed like someone was always passing a plate). Therefore, we had to tax Walter's generosity to the extreme. He never complained, however; and so we continued the series, which Walter subsidized heavily.

Applause was not generally acceptable in churches, either (except for the Pope on his visits); but Virgil's performance met with a loud ovation; and that novelty suddenly made applause acceptable at St. Mark's—despite loud objections from certain members of the vestry and the congregation who seemed to resent having "their" church filled with "strangers" who "didn't belong." Most importantly, Mr. Fischer was pleased with the concerts and the community outreach they produced. He helped us greatly with some of the more outraged parishioners.

Carlo Curley

The organ-builder Jack Burger used to tell the story of the preacher of a "society" church in Erie, Pennsylvania who explained to his congregation that since their church was God's House and Sacred Space in which there could not be applause, at the end of Virgil Fox's recital those assembled who felt so moved could quietly stand, clasp their hands together, and wave their arms over their heads. He even went so far as to rehearse this supportive gesture with the crowd, much to Jack's amusement.

As the Pastor walked away, Our Hero quickly entered, went to the front pew and proclaimed in his clarion voice, "Ladies and gentlemen! Contrary to what you have just been told, this performance is not a football game. You may applaud!"

The multitude responded with an overwhelming ovation even before the first note.

During the two seasons of concerts at St. Mark's, we presented the famous woman virtuoso, Claire Coci; Pierre Cochereau; Karl Richter and the Munich Bach Choir; the young African-American, Garnell Copeland (Garnell was a great friend of mine from San

Francisco, then attending the Curtis Institute, and was one of the greatest talents I have ever heard. He was killed tragically several years later in Washington, D.C.); Cherry Rhodes (then also at the Curtis); and my good friend John Weaver (who became head of the organ departments at both the Curtis Institute and the Juilliard School of Music—in addition to being Music Director and Organist at Madison Avenue Presbyterian Church in New York).

All these young players were well known and loved by Virgil, who encouraged their budding careers. Virgil headlined the series and played at St. Mark's two years in a row. He was the "shot in the arm" that our series needed. Without his charisma and artistry, most well-intentioned series faded and died after the first or second concert!

Meanwhile, in New York, things were going extremely well. The exciting new organ in New York was the long-awaited 98-rank Æolian-Skinner organ that had been installed in Philharmonic Hall (now Avery Fisher Hall at Lincoln Center for the Performing Arts). During the installation of the organ, Æolian-Skinner had a difficult time with the different unions involved in the construction of the hall. Nevertheless, in spite of delays—and one near disaster that caused the console to catch fire and have to be re-built—the organ was almost ready for its inauguration.

The actual completion of the installation took place several months afterwards; and portions of the organ continued to be revoiced to accommodate the oft-revised acoustics.

Richard Torrence

The organ was to have been ready for the opening concert of the hall in September 1962. E. Power Biggs was to be the soloist with the New York Philharmonic, Leonard Bernstein conducting, playing Samuel Barber's "Toccata Festiva" on the new Æolian-Skinner organ. Because of the union situation, however; and the fact that Joseph Whiteford made a decision that the organ would be installed only after the hall was officially opened (so that his own team wouldn't have to cotton to the various plumbers', electricians', and carpenters' unions), the Æolian-Skinner organ was definitely "not ready" for the Grand Opening.

In its place, they brought in an Allen electronic organ!

One snobbish New York organist told Virgil that it was "absolutely tragic!" that E. Power Biggs would agree to play such an inferior instrument.

Virgil quickly put the "tragedy" into perspective: "Why, any organist would have sat on the back steps of Philharmonic Hall banging a wooden spoon on an inverted pee-pot just to play there opening night!"

On the day of the official opening, Virgil and I ordered some soft drinks in an Irish bar across the street from Lincoln Center so that we could watch the proceedings on television. From the window, we could see the limousines arrive at Philharmonic Hall. On television, we could see the First Lady, Jacqueline Kennedy, arrive.

The formal Organ Inaugural Concert was finally scheduled for early December of 1962. It was "by invitation only," and turned out to be a splendid event in the history of the organ world. Here, in New York, at last, there was a proper organ installed in a concert hall, which was a dream come true for Virgil, who had always lamented the fact that there had never been a great concert hall organ in Manhattan.

Virgil had played the "horror" they called an organ in Carnegie Hall. In 1936, he played the first organ recital given there for a paying audience. He loved to tell of the large Kilgen organ they had installed in Carnegie.

"It had absolutely no impact or volume! How could the poor thing? It was installed high above the stage, nearly a city block away, and had to play through some kind of a filthy "tone chute." Here I was, on the stage on 57th Street, and the organ sounded like it was coming from somewhere on 53rd Street! It did have one hell of a 32-foot Bombarde lying on the grid above the stage house, however. It sounded like a B29 coming in for a landing! That's about all you could hear. Once you used it, you had to keep it on, or people thought the organ had quit!"

Virgil had similar feelings about the modest three-manual E.M. Skinner organ he had played in Town Hall—and it lacked a Bombarde! Finally, there would be a splendid organ in the newest concert hall in Manhattan.

The dedication concert consisted of three organists, all of whom would play in a single Saturday afternoon. They were E. Power Biggs, Catherine Crozier, and Virgil Fox. What a line up! Virgil was determined to play last, and got his way. In the end, it was a bad idea.

Lincoln Center for the Performing Arts had commissioned three composers, Henry Cowell, Virgil Thompson, and Vincent Persichetti, to write pieces for the opening of its new organ. Each artist premiered one of these works. Virgil was assigned to play Persichetti's "*Shimah B'Koli*" (which is the line following "*De Profundis*" from Psalm 130). I can remember coming up to New York from Philadelphia, and hearing Virgil practice the piece. He could make neither head nor tail of its dissonant wanderings. He even telephoned Vincent Persichetti, whose compositions for choir he had previously admired, and said, "Honey, what do I do with this? How does it go? What does it mean?" Later, Virgil gave the piece his own title: "Notes at Random."

I've always thought it curious that here was a golden opportunity for three well-known American composers to write works for a brilliant new concert hall organ; and all three of them created works more suitable for a house of worship. None of the works are memorable to me now except for their hideous dissonance. I would have been fired for playing any of them in a church for an ordinary congregation! I do give Virgil credit, however, for working so hard on the piece, and for inviting Persichetti to the final rehearsal to coach him on it, thereby giving it the best possible performance he could muster.

The hall was packed for the dedicatory concert; and all the "Major Players" in the organ and New York music world were there—not only to hear the new organ, but to see what these disparate (almost rival) performers would do at this lengthy marathon.

E. Power Biggs played first. I must say, I never heard him play better at a public concert! The organ sounded thrilling, despite the strange acoustics of the hall.

The lighting of the instrument was magical! Before the concert began, no one was aware that there was an organ in the hall—except, of course, for the imposing four-manual ebony console in the center of the stage. Just before Biggs came onstage, the house lights dimmed, and from behind the metal and wood screen above the stage, the great organ gradually came into view. Shades of blue, purple, and red made the silver pipes shimmer, and showed off the gold-leafed Positiv division casework and the gilded 32-foot Kontre Geigen stunningly. It was breathtaking!

Biggs inherited the Cowell work; but the work he played that I remember most vividly was a rip-roaring performance of Charles Ives' "Variations on America." It was the first time I had ever heard the work, and Biggs actually had fun with it and let the organ roar. The audience loved him and the organ!

The first intermission was long, as Catherine Crozier had to re-set every combination piston on the organ for her section. (Unfortunately, this concert took place long before the days of multiple memories and computers.) Her performance was worth waiting for, as she played to perfection (as she usually did). Not a note was out of place. To my taste, however, there wasn't much excitement or personality. My impression was that she was as lovely and poised as a marble statue. I recall her somewhat drab performance of the Franck "Chorale in B Minor," and an interesting fantasy of Jehan Alain, whose works she championed. One had to admire her effortless technique and scholarship, but I thought she lacked drive and flair.

During the next long intermission, Virgil slipped onto the stage, shielded by a screen, to change all the buttons on the organ for his section coming up. It was one of the few times I saw him wear his famous cape onstage. (Despite the many stories about his wearing a cape while playing, Virgil usually wore the cape only after concerts while greeting his multitudes.)

The concert was well into its third hour before Virgil started playing. (The intermissions became boisterously long cocktail parties!) The tension backstage must have been huge. Nevertheless, Richard told me that "Jimmy" Biggs and "Kitty" Crozier were being nice to Virgil; and Virgil was being cordial to them—even though he intended to outperform them in every possible way!

He must have felt like a racehorse at the starting gate, for when he came out, he tore into the Bach "F Major Toccata" at a tempo faster than I had ever heard it played. (The word "frantic" came to mind.) All went well until, during a de-crescendo midway in the work, Virgil closed the crescendo pedal (the device that automatically adds and subtracts stops), only to find that no other stops were on!

There was dead silence for a second or two, as Virgil's fingers and feet continued to fly over the mute keyboards! He recovered miraculously after this minor train wreck, and finished the work in record speed. The audience roared its approval, but Virgil was shaken and definitely not pleased with his performance so far.

He next gave a stunning account of the "E Major Chorale" of Franck, and was as creative and musical as he could be with the Persichetti "Notes at Random." His performance concluded with a frenzied, hysterical account of the Duruflé "Toccata." It was definitely *not* vintage Virgil, but his fans went wild! Unfortunately, it had gotten so late in the afternoon, that many people in the audience had left by the time he got to the end.

46. He Kisses Everyone! Both Boys and Girls!

Virgil would have another chance in less than a month's time when he would give the first solo recital at Philharmonic Hall. It was an historic event, and was one of the greatest concerts Virgil ever played.

The house was packed when Virgil walked onto the stage to address the audience on that Tuesday evening, the 7th of January 1963. He spoke only once, briefly, at the beginning of the concert when he introduced the first piece, which was Bach's monumental "Passacaglia & Fugue in C Minor." He recalled that Leopold Stokowski had made the piece famous with the Philadelphia Orchestra; and he ended by saying that for the first time it was possible "to play the 'Passacaglia' in a concert hall in New York on the instrument for which it was composed." He then proceeded to give one of the greatest performances of his career.

The twenty-two variations and double fugue on the "Passacaglia" theme of Bach were like the great architecture of a celestial monument under Virgil's hands, building and building, then backing off, then building again to enormous climaxes until the great ending of the fugue. I don't exaggerate when I recall that even with every stop drawn on that large instrument, and the mighty roar that it produced, Virgil could not drown out the frenzied standing ovation that occurred during the final chord!

It was as if the audience could not contain itself. It was compelled to erupt in this remarkable way even before the work was complete. It was electrifying!

Virgil went on to give astounding performances of Bach's "Trio Sonata VI," the "D Major Prelude and Fugue," and—after the first intermission—the *"Grande Pièce Symphonique"* of César Franck—from which he extracted every drop of its considerable beauty and symphonic style. Then followed a staggering performance of Olivier Messiaen's *"Dieu Parmi Nous"* ("God Among Us"), which, under Virgil's hands, became almost a new, delirious paean to the great

Creator of the Universe. This brilliantly dissonant work, following the melodic and tonal Franck, brought the audience to its feet for the fifth standing ovation of the evening (for a concert that was only two-thirds over, not including encores! "Don't forget the encores!").

After the second intermission, there were several Bossi and Vierne favorites. Then, the concert ended with the mighty "Fantasy & Fugue on 'How Brightly Shines the Morning Star'" of Max Reger. It was an astounding evening of music making. It seemed like it wasn't possible for Virgil to make even the slightest mistake, or play even a single "split note," that evening—he was so "on." Although the acoustics of the hall had turned out bad for all the other musical instruments, the organ sounded wonderful. The secret was that the organ was voiced after the hall was finished. Joseph Silver Whiteford, head of the Æolian-Skinner Organ Company, compensated for the lack of bass response in the hall by beefing up the pedal.

The lighting of both the organ and Virgil was magical. You knew you were in a proper theatre-concert hall because of the contrast to the often inadequate lighting available in churches. However, short-ly after this great concert (which got rave reviews), some of the crit-ics referred to the lighting of the organ pipes as distracting. "It looks like something out of a set for a Wagnerian opera," said one. For this reason, the lighting was never again used—ever! How sad, for the lighting was so beautifully and tastefully done. In no way was it dis-tracting. Organ pipes should be seen when they're not in enclosed divisions. Here, a great opportunity was lost.

Back to the encores! The crowd at Virgil's concert was delirious, demanding more and more. Virgil, as usual, gave generously of him-self, enjoying ovation after ovation. After the long concert, the greet-ing line went from the Green Room almost to the lobby as Virgil spoke to, and embraced, every single person. Richard later told me that he heard one of the more famous quotes about Virgil after that concert when a woman exclaimed, "He kisses everyone! Both boys and girls!"

One of the Philharmonic Hall ushers said there hadn't been a scene like that in the Green Room since the hall opened for soloists and the orchestra under the baton of Leonard Bernstein, four months earlier. It was after midnight before Virgil left the Green Room for the shower!

Richard had arranged to record portions of this concert later in the month. He was wary because the only recording dates available were during daytime hours—in fact, early morning hours, which Virgil avoided like the plague! I wasn't there for the recording sessions (Bob assisted Virgil at the console), but it was quickly apparent that the sessions were proceeding perfectly. Richard said that Virgil closed his eyes as though he were asleep when he began the "Passacaglia."

With such extensive preparation several weeks before, the first take was perfect! Everyone in the control room loved the recorded

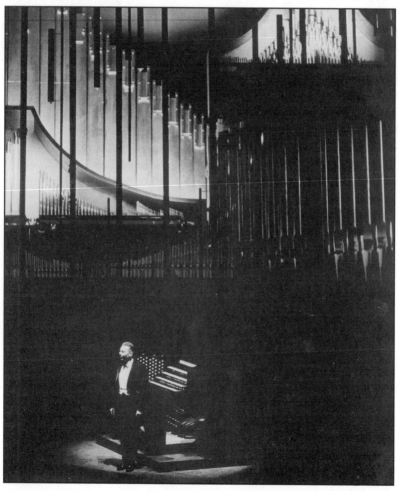

First solo concert of Virgil Fox at Philharmonic Hall,
Lincoln Center for the Performing Arts; with lights on the Great, Positiv,
and Pedal divisions of the Æolian-Skinner organ (January 7, 1963)

sound; and so the sessions were entirely productive—despite that "ungodly hour." Almost all of the excitement is there to experience, except for the roar of the huge audience, on the splendid Command recording. Anyone lucky enough to own one of the original releases (either the Command LP or the 4-track tape—remember 4-track tape?) can see the brilliant, full-color photo on the front cover of the great Æolian-Skinner organ before its dramatic façade darkened into oblivion.

Richard Torrence

The fact was, that shortly after the hall opened, temporary acoustical work was done on it; and a complicated set of shades was put in front of the organ. The mechanism to move these shades wasn't attractive, and could be seen whenever lights on the organ pipes were turned on. (Thus, they were kept off.)

The shades were erected under the theory that the organ did not make a proper "acoustical background" for the stage house—which was a ridiculous assertion when one considered the great concert halls in the world that have organs at the back of the stage (for example, Boston Symphony Hall). The new shades closed off the space that contained the organ, thereby (some people vainly hoped) better reflecting the sound of the orchestra on the stage into the room.

Bob Fine, the recording engineer for Command Records, summed up the problem better. "Acoustics, which are God-given, result from using honest materials in construction. This hall isn't made out of honest materials!" Nevertheless, Bob, with his brilliant knowledge, still recorded what John Coveney of Angel Records told me was, in his opinion, "the best organ record ever made." Bob psyched out the room, and made the best of a bad situation.

It took more than ten million dollars to "correct" Philharmonic Hall's "new" acoustics. Thus, the hall is now named after Avery Fisher, who was the fine man who put up the money. In fact, David Rubin of Steinway Piano summed up the hall's acoustics, after the work funded by Mr. Fisher was completed, as "Adequate. The former acoustics were not adequate."

During the major renovation of Philharmonic Hall to improve the acoustics, the hall management removed the organ entirely. Now, again, there's no great pipe organ in a major concert hall in New York!

Alice Tully Hall at Lincoln Center has an instrument, made by a Swiss company, that's only suitable for limited repertoire. Neither the organ nor the acoustics add much to the musical life of the city.

Carnegie Hall finally got a large electronic instrument in 1974. Built by the Rodgers Organ Company, the five-manual instrument was designed by Virgil (and revoiced by Ted!). It was also removed when the hall was renovated and never replaced. The renovation unfortunately created a near acoustical disaster that required an expensive, subsequent correction. The hall sounds good now; but there still is no proper concert hall organ in the entire City of New York!

47. Foam All Over His Face, Raving Like a Madman!

During the concert seasons of 1962 and 1963, there were significant changes in Virgil's personal life. As I mentioned, Virgil's relationships with Richard Weagly and Richard's mother, Grace, at 394 East Palisade Avenue in Englewood, New Jersey were far from tranquil. With Fred Swann firmly implanted at the Riverside Church, Richard Weagly and Virgil had become increasingly estranged over personal and musical matters. There were matters of musical taste, of course; but the confrontations in front of the Riverside choir at rehearsals grew increasingly nasty.

The Riverside choir was generally noisy at rehearsals. Richard constantly lectured them on matters of form and style—or shared the details of a current (some thought imaginary) illness. The choir had endured these lectures too many times, and was bored with them.

However, whenever arguments erupted between Virgil and Weagly (usually because Virgil was unprepared for a rehearsal), you could hear a pin drop. "Listen here, Mr. Man!" was how Virgil would begin his replies to one of Weagly's accusations.

No one wanted to miss a single word of these ever more frequent flare-ups.

After a performance of the great Brahms *Requiem* that everyone seemed to think particularly moving, Richard declared to Virgil in front of the choir at the following week's rehearsal, "You know,

Virgil, we don't need a crucifix in this church! You crucify me and the music every time you play the organ!"

You can imagine the tirade *that* remark produced! These outbursts hurt Virgil's feelings a great deal; and the relationship between the two men—both artistically and personally—was rapidly deteriorating. The two men rarely ever saw each other at home. Virgil was on tour much of the time; and Richard had already completed two-thirds of a day's work in Manhattan when Virgil was just waking up. When Richard arrived home in the evening, Virgil would already have left for dinner and late night practice sessions at the Riverside Church.

Richard's mother, Grace, aggravated the situation. She was a dear woman most of the time. She was extremely devoted to her son, always immaculately dressed, with *pince nez* glasses aiding her piercing blue eyes that seemed to see through everything and everyone. She usually attended to all of Richard's needs, and cooked most of his meals. She could also turn icy, especially when Richard and Virgil were feuding.

Sometimes when we arrived at Virgil's house for ice cream or a late night snack, Virgil would behave like a prisoner in his own home. We would have to tiptoe around and talk in hushed tones (which was amusing, because Virgil's whisper was not soft). Cleaning up after these evenings had to be thorough, for Virgil was terrified of incurring the old woman's wrath.

Virgil liked to shave in the powder room just off the porte-cochere entrance on the main floor of the house. He used to use Burma shaving cream, smearing it all over his face, and leaving just his eyes and mouth peeking out of the white cream. He was quite a sight! I was there one day after he had had an altercation with Grace. He had just gone back into the powder room, where he had been shaving, when Grace looked at me, shaking, and said, "He came at me with foam all over his face, raving like a madman! He's the most selfish human being I've ever known! He doesn't appreciate Richard or me—and after all we've done for him! I don't see how you boys put up with him!"

She then stalked off to her favorite haunt, which was the "sewing room" off the kitchen, where she would rock in her chair and stare out the window at the drive, the back lawn, and the carriage house.

One of the most bizarre stories Virgil told about Grace and Richard Weagly happened the night Virgil had come home from a lengthy concert tour. He had left his car at the church; for his habit was to take a taxi from the airport, stop at the church on the way in, and then drive himself to Englewood. On this evening, there was a fierce snowstorm in progress. Virgil was lucky in his timing (or else he was simply more determined than anyone else), for his was the last car permitted to cross the George Washington Bridge from Manhattan into New Jersey. Virgil was as expert a driver as he was a player on an organ console; and so that night, he managed to maneuver the Cadillac with relative ease. (Actually, he claimed he could only follow the highway by steering into the open space between the trees!) He succeeded getting all the way home; but when he reached his own driveway, the snow was completely piled up. He got as far as the porte-cochere, when he stopped to leave his luggage on the back porch. When he got back into the car, he couldn't get it to budge. He had to start digging around it to make a pathway for the car through the driveway to the carriage house, some ways away.

He was exhausted. He recalled that all the while both Richard and Grace were watching him struggle from the windows of the house. Grace was in the sewing room on the first floor, and Richard stared down from his comfortable bedroom on the second floor. As Virgil said, "Nobody moved Muscle One to help!"

After more than half an hour of shoveling, Virgil finally got the car into the heated garage (which was a rather grand four-car affair, with three car spaces in the front, one in the rear, and a real gas pump!). He trudged back to the house, and entered by the back door. He had arrived home for the first time in two weeks. Grace greeted him with, "What were you trying to do? Dig up the drive?"

Richard said nothing, having turned off the lights in his bedroom some time previously, and gone to bed!

Tensions flared around the house. Sometimes they occurred over petty matters. For example, Virgil would often leave copies of his new recordings on a table in the music room for Richard Weagly to enjoy. Richard would toss them on the floor, and ask his friends, "Why would I want to listen to him play more than I'm forced to?"

It was obvious that Weagly and Grace were jealous of Virgil's continuing success and fame. Nevertheless, Weagly behaved loyally whenever an organist or student attacked Virgil or his playing. Weagly would be vicious defending Virgil, humiliating the author of the offending remark. Richard felt personally free, of course, to make the unkindest remarks himself, whenever he chose.

Weagly would continuously rail against Virgil for being self-centered and rebellious, always doing as he pleased. "He never paid any attention to his teachers. He wound Hugh Price around his little finger. Middelschulte was putty in his hands. I can remember after his first concert at the Peabody, Louis Robert was furious at Virgil for doing almost everything just the opposite from how he was taught. He paid no attention to Dupré, preferring to fawn over Louis Vierne. Virgil simply has no musical taste!"

We would shriek at Weagly's stories and at his disdain for Virgil's genius. Of course, it was true that Virgil preferred doing things his own way. He almost couldn't do otherwise—and thank God for that! One of the reasons the services and oratorios at Riverside were so thrilling was the tension between Richard Weagly and Virgil Fox. Weagly was traditional and formal. He tended to conceal any "personal" interpretation he might have, almost to the point of blandness. Virgil fired his imagination in order to bring these works vividly to life.

Perhaps the straw that broke the back of the Fox-Weagly relationship came one night when Richard Weagly woke Virgil by bolting upright in bed. He let out a wail.

"What's the matter?" Virgil asked, alarmed.

"I'm... I'm in love with Fred Swann!"

Weagly was bawling. Apparently, the problem wasn't guilt, but lack of reciprocity.

"Oh, my God! Go back to bed!"

Richard Torrence

Despite the ridiculousness of this story, when Virgil told it to me, I could tell how seriously he took it. Apparently he was extremely upset to learn that Weagly would even consider being unfaithful to him, as he had never considered it possible for either of them, after more than 30 years together, to be unfaithful to the other. It was the first time, he told me, that he realized it was possible for either of them to fall in love with someone else. In other words, Virgil came to believe that Weagly's silly bedtime scene was the beginning of the end of the relationship between the two old friends.

48. Enter Adonis

By the summer of 1962, the stage was set for an entrance by someone Virgil could enjoy being with on a more personal level. Virgil had played at Ocean Grove, New Jersey, where he met a young man (I'll omit the details) who had become his friend. Although this fellow had a summer job as a desk clerk in the hotel where Virgil stayed, he was, in fact, an intelligent, charming professional with a growing career in public service during the regular season. Virgil was smitten. He talked endlessly about his new friend, who soon became part of all of our lives. It was obvious, however, that the man wasn't the kind who would submit easily to Virgil's whims. I'm not even sure their relationship progressed very far. Virgil was a prude. A kiss goodnight for him could signify a major romance.

Virgil was obviously thinking about augmenting, if not replacing, the Weagly relationship for some time. He'd finally tried to do something about it. His first excursion didn't work out as he intended; and so, almost a year later, after he played a return engagement in Kitchener, Ontario, he returned one day to New York, beaming. He reported to Richard Torrence that he had met a new, young friend. This young man had obviously thrown himself at Virgil (meaning, he had sat through extensive practice sessions, accompanied Virgil to meals and on long walks, and who knows what else?).

Virgil's description of his Canadian friend was glowing. This ardent admirer was an "Adonis" whose attentions had swept Virgil off his feet.

We were amazed when Virgil announced that his new friend, "David," would arrive in New York soon for a visit. For one thing, Richard Weagly was still living in the house—which would make things awkward, to say the least.

Earlier that year, in February 1963, Richard Torrence was joined in New York by his friend, Marshall Yaeger, who had just left San Francisco after graduating (Phi Beta Kappa) from the University of California at Berkeley. They moved into the same building that Bob Hebble lived in, the "Cambridge," an apartment house at 13th Street and Seventh Avenue. Both apartments were quite elegant. They were most certainly my home away from Philadelphia, and I visited as often as possible.

I remember visiting from Philadelphia during the early summer of 1963 when Virgil came over to Richard's—as he often did when we weren't "in attendance" at the church with him. He had already met David, but David hadn't arrived yet. He waxed on and on about the virtues of this "dear child"—a boy who could obviously do no wrong in Virgil's eyes. Virgil's emotions had obviously overtaken his reason, which explained why he was breaking moral codes regarding committed relationships that he had stood by for more than 30 years. We didn't question or criticize him at the time, but we were all astonished (and, I might admit, titteringly amused) at this strange turn of events.

(Skipping ahead some years, I recall a question that Marshall posed once, following Virgil's claim that he had always been constant to his partner.

"I'm one of a kind!" Virgil said.

Marshall was leaving the room at the time. He looked back to rebut, "Did you say 'one at a time,' Virgil?"

"Oh, you!" came back the irked response.)

"Adonis" arrived in New York a few days later. Richard was the first of us to lay eyes on him. He couldn't wait to report the details of a dinner he had with Virgil and David. Apparently, there were some cracks in the façade of this perfect specimen of manhood that upset Richard right from the beginning—especially when he noticed David and Virgil holding hands in the restaurant. Expressing affection like that was something grown men didn't do in public in the 1960s!

David was neither unpleasant nor ugly; but he certainly wasn't the Adonis that Virgil had described! Rather, he was an almost shabby youth who was nowhere near Virgil's level of intelligence. He gave Richard the same kind of impression any of us would have gotten from a 42nd Street hustler.

Richard saw how infatuated Virgil had become, and feared real trouble ahead. Still, he tried to be nice, as did we all. He and the rest of the "family" played along during this early—and we assumed, short—period, not wanting to hurt our dear Virgil. However, we prayed that this "fling," like the one that preceded it (with a much more suitable candidate), would soon end.

We were all frequently thrown together with David, for if we wanted to be with Virgil, David would invariably be present. He tried hard to be pleasant, and to enter our circle of friends; but he was always uneasy—and I'm sure we weren't easy either! Finally, we came to agree with Richard's negative assessment of the boy, and grew increasingly impatient for him to return to Canada. He was doing what Roberta Bailey had been accused of doing: cheapening Virgil, which worried and embarrassed us. Richard Weagly was appalled. He shrieked, "Why, the boy could be his grandson! Has he gone mad?"

Virgil's infatuation did not diminish, however; and it quickly turned into adoration. He even nurtured a delusion that David was a descendant (or at the very least, a reincarnation) of Richard Wagner!

We surmised that Virgil hadn't had much experience in sexual matters, except with Weagly, during his entire life. Whatever he did with Weagly, from what we could imagine, was probably not much more than what they call "vanilla" these days; and it was probably infrequent. Virgil used to mention "having family," which was his term for having sex; and there was one person's story (I pray, apocryphal!) about the use of a rubber sheet and Mazola oil (although another person swears it was Hershey's chocolate sauce) being poured on compromising portions of the male anatomy. These stories produced more howling laughter amongst us than erotic titillation, however.

I must also explain that if Virgil had ever "come on" to any of us "chicks," still in our 20s, we would have been intensely embarrassed. His sexuality was something that amused us; but the thought of being intimate with him was a bit horrifying. Thus we couldn't understand how "sweet, young David" could possibly have been interested in "the old man."

At one point, David went back to Canada, and the situation became even more intense. Virgil couldn't bear to be without him; and so the telephone lines between New York and Canada hummed. Soon, a second visit was arranged. This time it was to be permanent. Virgil intended that David live in the house on Palisade Avenue—not just as a guest!

No amount of reasoning would work on Virgil. In fact, the more we tried to dissuade him, the more determined he was that he would have this young man at his side come hell or high water. Both Weagly and Caméo were horrified at the prospect.

Since Richard Weagly's mother, Grace, had died several years before, Weagly was able to concoct a plan to leave the house "in a snit" and move into his own apartment in the city—temporarily—until Virgil's "latest insanity blows over." He announced that he would move everything out immediately and take an apartment near Riverside; and he did so with many unpleasant scenes, name-calling, tears, and tantrums. (He had already moved all his music and belongings from his rather sumptuous office in Englewood to his office underneath the Riverside nave.) He probably thought he would shock Virgil back to his senses; but his plan was fatal to their relationship, because with Richard no longer around to fight against the interloper, the interloper won—easily.

The crisis strengthened Weagly's friendship with Fred Swann, who provided a comforting shoulder on which to cry. It also brought Weagly and Caméo much closer. They had always gotten on well; but here was a cause that brought them even closer. "Get rid of that boy, and soon!" Weagly begged.

Frederick Swann

David's entry onto the scene, of course, brought about the somewhat violent and tragic end of Virgil's relationship with Richard Weagly. Within a year, Richard suffered a nervous breakdown, after which the Riverside Church paid for him to live under doctors' supervision in London for a year while he worked toward recovery.

49. Caméo Goes Berserk

One can imagine how the crisis affected their already shaky musical partnership at the Riverside Church. Everyone at the church knew almost everything, because Weagly nearly screamed the details in the hallways to anyone who would listen. The gossip flared up hot and heavy. The music committee, pastors, and especially the chief pastor, Robert James McCracken, had personally witnessed many of the squabbles during Virgil's and Richard's nineteen-year partnership at the church.

Once, in 1957, they were both fired from the church because Dr. McCracken had gotten so upset by one of their fights that he could hardly preach! Weagly went berserk, shouted oaths, and went into major tantrums with his office door wide open for anyone to hear—

and there were plenty of interested ears around to listen! Virgil maintained a steely calm throughout the crisis. Although he was away on tour most of the time, he pulled the right political strings, and managed to calm the "ruffled feathers." Virgil had many powerful and rich friends on the governing board of the church. He finally got them to reverse the dismissal at the last moment.

With David's being ensconced in the Fox mansion, all reasoning between Weagly and Virgil was impossible. David occupied the suite of rooms adjoining Virgil's.

David's idea of tasteful décor was to line the walls and windows with heavy brocade draperies, shuttering out any possibility of daylight. He claimed to be a member of the Rosecrucian Society (receiving periodic mailings from them). One might have guessed that he was an Orthodox priest, as he often wore a black cassock around the house with a large metal medallion around his neck. None of us, including Virgil, could fathom the role he was trying to portray. He was pleasant enough to everyone; but his behavior was often decidedly strange. Caméo was becoming increasingly worried. He forecast dark storm clouds brewing.

Richard Torrence

With Weagly out of the Englewood mansion, Marshall and I moved from Greenwich Village into the Weagly suite of rooms on the second floor of 394 East Palisade Avenue. We redecorated the large bedroom as our living room, made Grace Weagly's old adjoining bedroom into our bedroom, and used a large connecting sleeping porch as a comfortable den.

Having two bathrooms was a luxury, especially since the large one—off the living room—measured 9 feet by 12 feet, and had both a huge bathtub and a stall shower!

Virgil and David had far more room than we did, although, usually, when they were out of town, they covered all the furniture on the main floor and rolled up the rugs. Nevertheless, we had a sumptuous "apartment" on the second floor all to ourselves. Furthermore, Marshall fixed up a small room on the third floor as his writing "aerie," where he mainly worked on plays (he was a member of the Actors Studio Playwrights Unit around that time).

If it hadn't been for the fact that we usually had to put up with David, the living situation would have been idyllic. When Virgil and David were home, however, there was always tension in the air. The kitchen was always "common ground," and so we usually ate out.

Virgil informed us that David had spent some time in a mental institution (possibly, to garner sympathy for his new friend). This period seemed to have been limited to a one-month observation period in Canada. Richard Torrence saw a written report about the episode that indicated problems, but that wasn't alarming.

Virgil also let it be known that David was a married man with children. Virgil was determined that David get a divorce. In time, Virgil paid a lawyer to carry it through. From what Virgil told us about the divorce hearings, David's wife wanted to refuse any alimony. All she cared about was being rid of him!

David didn't accompany Virgil on long tours, at first, mainly because Virgil didn't want to bear the considerable expense of having him tag along.

Virgil had promised Caméo faithfully that his new boyfriend was merely an ardent admirer; and he promised that David would never interfere with their business relationship or friendship. It soon became obvious to Richard, however, that David had to be present whenever Virgil had business or financial matters to discuss. David always voiced his opinions freely, whether or not he understood the subject. Anyone who knows our dear Richard knows how highly he valued such advice. It hovered over his relationship with Virgil like a lead balloon. In short, Richard hated David's interference, and begged Virgil to "include him out" of their business! Virgil would simply dismiss these entreaties with "Honey, the sweet child is just trying to be helpful. He doesn't understand. Pay no attention to him!"

The business interference accelerated, agonizing and angering Richard to distraction. More than once, he threatened to quit; but Virgil remained oblivious to the trouble David was causing. To paraphrase Andy Crow's description of the situation, "David knows how to keep people in a constant state of agitation!"

David was now traveling with Virgil on all his tours. (It seems that Virgil had heard about some 42nd Street "wanderings" in Manhattan while he was away on tour, and decided never again to leave the "dear boy" alone where he could get into trouble.) Richard believed that his relationship with David could only harm Virgil, and that it would ultimately do nobody any good whatsoever. We all wanted David simply to vanish; but Richard was more insistent about it than anyone. He finally decided that it was going to be either David or Caméo. Virgil would have to choose between them.

Shortly after Richard made this decision, an opportunity arose. Virgil and David had been having serious arguments, and a breakup seemed imminent. Virgil had even promised Richard that, after the next tour, David would return to Canada permanently.

The two had gone off together on a short, East Coast concert tour, and would only be gone a week. One evening Bob, Marshall, Richard, and I were all at Virgil's house on Palisade Avenue. We had just returned from dinner at Baumgart's, which was a favorite haunt of Virgil's in the town of Englewood. The main topic of conversation was whether Virgil would stick to his word and finally send David "back to the Canooks."

When we got home, it seemed to me that Richard was going berserk. He went into David's bedroom and began tearing down the heavy, dark brocade drapes, and all of the room's decorations—all the while making sounds like a crazed beast on a rampage. We were laughing hysterically, until we realized how deadly serious he was! He broke into the locked closets that contained David's belongings, and dragged everything out to place in boxes. He intended to send all of David's belongings back to Canada preemptively, leaving Virgil no opportunity to renege on his promise. We were both delighted and horrified at Richard's outrageous courage, and at what we knew would be Virgil's reaction.

We tried to calm him down; but Richard would not be deterred. He felt this opportunity was the only way to get rid of a parasitic and sociopathic personality who would, however inadvertently and well-meaningly, severely damage Virgil's life, career, and what could have and should have been his exalted position in the history of Western civilized culture.

Richard was correct in his strategy. Virgil *would* have reneged on his promise to send David back to Canada if no one had done anything. It was Virgil's way. Moreover, David *did* have a pernicious effect on Virgil's life and career, without question. He contributed no small share of the vulgarity that made many people consider Virgil Fox to be a laughingstock instead of a serious artist of considerable genius that he truly was. Nevertheless, the decision to send all of David's things back to Canada sent shattering shock waves throughout our relationships. Things were never the same thereafter.

When Virgil returned from the tour and realized what Richard had done, his rage and hurt were monumental. David mailed his household goods immediately back to Englewood—"Collect," in care of Richard—who refused the cartons when they arrived, and sent them back to Canada again, this time at David's expense. David kept fighting viciously. For example, Marshall's father had had a heart attack a few weeks before this incident. Rather than being sympathetic, David wrote a letter to Richard threatening to "out" Marshall to his 70+ year-old parents (who lived in California) in retaliation for what Richard had done. Marshall was so incensed that he immediately moved out of his living quarters in Virgil's house and moved in with Fred Swann for ten days (Virgil never knew where he went). He then left for California for several months while his father recovered. He returned to the Englewood estate to live again with Richard, who by this time had moved out of Virgil's house into the carriage house on Virgil's property. David apologized for his letter.

When Virgil and Richard finally met face to face, there was only straight talk out of both parties. Richard said, "It's either got to be me, who loves you, and has your very best personal and business interests at heart, or this temporary trick of yours!"

"Trick!" Virgil screamed. "Tricks are what *you* have! David is my *mate!*"

The fur flew for half an hour. Virgil was not about to lose Richard, and he was determined not to give up David. The outcome was Virgil's promise to keep David out of business matters completely, if Richard would accept the fact that David was there to stay, and promise to get along with him.

David abided by the rules for at least a few days; but Richard and the rest of us resigned ourselves to the fact that "the snake" was probably going to be a permanent feature in the family.

Thus began an era of quiet animosity between Richard and David for the rest of Virgil's life. Sometimes the two were cordial and friendly; other times they wouldn't speak. Sometimes Richard would just glare at David.

David constantly plotted against Richard and his many pregnant ideas for the ever-broadening career that he envisioned for Virgil. Richard had a hard enough time convincing Virgil about some of his innovative ideas; but a few days later, after David had time to work on Virgil to dissuade him, Virgil would slide back and question

Richard's wisdom—which was not the thing to do. Then they would go at it again.

(There's a saying that the last person you speak to at night always has the most convincing argument!)

Usually, Virgil gave in to Richard, as it was quite impossible to change Richard's mind. Caméo was usually right; and Virgil knew it. David, however, as Andy put it, continued to keep Virgil in a constant state of agitation. David obviously wanted Richard's position in Virgil's life, but he lacked the talent, intellect, creativity, or imagination to supply what Virgil needed. Virgil was simply too smart for him. In fact, more than once, he told us to have patience with "dear David—he's not very bright, you know; the poor child!"

---

50. How Much Extra for the Cream and Sugar?

An uneasy truce prevailed. Meanwhile, there were many festive dinners, lunches, and brunches in New York at Bob's apartment as well as in Englewood where we all ate, talked, and laughed a lot. Bob Hebble accompanied and arranged for many young singers and Broadway hopefuls; and musical evenings spent with him were unforgettable and inspiring.

When Bob was at the keyboard of his elegant Steinway "B," accompanying a wonderful young talent, or if he just played a medley of well-known show tunes or popular songs, his music took on an entirely new dimension and character. Bob's ways of altering harmonies, and playing as fulsomely as an orchestra, were astounding, and evidence of pure genius. He had a truly God-given gift that few musicians possess. I was always awed by what this great artist could do both at the piano and the organ.

Virgil also admired Bob's gift greatly, for he didn't have that kind of talent. Nevertheless, he seldom acknowledged how highly he thought of Bob's musicianship, as it was usually put into service for popular music or for re-harmonizing hymns or other composers' melodies. Virgil would often say such things as, "That boy can sure play cocktail music!" He probably never took Bob seriously, only thinking of him as his "first born." He certainly used many of Bob's harmonizations and "crushing chords" in his recordings—especially in the Capitol Records "slush albums." Had it not been for Bob, the world would never have heard most of Virgil's arrangements and transcriptions.

It wasn't until much later that Virgil realized Bob was a serious composer, and began to perform and record his works. Bob continued to transcribe and edit Virgil's repertoire right to the end of Virgil's life in Palm Beach (where Bob had moved). Virgil had intended to make his own editions of his vast repertoire—especially his legendary performances of Bach and Franck; but there wasn't time before his life ran out.

We spent many exciting evenings at Bob's and/or Richard's apartment in New York (they were a few floors apart before Richard's move to Englewood)—many of them graced by an appearance by Virgil and David when they were in town. Virgil couldn't stand the thought of his "chicks" having fun, laughing, and eating divine food without his being there. I must say we all felt the same most of the time.

I remember one evening when Richard had a group of particularly fun people over for dinner. Everyone was bright, entertaining, and amusing; but the group was definitely not an "organ crowd." Virgil had not been invited; but shortly after dinner, around 10:00 p.m., Richard's house telephone rang. The door attendant announced that Virgil and David were on their way up. Virgil arrived, his usual ebullient self, announcing that he had just purchased "the most divine fruit salad" at the delicatessen around the corner. "It's simply the best fruit salad money can buy," and "anyone is welcome to partake of this rare treat who's willing to contribute 75-cents per serving!"

Richard was mortified. His friends had just finished eating an elegant dinner and huge dessert, and Richard was about to serve coffee when Virgil exploded on the scene with his delectable offering. Richard's guests were too full, and too astounded to accept Virgil's generous gift. Virgil pushed and pushed, however, even lowering the price, but there were no takers. He was not amused!

Richard finally served the coffee from a large tray, and was filling cups when one bright young man (Eddie de Pasquale, who worked for Richard's management) asked, "And how much do you charge for the cream and sugar?" The room burst into laughter, including Virgil's, but blended with the forced "Ho! Ho! Ho!" he used when truly annoyed.

Virgil could be unbelievably cheap sometimes, especially around strangers. He would never have pulled anything like that on us; but here, he thought it would be fine, since there were people around he didn't know. I think it was part of an act; or perhaps it was like behavior he observed Anne Archbold or Florence Candler (whose husband's family had bought the formula for Coca-Cola years before). He may have believed that the more bizarre and eccentric he was, the greater the attention he would attract. Such behavior generated countless stories, of course (including this one) to be elaborated on by his many good friends—and just as many detractors.

Virgil always had said "Be worried when they stop talking about you!"; and he always made sure there was plenty to talk about, whether it was a staggering performance or a recent public antic. It was never dull being around our extraordinary, dear friend.

Richard Torrence

> *Virgil kept hearing about twin sisters from Somerville, New Jersey who had been advertising to potential organ students that they had studied with him—which they had not. When he realized that these two eccentric sisters truly worshipped him, and that they were rich enough to be financially helpful, they all became great friends.*
>
> *The sisters began to cook for him in Somerville, constantly dragging Sunday lunches and dinners to him and his many guests in Englewood, doing all the dishes (by hand), and returning to their home with all the pots and pans.*
>
> *One Christmas they gave Virgil the most expensive Kitchenaid dishwasher they could find. When they proudly revealed their gift, Virgil said: "Well, that's fine, Girls, but who's gonna pay to have it installed? You're just making life easy for yourselves. It has nothing to do with me."*
>
> *The sisters paid $300 to have the dishwasher installed!*

---

51. Hollywood Neon Flames Out

In the early summer of 1964, the Philadelphia organ community was getting ready for the biennial National Convention of the American Guild of Organists. Although St. Mark's, Frankford wasn't part of the actual convention, my church did hold the most ambitious pre-convention event on the day before the opening. I had planned a festival evensong honoring the life and work of Richard Purvis, with a choir of thirty, plus brass and tympani drawn from the Philadelphia Orchestra. Richard Purvis conducted, and I was the organist (and producer). Purvis generously composed a new *Nunc Dimitis*, "The Song of Simeon," for the occasion, and conducted many of his best-known compositions and hymn arrangements.

Richard was gracious during rehearsals, and kept his caustic tongue in check—except when directed toward the organist! "Mr. Worth! Whoever told you that you could play the organ?" we heard, much to the delight of my choir and friends at one of the rehearsals.

The church was packed, despite the 100-degree July temperature and famous Philadelphia summer humidity. Everyone who was anyone in the profession was there, and the hymn singing and entire service were a smashing success. I do believe R.I.P. (that's what we used to call Richard Irwin Purvis) was moved and very pleased. He was also a delightful houseguest of Walter Mellbourne's on nearby Penn Street. I think he enjoyed being back in Philadelphia, where he had been a student of Alexander McCurdy at the Curtis Institute and held many positions in the city before entering the United States Army.

After the festival evensong, the church hosted a dinner for those who stayed for the evening solo concert. My good friend, and a brilliant performer, John Weaver, played it. The church was again packed; and I remember a standing ovation after John's electrifying performance of Franz Liszt's "Fantasy and Fugue on the Chorale '*Ad nos, ad salutarum undam.*'" The whole day was an unqualified success—except that the following day, The Rev. Mr. Fischer called me into his office and fired me! He had on dark sunglasses in his office, which was unusual, and simply said that I was too "big" for this parish. "You belong in a Main Line parish where they appreciate this sort of thing. This is too much for us!"

I was struck dumb, and immediately thought, "This is the end. What will people think?" Mr. Fischer assured me that he would squelch any rumors, that he had been entirely pleased with my work, and that he would give me the highest recommendation. I still couldn't figure out why I'd been fired, for the concerts and the entire Sunday's pre-convention events had been underwritten by sponsors, first among whom was dear Walter Mellbourne. The events cost the church nothing—only the use of the building and the organ.

Eventually, I understood that several powerful members of the vestry didn't like me or the "strange and different people" who attended the concerts in "their" church. They resented and probably feared the large crowds that attended and, for the first time, were made familiar with this magnificent building and organ. In their opinion, the church was meant to be shared by people like themselves. Outsiders—especially "artistic" outsiders, whose passion for music may have exceeded their devotion to Jesus Christ—weren't welcome.

Albert Fischer had always supported our efforts, and was proud and pleased with the throngs that attended the concerts. I imagine he had grown tired of the petty infighting in the church, and looked forward to his retirement, which would soon come. With my champion gone, I was now unemployed. As usual, I was near penury. The prospects were not good. In fact, they were grim.

Both Richard and Virgil were outraged at what happened; but there was no way they could help. They were supporters, as always—as was Walter Mellbourne, who never lost faith in me, and who helped me immeasurably through this dreadful period.

Luckily, I heard from a friend of Richard's about a job opening for Choirmaster and Director of the Chapel Music at a famous prep school, the Kent School for Boys in Kent, Connecticut. With encouragement from all quarters, I jumped in my Jaguar XK 150. This lovely used automobile was ten years old and very sporty. Unfortunately, it ate oil—cans and all. I drove up to Kent to meet with the headmaster; and I came away with the job. The position wouldn't begin until the school opened in September; but the situation seemed ideal (except for one thing—the organ), and the position would pay me a sizable salary!

Life brightened considerably when Richard and I set out that summer to drive the Jaguar (I called it "Rex") to California. We had a great time, and I almost forgot the terrible shock and tremendous hurt of St. Mark's, Frankford.

During the first week of September, I prepared for my move to Kent. When I arrived there, I went to a lovely suite of rooms; I greeted some of the students; and I went to see the head of the music department to see about my duties and meet again with the headmaster.

My stay at the Kent School was short. In fact, it didn't last the night. When I realized what they expected of me (which explained why they offered to pay me paid so well!), I was horrified to realize that I would have no time to practice music. My duties would last the entire day, beginning with matins. I was expected to chaperone the boys to soccer games and even to the Henley Regatta. I would be coaching several sports (which truly frightened me, for I knew nothing about the subject, except how to float while swimming). Then I met a few other members of the faculty who told me that the chapel choir was "nothing," and that the school would never get serious about serious music.

The most popular activity there, musically, was the school glee club, which sang at many of the functions and was permitted to visit the neighboring girls' school. Those who couldn't make the grade for the glee club were directed to the chapel choir.

The chapel was quite beautiful, with Norman architecture, lovely stained glass windows, mediocre acoustics, and a perfect horror of an organ. It was a tiny, neo-classic "screecher" that could never play an esthetic role in my musical life. I had played it before during my original visit, and I thought that I might use it mainly for practice, then concentrate on leading a magnificent boy choir. I now realized I was dreaming.

By five o'clock on the afternoon of my first day, I made up my mind to see the headmaster. I asked him why he had so grossly misrepresented my actual duties. He had said nothing about sports, chaperoning, or the state of the choir. I realized that I had to decline the position mainly because accepting it would end my aspirations for a concert career—which I had explained earlier was a major consideration in my accepting the job.

He was upset, of course. He offered to double the salary. When I still refused, he threatened to sue me. However, he wouldn't alter the workload. I would have none of it.

Around eight o'clock, I called Richard and asked him to come help me move out. "The Halls of Ivy aren't for me," I told him. "I'm Hollywood Neon, and I won't stay here another minute!"

52. Pray for Rain!

Richard was shocked. Nevertheless, he understood and supported my decision. As ever, he proved himself my most loyal friend, coming that evening to help me move my belongings out of the school and back to Englewood. The next day I drove back to Philadelphia to Walter's house where I sank into a brief period of despondency.

A bright spot suddenly appeared. Richard had contracted Virgil to make a Reader's Digest recording of the magnificent, huge Harrison & Harrison organ in Royal Albert Hall, London. Since the combination action wasn't reliable, Virgil insisted that Reader's Digest provide two assistants for him during the recording sessions. They were to be Richard and I.

What a great opportunity for an all-expense paid trip to Europe, again with Virgil as a guide! Virgil and Richard left before me—first to Paris and then on to London. I, and a good friend and great fan of the organ and Virgil, Alan Langord, flew to London together. Alan went on business, and so he could afford a fine hotel. Richard and I moved into a far more modest bed-and-breakfast house called the New Bentinck Hotel in Kensington, near the Albert Hall. (I'd have hated to stay in the "Old" Bentinck!) Reader's Digest was generous with us, but not as generous as it was to Virgil!

They arranged for him to stay at the Westbury Hotel in Bond Street, which he loved, because that's where Judy Garland had just been staying. The American recording producer, Charles Gearhardt, was also at the Westbury. Richard and I had planned to meet Alan Langord at Royal Albert Hall when we had finished unpacking, and then go inside to meet Virgil, who was already at the hall practicing. It was almost midnight when we met outside the great round, domed, red brick hall. It was quiet as we searched for a stage or back door entrance, when all of a sudden we heard the mighty roar of the great organ and the strains of Widor's "Toccata" from the *Fifth Symphony*! My spine tingled, and the earth shook even out of doors!

We found the entrance, and the sound became more intense and thrilling. It was almost completely dark in the cavernous room, which was painted a deep blue and cream color at that time, except for the area around the organ console which was embedded in the center of an imposing organ case. We "Yoo-hooed" and yelled to Virgil that we had arrived. He howled back with delight. We made our way to the old but sturdy console, and Virgil immediately treated us to a tour of that grand example of English organ building.

"Honey, listen to that full Swell. It's miles away, up there on your left on the eleventh floor! Oh that smothered rage!" It was. The console sat right in the middle of the Great, which was very "present." The Choir Organ was miles away and rather timid. The Solo boasted the famous English tuba sound, and a fiery French trompette. The great Solo Tuba Magna was, according to Virgil, "On 50 inches of wind!" It was the most powerful stop on the splendid instrument. Then came the gargantuan Pedal division, with four or five 32-foot stops, including two 32-foot reeds. There was even an enclosed Trombone in a swell box! There were many wood stops in this division. Believe me, they were serious, and provided a true foundation and underpinning for the huge instrument.

It didn't hurt that the hall was reverberant. It could hold more than 5,000 people, and was the home of the famous Prom Concerts. Other festivities it hosted included prizefights and other sporting events. Just below the stage area was a sizable round area that looked like a pit. It reminded me of the Coliseum in Rome. The boxes and other seating areas surrounded and soared to a great height above this pit. During the Prom Concerts, the young crowd claimed this area as their spot. It became something like a standing room section in the middle of the hall.

Virgil showed us the softer strings and the color solo stops, which were beautiful, but faint and distant. He didn't like the tremulants (of course), but an organ tuner was due the next day. As usual, Virgil had compiled a mile-long list for him.

At about 3:00 a.m. in the morning, we all returned to Virgil's hotel where he treated us to fresh fruit drenched in sinfully rich Devonshire cream. We all went mad for it.

"Teddo, they're going to start sound checks with the microphones in the early afternoon. I'm sure you'll play for them. I'll meet you all there after six, and we'll dine and then go to work."

What a thrill to be able to play that organ as much as I pleased during the late morning and afternoon! It was an unusual autumn in London that year. There was neither rain nor fog; just radiant, sunny, dry days.

We loved the weather; but we stopped loving the Albert Hall organ! From the first evening, while Virgil was preparing the "Toccata and Fugue in D Minor" of Bach, we began to hear a perceptible sag in the pitch during full organ passages—of which there were many. It sounded painful and piteous, like a monster gasping for air—which, in fact, it was. Virgil was right to be upset, as the recording sessions were about to begin, and the sagging wind would ruin the recording.

It turned out that all of the wind lines of the organ were made of wood. Because of the unusually dry weather, they were beginning to pull apart, which caused the wind to leak. I heard the leaking noises from inside the pipe divisions, which sounded like a hundred electric vacuum cleaners gone nuts!

"Dear man, what can we do? We can't have this!" Virgil cried. The poor organ tuner was in agony. He had worked his butt off and turned himself inside out to please Virgil—he had clearly never seen an organist like Virgil before!—and Virgil's handling of the huge instrument mesmerized him.

"We must pray for rain," said the tuner.

"We'll put on feathers and do rain dances if necessary," Virgil said, "but we don't have much time left!"

"We could pump in live steam," the tuner suggested, "but that might be very bad for the organ if we overdo it."

That's exactly what the tuner did. It worked like a charm—almost. The problem was that the steam could only be pumped in while the organ was turned on. However, it couldn't be pumped in while anyone tuned, rehearsed, or recorded the organ. Thus, the motor on the blower had to run 24 hours a day in order to get in enough steam to swell the wood, which presented new problems of the motor overheating. Nevertheless, the system of pumping live steam into the organ—judiciously—worked. After several days of on-again, off-again steaming, tuning, and practicing, we were finally able to begin the recording sessions.

Virgil was relieved and pleased as he began to prepare the repertoire. He intended to include many famous "war horses" for the Reader's Digest: Bach's "Toccata and Fugue in D Minor," "'Little' Fugue in G Minor," "Jesu, Joy of Mans' Desiring," "Air for the G-String," "Sheep May Safely Graze"; Purcell's "Trumpet Tune and Air"; Widor's "Toccata from the *Fifth Symphony*," and Franck's "Final in B-Flat" were what Virgil decided on.

53. Listen, Fatty!

All was going well with the preparation. Virgil was in a great mood, looking better than we had ever seen him. Richard had persuaded him to refurbish his wardrobe, and so he had purchased many new clothes. I remember one evening he was dressed in a fashionable new suit and wrap-around overcoat with a rakish hat. He looked like a magazine model. Hats (except for an occasional beret or Turkish towel) were unusual for Virgil; but he and Richard had bought it at Pierre Cardin in Paris.

We had great times together, laughing and eating; but Virgil's missing David (he didn't take him to Europe, for it was "too expensive") began to get him down. Charles Gearhardt, the producer, was a charming chubby person, a great fan, and easy-going. He loved Virgil's playing, and was pleased by the end of the second day of recording. Unfortunately, while we were recording, the only method Virgil could use to communicate was to speak in normal tones, which Chuck would hear through earphones sitting somewhere in the bowels of the hall. When Chuck responded, it would be through a giant loudspeaker set up somewhere distant in the vast, dark hall. It was an eerie system, but it was generally satisfactory—and loud!

Virgil hated hearing things like, "Take 23 of the Purcell Air!" in Chuck's loud voice, which reverberated around the room. "Why, I could play this thing in my sleep! This damned organ isn't responding!" Then Virgil would re-rehearse, and re-register this or that sound of the "Air."

"Which do you like, kids" he would say, "registration A or B?"

Richard and I were too weary to pay attention. It was late, and Virgil was getting tired, and more than a little annoyed at a particularly sticky passage. He asked the question again, and again we failed to respond. Then, with a great roar, he said, "Answer me!" Richard and I perked up immediately.

Virgil was staring straight ahead toward the keyboard, the hair on the back of his head sticking straight up in the air, as it always did when he was really pissed.

I looked at Richard, terrified, then started to scream with laughter at Virgil's roar of indignation. So did Richard; and finally Virgil joined in. This incident broke the tension, and Virgil came alive and completed two more pieces that evening.

Up until now, all the works Virgil recorded at Albert Hall were big and loud. He hadn't rehearsed the softer works still left to be recorded. Next evening he began to work on the brilliant "Final in B-Flat" of César Franck. Virgil loved the work, and played it better than anyone I have ever heard. He simply tore into the opening pedal solos ("Ba-BUM; ba-BUM; ba-BUM-ba-ba-ba-bum"); and this organ was just the vehicle for such a brilliant showpiece.

He always spoke of his teacher, Louis Robert's, interpretation of the work. "Robert always took this tempo; and believe me kids, he was right on target!"

Virgil was cooking with gas, when all of a sudden the "Great Voice" came out of the loudspeaker. It was Chuck Gearhardt, who asked, "Virgil, what is that piece?"

Virgil said, "It's the Franck 'Final in B-Flat.' Isn't it stunning on this beast?" Virgil proceeded to play another section that was marked on the music in Virgil's hand "WIDE OPEN."

"Virgil," said the Great Voice, with an edgy tone to it, "We haven't discussed recording the Franck 'Final.' Where are the soft pieces? Where's 'Sheep May Safely Graze,' 'Air for the G String,' and 'Jesu, Joy'? We need the contrast!"

"We'll get to those Charles, dear; but we must have this wonderful Franck piece on the record," Virgil said.

"We don't want the Franck! I want the other works we discussed!"

"But, Honey—!"

"No!" came the reply.

A long pause ensued. Then Virgil, in his most stentorian, self-righteous tone, roared, "Listen, Fatty! I'm sick and tired of you, this country, this unheated mausoleum, and this organ—which will not do for that kind of repertoire. If we don't record the Franck, and now, I shall return to the United States of America on the first plane tomorrow! If you wish to record the other repertoire it will have to be done on my beautiful organ at the Riverside Church in New York!"

There was no answer. Richard and I were speechless. Virgil was livid. He meant what he said, which was clear for all to see. Richard had just encountered his first crisis between Virgil and a record producer. He then went on to calm the "ruffled feathers" as best he could. We did not record the Franck (which was a pity, for it sounded stunning on the Albert Hall organ). Virgil went back to New York the next day.

He was obviously pining for David, and he truly felt that his type of symphonic interpretation on the lush stops of the Albert Hall organ didn't sound right. Some of the sounds on the organ were quite lovely; but they were mostly distant and miniature, which was not to Virgil's taste. The tremolos were also not adequate, and were missing in parts of some of the divisions.

If you own this superb recording, you can hear a sample of these distant color stops in the recitative just before "Sheep May Safely Graze." The recitative was recorded on the Albert Hall organ; but the verse—along with the other entire soft repertoire—was recorded at Riverside. The parts were joined together through the wonders of electronics. Thanks to Richard's persuasive powers, Charles Gearhardt came to Riverside, completed the record, and all was forgiven! He and Virgil collaborated again at Royal Festival Hall on a Christmas album for Reader's Digest Records; and they remained the best of friends.

Richard and I, with Alan Langord, went on to Amsterdam. Richard and I stayed in a canal house, while Alan checked into the grand Amstel hotel after one day of arguing with the tiny hot water heater in the bed-and-breakfast.

Richard and I then went on to Copenhagen, Munich, Paris, and back to New York. While in Munich, we visited Karl Richter, the great German organist and conductor. He was fond of Virgil; and he greeted us warmly. He invited us to his church to hear a few of his students play at their lessons. He was particularly hard on the first American lad, and sent him packing to practice some more. The next student in line was our friend, the "long-stemmed" Cherry Rhodes, who was then studying with Karl for a whole year.

Richard and I were delighted to see her. Although she was a great favorite of Virgil's, we were amazed that Richter had her play only works from the *Orgelbuchlein* of Bach. Here was one of the most brilliant graduates of the Curtis Institute in Philadelphia playing only minor pieces of Bach! Then we learned that his assignment was for her to play each piece in many different keys before he let her study the larger Bach works with him—no small feat!

Cherry had prepared well, and breezed through the pieces with ease. We were proud of her; and Karl seemed pleased as well. It was cold in the organ loft, and there were infrared lamps to warm

Cherry's hands before she played, which didn't seem to please her. Richard and I were amused when we spotted several empty beer bottles and cigarette butts in the loft. Karl Richter liked to smoke and drink while he listened to his students, so it seemed.

Karl invited us to dinner that evening, which turned out to be a sumptuous meal in an elegant restaurant. The staff treated Richter like a prince, for he was famous in Europe for playing the organ and also founding and conducting the famous Munich Bach Choir. That evening at the restaurant, two dear children came up to the table to greet "Herr Richter." Karl seemed confused, and it took some time for him to recognize that they were his own children! We never found out the true story behind that incident!

The next evening, Karl invited us to attend a memorial concert for Karl Gerstenlager, the manager of the Munich Bach Choir. Since the man was Roman Catholic, the concert would be held in the Catholic cathedral, called the *Frauenkirche*. It was the first time the Lutheran Bach Choir had performed there; and so it was an historic event in Munich.

The cathedral was crowded, and the singing was heavenly. A Brahms motet, *"Warum,"* and an extended Reger motet were beautifully done. Strangely

Signed: "Karl Richter"

enough, following these superbly performed pieces an organist began to weary us with droning, dull music. After such sublime choral singing, in such a musical ambiance, why did we have to endure boring organ music on a modern German organ of small distinction?

We went on to Copenhagen, spending the last few days—and the last few dollars—in Paris before we headed home. We had a grand time; and we owed it all to Reader's Digest Records (which were recorded by the RCA Victor staff in New York, and the Decca staff in London) and our dear Virgil, who simply "couldn't possibly do this recording without my boys."

Steven Frank is a virtuoso organist. He is also the president of the Virgil Fox Society, which commissioned the development and publication of this book.

Steven Frank

It was "Joy To The World" from the second Reader's Digest album that changed my life (with the magnitude of a huge meteor hitting the Earth!) the day my junior high school band director introduced me to the music of Virgil Fox. Some years later, I took a long bus ride from Albany, Georgia to Miami because I knew I had to hear the man in person.

I tried sneaking into the church beforehand to hear him practice. It didn't work. I tried breaking into the front of the line after the concert. That didn't work either. It was the end of the line or nothing.

I began losing my nerve as I watched this magic personality greet dozens of people, all of whom seemed to have some connection to him. What could I possibly say to him, or he to me—a total stranger?

When I finally got close enough for him to see me, his eyes lit up and he blurted forth, "Steven Frank!" He came toward me with outstretched arms.

How could he know who I was? He'd never laid eyes on me!

As it turned out, in a way, he had; for my mother insisted I enclose a small photograph in my first fan letter to him so he could see "what a nice boy" I was.

Thus began a long and amazing relationship "up North" coaching with Virgil while studying more formally at the Guilmant Organ School. My regular teacher, George Markey, grounded me in a firm technical foundation, while Virgil helped me reach deep inside to touch what one commentator recently called "the Eternal Flame."

Although I've played five Virgil Fox memorial concerts over the years, every note I've ever played has been a memorial to Virgil. I can't separate his memory from my music.

54. The Holy Terror

W hen I returned to Philadelphia, I was jobless! One or two days later, I got a call from the rector of St. Mary's Episcopal Church in Wayne, Pennsylvania—which is a beautiful suburb on the Main Line of Philadelphia. I had met Father William Kier and his attractive wife, Hope, once or twice, after my old friend Paul Fitz Gerald had taken the job of organist and choirmaster of St. Mary's a few months earlier. I had visited Paul and my good friend, Bill Marsh, who were sharing a charming carriage house a few blocks from the church.

Father Kier asked if I would be willing to take the job, at least temporarily, as things weren't working out between him and Paul. He didn't give me much time to think about it, for he had already dismissed Paul. He wanted me to start immediately by taking the boy choir rehearsal the next day, and to play the services that coming weekend. I said I would certainly help until he could find someone suitable.

When I arrived at the church the next afternoon, the boys of the choir were running amok. They were jumping in and out of the windows of the parish house, yelling and roughhousing, as boys will do. This behavior was not acceptable to me; and so, in the best Richard Purvis autocratic fashion, I walked over to the grand piano in the parish hall. I raised the lid over the strings as high as possible. I paused; and then I let it slam down with a resounding crash!

I had stunned the little demons. One by one, they cowered to their seats for the rehearsal. I introduced myself, and told them that the remainder of the rehearsal would be spent in total silence. Not one sound would be uttered for the next hour! I also informed them that any infringement would cause them to stay an extra hour.

One timid little chorister said, "What will my Mother do when she comes to pick me up if we have to stay later?"

"She will wait; and she will be told why!"

Thus, the rehearsal ended on time; and they had their first taste of the discipline they so sorely needed. I'm sure that, although they didn't realize it at the time, they appreciated having someone finally lay down the rules.

I went to Father Kier and Hope, and told them what had occurred. They had already heard the story, since their son, Sam, was one of the choristers. They were delighted; and they howled when I described the expressions on those little monster's faces.

The first Sunday services went well. We kept everything simple for the first few weeks. The main choir was a mixed choir of volunteers, with a paid professional quartet to help (there was one professional in each section). The boy choir sang at the early service at 9:30 a.m., and the mixed choir at 11:00 a.m. Hope and Bill Kier were lovely people to work for and be with. They weren't the slightest bit pretentious, and their household was filled with laughter and love. In addition to Sam, their family included Mary, their daughter, and a ferocious looking, but lovable, English bulldog called "Wrinkles."

I spent a lot of time at the rectory. Father badgered me to accept the job for at least a year. He was pleased, and the people in the parish were lovely to me. St. Mary's was charming. It was small in comparison to St. Mark's, Frankford. The "churchmanship" was "high church," which was unusual for an affluent community like Wayne. There were several other Episcopal churches within a radius of a few miles, however. Therefore, one could choose the degree of "high" or "low" with which one was comfortable.

There were two serious drawbacks musically as far as I was concerned. The acoustics were uninspiring (in fact, they were deadly dry); and the organ was a horror! In its day, the three-manual Haskell was probably fine; but it was showing its age. Its sound was dated at best; and the ivories on the console kept coming off with every piece I played. Trying to control it was like driving a Mack truck. The swell shutters were mechanical, and I'm sure I developed terrific muscles in my calves while trying to open and shut those monsters. They regularly creaked; and they either slammed open or slammed shut.

Father Kier promised that if I stayed at St. Mary's, he would fight for a new organ within the coming year. He would also try to rectify the acoustics, if possible. These promises, together with the fact that Bill Marsh had offered to let me live with him in his beautifully furnished, charming carriage house, persuaded me to consider staying in Pennsylvania for awhile. I'm glad, now, that I did, because the next years were among the happiest and most productive of my life.

A few months after my arrival, I had convinced the music committee to make the boy choir the main focus of the musical life of the parish, and to use the volunteer men of the church (with a few additional paid men) to fill out the tenor and bass sections. The volunteer mixed choir plus the paid quartet weren't exceptional. As with almost every volunteer choir, there's always an excuse why many of them fail to show up for rehearsals or services. We paid the boys, however, a minimal amount for each of three rehearsals per week and the two Sunday services. I believed that the serious training they would have to endure would be an important part of their education; and they deserved a stipend for committing to doing so much work. The stipend (although small by any standards) gave me a formidable stick to "fine" them for lateness, absence, or improper behavior. I think some of them were fined so often, they never were paid!

They were a great bunch of lovable urchins who worked hard. After a year, they became quite good; and they knew it. Because there was no choir school, it wasn't feasible to teach them how to sight-read; but they learned by rote quickly, and they took great pride in their achievements. I was often hard on them, quite strict, and I managed them like an army. I never tolerated any nonsense!

Few parents ever complained. Those that did were told to remove their child if they really disapproved. No one did. The parents and the boys appreciated and enjoyed the discipline, for they knew it was for the good of the choir. Although I must have sometimes been a "holy terror" with them, I loved every one of them dearly! I'm afraid they quickly figured out how I really felt, and realized that my bark was always going to be worse than my bite. They obeyed me in order to avoid the consequences of not doing so; but I think the true reason was they secretly adored me.

55. The South Wind Over a Field of Empty Bathtubs

After the first six months, Father Kier was determined to get me to stay. He started the wheels turning concerning a new organ. Virgil was delighted, of course, that at last I could be happily ensconced somewhere, and was thrilled with the prospect of advising us on the new organ. We never doubted that the organ would be built by Æolian-Skinner; and so I immediately contacted Joseph Whiteford to tell him the good news and start planning for the new organ.

Joe was enthusiastic, but told me that he was seriously considering leaving the firm. (Virgil and I started to worry about the consequences of such a drastic move.) Even worse was that he told us we had to wait more than three years for a new organ to be built! Finally, he told us that the price of a new Æolian-Skinner organ would exceed the cost of any other American builder. Since we believed that Æolian-Skinner's quality might have been declining during that time, Virgil and I decided to consider some alternatives.

The bid from Æolian-Skinner turned out to be outrageously expensive. By the time we received it, Joe had already announced he would leave. He, himself, advised me to look elsewhere.

When Father Kier, upon hearing the price and the situation, announced, "We'll have to look elsewhere," we found ourselves in a real dilemma! The organ world had been going through drastic changes. The neo-Baroque movement had taken hold. It seemed like everyone insisted on having the "North German sound."

This particular taste in organs may work well in acoustically superb churches and cathedral spaces in that region, but I consider the results (which are thin and often ugly sounding) as utterly unsuitable for most American churches—too many of which have the acoustics of a carpeted telephone booth!

Virgil had a lot to say on this subject. He had inaugurated many of what he used to call "those gutless wonders." He often made emphatic statements, such as, "Where was the 8-foot tone? There was nothing but 50 tierces, and no wood in the pedal! Where was the power? The organ was hollow sounding, like an old woman blowing through ferns, or worse—like the south wind blowing over a field of empty bathtubs! Moreover, the strings were as weak as an old lady's purse strings!

"Why," he would go on, "I just played an enormous new organ! It was pitiful! There was no body, no color, except for a portion they'd saved from their old E.M. Skinner. And the weak 32-foot Bombarde sounded for all the world like a rattlesnake peeing down an eave trough!"

Virgil could outdo even Sir Thomas Beecham with his withering descriptions!

Carlo Curley

To this day I start to giggle when I think of being with Virgil at a venue where a 32-foot Bombarde had gone badly out of tune and regulation. Virgil leaned over and remarked, "Oh, Honey! It sounds like a gaggle of rutting orangutans!"

Richard Torrence

Virgil's wit was legendary. Once, he and I visited the Saville Organ Company's offices in Northbrook, Illinois during a period when Rodgers was waffling on keeping the touring organ program alive. (Eventually, when I advertised that the management's artists would be touring with a Saville organ, Rodgers snapped to!)

During our visit to Saville, we met with the company's president, who didn't seem particularly knowledgeable about music. (He mispronounced Nadia Boulanger's name horribly!) Virgil was bored, because there was little to see but consoles, until we got to a large room filled with a wild collection of organ pipes that were not in good condition, sitting on old chests that once upon a time had pumped air through them.

The president said, "This is where we take samplings of the pipes so we can electronically recreate, perfectly, the sound of a pipe organ."

Virgil was amused. He gave his low "Ho! Ho! Ho!" and said, "Finding organ pipes in an electronic organ factory is like finding birdshit in a cuckoo clock!"

This dismal state of organ building in America lasted from the mid-1960s until some sanity returned to the scene in the mid-1980s. Even now, however, we're still plagued with the group that will not hear of an organ that doesn't have mechanical action. Virgil hated these "tracker backers."

I often thought it inconsistent that these purists tolerated electric blowers. They should have been made to pump the organ bellows themselves; for my ears convinced me that they would demonstrate more talent pushing long wooden handles than operating musical keyboards.

I didn't know what to do. I would not have a Möller of that period. I was intrigued, however, at some of the work a newer firm, called Gress Miles, was doing. We examined a few of their instruments, and were almost ready to do business with them, when they decided to reverse their approach to our scheme. They were rude to me and the vestry of St. Mary's, and were even asked off the property by the rector, much to my wicked delight!

What to do now? Father Kier had heard that Virgil had played some nicely made Casavants (which was a distinguished Canadian firm). He said, "Why not go to Casavant Frères and beg their tonal director to give you some of the things you want, and see what they'll agree to."

He said, "I'll pay for you to go to Ste. Hyacinthe and convince them." We quickly decided that Richard and I would drive to Canada in my pride and joy, "Rex," the Jaguar that Walter Mellbourne had helped me purchase.

We decided to drive first to Montreal to visit a friend we had there by the name of Denis La Chapelle, who worked for Air Canada. Denis had invited us to stay with him and enjoy a few days of vacation. Richard had also wanted to scout out some places for Virgil to play, for he hadn't appeared in Quebec for several seasons.

Montreal was glorious, and both Richard and I fell in love with this marvelous city—and the food, which was heavenly! Shortly after we arrived, Denis told us of an article in the paper he had saved about a new concert hall that had opened in town. There was a large pipe organ in the new hall. Richard was intrigued, of course, for it might be an ideal place for him to book Virgil—and me! By that time, I had become an artist on Richard's management roster.

I was interested in hearing what a large, new Casavant would sound like in a concert hall, which obviously didn't have the acoustics of a cathedral. (We were sure it would be a Casavant, for their foremost builder built nearly all the organs in Canada.)

56. Sister Jeannie Jesus

The concert hall was named *Salle Claude Champagne* after the contemporary Canadian composer. It was located in a music conservatory run by the Archdiocese of Montreal: *l'École de Musique de Vincent d'Indy*. The beautiful hall seated 1,000 people. Across the stage, there was a stunning display of façade pipes with a wonderful, "belled" *en chamade* trumpet splaying out of the top of the façade. (It was the first *en chamade* trumpets I had ever seen that actually looked like real trumpets.)

We were greeted warmly by the dear little nun that ran the hall. She introduced herself as *"Soeur Eugenie de Jesus"*—soon to become known by the name Virgil gave her, "Jeannie Jesus." We asked about the organ, and she told us that it was an Italian organ, a "Ruffatti."

I remember grabbing Richard's hand and whispering to him, "It looks magnificent! But I'll bet it sounds like shredded tin!" She asked if we would like to play it. Suddenly some stagehands appeared, pushing the movable console on stage. So far, so good! It was movable!

The console was handsome looking, with four manuals and tilting tablets arranged in terraced side jambs. It looked a little foreign to us, but nicely done. A closer look revealed that almost every control on the console had been placed wrong! Still, the organ was sizable—80 ranks—and so it couldn't be ignored!

I was afraid to start playing, thinking we might start laughing at the instrument in front of our kind hosts. I climbed onto the bench and turned on the 8-foot Principal on the Great. A rich and warm, singing tone poured forth from the pipes. I was pleasantly surprised. I then proceeded through the principal chorus of the Great, beginning with a handsome 16-foot and ending with two brilliant but transparent mixtures. I then added the three independent Great chorus reeds at 16-, 8-, and 4-foot. A blaze of tone raged from the Great division alone. We were flat out impressed!

The tone reminded both Richard and me of the best of Æolian-Skinner, but there was a difference; the tone was more "singing" in its naturalness. None of the individual stops were particularly loud by themselves, but they all added up to a thrilling richness.

I was pleased to see Great sub- and super-couplers, devices that the Baroque enthusiasts would completely reject. Moreover, there were "subs" and "supers" within every division. Every manual coupled at 16-, 8-, and 4-foot! Casavant would have balked at this decision; but I was determined to have these couplers in Wayne. I had grown up with them, and my style of playing (as well as Richard Purvis's and Virgil's) required these couplers.

We believed that the American and Canadian builders of the day had fallen prey to the "classic" movement. Therefore, most of them preferred not to include these couplers and other valuable assists to the player because of certain academic theories. By eliminating these features, they were imposing restrictions on the player's artistry—restrictions that were often unavoidable with earlier, less well developed instruments that were mechanical in operation (as opposed to electrical, as most American instruments had come to be).

These organ builders, academics, and critics declared themselves the arbiters of taste and style, yanking away the roles that more rightfully belonged to performing artists and their audiences. These "purists" argued that since these devices were not "historically correct," they were often "misused." Therefore, the builders would prevent the possibility of any "bad taste" occurring.

Oh, how Virgil and I deplored this new thinking and the large and small "gutless wonders," to quote Virgil, that resulted! These builders saved lots of money, of course, for they were erecting organs that had no "weight" and very little color—except for a few, new "quacky" classic-type color reeds, and a Pedal Organ (which should be the glory and foundation of any great instrument) that could barely sustain even modest hymn registration. We declared all these organs to be just plain blah and boring!

When I finally got the entire organ going in the Salle Claude Champagne, the place was on fire with a rich and full organ tone. It was a blazing, thrilling rage! Pausing to compliment our hosts, Sister Jeannie Jesus told us that the organ had been designed by the organist of the Roman Catholic cathedral, *Marie Reine du Monde*, in Montreal. The organist's name was Georges Lindsay. The specification was very French, with complete principal, flute, and reed choruses at 16-, 8-, and 4-foot.

The Swell had a very nice Oboe and the Positif a European Cromorne. The celestes were French and kind of scrappy but nice. The tremulants were a horror, and did far too little. Even worse, the organ had "ventil"–type chests, which I felt were too slow and failed to respond to the keys quickly enough. The *en chamade* was good, but nothing to write home about. The Pedal was solid and rich. There were no 32-foot stops except for a Resultant; but there were 16-, 8-, and 4-foot Pedal reeds that were made of wood and were definitely French—and thrilling!

We asked Sister how they came to buy a Ruffatti, and what the price might be. She told us they had paid $80,000 for the instrument, or about $1,000 per rank. We were astounded! This price was less than half of what other builders were asking. Our wheels began turning, and I considered an instrument like this one for St. Mary's, Wayne.

The person who maintained the organ, Franco Teletin, was the North American agent for the firm, and Sister told us he would be at the hall within an hour or two. I continued to play the organ, and the more we heard, the more we were impressed and thrilled with the tone.

When Franco arrived on the stage, he greeted us warmly. He had tears in his eyes. He had been sitting in the hall for some time, and he said that he'd never heard an organ played like that! He was a wonderfully open, simple, and kind man; and he proceeded to show us through the instrument and tell us all about the Ruffatti Family and their splendid factory in Padua, Italy, near Venice.

One thing that struck Richard and me was the quality of workmanship both inside and out. All of the wind chests were finished like fine furniture. Franco told us that the head of the firm, Antonio Ruffatti, had decreed that his instruments must look as good on the inside as on the outside; and that the interior must be as beautiful as the strange-looking (to us) console with its French-polished rosewood interior and parquet floor on a movable platform.

We got on so well, and Franco was so personable, that he invited Richard and me to his home that night for dinner. His wife, Lucia, was a total delight. She prepared a sumptuous feast (the best ravioli I've ever eaten!). It was a splendid and momentous day in Richard's and my life!

The first thing I did the next morning was to telephone Father Kier to tell him about what we had heard and seen. By that time, I wanted nothing further to do with a Casavant, or any other builder. I told Father that Franco had mentioned he could probably arrange for the Ruffattis to come to Wayne at their own expense. What could we lose by investigating this firm? Neither Richard nor I knew of any other builder who offered a similar quality or tone—especially at that price.

Kier said, "Get them over here—now!" Thus, it was arranged that the Ruffattis would arrive in Wayne a week or two later. I've always thought that Divine Providence had led us to the Ruffattis!

We returned to the hall the next day; and I played and played. As luck had it, Sister Jeannie Jesus brought in the composer for whom the hall was named, Claude Champagne, who was a wonderfully dignified and personable man. He was so impressed with what he heard that he recommended I appear at the hall in concert the next season! Richard also arranged to rent the hall in order to present Virgil later that year; and so it was an exceedingly fruitful trip, thanks to dear Denis La Chapelle, Sister Eugenie de Jesus, Franco Teletin, Georges Lindsay, Claude Champagne, and the marvelous Fratelli Ruffatti organ!

It was decided that Franco Teletin and Georges Lindsay would also visit Wayne in order to join the Ruffattis in their initial meetings with Father Kier and the formidable vestry of the parish. The Ruffattis actually flew to Montreal and drove to Philadelphia with Franco and Georges—by way of New York, where they picked up Richard. Of course, it was essential to have Richard along so that he could contribute his considerable talents and knowledge, and could bolster me—for I was wary of what the vestry might think and do. "This boy is mad! Why should we consider an Italian instrument for this parish? The Italians aren't known for organ building! They've only got one organ on the continent—in Canada!"

To complicate matters even more, we found out that Papa Antonio Ruffatti spoke no English! Franco spoke Italian and broken English; Georges spoke French, Italian, and broken English. We were also informed that Papa was bringing along his twenty-year old son, Francesco, who spoke "some" English. (At that point, he spoke very little. He had studied business—but not conversational—English!)

The whole situation was laden with problems; but I believed in the superb sound I had heard, and Kier said that both he and God would take care of "the old geezers on the vestry."

57. Debbie Does St. Mary's

During this period, we had explained to Virgil what our impressions were of the Montreal trip. Although he was skeptical, he agreed that the world could use a new organ company to take the place of Æolian-Skinner. He admitted he had grown less and less impressed with new Æolian-Skinner organs. He agreed we should consider an alternative.

When the Ruffattis, Franco, and Georges arrived, they charmed the staid and sometimes gruff members of the vestry into submission. Although Papa spoke no English, his manner, openness, expressive face, and body language sold him completely. He was a robust and stocky man (he looked German to me) who seemed thrilled and interested with everything and everyone he saw and met. We all loved him and his young son, Francesco, immediately.

Francesco was enormously helpful, and he struggled with his English valiantly. He worked hard, for there were endless complicated questions that had to be translated into Italian, after which the answers had to be translated back into English. It was trying and tiring, but everyone did a superb job. We surely communicated everything we had to!

Richard Torrence

> *Ted wanted an 80-rank organ; but because of space and money considerations, the specification had to be reduced to 50 ranks. In one meeting, Antonio suggested (in Italian) that to economize, the 32-foot Bombarde should be removed from the specifications. No one needed to translate this suggestion to Ted! He dramatically declared, "If there is only one stop on the organ, it will be a 32-foot Bombarde!"*
>
> *Antonio understood Ted's English perfectly well, and we all started to laugh.*

Finally, the decision was made that St. Mary's would contract for a 50-rank instrument to be built by the Ruffattis and installed in the autumn of 1967. The Ruffattis were so surprised at their good fortune that they immediately asked Richard and me to become their agents in the United States. We agreed to work through Franco, although he didn't stay involved with us for long, because he became too busy in Canada. The Ruffattis also informed me that they expected to pay us a sales commission and me a design commission since I had drawn up the organ specifications. I was pleased with the offer, but I explained that in America it would be considered a conflict of interest for an organist to recommend a particular organ to a church and then collect a commission on that instrument.

Father Kier, in his usual direct way, said "Take it! You deserve it!" I decided, however, to put the money for the design into the instrument itself; and the Ruffattis agreed to add another 10 ranks to the organ!

The Ruffattis agreed to several other conditions, also. They assured us that the console would conform to American specifications, with every control in the right place and every measurement correct. The Romantic color reeds and celestes would have to be of the American style, after E.M. Skinner and Æolian-Skinner. We agreed to provide the necessary "scalings," and the information on how to build them. The chests would have to be of the American "Pitman" style, and lightening fast! The tremulants would also have to be Æolian-Skinner style, not the puny "motor boat," ineffective horrors we heard in Montreal!

The church had the Ruffattis sign a contract that placed all of the money in escrow in an American bank. They would not receive any of it until the organ had been installed, voiced, and accepted by me! This condition was unheard of, for the Ruffattis had to deliver everything to our liking, with everything accomplished on time! Few companies would have agreed to entirely revamp their methods of building a console and chests, as well as erecting quite a few ranks with which they were unfamiliar. However *"Fratelli Ruffatti, Famiglia Artigiana di Padova, Italia"* were motivated to get into the American market. They agreed to everything.

As if the organ project for St. Mary's, Wayne weren't enough, Richard and I persuaded the Ruffattis to begin advertising in the organ magazines of America, and to provide important displays of their work at the next National Convention of the American Guild of Organists, which was to convene in Atlanta in June 1966.

We decided that they should build and show a twenty-five rank, two-manual organ for that convention, although there wasn't a single buyer in sight for such an instrument! What a risk: to install an organ, temporarily, for a convention! We discovered that the instrument wouldn't fit in the convention hotel; the exhibition space ceiling was too low. Fortunately, there was an African-American Methodist church near the convention headquarters; and so the instrument was installed there in record time. Then it was up to Richard and me to try to sell it!

These times were exciting and creative for Richard and me. Virgil was wryly amused at our little venture. He thought it "cute" that "Richard and Teddy have found this funny Italian organ company" to represent. Who ever heard of an Italian organ builder in the U.S.? "I hope you chicks know what you are doing," he said; but he also wished us luck. It wasn't until he played the concert at Salle Claude Champagne that he knew how serious we were. He was highly impressed with the sounds he heard.

I think he may have been jealous of Richard's and my involvement with the Ruffattis. I know he resented any time we spent on their behalf—especially when it involved Richard. The thought that we both might make some money out of this venture also rankled him. It was part of his nature, which could be controlling; but he didn't protest too much, because he figured this business might bring in more concerts for him to play!

When the organists around Philadelphia heard about the proposed organ for St. Mary's, some would laugh and make jokes about "Ted's spaghetti organ." Richard and I had no capital to invest in this new venture, and so I went again to our dear friend, Walter Mellbourne, to see if he might be interested in our new project. He was interested, and that was how we formed the first sales organization in the United States to represent the Ruffattis in America. The company was called WTM, Inc. for "Worth, Torrence, and Mellbourne."

Shortly after the organ contract was signed, I met a woman from the parish who had come to pick up her son from choir rehearsal. Her name was Deborah Eldredge duPont. I had her son, Henry in the boy choir. (She called him "Larry," however, which was his middle name.) Her eldest daughter, another Debbie, was in the adult choir. I had never met Mrs. duPont before that time, as she didn't come to church "very often." Her two children, however, were always there, on time, and lovely to work with.

Mrs. duPont was an attractive woman, youthful in appearance and dress. She looked and behaved as if she'd been "little Debbie's" sister, rather than her mother! She was outgoing, friendly, and unpretentious, despite her relationship to one of the most important families in the country. I can still remember her arriving at the parish hall, asking for "Larry and Debbie."

It was a warm, late spring evening; and she was in a light windbreaker, her long hair flowing. She held a cigarette in a long holder, seeming oblivious to the heavy rain that was falling. On her face was a beaming smile. Her voice had a distinctive, throaty quality that didn't seem to go with her slight build. She collected the children, said she was so happy to meet me, and went off with them to her car in the parking lot.

I suddenly noticed that she was barefoot—which wasn't a typical Main Line style! She seemed to be a free spirit, and very Bohemian! I immediately ran to the rectory (which had become my second home by then; Hope and Father Kier, and their entire family, had practically adopted me) to inquire about the eccentric Deborah duPont. Father Kier said that she had recently been divorced from William Henry duPont, and had moved back to the Main Line from the Wilmington, Delaware area. She now lived in St. David's, and had joined St. Mary's only a short time before. Her parents lived in Bryn Mawr, on the Main Line; and her father, Laurence Eldredge, was a famous jurist. In fact, he wrote the book, *Trials of a Philadelphia Lawyer.*

"You should get to know her, Ted," said Father Kier. "She might give a stop or two to the new organ. She certainly has been generous to the church. I think she's loaded!"

We laughed, and I thought no more about her until two or three weeks later. I got an invitation from her to attend a dinner dance at the St. David's Golf Club. I was to be her escort at a formal affair!

I was horrified and petrified! Here I was the village organist! What did I know of formal dinner dances? Kier said, "Take her, it'll do you good. She obviously likes you!" I considered it, but as it turned out, I had promised Richard to be in New York that night. Mrs. duPont was disappointed; but she understood, and insisted that we lunch together the minute I got back.

Thus began my lifelong friendship with the incredibly wonderful, generous, eccentric, and fabulous Debbie duPont!

At our first lunch, she inquired about the new organ. "Do you need money?"

What a question!

"What can I do?"

She decided that she would give the *en chamade* trumpets, and a few other goodies—including an elevator under the console so that we could move it front and center for concerts! On top of this generosity, she wanted to encourage my dream of having a concert series at the church. She said she'd help that project when the time came.

She made the commitment to Father Kier the next day! I was flabbergasted and delighted! From then on, I was a regular guest for dinner several times a week in her lovely home, and we became great friends. I could never quite figure out what appealed to her, for although we had plenty of good times together, and although she loved to hear me play, I don't think she was interested in the organ or in church music. Her tastes tended more to rock'n'roll than Buxtehude; and she was wild for baseball! She was interested in Oriental art, and had a passion for jade. She also was knowledgeable about fine antiques. She had just taken up *ikebana*, Japanese flower arranging, and she collected *bonsai* trees—some of them quite old.

58. Electronic Device Deafens Audience

While all these plans for a new organ in Wayne were going on, the Rodgers Organ Company was building a large electronic organ for Virgil to take on tour. The instrument was nearing completion in 1967, and Virgil anxiously awaited its arrival for his approval. He had visited the factory; and people from the factory had visited him at Riverside Church; but he had yet to examine what they had produced.

Richard Torrence

From the moment I entered Virgil's business life, he never stopped encouraging me to help him acquire a large movable pipe organ for the road. I realized how complicated such a large instrument would be to tour, and so I investigated the possibility of procuring an electronic organ.

Ted had introduced Virgil (and me) to Rodgers Jenkins, the inspired leader of the Rodgers Organ Company; and Bob Hebble had introduced me to Paul Berlin, one of the Rodgers representatives in the New York area. Paul and I felt that a Rodgers electronic organ was the only practical solution to Virgil's problem, and so we arranged a meeting between Virgil and Rodgers Jenkins at Virgil's house. During the meeting, "Rodg" actually committed his company to build an organ for Virgil!

Virgil didn't like the specifications of the organ once he saw them, however; and so he asked to meet with someone from the company. Soon, a young executive appeared at the Riverside console, and Virgil proceeded to demonstrate his mastery over what he always loved to describe, tongue-in-cheek, as the "biggest organ in Manhattan."

The young man said nothing while Virgil proceeded to dazzle everyone with outstanding demonstrations of virtuosic German and French music. Finally, visibly moved, the young man said, "Gosh, I had no idea you could really play! I always thought you were just a showman!"

Virgil remained calm for the remainder of the meeting, holding back an explosion of utter rage until after the young man left. From that day on, despite Virgil's phenomenal talent for remembering people, he was never able to recognize this young man's face. Despite the many times they met again, Virgil always had to be reintroduced. The young man was always devastated.

The Rodgers people, led by Rodgers Jenkins, had spared no cost in developing as perfect an organ as was technologically possible at that time. They were anxious for Virgil to be pleased with the new instrument. The original arrangements were that the company would supply Virgil with his organ at all the concerts that required a touring instrument—free! They would transport it, set it up, and voice it according to Virgil's instructions in order to match the acoustics of every hall. All they asked for was a mention in the program.

Rodgers Jenkins then made a serious tactical error in judgment. He decided to try out the organ in a concert in Canada before Virgil heard it. He engaged a hall in Montreal, and hired a woman organist (of whom no one had ever heard) to inaugurate "The Virgil Fox Touring Organ." He probably thought that Virgil would never hear about the concert, and that everything would go well at the trial run. As Virgil used to say, "He was *totally* in error!"

News travels fast in the organ world. Within days, Virgil and Richard knew everything about the whole affair.

Virgil was livid. "That Rodgers W. Jenkins is a liar! I'd like to yank the tongue right out of his head! How dare he do a thing like that to me, using my name! I'll never touch that filthy electric device; and he'll wish he'd never been born when I finish with him! Caméo! Call him and demand an explanation!"

Richard, with his usual aplomb and will of steel—and the touch of a velvet glove—was able to smooth things over by convincing Virgil that he should at least hear the instrument and try it out at the few concerts that had already been booked.

Thus began the rocky beginning for the greatest concert organist in the world and the new instrument that was destined to become one of the most famous and most frequently heard organs in the world! It was to create a new venue for Virgil—as well as many other organists in its colorful history. It put the organ right onto the concert stage, which was where Virgil longed for it to be.

For some time, Richard had been contemplating how to reach an entirely new (and immense) audience that would be thrilled and inspired by the spell and literature of the King of Instruments. It almost didn't happen, except for his determination and his fast-talking!

A young and gifted artist named Joyce Jones, who had been a professor of organ at Baylor University in Waco, Texas, had been touring for several years through an organization called Community Concerts. This extraordinary, immense, grass-roots concert network was owned and operated by the giant concert management, Columbia Artists Management Inc. ("CAMI") of New York.

Community Concerts were presented before "organized audiences" in cities and towns all across the United States and Canada. At one time, there had been 1,500 of them; but by this time, due to a government decree that the organization was a monopoly, there were only about 750 cities and towns left that were associated with CAMI. Each town would present three to six concerts per season on a series basis. All of the people interested in "good music" in each community would subscribe to the entire year's concerts. ("Organized" meant that tickets were sold in advance before the actual series was announced, thereby eliminating risk for the organizers.) Series included such groups as Fred Waring and The Pennsylvanians, Guy Lombardo and His Orchestra, and the Roger Wagner Chorale. They also included famous dance companies, soloists, duos, and small chamber groups. Brilliant pianists, famous string quartets, harpists, and well-known singers appeared on these "meat and potato" series. Most of the artists and groups presented were under management by CAMI.

Each community would have decided on one or two of the more famous ensembles or concert artists—which they would announce as their sales campaign began. When they knew how many tickets they had sold, they added some less well known artists, and often an up-and-coming young virtuoso.

Joyce Jones had done a great deal of work to market herself to this system of organized audiences. She therefore blazed new trails for the organ world. Since most concerts were held in high school auditoriums not churches, Joyce was only able to perform on the Community Concerts circuit because she used an electronic organ. Her terrific talent and effervescent personality made every appearance a success. Eventually, she contacted Richard—who had become famous as Virgil's manager—because she knew she would need professional help to expand her career beyond "Community."

Among other things, Joyce gave Richard her past lists of all the officers of the Community Concert associations around the country. As the new names and addresses of each season's officers became available, Richard copied them at the Columbia Artists Management headquarters on 57th Street. (Because of an antitrust settlement, CAMI was required to provide competing managers these addresses; but the company only made them available on Wednesdays—and in the foyer of its ladies room, where Richard had to sit, week after week, under the watchful eye of a CAMI employee, copying out the 1,500 names and addresses by hand, two for each association.)

Richard was therefore able to mail out literature about each of his artists (including Joyce of course) to the latest officers of these associations. In this way, and solely because of Joyce's success—despite the inadequate instruments she had to play!—Richard was able to enlarge the market enormously for organ concerts all around the country.

Joyce usually played a Baldwin electronic organ, which was provided by a nearby local dealer. There were many Baldwin dealers around the country; for Baldwin, which was most important as a manufacturer of pianos at that time, had put a great deal of money into developing a market for their organ. Joyce told me some horror stories about being provided with tiny spinet models, sometimes with only 12 pedals! (A classical organ has 32 pedals.) That she was willing to play standard literature on so many electronic organs that produced inferior sound testifies to her dedicated search for new and larger audiences for our instrument.

Audiences that heard Joyce's concerts invariably asked her back again—and again. She created considerable interest in the instrument and its literature with an audience that had rarely paid attention to the organ. She was a trooper; and the entire organ world owes her considerable tribute!

With Richard's help, Virgil made a wide swath through this new-found source of bookings; and he soon had many more engagements at higher fees than ever before. He wasn't familiar with how electronic organs were supposed to be voiced, however; and too often, especially in the beginning, he would face the 144 speakers directly at the audience. He wanted to dazzle them by showing off the immense power and rage that he had at his fingertips. Not sitting in front of the speakers himself, he didn't realize what a bad idea it was for him to instruct the organ technician to turn the overall volume up to what, for the audience, approached the level of pain!

The first reviews were not favorable. "Electronic Device Deafens Audience" was typical of some of the first critiques Virgil got on the inaugural tour of the new Rodgers. He realized the sounds that the organ produced weren't satisfactory (although not why). "The electronic burn that comes from that *thing* is annihilating!" he exclaimed one day.

I remember one of the first times I ever heard Virgil's new Rodgers touring organ was in Merion, Pennsylvania, at a Community Concert. He was, as usual, his ebullient, staggering, virtuosic self; but the organ didn't come off at all. It sounded ugly, loud, and definitely "electronic." Virgil was mostly to blame. In Merion, there were perhaps 1,600 seats in extremely dry acoustics. Virgil had turned up the organ way too loud, with every tweeter at its highest level. (This kind of small speaker accentuates the high frequencies that produce the most painful frequencies.)

The sound was dreadful and unmusical. No one could stand it for long. The biggest, loudest reed on the organ was in the Choir division, the Trompette Harmonique. Virgil had it voiced as a large English tuba, and turned it up as loud as possible. The sound came through a metal horn that was attached to a J. B. Lansing mid-range driver. The whole thing was pointed directly at the audience. It was like a hammer that bludgeoned. It did anything but thrill the audience. It was no wonder that Virgil was upset.

As always, Virgil was stubborn. He couldn't understand why the instrument didn't thrill people in the way that the Rodgers he'd played a few years before in Berkeley did with such success; but he paid no attention to what anyone said. Some tried to reason with him to improve the sound of the organ by turning it down. He asked me what I thought, and I told him that the sound was too direct. I suggested that he lay the speakers down and point the sound upward. At least he needed to stop pointing the speakers at the audience! My suggestion was to deflect the sound, and let it mix and diffuse as all good organ sound does. Virgil was unconvinced. He wanted a clear delineation between the notes.

He certainly got it! It just sounded like smashing glass!

59. More Tales of the Toaster

The executives at the Rodgers Organ Company were horrified at the reviews of the new organ. Richard Torrence was also dismayed, and didn't know quite what to do about it. Virgil found comfort in deprecating "the electric"—which is what he always called it. I'd say, "Virgil, they're called 'electronic,' not 'electric!' It sounds like you're talking about a clock!"

(At least he didn't call it a "toaster," which is what passes for humor in the snooty organ world these days.)

When the Rodgers Organ Company decided to build the organ for Virgil, they naturally wanted to enhance their image. They didn't expect he would play more than a dozen or so concerts each year. Eventually, they figured they would sell the organ, and that would be that.

Richard Torrence had a better idea for the touring organ than mere publicity, followed by the sale of a used instrument. Virgil's reviews weren't good, and Virgil was immovable about how he wanted the organ to sound. At the same time, he understood that he

On top of the Black Beauty console (Photo by Donald Sipe, late 1960s)

could increase his income, which he needed to do just then. The only way to do it would be to increase his use of the touring organ.

Although Richard was also my concert manager at that time, he never took the compensation he had earned for his hard work and tremendous effort on my behalf. He figured I was a young, poor, aspiring artist playing a weird instrument who could hardly command a fee large enough to cover career expenses. Basically, I was playing almost no concerts, because I couldn't afford to subsidize my own career any more than Richard could.

Richard persevered, however, and managed to get me several Community Concert engagements. I was thrilled with the opportunity! Originally, I was scheduled to play on a Baldwin, like Joyce Jones; but in the back of his mind, Richard had decided that I would use Virgil's touring organ.

In the midst of the dilemma, Eugene Zarones, director of marketing of Rodgers, arrived in New York to meet with Richard—and to drop a bomb on him. He said that Rodgers had decided to take the Virgil Fox Touring Organ off the road, move it around among some of their dealers as a publicity ploy, and supply it to Virgil two or three times a year, only for "important" concerts.

Richard, ever quick on his feet, said, "Oh I understand! You want only *bad* reviews!" Gene Zarones said he didn't understand. Of course, they didn't want bad reviews.

"Well," said Richard, "that's what you're going to get with your plan. More bad reviews—just fewer of them! What I can give you is a grass roots, Community Concert tour with Ted Alan Worth and others that I guarantee will get only *good* reviews."

The truth he was getting at was that most of the Community Concerts were played in small towns where the society writer was also the music, dance, and theatre reviewer. Richard knew that they almost never gave bad reviews. To them, a concert was a social event, not an artistic statement. Few of these small town reviewers knew much about music, much less organ music. There was no point in a writer giving, and almost no chance of an artist getting, a bad review for a Community Concert.

Gene was impressed with Richard's argument, but said that he would have to discuss the idea with Rodgers Jenkins and the other top executives. Richard told me that he received a call from Gene several days later—just as Richard was nervously trying to decide whether he should arrange for a Baldwin for me and my few concerts, or wait for the Virgil Fox Touring Organ. Finally, it was agreed that Rodgers Jenkins would inform Virgil that the decision of the company was that other artists would use the organ, and that there would be a $300 charge for each use.

I happened to be staying with Richard in the carriage house on Virgil's property the day he was informed of my engagements. When Virgil realized that I would use "his" organ, he became thoroughly enraged!

"That's *my* organ, and no one else will touch it! It's bad enough that that woman in Canada has befouled it. Never again! *No one!* Or else I'll not set my finger to it again!"

Richard was aghast. He said he understood Virgil's feelings in general, "But this is Teddy! It's family! I thought you'd be delighted and pleased for him! After all, he introduced you to the Rodgers Organ Company!"

There was a long pause in the conversation. "I *am* pleased for him; but he can get his own organ just like everyone else! Teddy is 'Mr. X' in this matter. No one may touch my organ, or they can remove my name and I'll not play it again; and that's final!"

We were all stunned at Virgil's response, and we considered looking elsewhere for electronic instruments for these concerts. I was hurt, of course; but I was also used to Virgil's habit of being incredibly selfish and obstinate at times like these.

I don't know exactly what Richard did or threatened to do, but I got to use Virgil's touring organ. It may have helped that Richard and Rodgers agreed to inform Virgil that the truck would immediately be repainted to say "Rodgers Touring Organ" rather than "Virgil Fox Touring Organ." On the other hand, what probably led to his capitulation was that Virgil realized that the Rodgers Organ Company didn't care whether he played their instrument or not.

Richard Torrence

Despite continual undermining protests by David—who thought that Virgil was the most important musician on the face of the earth, and consistently told him so—I gradually persuaded Virgil that the Rodgers Organ Company could not, and would not, keep the touring organ on the road solely for him. It was just too expensive for them to have a truck and driver available at all times without at least 100 concerts at $300 per con-

cert just to cover the driver's salary, not to mention the cost of the truck.

One year later, Virgil was playing 60 concerts a season, half of which were on the Rodgers Touring Organ. One day, he told me that the touring organ was not adequate, and he wanted to stop playing it! I pulled out all the contracts for the first season, just concluded, and separated the pipe organ from the touring organ recitals. Then I asked Virgil how many of the pipe organs he had played that season were actually better for him as a concert artist than the Rodgers Touring Organ. He admitted that only one of the organs (which was located in Charlotte Garden's old church in New Jersey) was better. I responded that I had been present at that concert, and he was wrong! The console in that church was located underneath an entire division of the organ, which meant that the organist couldn't hear the organ! In fact, Virgil hadn't played well at all at that concert, which Virgil did acknowledge. (Even at that time he had claimed it was the fault of the organ.)

In spite of all my arguments, I finally had to offer to pay the $300 touring organ fee out of my own commission. Then Virgil was interested!

In fact, I paid the money for almost a year on behalf of all the artists I managed. Eventually, this arrangement cost me $12,000, and it brought the management close to bankruptcy. (I personally earned only $4,000 the entire year!) I then informed all the artists that henceforth, I would deduct the $300 touring organ expense from their fees. By that time, all the organists were hooked, and so they all agreed. The touring organ program then continued successfully for another decade!

60. Andy Turns Down the Volume

My first Community Concert took place in Berlin, New Hampshire (accent on the first syllable: BER-lin, I was told). I was finally able to meet the agreeable Rodgers technician about whom Virgil had spoken many times. He was also the driver of the truck, Andrew Crow. I had never met him; but Virgil said "You'll love him, Honey. Andy is a sweet, dear child who will do anything for me!" I had also heard that "Andy" was a brilliant theatre organist.

Two nights before the concert, I was waiting for Andy to arrive at Virgil's house in Englewood—or, actually, at Richard's carriage house on Virgil's property. I was naturally anxious about this important concert, worried whether or not Andy would like me, and nervous about how the organ would sound. We had decided that Andy and I would drive together to Berlin in the truck with the organ. (The truck was actually a utility wagon that pulled a horse trailer that had been converted into a home for the organ on the road). BER-lin didn't seem that far on the map.

Andy arrived. Richard had prepared a sumptuous feast for us. Even before the salad course was served (which usually came last in Richard's house), it was clear that Andy was a gem. He was absolutely one of us, so funny and so easy to know. It was as if we had known each other for years, and had worked together a lifetime. He could also imitate Virgil's voice and gestures far better than anyone I had ever known (and many tried!). Andy was a good omen of my life to come!

The trip from Englewood to Berlin was interminable. We left about 9:00 p.m. and didn't arrive until 8:00 a.m. the next day. It didn't seem that long, however, because we entertained ourselves with non-stop conversation.

In the early days of the touring organ, all the speakers, amplifiers, cables, and console were packed tightly in the small trailer that was hooked to an International Harvester "wagon" (a forerunner of the SUV). I remember that the trailer had been painted a baby diaper delivery service blue; and it now advertised the Rodgers Touring Organ. Everything was a little makeshift in those days, for the project was still an experiment. No one knew if it would work.

We arrived at the school auditorium where the concert was to take place, and were both pleasantly surprised how nice it was and how generous the acoustics were. We were astonished to find another organ console in the orchestra pit! It was a fine Wurlitzer theatre organ. After the Rodgers had been unloaded and was being moved in, piece by piece, by the stagehands, I said, "Go to it, Andy! Show us how this old Wurlitzer sounds!"

It sounded magnificent; but what was even better than the organ was the dazzling artistry of Andrew Neal Crow! He was truly gifted in his field.

We got the Rodgers all hooked up, and placed the speakers so that they pointed away from the audience: upwards, at an angle, taking into consideration the generous, high auditorium ceiling. We then fired her up, and the sound came out rich and beautiful in the large room. However, when I added the big 8-foot Trompette Harmonique, the noise was so loud and bludgeoning that it completely dominated and blotted out the rest of the full organ sound.

Andy had received strict orders from Virgil not to touch or revoice any of the stops. We were to confine ourselves only to the main volume controls and the tweeter controls on the speakers themselves. Although these instructions gave us a general leeway, the minute I heard that hideous trumpet stop on the Choir, I had Andy open the back. "We're going to work on that awful sound whether Virgil likes it or not!"

Andy agreed; and within an hour, we had "thinned" out the sound of the stop in order to place a beautiful "crown" on the full organ—not a giant horn that obliterated the rest of it. We made a few more tweaks here and there. Once we got inside, we couldn't stop ourselves from attending to several other offending stops. Finally, the entire organ sounded much better than I had ever remembered. It was an instrument that all but the most precious of organists would have been proud to play.

The audience was thrilled with the sound. The concert was a huge success; and the president of the concert association sent word backstage requesting me to play on the Wurlitzer as well. I told the audience that I would love to play more for them on the instrument of which they were so justly proud, but that the classical organ and the theatre organ are two very different beasts ("...like a symphony orchestra versus a big band"). Both instruments are wonderful; but, for the most part, they're limited to different literature.

Then I added that my road manager, Andy Crow, could do far more justice to the Wurlitzer than I could; and Andy graciously consented to play. The audience loved him, also, and gave us many standing ovations.

That same evening I extolled the virtues of the electronic organ to the audience, and paid tribute to the wonderful "Black Beauty" (which is what we called her ever since that night, paying tribute to her ebony console that looked as good as any concert piano). The review was also terrific, coming out exactly as Richard had predicted it would!

Rodgers was pleased, of course. CAMI and Community Concerts was pleased. Virgil "got used to it." Moreover, before I "passed" the organ back to him from my tours, I always revoiced the hideous reed, according to his taste. He eventually gave in, however—quietly; and the reed stayed the same for all concerts. (There were some exceptions, when he was in one of his infrequent cantankerous moods.) Community Concerts provided a terrific new venue for all of us fortunate enough to be booked through them. These concerts also paid far more money for presenting us than I had ever known about before.

Andrew Crow, who was hired as a staff organist at the Rodgers Organ Company in 1964, was the first "driver" assigned to transport the Rodgers Touring Organ around the country. He toured with the Rodgers Touring Organ for more than 15 years—but for the first years, only as a driver. With the Worth/Crow Duo, he played 366 mostly Community Concerts throughout North America, composing the musical arrangements for all of the organ duets. Virgil and Ted adored him.

Andrew Crow

My first contact with Virgil Fox was in 1953 when two friends and I crept up to the balcony of the University of Redlands Chapel, where my friends had told me "the greatest organist in the world" would be practicing for a concert the following evening. We sat there, as quiet as mice, until three in the morning. I'd never heard such organ playing in all my life!

Next night, Virgil bounded out, cape and all, to play the concert. We were seated right in front. He had obviously seen us the previous night, for he immediately spotted us and seemed delighted to see us again.

The concert was staggering, all from memory, including the Reubke "Sonata." At one point, he turned his head to us and said, "Kids, listen to this gorgeous part!"

Mercy!

In 1967, I met Virgil again when the Rodgers Organ Company assigned me to drive the truck, trailer, and new touring organ to St. Petersburg, Florida. Virgil was about to play his first concert on the new instrument. The stagehands couldn't believe the size and weight of the console, which was slightly less than 1,800 pounds. There were 14 individual speaker cabinets and two large bass cabinets: one with two 15 inch-speakers, and the other containing a 30-inch speaker for the 32-foot Pedal Bourdon and Principal. All of these speaker cabinets had to be connected to a box containing 16 amplifiers. From there, all the wires went to the console.

Virgil astonished me when he addressed me by name, recalling instantly that it was I who sat directly behind him 14 years earlier at his concert at the University of Redlands when I was a sophomore. (Of course, I had introduced myself when the concert was over.)

Virgil often used to ask me to stand next to him during his practice periods (usually in the wee hours of the morning) in order to push or pull some stops at "just the right moment." He would also have me stand at various places in a room to help him adjust the placement of the speakers for minimal "antiseptic burn," which was a term he used to describe the reflective, stinging electronic sound as it bounced from a cove or wall surface.

I learned more about organ playing from Virgil Fox than from all my years of formal study; and I'm so proud to have had him as my friend. He was the greatest organist in the world, and I loved him very much.

61. Virgil Takes a Break

Community Concerts offered a refreshing change for organists. I began to get 20 concerts per season, then 40, all because of the touring organ.

Shortly after the first successful season of concerts on the Rodgers, Joyce Jones changed from performing on "parlor Baldwins" to playing on Black Beauty, continuing her successful career playing Community Concerts. She surely deserved a better instrument, because she had pioneered the market, thereby blazing the trail for us all.

Of course, as far as Virgil was concerned, his fee was now quite large enough (Richard had been pushing it up, season by season), whether for a church concert or for an AGO chapter event. Virgil had the drawing power, provided enough advertising was done. Although many churches and guild chapters were unaccustomed to paying to advertise in the newspapers and on radio stations, they were almost forced to do so in order to be able to afford to pay Virgil's fees. He therefore became the main draw on their music series, even when his style of playing conflicted with their own ideas about proper "performance practice."

I remember the Detroit Chapter of the AGO wanting to book Virgil—but only on their terms. They wanted him to play a solo concert on the new Ford Auditorium Æolian-Skinner mainly because they knew it would swell their coffers by drawing in the public. They presumptuously demanded that Virgil play only French Romantic works, however, as they believed that his Bach was "unacceptable." According to them, he distorted the line, blew everything out of shape, and completely ignored the proscribed "performance practices" of Bach's time. The truth was that these "purists" were victims of poor academic training. Their theories were flawed, and their knowledge was often inaccurate. In the case of French Romantic organ music, for example, Virgil almost never paid attention to the composer's registrations or the tempo markings. Nevertheless, the "purists" never realized it because they knew so little about the subject, confining most of their critiques to the Baroque era.

The Detroit Chapter asked Virgil to play only Franck, Widor, Vierne, and Dupré—which he certainly could do outstandingly, and did. Virgil agreed to these terms; but at the concert itself, he announced that he would change the program slightly, and he included a large serving of J. S. Bach. Although a dozen or so organists may have cringed in horror, 3,000 people stood up and screamed for more!

Marshall Yaeger

Ted's illustration here is interesting, since it shows that the organists "on the other side" of the controversy that raged throughout the organ world during this era, and that damaged Virgil Fox's reputation in music academies throughout America, thought of their musicianship as "classic" and Virgil's as "Romantic." (They even used to call him a "Romantic.") What is clear to any cultural historian, however, is that these purists' ideas were Romantic in practically every respect when compared to the characteristics of Romanticism and the Romantic movement of the Nineteenth Century—one of the most glaring characteristics of which was a slavish and unrealistic respect for the "past." Most of these purists never bothered to study (much less teach) Romanticism in college. Unfortunately, Virgil didn't study any cultural history either; and so he never quite understood that he had earned a significant chapter in the cultural history of Western Civilization. He only saw the controversy as a conflict between talented outsiders and untalented academicians who hid the limitations of their musical abilities behind intellectual theories that demanded less virtuosity from their performances than Virgil always demanded from his.

Richard Torrence

In 1949, Albert Schweitzer came to the United States (for the first and only time), performing organ recitals in order to raise money for his hospital in Lambaréné. When Virgil met him, he asked, "What is this 'Baroque' organ they talk about?"

Dr. Schweitzer responded, "There is no such thing as a Baroque organ." ("L'orgue baroque n'existe pas!") When Virgil urged Dr. Schweitzer, as the great authority on Bach, to repeat that statement to the world, Dr. Schweitzer responded, "You tell them."

Virgil always kept a copy of Dr. Schweitzer's book, J.S. Bach (Vol. 1) next to his bed for late night reading. He often quoted Dr. Schweitzer about Bach in his concert presentations.

Virgil's schedule continued to expand in all directions as early as 1963. He was in more demand than ever. Richard was dropping hints that Virgil might consider reducing his activities still further at the Riverside Church in order to free up more time for his concert career. Richard even went so far as to suggest that Virgil consider leaving Riverside altogether.

"And leave my beautiful organ? Impossible! That, my dear child, is out of the question!"

At that time, Virgil played only half of the church services, and even less than half of the oratorio performances, as Richard Weagly was more and more inclined to use Fred Swann because of his deteriorating relationship with Virgil. Many fans of Virgil's would telephone the church on Sunday morning to find out who was playing that day. The atmosphere around the church grew chillier, as people began to take sides either with the Weagly/Swann camp, or with Virgil's entourage. Gossip was hot and heavy, though Virgil seemed oblivious to it all. He couldn't believe that those who had been close to him, especially Richard Weagly, would turn on him and foment constant trouble, especially when he was out of town, on tour.

Richard knew exactly what was going on, however. Virgil had definitely become a star, and often a prima donna, but never deserved the kind of abuse the mere mention of his name elicited in some of the more powerful circles around the church. Richard kept bringing up the subject of "life after Riverside" with Virgil, and finally got him to agree to a year's sabbatical "to see if you can stand not being there," as Richard put it.

Virgil agreed; and in the autumn of 1964, the sabbatical began. I plan to ask Richard to write the story behind Virgil's finally leaving Riverside, because he was so much a part of it.

Frederick Swann

In 1957, the senior minister of the Riverside Church, Dr. Robert J. McCracken, asked if I would come to his office at the conclusion of the service. I walked in to see not only Dr. McCracken, but also the chairman of the Music Committee and several church officials. In a rather blunt manner, I was told that because of the legendary feuding between Virgil and Richard Weagly, and the uproar it was causing (sometimes even during a church service!), the church would not renew these two men's contracts—and, by the way, would I agree to take over?

Of course I would not!

A few months later, I received word that the proposed ousting of Messrs. Fox and Weagly had created a revolution in the congregation! It had been determined that the "fault" was Virgil's, and that after much prayer and meditation it had been decided to retain both of them as long as another organist could be hired to do most of the playing.

The only candidate that Virgil and Richard could both agree to was me. Virgil would retain the title of Organist, but play only a third or less of the services and oratorios.

From then on, until 1964, Virgil and I shared the post, both being listed as "Organist."

Our relationship was always cordial and supportive, with almost no problems. However, on a spring Sunday in 1964, Richard and Virgil had a Super Altercation during the service that so enraged Virgil that he pushed on the Full Organ button and launched into a fiery toccata during the choir's a cappella Benediction response (a soft, ethereal series of Amens) from the North Ambulatory.

At that point, two prominent female members of the congregation who hated Virgil charged up to the organ, one to beat his back with her umbrella, and the other to pull him backwards off the bench!

He never finished the piece, and was soon strongly advised to take a sabbatical while things cooled down.

Many years passed before Virgil returned to The Riverside Church to play his final concert on the instrument he loved so much and that he helped create.

Robert Hebble remembers a similar incident.

Robert Hebble

In the mid-1950s, a "Mrs. Green" struck Virgil with a parasol. She was the second wealthiest person in the Riverside Church after Mr. Rockefeller; and despite her deafness, she hated loud organs.

Every year at the campaign for funds, the powers-that-be would ask Virgil to lower the volume just to make sure that Mrs. Green would honor her financial pledge. Virgil would just smirk and make a point of taking off the 4-foot flute in the Echo Organ and nothing else.

Once, when Mrs. Green couldn't take it any longer, she entered the chancel area through the curtained entryway just behind the console.

Beating Virgil on the shoulder with her parasol, she kept screaming, "It's too loud! It's too loud!"

Mrs. Green now lies within the walls of the Riverside Church in a small urn.

Richard Torrence remembers a different situation.

Richard Torrence

During the three years I worked with Virgil at Riverside (from June 1962 to June 1965), Virgil played half of the services and slightly less than half of the oratorios (except during his sabbatical, when he had no duties). He also played several recitals each year, which made him approximately "even" with Fred Swann. (I had to know exactly when and how many services Virgil was responsible for playing in order to schedule his recital bookings.) Fred did, however, earn $100 more each year than Virgil because he took over the administrative duties of the organ department—so Virgil told me.

The idea for Virgil's sabbatical was actually my solution to one of Virgil's career problems, and I had to argue him into it! He simply couldn't find the time to memorize the Poulenc Organ Concerto for an orchestra concert in California. I pointed out that his problem would have been the same for Artur Rubenstein if that great pianist were committed to playing at a piano bar every Friday and Saturday night! Virgil knew how hard I was pushing for him to have a career like Rubenstein's, and he got the point. He soon informed the church that he would take a sabbatical from September 1964 to June 1965. He asked for no salary during that time (it would have been $3,000); but he kept his office, and he continued to use the Riverside organ as his practice instrument.

Midway through the sabbatical, I realized that, after 19 years, the church's "anti-Virgil forces" had finally taken over when I opened a letter from the Music Committee addressed to Virgil, who was vacationing at Anne Archbold's in the Bahamas at the time. The letter briefly accepted Virgil's resignation from the Riverside Church "effective immediately." I called Marshall, who was in Englewood, and read him the letter. He was appalled by how impersonal and brutal a religious institution could be when dealing with a great artist, and he suggested that the situation would undoubtedly warrant a sympathetic article in The New York Times. Specifically, he said, "Threaten the bastards with publicity!"

They backed off immediately, and scheduled a hearing with the committee's chairman (in the executive offices of a New York bank, where he worked). "You've gotten too big for Riverside," this bank officer said. Virgil teared up, but he had to agree that a parting of the ways would be best for everyone. However, he would not announce his resignation until the conclusion of the sabbatical.

As one of the staff people said, "There used to be room for everyone at Riverside: Harry Emerson Fosdick, Dr. McCracken, and Virgil Fox. Now there's only room for one!"

I moved all of Virgil's files, music, his rollaway bed, and my management's office from the fourth floor of the Riverside Church to Virgil's house in Englewood, where we all worked and flourished for another decade. However, many years had to pass before any of us would enjoy again the great music and beauty of the Riverside Church.

62. Virgil Performs with His Toes

Virgil inaugurated the new Æolian-Skinner organ in the venerable Academy of Music, Philadelphia, in the early 1960s. The hall, although beautiful and ornate, was as dead as a doornail, acoustically speaking; and the organ, therefore, was never a success. Nevertheless, Virgil had a real triumph in a solo concert. Because of the acoustics, and also the fact that it moved on and off the stage on carts (which led Æolian-Skinner to emphasize the upper, and therefore less bulky registers of the organ), Virgil thought the instrument to be "rather thin, brittle, and white hot." He was delighted, however, to be able to perform on the stage of the Academy!

Virgil looked forward to appearing again with Ormandy on the new instrument, now that the Academy had a proper organ. It was not to be, however, because of another concert Virgil had played with the Philadelphia Orchestra a season or two before the new Academy organ. It was at the Worcester Festival in Massachusetts. Worcester Auditorium had a fine five-manual Kimball organ—which, although from another era of voicing, was quite grand, and in first class condition. William Smith, the orchestra's gifted associate conductor, was on the podium that evening. Bob Hebble and I were in the audience of several thousand. Eugene Ormandy was also somewhere in the throng. Virgil played the first movement of the Widor *Sixth Symphony*, as arranged for organ and orchestra. It was a knockout performance, and the audience loved it. After the intermission, Virgil played the entire Jongen *Symphonie Concertante*, and there was near pandemonium as the audience erupted into stomping and shouting their approval. Virgil responded with several encores while the orchestra remained on stage, waiting to complete the program. It seemed like a love fest for all concerned; but Virgil extended his welcome by one or two encores too far. The hour was late, and the union-ized musicians would be going into overtime. Virgil was impervious to the problem; and as usual, he felt compelled to give the people what they wanted. Unfortunately, he gave them more.

He also had a new costume for the evening, of which he was proud. It was a gray shantung silk tuxedo, which Bob and I thought was hideous. He loved it, as it made him stand out from the orchestra and conductor, who were in white tie and tails.

Virgil's histrionics at the console that evening were even more dramatic than usual. During orchestra sections, he constantly pulled on stops and couplers, drawing attention to himself in a non-musical way. When he wanted all stops and couplers off, rather than use the general cancel to do the job quickly, he would dramatically lunge like a wild animal, and throw his whole body against the knobs in each division. He became a kind of human General Cancel! Meanwhile, the audience's wild response to his virtuosic performance threw gasoline on the fire, and he pulled every trick he knew to attract attention to himself. This entire non-musical behavior was unnecessary.

When Maestro Ormandy greeted Virgil in the green room after the performance, he exclaimed, "Well, Virgil, you won!" Then, "Virgil, can't you afford the price of a proper set of evening wear?"

Later, telling Bob and me of his encounter with Ormandy, Virgil said, "The old dear was green with envy! They just can't abide an instrument that can stand up to their precious orchestra, or someone who'll really play the damned thing!"

Although Virgil finally started performing with the Philadelphia Orchestra in the Academy of Music on their new Æolian-Skinner organ, it wasn't with Ormandy. Only a guest conductor or William Smith, who loved Virgil, would have him. Virgil would say that "Poor Eugene never got over Worcester," and I could see that he always regretted this fact. Ormandy was surely a giant, and a powerful man in music. He also led the orchestra that Virgil most admired!

I remember attending one rehearsal with the Philadelphia Orchestra in the Academy of Music during the mid-1960s. Virgil was playing the Jongen *Symphonie Concertante,* and had asked me to be there to check the balances. The orchestra was onstage, rehearsing another work. When I met Virgil backstage, he told me he was going out to prepare the console; and so I went out into the house to get ready to listen.

The orchestra played away while Virgil sat in a chair next to the console. He started to change his patent leather shoes (which he used to use for concerts in those pre-rhinestone pump days). However, not only did he change his shoes, he also removed his stockings! Then he pulled out several sheets of toilet paper, which he carefully folded into long, thin strips. All this went on while some of the members of the orchestra watched in disbelief. He began to thread the strips of paper between his toes, first on one foot, and then on the other. He put his stockings back on, and then his shoes, and climbed onto the console bench.

By this time, several members of the orchestra were laughing hysterically! I was amused, too, but also embarrassed for Virgil. I asked him later what in the world his paper winding, toe performance was all about. In all the years I'd known him, I'd never seen such an exhibition.

"I'll not have perspiration between my toes!" he said, emphatically; and then he roared with laughter. I realized that he didn't much care what others thought of him, as long as he stood out on front and center stage.

The performances with organ and orchestra that week included the Saint-Saëns *Organ Symphony* in addition to the Jongen. Thank God, William Smith was conducting, and Ormandy was out of town! The Saint-Saëns went before the Jongen, just before intermission. Although Virgil loved the work, he was always annoyed with having to sit at the console doing and playing nothing for what seemed like an interminable time before the organ entered.

He decided on a bizarre solution. The first evening, as the Saint-Saëns began, the organ console was front and center, just to the right of the conductor and in full view; but there was no one sitting on the bench! I panicked, thinking something had gone wrong. The orchestra was beginning without Virgil! However, a few minutes before the entry of the organ, Virgil appeared and tiptoed across the stage in front of the packed house. He sat down, pressed a piston, and started playing the soft entrance of the organ part.

What that audience must have thought, I can't imagine; but I'm sure they never forgot Virgil's entrance! Probably no other soloist ever pulled such a stunt, before or since!

Obviously, Virgil's constant efforts to find new and startling ways to draw attention to himself were part of his nature. He particularly enjoyed the "chicks'" reactions to these bizarre antics, which usually resulted in irrepressible, audible squeals of laughter.

Virgil loved to laugh and cause laughter of any kind. Now that I think of it, I must admit that our squeaks and squeals may have unwittingly provided more than our share of necessary fuel to cause such a towering genius to light up and shine in such puerile ways.

63. That Hog-Eye-Stink-Crotch!

Despite all these antics with the Philadelphia Orchestra, Virgil finally did have a chance to play with Ormandy in the mid-1970s. After Virgil had become a salable commodity with Heavy Organ, RCA Victor wanted him to perform with the Philadelphia for a new recording of the Saint-Saëns *Organ Symphony*. He was also invited to perform with the orchestra and Ormandy in the Academy of Music before the recording sessions. However, Heavy Organ was booked in Missouri for lots of money. The orchestra arrogantly paid miserable fees to its soloists, and demanded performances at three subscription concerts for a single concert fee! Richard had to turn down the orchestra for the concerts, but he accepted on Virgil's behalf for the recording sessions.

They couldn't use the Academy of Music or its organ for the recording, as the hall was too dry acoustically; and, by that time, the Æolian-Skinner organ was in disrepair from being moved so much on its carts, as well as from lack of use and attention. The Scottish Rite Temple, where the Philadelphia Orchestra usually recorded, was used. Black Beauty was brought in.

Virgil wanted the sessions to be recorded at Yale University's Woolsey Hall on its behemoth E. M. Skinner, which Virgil adored. However, the expense ruled, especially when the fact that Ormandy wouldn't hear of changing the orchestra's sharpened concert pitch of A-443 was taken into account. The Woolsey Hall organ was tuned at the standard A-440; and that specification couldn't be changed, either!

The Scottish Temple was marvelous acoustically; and Black Beauty sounded great. Virgil was delighted, and Ormandy seemed overjoyed at their first rehearsal together. Ormandy proclaimed to the orchestra that Virgil was the greatest and most musical organist in the world, and he claimed that he heard things with Virgil playing the Saint-Saëns that he had never realized were there or ever heard before. (I think Ormandy was thinking of inner voices and of Virgil's interpretation of the organ part, because Virgil was a master of both.)

There is tremendous power and majesty in the big moments on this recording; and rich support in the soft, magic moments. Ormandy was delighted with the results, as was Virgil; and all was forgiven! They spoke of wanting to collaborate again in the future, and finally did perform together one more time at the summer home of the Philadelphia Orchestra in Saratoga Springs, New York.

Richard Torrence

Virgil had demanded that the Rodgers Organ Company pay him for recording the Organ Symphony *on their organ. He said to Jim Walls, the president of Rodgers, "I'm just a prostitute, Dear Boy, and I want to be paid."*

Jim responded, "I'm sorry, Virgil, but we're not in the business of dealing with prostitutes. Make the recording if you like. We'll only supply the organ."

On the other hand, when Virgil's publicist, Alix Williamson, met resistance from Virgil to making a hymn recording on the touring organ, she said, "I'm reminded of a joke, Virgil. This man walked up to a beautiful babe on the street and said, 'Will you go to bed with me for $10,000?' She answered, 'Of course!' Then he said, 'Will you go to bed with me for $1,000?' She thought for a moment, and said, 'Okay.' He said, 'Will you go to bed with me for $10?' She said, 'What do you think I am?' He said, 'We know what you are. We're just negotiating the price!'"

"So how much money do you want to make the album, Virgil?" she asked.

Virgil made the album.

Virgil made his legendary recording of the beloved Wanamaker organ for Command Records in 1964; he asked Richard and me to assist him at the sessions. The combination action on the famous behemoth had ceased to function at least twenty years before. Imagine the largest playing organ in the world, with hundreds and hundreds of stops, and no combination action!

Virgil was well acquainted with the beast, of course. He knew what he wanted and how to get it. He especially loved to improvise on that organ, and run the instrument from pianississimo (triple piano) to quadruple forte simply by opening the crescendo pedal.

Virgil traveled from Englewood to Philadelphia by car several times before the Wanamaker sessions in order to rehearse. It was a revelation to hear him practice on this unique instrument after the store had closed, and to hear many of the magnificent soft stops that were usually inaudible above the din of shoppers and ringing cash registers during store hours.

The recording sessions were arduous, because any extraneous noise could be heard. Some stops wheezed; and there were dead notes here and there despite the heroic efforts of the organ tuner and curator of the Wanamaker organ, and his devoted crew.

This tuner (he's dead now; but I'll name him "Perry" anyway, for reasons that will be evident) was sometimes a little slow for Virgil's requirements. Virgil derided him constantly, despite the fact that the poor, overweight man had devoted his entire life to that organ and had great love and affection for it. Virgil loved to tell the story of how Perry (whose father had been a milliner) was vacuuming the organ one day, and accidentally dropped the vacuum cleaner down the low pipe of the 32-foot wood Diaphone.

"They had to find a whale fisherman to haul it out of there," Virgil roared. (Staffers actually used fish hook and line from the store.)

Richard stood on the right side of the console, and I stood on the left. My side contained the famous String Organ and the Pedal division. Virgil had prepared well for these sessions, and made copious notes in the music for Richard and me to do this or that at specific moments. We usually did them well, after we had fully rehearsed.

The sessions were grueling at first, however. Virgil would record and re-record each piece, hearing a dead note here or there, or an extraneous noise that emanated from the organ or the cavernous Grand Court of the store below. In addition, it was extremely hard for him to play this daunting instrument. The console was too far from the pipes. Therefore, when he depressed a key, the sound didn't begin for almost another second. Articulation was difficult, but Virgil thought he had prepared and chosen his repertoire well.

Virgil expected that the first night of recording would be a breeze. For example, he thought he could record the Mulet toccata, "Thou Art the Rock," in one or two takes; but I saw the hair on the back of his head stick straight up when someone in the control room announced, "Take 29!"

"Must those people announce the number of takes each time? I mean, really!"

Then he'd light into Perry (privately, to us): "That hog-eye-stink-crotch! How dare he leave this stop sounding that way? Well, his father was only a cap maker!"

Richard stepped in after the first nearly disastrous evening, and on the second night, we recorded every piece in exactly two takes. The "Come, Sweet Death" of Bach was ravishing, of course; and the "Liebestod" from *Tristan and Isolde* will never be played better!

During non-recording times, Virgil reminisced about the first time he ever played the Bach chorale, "Come, Sweet Death," on this great instrument.

"Kids, in those days there was much more resonance in the room; and the full organ was much more powerful! There were none of those miles and miles of that filthy, heavy green velour hanging from the ceiling to deaden the sound!"

Command Records managed to capture extraordinarily fine sounds on their recording; and Virgil was extremely proud of the Wanamaker album that resulted. Moreover, we celebrated when the album was finally finished.

After we had been entering and leaving the Wanamaker console through the stock room in the women's shoe department constantly, Virgil decided that he, Richard, and I should try on some of the shoes. I think he simply wanted to generate some mirth by seeing how ridiculous we'd look; but I also think he was interested in finding out what it was like to play a pedal organ in high-heels, which the noted woman organist, Jeanne Demessieux, was famous for doing. We then proceeded to jam our feet into several pairs of the largest and most expensive shoes by Delman. (When Virgil recognized the label, he insisted we all try on only the best!)

After hobbling around in a pair of stiletto evening pumps, he said, "I wonder if I can play like Jeanne Demessieux did." He then proceeded to the console, and did a credible job (although I think he wrecked the shoes in the process). He then went into the women's clothing department to find a nice mink coat and a sequined handbag to complete the picture.

We were completely out of control with laughter when we heard approaching footsteps and the menacing growl of a fierce-sounding animal. The store was patrolled at night by armed guards accompanied by vicious German Shepherd attack dogs. We sobered up quickly, and Virgil calmly faced the gruff-looking guard and announced, standing as proud and tall as he could in high heels, "We thought we'd try on a few of these lovely things. Ho! Ho! Ho!"

As he ran to return the coat and handbag to its proper place, the guard replied, "Yes, lovely!" and mercifully went on his way leading the dog.

"Kids, let's get out of here!"

We made a fast retreat, throwing the shoes and boxes back into the stock room, and later shrieking at the thought of the puzzled faces of the staff when they found three pairs of pushed-out-of-shape shoes with broken heels!

Richard Torrence

We had exactly three nights in Philadelphia's John Wanamaker store to make the historic recording on the organ that had helped establish Virgil's career many years before.

The first night was spent entirely on hanging microphones in the vast Grand Court. No recording was done except for sound tests.

On the second night, Virgil started to record the first piece on the album (the "Nocturne" from Fauré's "Incidental Music for Shylock").

"Roll the tape," Virgil told the engineers.

"Take One," came back the response.

Not much later, when we heard "Take 38!", Ted put his hand over his mouth to stifle an audible shriek.

"Shut up, Brat!" Virgil snapped.

Tension hung in the air. It took two more hours to record the "Shylock," and then another two pieces (the Mulet toccata that Ted refers to above, and Vierne's "Carillon de Westminster"). At that rate, we'd never finish!

Virgil was a wreck. He had recorded less than a third of the album, and there was only one more night to go. Not only were we wasting valuable time, but also Command Records was using the most expensive recording process ever devised! (The record was made on 35mm sprocketed magnetic tape, run unusually fast.) All costs would be deducted from Virgil's future royalties.

That night I lay awake. I remembered how much easier Virgil's Lincoln Center recording had been. Virgil had played most of the pieces in his concert at Philharmonic Hall only two weeks before the recording sessions. Thus, he had them all at "concert pitch."

I theorized that the ideal recording process for an orchestra would be to play a piece complete, and to everyone's satisfaction, before beginning to record. Given that idea and the Lincoln Center experience, I imagined a new system that required a perfect run-through (with the console assistants) of a specific work before turning on the tape. (Virgil had gotten into the habit of saying, "Go ahead and tape. Maybe we'll get something." It meant he wasn't ready. By trying to speed things up, he slowed them down.)

Next day, I asked Virgil to allow me to run the sessions. He said, "I'm at my wit's end! I'll do anything!"

The engineers didn't want to sit around and do nothing while Virgil perfected his performances; but my arguments prevailed. Virgil carefully rehearsed each piece with Ted and me assisting. We ended up recording each piece twice. On the third and final day, we completed the final two-thirds of the album!

From then on, Virgil used the system for all the recordings in which I was involved. Ted also used it.

It always worked!

---

64. Molto Bellissimo

The new organ for St. Mary's, Wayne was scheduled to arrive in the early fall of 1966. During the late spring, I had gone to Italy on behalf of the church to see and hear the instrument as it neared completion. Traveling by train from Milan through the north of Italy was magic; and by the time Francesco Ruffatti had taken me on a tour of Venice and then driven me to the medieval city of Padua, I was intoxicated. The food, architecture, works of art, and atmosphere astounded me.

The Ruffatti factory was a revelation. Two-thirds of the instrument for St. Mary's was up and playing. The console, one of my chief worries, was perfect and handled like a dream. Everything was in the right place, and everything was first rate. It was elegant to look at, and it "felt" elegant! The twenty-five rank instrument they had built for the National AGO Convention in Atlanta was also set up and playing. The compact two-manual console was set up in front of the simple, handsome case that enclosed the entire instrument. It was a knockout! The organ for the Atlanta Convention was the first organ they shipped to the United States; it had to be in place and voiced before the convention began, in late June. The factory was jammed to capacity with the organ for St. Mary's, the convention organ, and the final section of a five-manual instrument they were completing for the Cathedral of Monreale in Palermo. Behind the case of the Atlanta organ was the elaborate façade of an ancient Italian Renaissance organ they were restoring. It was painted gold and various shades of green—stunning. Every place I looked I saw treasures, including beautifully decorated, small choir organs dating from the 1600s and 1700s.

Papa Ruffatti took me on tours to show me the wood that was used for consoles, chests, and pipes. He had personally selected these fine aged woods; and there was an enormous, high room where great wooden slabs were kept. Then we went on to the chest makers, the wooden pipe makers, and so forth. I remember one veteran artisan in the woodworking department constructing a large-scale 16-foot open wood pipe. He was sanding around the large mouth of the pipe, and I noticed as he worked that both his left and right thumbs were greatly enlarged and flattened. They looked like a fifty-cent piece had been inserted inside his thumbs. He had a look of absolute devotion on his face as he worked on the wooden pipe. He must have done this work for at least 30 years. I smiled and said *"Molto bellissimo"* although I didn't speak Italian. *"Bellissimo"* would have sufficed; but I liked to add *molto*, correct or not, to show my appreciation.

Papa indicated that I shouldn't smile at the workers. It might distract them from their work, and such distractions weren't tolerated. He was obviously the ruler of the entire place; and everyone held him in high esteem because it was his custom to work harder and longer than two of his workers combined. He was known to all as *"Principale."* I couldn't help myself from smiling at all of the workers, however, to show my complete delight and appreciation for their craftsmanship; and I continued to do so—much to the displeasure of Francesco and *"Principale"*!

One day, Papa Ruffatti selected the metal to boil down in order to make the sheets of tin, zinc, and other alloys for the metal pipes.

This operation was part of the pipe-making process, which was entirely in his domain. He took me first to a room that contained piles of silver-colored ingots. They looked like the gold bricks stored in Fort Knox. He chose several types of ingots, and ordered them carried to a large boiling caldron where they were deposited in the giant pot to liquefy. Sometime later, he prepared long slabs of marble covered with cloth. When the molten metal had reached the desired temperature, he poured a generous amount on the surface of the cloth-covered marble with a large ladle. Then, with what looked like a giant rolling pin, he rolled out a large sheet of gleaming, spotted tin. He then checked the sheet for the desired amount of thickness and uniformity. He obviously enjoyed this exacting work, and went on to produce more large sheets of pipe metal. The sheets then went to the various pipe artisans for cutting, shaping, and the painstaking work of soldering pipes of 32-, 16-, 8-, and even the tiny 1-foot length pipes, the smallest of which are the size of a small lead pencil, which appeared to me to be incredibly difficult to shape. Nevertheless, all the solder seams looked perfect. Then came the painstaking work of getting each of these pipes to speak at the correct pitch, and to speak promptly with the right speech characteristics.

I had never realized how much hard labor in so many departments—console, chests, design, structure, wind chests, pipe making, and voicing—is required to build a fine pipe organ. The attitude of the artisans was rewarding to observe, for they obviously took pride in their creations. In those days, there were about one hundred workers at the factory. They enjoyed their obligatory afternoon nap after the noonday meal in a large dormitory-style room. Then they would work until 7:30 p.m., and a half-day on Saturdays. Nowadays, however, this schedule has changed in Padua. The workers follow a more American schedule.

The Ruffattis treated me like a king. Mrs. (Costantina) Ruffatti was a lovely, gracious host, and a sensational cook! Francesco was my lifesaver and guide, and took good care of me. It seemed we were always eating. The food was magnificent! Whether at breakfast every morning at the Café Pedrocchi, (which is the oldest café in the world, where we would drink cappuccino and eat brioche in the outside terrace), or for lunch at country inns in the hills surrounding Padua, everything was tasty and fine. Francesco's brother, Piero, was in the Italian Army at that time; and so I didn't meet him until a year later.

The Ruffattis produced a concert for me on one of their new instruments, near Florence at the Cathedral of Prato. There were handsome posters advertising the concert all over town. Francesco had worked with the Prato Tourist Bureau; and this concert, which was also the inaugural concert of the new Ruffatti organ, was well publicized and an important affair. I felt like a star playing my European debut!

The Cathedral of Prato was a magnificent 15th Century structure set in the middle of the main square. It boasted an outdoor pulpit by Donatello, several Della Robbias, and incomparable frescoes by Fillipo Lippi. The exterior and interior were made of alternating layers of green and white marble. The main floor extended to several levels, each one three or four steps higher than the other, leading ever upward to the high altar. I spent several days practicing on the new Ruffatti, which sounded elegant in the reverberant acoustics. Between the breathtaking surroundings of the Cathedral, and the seemingly endless fabulous meals that Francesco hosted, I felt I was in quite another world.

The concert took place at 9:30 p.m. Much to my amazement, the Cathedral was filled with over two thousand people! I got favorable press in the Florence newspapers, which provided my first European reviews. Both Richard and Virgil were delighted to hear of my success, and they wanted to hear all about Italy the minute I reluctantly returned after three weeks. Virgil was particularly interested in the organ in Prato, and, of course, the organ for Wayne. He had never played a formal concert in Italy, and I think he was a little jealous that I had gotten to play one before he did.

He also appeared envious when I related the details of a short trip I had taken with Francesco to nearby Treviso, to see an organ in a prominent residence: the villa of the world famous tenor, Mario del Monaco! We drove up to ornate gates, and announced ourselves through a telephone. The gates swung open, and we drove down a long, sweeping driveway lined on either side with cypress trees. The villa appeared, and we entered a circular driveway and parked the car near the garage. There were several Mazerattis, Lamborginis, and a Rolls Royce parked there. (It appeared that the world famous singer loved fast and expensive cars!)

Del Monaco greeted us at the door, and asked what we would like to drink. Then in his middle to late fifties, he was a strikingly handsome, fit man, with an expansive personality and ebullient sense of humor. The villa was enormous, impressively beautiful, and crawling with servants. We took a tour, including the ballroom, which had walls of velvet and a marble floor. A two-manual Ruffatti organ was at the far end of the ballroom; and it had a lovely façade framed by two Baroque cupids. The organ wasn't large, but it had an appropriately singing tone. Del Monaco loved hearing the organ, and he apparently enjoyed my playing! We had light refreshments, met his charming wife, Teodora, and he autographed a picture for me. He handed me his card, with several more addresses (a residence in Rome, an apartment in Paris, etc.), and told me he would like to collaborate with me and perform some church concerts in the United States some day! I nearly fell over! Surely, I was dreaming!

The visit only lasted two hours, but it was a thrill. (I think it was the prospect of concerts with del Monaco in America that made Virgil envious, but he need not have worried. Del Monaco passed away before any collaboration became possible.)

65. The Atlanta Doyennes

The Ruffattis delivered the twenty-five rank display organ we specified for the AGO National Convention in Atlanta in June 1966. During the convention, which was a gala affair, there were several mini-concerts on the instrument; and a famous teacher, Mildred Andrews, gave several master classes using the instrument. We later sold the instrument to a church in Canton, Ohio, which seemed to please Virgil. He was always eager to know how much commission we got, thinking we were all becoming instant millionaires! (He was woefully off the mark!)

Virgil performed the best concert at the convention. It took place at a Jewish Temple on Peachtree Street, on a fine Æolian-Skinner organ. Virgil's close and dear friend, Emilie Parmalee Spivey, was the organist there. She arranged to have him play his convention concert there. The instrument was surely the best organ in Atlanta at the time. Virgil knew the instrument well. The temple was jammed for the concert. It was a hot and humid July, and Virgil insisted on playing his usual marathon program, although the church wasn't air-conditioned. He couldn't be seen, which was probably just as well. Even in his shirtsleeves, he was soaking wet. He constantly had to wipe himself off with Turkish towels because of the hot and sticky weather. (He had made a deal with the convention program committee that if the day of the concert was hot, the concert would be moved to an air-conditioned building. But he so preferred the Temple organ to any alternatives, he decided the concert would take place there nonetheless.) The top sections of the windows throughout the auditorium were open in hopes of a breeze; but the open air brought in traffic noises that annoyed Virgil. He instructed David to go around the room and close the windows just before the soft passages, and open them just before the loud—to the horror of the wilting audience! I saw several people (including E. Power Biggs) make a hasty retreat at intermission. Nevertheless, those who braved the Turkish bath conditions were treated to vintage Fox, and a heroic Reubke "Sonata."

During the convention, Florence Candler, another one of Virgil's old and dear friends in Atlanta, gave a great reception for Virgil at the Capital Cities Club, which had a posh country club. Florence was well known in Atlanta; and she was eccentric. Several days before, she had asked Richard and me to the reception with, "You'll get all you want to eat; but if you want alcohol, you'll have to have plenty before, because I'm not serving any booze! You know how Virgil feels about booze! Besides, it won't cost me as much if I don't serve liquor!"

Florence was the second wife of Asa G. Candler Jr., son of the founder of Coca-Cola. While Mr. Candler was alive, the couple owned one of the largest and grandest houses in Atlanta. Inside was a four-manual pipe organ of 100 ranks that Virgil had played many times. Florence was a hoot, and could be great fun. Sometimes she was almost crude in her social behavior, which endeared her even more to Virgil! He enjoyed her eccentricities and loud outbursts.

Virgil's other favorite person in Atlanta was clearly Emilie Spivey. Emilie was a comely, gracious, and talented woman. She was immaculately groomed, and she dressed stunningly. She was also a first-rate organist and choir director. For many years, she had been the organist and choir director of the opulent North Avenue Presbyterian Church in Atlanta (in addition to her duties at The Temple). She was married to Walter B. Spivey, a prominent dentist; and they lived in the suburb of Jonesboro. She hardly needed to play the organ for a living, for they were wealthy. They had purchased acres of land in Jonesboro, and built a large manmade lake, which they ran for years as a successful recreation park, called Lake Spivey.

They had a fabulous French-style house on a choice piece of property overlooking the lake. It was there that Virgil often stayed when he went to Atlanta. Emilie had studied with Virgil on and off when she visited New York. Virgil was so impressed with her playing that he invited her to give a concert at the Riverside Church! The concert went quite well, and it had to be one of the highlights of her life. She had been honored as "Woman of the Year in Music" in Atlanta, and enjoyed everyone's friendship. She adored Virgil, and was equally gracious and loving to Richard and me. She was as loyal as they come, and God help anyone who made snide or uncomplimentary comments about her dear Virgil! She had a lot to do with keeping the love of the organ alive in Atlanta.

After Walter and Emilie had run Lake Spivey for several years, they decided it was too much work for them; and so they sold most of the property, including the park and the lake itself. Soon after it was sold, rock'n'roll impresarios held enormous concerts on the site, the decibel levels of which nearly drove Walter and Emilie crazy. As providence would have it, the rock promoters got into financial trouble and the property reverted back to the Spiveys. At that point, Emilie and Walter began to develop the property for high-priced lakeside homes. They also owned hundreds of acres around nearby Lake Jodeco, which they developed in the same way. In all these negotiations, Emilie proved that a dear, sweet, demure, southern belle could also be a smart and savvy businesswoman as well as a talented musician with considerable gifts.

By this time, with all their lakefront property, the Spiveys were "loaded." Virgil never ceased trying to find out just how much money they had, and how he could get his hands on some of it for his many projects—especially his life-long pipe dream of owning a large touring organ. With Black Beauty at his disposal, however, he had calmed down considerably.

66. False Alarm!

The fall of 1967 saw the arrival of the new 60-rank Ruffatti for Saint Mary's Episcopal Church in Wayne. Papa Ruffatti, Francesco Ruffatti, and seven workers from the factory descended on my little carriage house. (I had offered them housing as a condition of the contract.) By that time, Father Kier, St. Mary's zany and wonderful rector, had lent me the money for the down payment on the beautiful old carriage house, which included an acre of wooded property. He was determined to keep me there! The former owners removed the furniture we had used while renting the house; and so it was now quite utilitarian to say the least, with garden furniture and other temporary movables. My good friend, Bill Marsh, was my long-suffering (and well-entertained!) roommate; and he was patient and understanding when the Italians invaded.

The living room looked like a dormitory with rented beds, but no one seemed to care. Papa Ruffatti and his troops worked hard, and the organ was up and playing in no time. Francesco was worried about his father's health, as *Principale* always worked too hard, lost weight, or developed some other nuisance condition that didn't deter him for a second. Whenever he was not working, he was busy socializing. Many parish members wanted to have him and Francesco for dinner. Papa was an especially attractive guest; and he had no trouble communicating by means of his European manners if not through his language. He was an excellent salesperson and public relations department in one.

It soon became evident that the workers were homesick and disliked being away from their families for such a long period. Final voicing of the pipes in the church was a problem. Since I spoke no Italian, it was difficult for me to communicate to the Italian voicers exactly what I wanted. The unusually dry acoustics of the room didn't help, either. Richard, Francesco, and I decided that Ruffatti should employ American voicers. We were striving for the American sound. Therefore, *Principale* reluctantly agreed that in the future we would use American installers. We then set out to locate the best people possible to voice the organ at St. Mary's, Wayne.

The famous flue voicer, Allen Van Zoeren, and the young reed voicer, Jack Steinkampf, joined us from New York. Then the gifted, young Roger Hardesty, who had taken loving care of the Æolian-Skinner organ at St. Mark's, Frankford became their able assistant who would be trained to handle future maintenance of St. Mary's, Wayne after the organ was finally installed.

Virgil was pleased to hear the good comments about our progress. Down deep, however, I suspect he may have thought that Richard and I had lost our minds at backing an Italian organ!

Actually, the only real difficulty we had with the entire project was the tremolos. They were awful! I had warned them that the "motor boat" type of tremulants would not be acceptable. Papa Ruffatti assured me that after his modifications they would be effective, adjustable, and noiseless. Every day Papa would make further modifications, and every day he would ask my opinion. *"No bene!"* I would reply. Crestfallen, he would go off and try again. By the sixth or seventh day of breaking his heart with *"No bene,"* he threw up his hands and agreed to have all new E.M. Skinner-type tremolos built by some friends of our American voicers. They were fine— just what the doctor ordered. The Ruffattis learned their tremolo lesson quickly, and never produced the "motor boat" type again! Every day I had been thinking of Virgil, and how he would want to find the trems!

The organ of Saint Mary's was opened in 1967 with a Festival Choral Evensong Dedication Service that used my choir of men and boys, the herald trumpeters from Valley Forge Military Academy, two Bishops, and a legion of clergy. There were bells and smells (lots of incense) and high drag galore, copes for days, and two mitres! One amusing incident happened while I was playing a short organ recital before the service. The Reverend Albert Fischer and his wife Betty (the very rector that fired me from St. Mark's, Frankford!) were in the front row. Albert caused a stir because he smelled smoke and was afraid the church was on fire! St. Mark's, Frankford was low in its churchmanship; and incense was unthinkable there, while it was the norm at St. Mary's. What he smelled was the incense being prepared in the sacristy which was right near his seat. It didn't stop him from going into the sacristy to report the fire!

Marshall Yaeger

Ted wasn't in the congregation before the service began, and so his memory failed him on this point (although the way he tells the story was definitely better). In the interests of history, I have to admit that it was I who smelled the smoke and was delegated by some others who sat nearby to go into the sacristy to report the fire!

67. Buckingham-on-Fox

Father Kier was thrilled with the evensong. Immediately after the Purvis "Psalm 150," which was a boisterous and jazzy affair that ended with a terrific crash from the organ, tympani, brass, and cymbals, he shouted to the congregation, "So how'd ya like that?" Father Kier was a character, and I adored him.

Virgil's inaugural concert on the new organ was stunning, and he loved the instrument. The church was packed, and the audience demanded five encores. My own concert went well to an equally filled church. The organ, Virgil, and I got favorable press from the Philadelphia newspapers.

"Ted's spaghetti organ" led us all into a new world, and eventually had an impact on Virgil's career.

Richard Purvis had been at St. Mary's a few days before the dedication to hear the choir and brass rehearse the setting of the 150th Psalm he graciously composed for the occasion. Unfortunately, he couldn't remain for the service because he had to get back to San Francisco and his duties at Grace Cathedral.

While he was in Wayne, he also inspected the new organ. In particular, he examined the new console; for a new console was badly needed for the famous and noble Æolian-Skinner at Grace Cathedral. Purvis was favorably impressed, and shortly after the opening of St. Mary's new Ruffatti, we signed a contract to build a new five-manual console for Grace Cathedral in San Francisco!

Another visitor to the new organ in Wayne was another San Franciscan, Father (later Monsignor) Robert F. Hayburn, the Archdiocesan Director of Music. He was in charge of purchasing a large instrument for the yet-to-be-built Roman Catholic cathedral. (The building finally constructed was the now-famous architectural wonder, St. Mary's Cathedral.) I had known Monsignor Hayburn since I was a chorister at Grace Cathedral. Wonder of wonders, we landed that remarkable project as well! Thus, in a few years, the Ruffattis were on their way to becoming major players in the American organ scene!

Things in New York were constantly changing. In 1964, Richard and Marshall had moved from the Cambridge in New York to Virgil's mansion in Englewood. On the second floor, in the half that

Richard Weagly had occupied, they created a gracious apartment for themselves. Then, when David was clearly going to stay, and the conflict between Richard and David escalated, Richard decided, in 1965, to move into one of the rental units in the Englewood carriage house. Shortly afterwards, Virgil offered to renovate a large area of the carriage house that was contiguous to the small rental unit. The corporate offices of WTM, Inc. would be located there as well. Richard created a wonderful and spacious apartment out of the small rental unit, which included the potting shed for the greenhouse that was attached to the carriage house, one of the heated garage spaces, and the coal bin that had once contained all the coal to heat both the carriage and main houses (through an underground conveyor belt that became unnecessary when oil furnaces were installed in both structures).

Everything was first-rate and done with taste. Virgil chafed at the cost, but kept his word and paid like a slot machine in order to keep Richard and Marshall close by! After the project was finished, Virgil would insist that all of his guests in the main house had to go and visit. Virgil always called their place "Buckingham Palace."

Shortly after the renovation at the carriage house, Virgil decided to build something for himself, and that what he most wanted and needed was an indoor swimming pool. He loved swimming, and always complained that the Riverside Church lacked one thing that St. Bartholomew's Church had: a swimming pool. Of course, Virgil didn't want a small pool, but an Olympic-size pool—at least in length. Since, when he swam, he was almost always alone, he figured he didn't need to pay for a wide pool; and so the result was a 70- by 20-foot strip that many thought looked like a ribbon of water. (I christened it "Fox River.") The room surrounding the pool was made out of cinder blocks that were unrelieved by any attempt at refinement. Virgil had engaged the service of a Florida contractor that he had heard was cheap. The result was architecturally undistinguished.

The street side of the building was solid cinder block. On the other side were large sliding glass doors; and covering everything was a glass and metal ceiling that was supposed to open and shut at the touch of a button to let in sunlight or air as the season permitted. The two-story affair was attached to the guestroom above the house's port–cochere, which allowed one to enter from the house itself via a stairway leading down. There was a seating area inside the sliding glass doors; but it was so narrow, one had to walk carefully to navigate down that side of "Fox River."

Nevertheless, Virgil was delighted with his new water works, and used the pool quite often whenever he was in residence. Swimming took place after he practiced the organ, usually from 2:00 a.m. to 4:00 a.m. If any of us were around, he invariably called us to join him. (David didn't like the pool as much as Virgil—and Virgil got lonely.) Virgil usually swam nude; but he always wore a bathing cap. When mixed groups were around, he wore colorful bathing suits; and he loved to show off his "excellent figure for a man of my years."

During the summer months of those years, Virgil was always interested in earning additional income, as concerts weren't so plentiful during the summer. "It costs a fortune to run this emporium," he would say—and indeed, it did. The house was always in need of plumbing, heating, or roof work; and now the pool required upkeep. The cost of heating the pool became a huge extravagance. Virgil insisted that the water temperature be kept at 85 or 90 degrees, winter or summer. It didn't help that the roof leaked, letting out valuable heat in the cold Eastern winters. The Florida contractor hadn't realized the special needs of Northern New Jersey. Apparently, David damaged the movable roof several times until it permanently froze in a closed position. Many times the pool building became so hot and humid inside that it actually rained real drops!

The swimming pool adjacent to the house in Englewood, New Jersey

Richard Torrence

In the early 1960s, Virgil met Huntington Hartford, who was an heir to the A&P fortune. "Hunt" was building his Gallery of Modern Art on Manhattan's Columbus Circle, and he wanted Virgil to be the organist. (An Æolian–Skinner organ was to be installed in one of the exhibition spaces.) As Virgil was no longer going to be at the Riverside Church, he thought it was lovely that a rich man would provide him with a Manhattan "drawing room."

Hartford made Virgil the Gallery's director of music, and I was in charge of the organ concerts that took place several times a month.

When it came time to dedicate the new organ, Hunt asked Virgil what he would play for the opening event, which was to benefit the Abu-Simbel project in Egypt. "How about playing some Egyptian music?" he asked.

Virgil said, "Well, there haven't been a lot of Egyptian composers who wrote for the organ."

"What about Aïda?" Hunt shot back.

Virgil played the "Triumphal March" from Verdi's opera at the opening performance.

---

68. Don't Pee in the Pool!

Virgil decided to run a series of master classes as he had done in earlier years at the Riverside Church. He held them at the great house in Englewood. "They all want to see the house, they can swim in the pool, gawk at the grounds, and pay me a fortune for the privilege!" A mailing was sent out to Virgil's fans, and many people were interested. In the end, around thirty dedicated Fox fans each shelled out money for four to six sessions during the summer. The classes were to begin at the unheard-of early hour (for Virgil) of 2:30 p.m. Virgil was never on time, and so they usually began around 4:00 p.m.

The members of the class were widely different in their playing abilities, which, overall, were disappointing. Many of them chose only to audit, just in order to bask in the sunshine of getting close to their idol. In addition, some exceptionally talented people attended the classes regularly.

Michael Stauch

Virgil used to say to his students, "Your performance should be twice as good as you 'play' the piece." What he meant was that besides hitting the right notes at the right time, the organ presented many other difficulties as well as vitally important opportunities not possible on any other musical instrument.

For example, there's the whole subject of registration, of which Virgil was the undisputed master (although Ted Worth was sometimes his equal). Besides selecting the "colors" of the sounds (of which Virgil was extremely conscious), Virgil always concentrated on an entire bag of tricks that could enunciate the music. Some of these devices included phrasing and different styles of accenting notes, for example. He envisioned music as the sum total of all the expressive musical devices he could bring to a piece, and he knew how arduously and long he had to practice the music in order to achieve his goal.

You often hear, "Talent does what it can, while genius does what it must." Virgil always knew exactly what he wanted the music to say (with no lame excuses about what he thought a dead composer "really wanted"); and he always struggled exactly as hard as he needed to in order to make the music say no less than he knew it must.

To watch Virgil play the organ was a life-altering experience. I can only describe my impression that this man could actually unite and become one with an organ console. For me, in his case, there was no separation.

Virgil tried his best to give personal attention to each person, regardless of their talent or level of artistry. He taught simple rules of pedaling, the rudiments of hymn playing, and how to approach the major works of Bach and the French Romantics. He also taught the proper orchestral approach to accompanying Mendelssohn's Elijah, *the Brahms* Requiem, *and Handel's* Messiah.

These lengthy sessions were often interspersed with singing lessons! Virgil loved to give singing lessons—especially to major singers, whether they wanted it or not! (He knew Leontyne Price, for example, when she was a professional singer in the Riverside choir; did he give her lessons? He insisted on coaching her ex-husband, the great baritone William Warfield, when he and Virgil made a Capitol record together!) In his master classes, Virgil taught organists how to get the most out of choristers, especially soloists. Sharing tips for training soloists gave Virgil the opportunity to demonstrate his own techniques of singing. He produced, thereby, one of the strangest and funniest sounds I had ever heard come forth from a human being. He had convinced himself that he had a fine singing voice. To the rest of us, he sounded like a braying animal. It wasn't that he didn't know exactly what he wanted; it was that his formidable vocal demonstration was unselfconsciously terrible. You could hear his noises all over the property!

Carlo Curley

The execrable sounds of Virgil's vocal efforts aside, I've never met a greater proponent of the art of voice leading than Virgil. His execution in this department was tremendously inspiring. To this day, I'm annoyed when I travel and hear organists who haven't the slightest sense of how to phrase the dear old pedal line. Every note is laughably separated—painfully détaché. It's as if the first three voices of the fugue played on the manuals are of international importance on which great care is lavished while the pedal line skips along in broken half-splendor as though an irritating afterthought. I remember how Virgil used to dig his "claw" into my arm while "busting a gusset" as some hapless organist treated the voice leading pedal line with unforgivable contempt.

Virgil was annoyed that neither Richard, Bob, nor I attended the classes. "You kids could learn something you know! And you don't have to pay!" We would occasionally appear in the back of the music room to listen for a while, and then head out to the carriage house to spend time with Richard and Marshall. We had lots of fun at Richard's, eating and—I'm ashamed to say—making fun of some of the eccentrics who attended the master classes.

There was usually an afternoon break for light refreshments and swimming. Virgil laid down rules when it came to using the pool, however. He was not going to have folks traipsing through the house; and he would only permit the changing of clothes in the bathroom off the port-cochere on the main floor. Since this small room was only a powder room that contained neither a bath nor a shower, Virgil insisted that before people enter the pool, they hose themselves off with the garden hose connected to the outside of the building. His most important exhortation was: "Don't you dare pee in my pool! I've had a special solution added to the water. If you urinate, the water all around you turns red!" The first time we heard him issue this serious warning, we ran screaming into Richard's apartment; for Virgil himself was close to guffawing at his own ridiculousness.

When it came time for refreshments, soft drinks were made available. They cost fifty cents per bottle. Straws were five cents extra. Cookies were free, as some of the students chipped in with edible donations. Often, Richard took pity and baked a pound cake or two!

One summer, Virgil installed Black Beauty in the house for an evening concert featuring some of the more brilliant students. Arnold Ostlund performed, as did Carlo Curley, whom I met at this per-

The Æolian console of Virgil Fox's four-manual organ in Englewood, New Jersey
(Photo by John Littlewood)

Some of the wind lines, cables, and reservoirs of Virgil Fox's home organ tended to intrude on the graciousness of his furniture arrangements

formance for the first time. Carlo, who was just as jovial and outgoing then as he is today, had been studying privately with Virgil, paid for by his patron and Virgil's good friend, Florence Candler. Arnold played the complete set of *Three Preludes and Fugues* of Marcel Dupré with great virtuosity; and Carlo brilliantly performed Bach's "Toccata, Adagio and Fugue." Carlo was a large individual; and Virgil thought it was amazing that he could play the pedals so brilliantly with such immense feet.

Virgil behaved like a mother hen around his students. His concerns went way beyond just the musical aspects of their careers. He was especially concerned about their appearance and deportment. He used to warn them about the importance of first impressions.

Albert Fuller is a harpsichordist, a long-time Juilliard School faculty member, and author of Alice Tully: An Intimate Portrait.

Albert Fuller

At the beginning of the Second World War, when Virgil was at Fort Meyer, he played recitals from time to time at the Washington

Cathedral. One Sunday, among other stuff, he played Reger's hugeosity on "How Brightly Shines the Morning Star." He hadn't had time to memorize it, and I was asked to turn pages. When he finished, I saw that he was soaked with sweat, and his army uniform was covered with wet splotches.

He turned to me and asked me to hand him the pile of dark cloth lying on a chair nearby. When I picked it up, I found it immense. One side was covered in scarlet silk, and I wondered what the devil it was.

He instructed me to hold up one end and put it around his shoulders.

Aha! Now I realized it was a cape! I instantly asked, "Sergeant Fox, Sir, why do you wear a cape?"

He looked me straight in the eye and said, "Honey, they see you before they hear you!"

Oh, yeah, I thought; that's right!

As I write this, I'm in the midst of my 38th year at the Juilliard School, and I can honestly say that I've told every one of my students never to forget: "They see you before they hear you! Got it?"

Virgil wanted everyone to dress nicely and to look clean and well cared for. The idea of body odor ("stinking to high heaven," as he would put it) to anyone who took as many baths as Virgil, and doused himself with as many splashes of Bonwit Teller Private Label and other exotic scents, was unacceptable. He would tell someone right immediately. "Honey! You stink!"

Carlo Curley

To provide a crystal-clear example of the documented forth-rightness of Virgil Fox: several years after we met, a recommendation he gave led to my appointment as College Organist at Philadelphia's Girard College. One late afternoon he arrived to visit the Chapel on what must have been the hottest day of the year, during which I had been holding notes and running up-and-down zillions of stairs for the tuner since late morning, perspiring like mad in sauna-like conditions. Rest assured that my deodorant had failed miserably and, after a hug of Herculean proportions and an hour or so of reminiscing and playing this inspirational instrument, Virgil took me to one side and said in the most pronounced of stage whis-

pers (clearly heard by those assembled round the console), "Chicken, I'm the only person who can say this to you: Soap and water are practically free! Use them!"

At that moment I desired not only a bar of Ivory and a tub but that a large fissure in the cool, stone floor would crack open so that I could vanish forever into a sudsy nether-region. He let out a sudden mad-cackle giggle that made it obvious that his frank pronouncement had been proffered in absolute friendship.

I raced off to cleanse. The organ playing and dinner-party that followed were memorable. Give me strength! I was not yet twenty years old.

Heaven help anyone with bad breath! Virgil was constantly cleaning his teeth with a toothbrush he carried in his coat pocket. He would ceremoniously cover his mouth with his hand at meals and go right to it; or he would go into the nearest lavatory and rinse out his mouth. Concerning some poor victim of halitosis, he would say, "Well kids, it's no wonder the poor thing has bad breath. Did you see those green teeth? Why, it looks like there's a garden growing in there!" To one hapless pupil he said, "Honey, you simply have got to do something about those teeth. They look like shattered glass!" Even the divine David didn't escape the Great Man's criticism, right in front of him and everyone else. "The poor kid's got bad teeth, and sometimes the breath won't do. Why are your teeth so rotten? Your brother has such nice teeth!" In such situations, Virgil could often be unbelievably cruel; but he felt it would do that victim some good; and often, it did. Thank heaven the most hideous comments he made were repeated only before "close family."

Frederick Swann

During the mid 1950s, both Virgil and I were losing more and more hair. At dinner one evening, he told me he had been in contact with a woman in Baltimore who said she could guarantee to grow our hair back! It required placing a potion on our heads and then being put in a dark room without food or water for 48 hours. The treatment was to be repeated at two day intervals for two weeks. Virgil offered to pay for my treatment if I would go first "to make sure it works." Later, over ice-cream at Rumplemeyer's, I persuaded him that we could spend our time in better ways. He continued to use dark shoe polish on his bald spot before recitals.

On the evening of the closing concert of the summer master classes, Virgil gave what he described as a "banquet" in his beautiful dining room. Hamburgers (made from what Virgil described as "The finest meat money can buy!") and hot dogs were the main attractions. All of this meat was served on fine china and pewter plates (which were supposed to be used for place plates). Midway in the meal, Virgil asked Richard and me to pass around a paper cup to defray the feast's expenses! Richard and I were horrified, and we refused. Completely unfazed, he enlisted the aid of a student who meekly passed around the cup for donations. Virgil always loved going just as far as he could with people, and then go one step further. We were appalled; but he was delighted! If, on the other hand, someone acted toward him in a stingy or niggardly way, Virgil would say, "Oh Chicks, that old S.O.B. is as tight as a bull's ass in fly time!"

Steven Frank

I, too, had to pay for cans of soda at the master classes! However, there was another side to Virgil not too many people knew.

While coaching with him in Englewood, he sort of took me under his wing. I thus spent many evenings at his mansion enjoying great companionship, camaraderie, conversation, and—above all—free meals, which were exceedingly welcome for an exceedingly impecunious student!

One dinner began with a fruit cup that had a lot of grapefruit in it. I had some sores in my mouth that were causing too much pain to chew the citrus. When Virgil insisted that I absolutely must eat the fruit cup, I had to admit I had a problem. He asked me if I'd sought medical advice, and I explained that I simply couldn't afford such luxuries.

He then insisted I go to a doctor, and I followed his instruction.

The problem turned out to be a vitamin deficiency, which the doctor relieved with a shot of "B" followed by prescription strength vitamins.

Virgil insisted on paying the doctor's bill!

Not only that, he never charged me for lessons after the first time.

69. The Blessed Child

Things continued to progress well at St. Mary's in Wayne. After the 1967 dedication evensong and great inaugural concert that Virgil gave, there was much interest in the new organ. Debbie duPont had contributed a good deal of money towards the organ, and had purchased the wonderful *en chamade* trumpets. She was now eager for the excitement and interest to continue, and offered to underwrite a concert series that turned out to be quite successful. She held receptions at her lovely home in St. David's after each of the concerts.

We had one difficulty with the concerts. Certain parishioners objected strongly—not to the concerts, but to the applause in their church afterwards. Although Father Kier sided with us, it became necessary to mount a campaign for applause at the concerts. One Sunday morning at the inevitable coffee hour after the services, I was campaigning heavily for the prevailing concert deportment in American churches. I was distracted momentarily by the sight of a strikingly handsome young man whom I hadn't remembered seeing before. He was with an attractive, young Asian woman. I immediately went over to him to find out who they were (which is to say, who *he* was). He introduced himself as Reid Betten, and the young woman as "Miss Republic of China"! He was a member of St. Mary's, as were his mother, father, and three brothers. When he expressed interest in the new organ, I immediately enlisted his aid in the pro-applause campaign! He said he would cooperate in any way he could. I began to formulate several ideas on how he could cooperate—not only in my applause campaign.

If ever there was love at first sight, it happened on this occasion. I was thoroughly and completely stricken, like a lovesick cow. He was so attractive and so likable and intelligent—such a gentleman. I found out everything I could about him. He was at that time going to Temple University for a master's degree in anatomy (he planned to be a doctor); and he worked at a research institute part time. I included him in every activity that had to do with music at St. Mary's. For example, he was my console assistant on Sunday evenings (not that he knew much about the pipe organ); and I saw to it that he attended all the concerts and festive parties at Debbie's. Debbie, too, was attracted to him, as were most of the people who met him. I saw to it that the multitude of my gay friends met him as soon as possible. Reid soon became one of the most popular guests at our parties and get-togethers.

We often visited the various Philadelphia nightspots. I couldn't wait for Virgil, Richard, and Bob to meet Reid. As I predicted, they were delighted with him. Virgil was particularly happy. "You have to have a mate, Dear Child, not just run around to those awful bars!" He expressed my desires completely, and referred to Reid as "The Blessed Child," which I soon shortened to "The B.C."

We had a rocky beginning to our relationship. Reid was too smart and too attractive to be tied down to one person so early in his life. I was prepared to wait, and suffer, and make all my friends suffer, until I could finally call The B.C. my "Lover and Best Friend in This World"! It was well worth the agonizing year or so that it took. The dissension over applause in the church (which we won handily) allowed me to meet the most important and wonderful person in my life. As of this writing, it is twenty-five years since we began sharing our lives together. Reid became an instant and much-loved "chick" and a full-fledged member of Virgil's family and inner circle! He was soon to become heavily involved with our Ruffatti business and with Richard Torrence Management.

The "B.C.," Reid Betten

70. The Virgil Fox Show

The last time I saw Virgil inside the Riverside Church was when he was to attend a concert I played (that he had invited me to give on the Summer Concert Series) in August 1965, shortly after his resignation became effective. Virgil told me he intended to come to my concert, but that he had decided to listen from the triforium level two or three floors above the nave. He felt I wouldn't want to put up with the mobs of fans and well-wishers he expected he would attract. I remember that just before the last work on my program (Max Reger's "Introduction and Fugue on 'How Brightly Shines the Morning Star'") he bowed and blew me a kiss from the triforium, his beaming face framed in the beautiful Gothic arches that line the third floor level along the entire length of the nave. I believe that was the last time he entered the Riverside Church until more than 14 years later, when he went to begin his rehearsals for a triumphal return concert in May, 1979.

In the meantime, it was difficult for him to pass by the church every time he drove in and out of Manhattan along the West Side Highway, glancing furtively in the direction of the great Gothic tower. He made funny faces of disgust, saying, "There's old Rubbersides," and inventing a few new disparaging names and ill wishes for his detractors there.

An era ended; but more exciting times were beckoning toward this talented musical giant. He played more concerts than ever in the coming seasons, partly because of the availability of Black Beauty. He also received national television coverage when Richard and Marshall arranged for Virgil to hire a nationally known music publicist, Alix Williamson. When he appeared on the "Ed Sullivan Show" with Black Beauty, a near disaster was averted after a donkey, who was part of the animal act to appear that night, stomped on one of the main cables bringing power to the organ. Nevertheless, all went well. His appearance on the "Mike Douglas Show" was such a success that he appeared several times. He always wanted to be on the "Johnny Carson Show," as Virgil especially liked him; but the answer was always "No." Johnny Carson didn't like the organ ("Too funereal"). Too bad, for Johnny would have had a hoot of a time with Virgil and his wicked sense of humor. During one of his appearances on the "Mike Douglas Show" the legendary Liberace joined him. For once in his life, Virgil was at a loss to know how he could outshine and outdress this legendary showman. Virgil and Liberace got on well. Liberace commented that he envied the rhinestones in the heels of Virgil's shoes. This comment amused Virgil, because he knew that Liberace actually had the same shoes! When Richard had spied them in Lefcourt's window while shopping with Virgil on Madison Avenue, the sales clerk told them that Liberace had previously bought two pairs. Liberace was gracious, and impressed with Virgil's gift and humor. Virgil's pet name for Liberace was "Lib, Honey." They played "Tea for Two" on the show as a duet for piano and organ. The audience roared its approval!

Dick Cavett was also fond of Virgil, interviewing him twice. When Virgil was on "The David Frost Show," in his usual fashion, he took over the interview. For example, Frost asked a question about the organ. Virgil didn't want to deal with questions about anything but himself; and so he went off on his own. After a commercial break, Frost welcomed back the audience to "The Virgil Fox Show."

Virgil quickly responded: "This always has been, and always will be, the wonderful David Frost Show," but Frost had made his point.

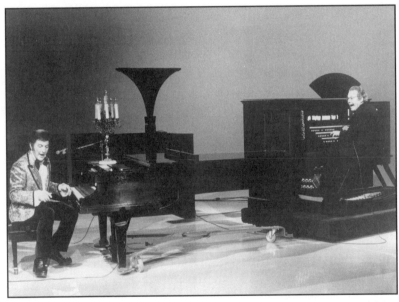

Virgil Fox's Rodgers organ speakers outperform Liberace's candelabra
(Mike Douglas Show)

Richard Torrence

Radio hosts loved to invite Virgil because he gave such good interviews—and got such good responses! For example, once, when Virgil was discussing his playing technique, an interviewer got the following written message from the famous virtuoso pianist Earl

Wild: "Dear Virgil. If you need help in fingering your passages, give me a call!"

Another time, on one of his many interviews with Bob Sherman, who hosted a morning show for many years on WQXR in New York, Virgil launched into one of his diatribes about "purists" and "maggots," comparing certain organists to "a pack of dogs, running around in a circle, smelling their...."

At that point, he broke off, and Bob went nervously on to a recorded commercial (for "Odal" mouthwash—which seemed unusually appropriate). Unfortunately, the engineers turned off Bob's microphone but not Virgil's. Virgil went on to say, "I was going to say, smelling their own bungholes!"

We were all listening back at the office, and we went into a state of shock.

Right after the show, Virgil called me. The first thing I said was, "Do you realize that you said 'bungholes' on the air?"

There was a second's pause; then Virgil said—emphatically, "Good!"

My own career was growing nicely, also, thanks to Community Concerts and Columbia Artists. I think Virgil was secretly pleased with my success, although he rarely let on. When I had my first tour of more than ten concerts, I remember Virgil said, "Ho! Ho! Ho! I hear you've been on tour! Were you able to buy a postage stamp when you returned?" He was fishing around to see what kind of fees I was getting. He couldn't bear the thought of my receiving money for a concert that possibly could have been his. "Don't let them get you too cheap, Kid!" That meant he would get fewer concerts in his mind, because his fee was getting higher and higher, and he was worried I'd give a similar concert for much less money, and he would suffer.

There was also the matter of using Black Beauty. "What if a date comes in for me later on, and Teddy's booked with my organ. What then?" He was wrong, however, because he actually got more concerts, even with the higher fee and the busy organ. The organ was so heavily booked, in fact, that Richard was able to convince the Rodgers Organ Company to provide a second touring organ for me, the Worth/Crow Duo, Joyce Jones, and some of the other artists that Richard now represented. Rodgers provided an additional organ in the new touring truck, a three-manual theatre organ for Andrew Crow.

Richard had created the Worth/Crow Duo in order to serve the Community Concert audience that appreciated popular music as much as (or more!) than classical. (Richard created a motto for us that claimed we were "Worth Crowing About!") I would begin each of the concerts on the classical instrument. Andrew would then play a group of solo pieces on the theatre organ, ending with a short silent film of the kind for which the theatre organ was originally developed. On the third section of each program, we used both consoles to play Andrew's arrangements of "Harper Valley PTA," "Pomp and Circumstance," and the "Stars and Stripes Forever."

Audiences loved the program, and Andy and I had great fun. Although Virgil seemed genuinely pleased with our success, if we were appearing in Great Bend, Kansas and Virgil was appearing at the Royal Festival Hall in London, he was still a bit piqued that he might have played our date as well—collecting both fees!

Columbia Artists had an important affair every fall when Community Concert salespeople would converge on New York for a week's conference of listening to new talent. Andy and I were fortunate enough to showcase for them in Carnegie Hall. We were also invited to a swank dinner dance at the Pierre Hotel. After dinner, the Columbia managers brought up their artists to be introduced to the salespeople. Michael Reis represented Virgil, the Worth/Crow Duo, and me. When he introduced Virgil, the crowd roared its appreciation. Then he introduced a few of his other artists. When he introduced me, they roared just as loud for me as for Virgil, and I took my place on the stage of the ballroom next to him. He put his arm around me and whispered, "I'm so proud of you, Teddo!" I was thrilled to stand next to this "King of Instrumentalists," for he had made me feel like a prince!

After leaving Riverside, Virgil's concert career was really able to flourish. His fees increased, and the number of his bookings grew. His fame, however—except for rare orchestra dates and recordings—was still mostly limited to the "organ world."

In those days, I used to refer to the world of organists collectively as "the worst world in the world!" Virgil would scream with laughter—and heartily agree! He said if I never played another note, I'd go down in history as having made the most comprehensive statement about the organ world that had ever been made in this century!

Andrew Crow

The following are excerpts from a two-week history of my activities moving the Rodgers touring organ around the country in March 1969.

March 13, up at nine for a concert with VF scheduled in Devils Lake, North Dakota. Hear about flooding road conditions and have to get to Jefferson City, Missouri in the next four days. I start about 10:30 a.m., and drive through lakes of water, sometimes as high as the hubcaps on the trailer. In some places, there are dikes on either side of the road with the water level higher than the road itself.

Five miles out of Topeka, have a blow out on the trailer. While changing wheels, I visit my Aunt, who happens to live in Topeka, leaving the trailer and truck to be serviced. Buy a new tire and scrounge around town until I find a wheel to fit the trailer. Find one that's bent, but the wheel size is wrong; obsolete, they tell me. A junkyard provides what I need for exactly one dollar.

Virgil's concert the next afternoon is so staggering as to warrant four standing ovations!

March 21, meet Ted Worth in the Toledo airport and we drive to Van Wert, Ohio. Those in charge of the concert have failed to carefully read the instructions that Richard Torrence sends in advance. (They're supposed to walk through the same pathway the organ console will take—with a measuring stick. It seems like no amount of telephone calls, either from the management or from me, gets people to follow the instructions!) Therefore, the organ won't go through the doors onto the stage. The afternoon is taken up rounding up cement blocks and plywood sheets to make a platform based on the floor that is high enough for the audience to see. By six that night, the lights are set and Ted gives his usual stunning performance.

March 24, Ted and I arrive in Rolla, Missouri at 2:05 in the morning to meet the movers. Unfortunately, those in charge at Rolla have failed to read the instructions at all, so the organ won't go through the door, not to mention up the 37 steps behind the door. There are some frantic telephone calls, but by noon, we get the organ installed into the local armory and I'm exhausted. The acoustics are as good as they can get—in a cement room with a dirt floor. Ted practices all afternoon and I try for some lighting effects with crude spotlights set on hat racks. Ah, show biz! Ted gets two standing ovations.

Next morning I meet the movers at 7:00 a.m., load the organ, and meet Ted at 9:30, and we start for Hot Springs, South Dakota, about 1,200 miles away.

Have serious engine trouble about 20 miles out of Columbia, Missouri, which is made obvious by an incredible pounding and knocking. Am able to ease the machine into a small town called Booneville. Tell them our plight and tight schedule. They stop the whole place and replace the main and rod bearings in the engine.

Next day, make it to Alliance, Nebraska by 2:45 a.m., about 900 miles. I drive about 700 of it and Ted the other 200. Hot Springs, South Dakota is about 150 miles from here but the snow is falling heavily so we rest at the Drake Hotel in Alliance for two and a half hours and start out again for Hot Springs. We arrive at 12:30 p.m., and I let Ted off at the hotel and go directly to the school auditorium where I meet the movers. In the meantime, Ted gets into his tuxedo, plays the afternoon concert cold to 800 people while I grab my suitcase from the truck, put on a suit, and play the encores. I must say, Ted's dialogue backstage to me is totally different from what the audience gets!

Load up the organ, and go out to supper with our hosts, who provide us with a few good belts. By 11:00 p.m., I'm sound asleep, and I mean sound asleep!

Next morning, March 28, we drive to Denver. Bed looks good about 2:00 a.m.

Arrive at Riverton, Wyoming about 2:30 p.m. An hour later, we move the organ into the armory and onto the "stage," which is a flatbed truck. Our movers are Indians who are prisoners in a local jail, supervised by the Chief of Police and a few deputies. These prisoners, I'm told, are thieves, and I catch one trying to run off with my hydraulic jack and stop him. (He must have made off with it later, because the jack is now missing!) The concert takes place that night, and it seems like everyone in the town is present. There are no lighting effects, just naked light bulbs blazing away, but the crowd is enthusiastic.

Arrangements are made to move the organ out the following morning. I'm there at 9:00 a.m., and so are the Indians, the Chief of Police, and his deputies. By noon, Ted and I are on our way to Rawlins, Wyoming.

In the afternoon, we meet the movers, who are prisoners from the state prison. The organ is moved into place in the Community Center. Someone finally read the instructions!

Sunday's easy. Nothing missing.

Next morning, Ted is supposed to catch the only daily flight out of Rawlins, 7:10 a.m. to Denver, but the plane never arrives for some reason, so he rides with me to Laramie, Wyoming, and catches another flight to Denver.

The Worth/Crow Duo with a Rodgers American Classic organ
and a Rodgers theatre organ

71. Heavy Organ

Richard and Marshall (who was in charge of handling Virgil's bookings and directing his marketing) had long tried to invent imaginative new ways to steer Virgil and his colossal musical gifts more toward the mainstream of the music world—and beyond. A gift and personality as great and vital as Virgil's deserved a broader and more varied audience.

Richard and Marshall felt that somehow the young people of this country had to be reached if the organ, Virgil's career, and indeed classical music were to continue and flourish in a healthy manner.

The rock'n'roll craze was in full force; and new audiences were accessible but not usually tapped by classical artists. So the two of them concocted the idea of Virgil's playing an all-Bach concert with a "psychedelic" light show. They believed that the concert should not take place in an obvious venue like Carnegie Hall or Lincoln Center, but in a "rock palace" such as Bill Graham's world-renowned Fillmore East on the lower east side of New York.

Initially, Virgil was not enthusiastic. Indeed, many of us who surrounded Virgil thought that Richard and Marshall had lost their minds! I, for one, pooh-poohed the whole idea. I have to hand it to Richard and Marshall, however. "No" wasn't a word Richard ever understood. He pushed and pushed, and then he pushed harder until Virgil agreed at least to try it.

Once.

"Oh, Honey," Virgil said to me. "Caméo and Marshall are insane! Ho! Ho! Ho! Can you imagine me in such a place with a light show? I told them that no one will come; but you know how stubborn and determined Caméo can be! If I lose a lot of money because of this, I'll take it out of his hide!"

In fact, Virgil was somewhat intrigued with the idea of lights. He had always adored the idea of color. (In his house hung a talented painting of a house and garden that he had done as a youth. Obviously, he had neglected a fine visual talent in order to concentrate on music.) He thought of sounds in terms of colors (often describing them in those terms); but he feared that his ideas, and those of the people who would be in charge of the lights, would conflict. Of course, they would at times; but by the time Virgil was on the bench playing, he always was too busy to watch!

Marshall suggested naming the concert "Heavy Organ" after the concert record title suggested by the Decca producer, Israel Horowitz. We all detested that name! We didn't understand or appreciate young people's lingo much, although we understood that the name was contemporary—too contemporary for the Virgil we knew! It turned out to be a perfect name, and a stroke of marketing genius!

Somehow, Richard got the great rock promoter Bill Graham interested in the idea and the proposed concert. Fillmore East was engaged. Joe's Lights, the resident light show of the Fillmore East, was hired; and the date was set: December 1, 1970. Of course, the Rodgers Touring Organ was used (no part of this event would have been possible without it). The advertising was heavy and impressive.

Richard did everything he knew to make the event successful; but this sort of show was an entirely new concept for a classical musician. No one had ever attempted such a departure and succeeded. None of us knew what to expect. I feared the worst.

When the day of the concert arrived, I took a morning train to New York because Virgil had asked me to go with Richard to the Fillmore East and play the organ for the recording technicians. Decca was recording the concert "live," and I was to advise them about what would be the loudest and softest levels of the sound from Black Beauty so that they could set the levels.

I was horrified at the way the organ had been set up! Every speaker was pointed directly at the audience, and the organ was turned up full blast—to pain levels! Someone had told Virgil that young audiences liked it *loud!* They would not be disappointed on that score! I was almost deafened. I imagined Virgil drawing blood from both eyes and ears!

To make matters worse, the hall, which was a large old legitimate theatre made into a movie palace, lacked all acoustical ambience. "Dead as a doornail!" I was heartsick, and so was Richard. Rock groups attached reverberation devices to their instruments; but Black Beauty had none, and was therefore at the mercy of whatever acoustical environment in which it was placed. The Fillmore East was certainly one of the worst places for Black Beauty I had ever heard—not a good omen.

There was too much lighting equipment and extraneous sound going on behind the mammoth screen on the stage. The semi-permanent light show installation was called "Joe's Lights," and was the successor to the "Joshua Light Show" created by Joshua White, who had originated the light shows at the Fillmore East. The equipment must have cost a fortune. Richard told me that at the rehearsal the night before, Virgil had made many suggestions to the head of the light show and his assistants—all of which, it was obvious, they would ignore. They were determined to "create" as the spirit moved them during the concert! By 3:00 a.m., there had still been no actual rehearsal with the light show accompanying the organ, and Virgil had to go home.

Virgil was upset. He said, "OK Kids, but don't you dare plunge me into total darkness! I've got to be able to see what I'm doing!"

He also admonished them for their incessant smoking. "What is that foul stink that comes from those cigarettes?" He thought he

"I feel like I've finally come home!"

smelled an exotic form of tobacco. What he smelled was, indeed, exotic; but it wasn't tobacco. Richard and Marshall recognized the odor of marijuana instantly, but kept Virgil in the dark for the time being. Better to let sleeping dogs lie than further depress Virgil's already waning enthusiasm for the concert.

72. Go, Virgil!

Richard checked the box office on the morning of the concert. He wasn't encouraged. The Fillmore East personnel explained, however, that the usual crowd didn't buy advance tickets for most events;

and this concert wasn't typical in any way that would allow for accurate predictions. After hearing the sound of the organ and the dismal report from the box office, Richard and I returned to his office in Englewood, where he tended to last minute details and tried to drum up some additional business by offering free tickets to anyone he could reach on the telephone. Richard and I decided to splurge and have an early dinner at the Edwardian Room of the Plaza Hotel. He was dejected and said, "Virgil will just love this! He said it wouldn't work, and I guess it won't. Oh well, we'll have to think of something else." I tried to assure him that, although this idea had been insane all along, he and Marshall had given it their best shot.

It was getting late, and so we took a cab down to the Fillmore East. "I don't know why we're bothering to get there early," Richard said. "There won't be any audience to speak of."

As we approached the theatre, we could see a large crowd surrounding the box office. The line waiting to buy tickets extended clear around the block! The cloud of gloom hovering over our taxi disappeared, and Richard went into high gear, his face beaming with anticipation. He walked with me to our seats, and then went backstage to see that all was well—and possibly to gloat to Virgil that with the hall already filling up, there were still a thousand people clamoring to get in. Hundreds would be turned away!

As I looked around me, I saw few familiar faces. This audience was young, eccentric, and new. Their mode of dress was bizarre, to say the least. It seemed like anything was acceptable in those days. The auditorium was filled with a blue haze of smoke, most of which was you know what. "These kids are going to enjoy and savor this concert," I thought. "If Virgil only knew what they were smoking, he'd die!"

The concert began thirty to forty minutes late because of the huge, sold-out throng settling in. Someone else took Richard's seat. Virgil walked out on the stage in a splashy dinner jacket and new silk shoes with rhinestone buckles that caught the light in a super-dramatic way. I don't recall a word he said before launching into the hushed, rhythmic opening portions of the "A Minor Prelude and Fugue." But I understand that he actually did speak.

The stage was dark, and some squiggly looking things in shades of brown and green, like cells one would see under a microscope, began to appear on the giant screen. "Horrors," I thought, "Virgil would hate those drab colors!" Then shafts of intensely colored light began appearing on Virgil himself from lighting instruments around the proscenium, and the screen became more active with colors and objects. The music intensified and grew louder. The power of the pedal was already shaking the whole place, and Virgil still had only half the stops on!

There was an ovation after just the prelude—which is a definite no-no in a classical music concert; but this crowd couldn't have cared less. They loved what they heard, and they wanted to show their appreciation! Before the fugue began, the light show people plunged Virgil into total darkness—which was exactly what he instructed them not to do. Therefore, it's a wonder he knew where his pistons were, or the keys for that matter. The stage was pitch black!

Yet, he began the colossal, rhythmic fugue at a terrific tempo. Gradually, the cell-like images began to multiply. Joe's Lights had discovered a counterpoint of their own! By the time the astonishingly virtuosic pedal passages rushed toward the end of the fugue, the entire stage, screen, and organ were ablaze with light and sound! The noise was intense; and around Black Beauty's red-carpeted platform, smoke poured forth that was illuminated by the shafts of light that streamed down on Virgil, creating a splendid rainbow of concentrated color.

The last chords of the first piece were completely inaudible, for the crowd burst into a tumultuous ovation, stomping and screaming its approval and appreciation. It was a surreal experience for me, and wonderful to witness: a rock'n'roll audience completely under the spell of Johann Sebastian Bach and our very own Virgil Fox!

At first, Virgil was taken aback by the unbridled enthusiasm. He was obviously quite moved, pleased, and delighted with their approval and the joy they expressed in what they were experiencing. One delirious fan shouted, "Go, Virgil!"

He did. The ovations continued after every piece, until pandemonium followed a virtuoso performance of Bach's "D Major Prelude and Fugue" that Virgil played just before the intermission.

To be honest, Virgil's playing that night was less than his greatest. (Richard put it more bluntly: "He played like a pig!") Being plunged into darkness several times, some of the proscenium lights blinding him, and being distracted by the never-ending colors projected on the giant screen within his sight-lines, took their toll even on his considerable talent. Black Beauty's volume was turned up to distortion levels (which only seemed to delight the enormous audience); and so the organ had none of the refinement and subtlety we had worked hard to achieve before this event. At first, I was distressed; but later, totally thrilled with the reception the audience gave to Bach, Virgil, and the organ. A whole new world was waiting: it would be a new era for the King of Instruments.

I caught up with Richard during the intermission and threw my arms around him and said, "This is an artistic disaster, but a managerial triumph!" The look of pleasure on his face was indescribable. We had *all* been wrong. He and Marshall had really hit on something great, and Heavy Organ would have an impact on Virgil's career and on the music world for years to come.

The rest of the concert was just as exciting, and the audience if anything became even more enthusiastic and boisterous. Naturally, this reaction only added more fuel to Virgil's unbounded energy and showmanship. He spoke to the audience as he always did, sermonizing to them about taking them "On a *real* trip—the towering counterpoint of Sebastian Bach!" He even spoke of an "out of body" astral projection he had experienced! He was the same Virgil that he always was in front of an audience—only more so—and the young people loved it. He played four encores, and still they screamed for more. He finally announced his "Goodnight Song," which was Bach's "Air for the G-String."

The entire evening was one of the most remarkable events in the history of the organ (and possibly of music); and I came to believe that it would give Virgil and the King of Instruments a new audience of wonderful zealots for generations to come. All of this new history could only have been made because of Virgil's genius, his genuine enthusiasm and love for the instrument, the music of his beloved Bach, and the genius, ingenuity, and true grit and determination of Richard and Marshall, and their vision of what the organ could mean to the broader world!

Richard Torrence

The moment that Heavy Organ was actually born occurred when Sara Tornay, another concert manager and friend, invited Marshall and me to the Fillmore East to attend a rehearsal of a Hilde Somer piano recital with lights. Hilde was interpreting the music of Scriabin, the Russian mystic who specified that lights should accompany certain of his compositions. (She played the actual concert later with a small rear-projection screen at Alice Tully Hall.)

Marshall and I had never seen the Fillmore East before, and so we accepted the invitation. As soon as the rehearsal began—literally within seconds—we turned to each other, wide-eyed, and said, "Not Scriabin!"

"No, Bach!"

"Not the piano!"

"The touring organ!"

Shortly after Virgil played his last "Fanfare for Organ" (with orchestra), we insisted he accompany us to the Fillmore East to hear a concert featuring the rock groups "Ten Years After" and "Zephyr," and the rock violinist Doug Kershaw. We didn't stay long, because Virgil thought the sound was too loud—even after he had stuffed Kleenex in his ears. But he got the point, and he agreed to play there!

The next step was to find the money to cover the up-front costs of the concert. Marshall had devised a clever scheme to finance Virgil's "Fanfare for Organ" series at Lincoln Center's Philharmonic Hall that same season (1969-70). We got Virgil to ask several of his wealthier friends that were eager to help him out to invest $1,000 or more in the series, which cost $20,000, and which would do little more than break even.

The investors actually lost a little money (1/4 of their investment), but I asked each of them to stay in the game—and they all agreed; and so we rolled over the $15,000 we had gotten back from Philharmonic Hall to produce two concerts at the Fillmore East.

Virgil's publicist, Alix Williamson (the doyenne of classical music publicists for many years) set up a lunch with Israel Horowitz of Decca Records and me to try to sell him Virgil and another of her distinguished clients, the great Metropolitan Opera tenor, Richard Tucker. She thought an album of the great organ and tenor arias would be splendid. Israel yawned. Then Alix brought up our crazy idea of presenting Bach at the Fillmore East with Virgil and a light show.

Horowitz immediately said, "I'll record it—live!"

Alix was thrilled, and I went numb. Then he said, "I'll call the album 'Heavy Organ.'"

Alix said, "Well, I know what's dirty about it; what's good?"

I explained that "heavy" in contemporary parlance meant "serious and important." So we ended lunch with a commitment for Virgil's first "live" recording.

We were going to call the Fillmore East concert "Virgil Fox Plays Bach with a Light Show at the Fillmore East." When Marshall heard the name that "Iz" Horowitz was going to call the album, he said, "Call the concert 'Heavy Organ,' too."

I said, "The Heavy Organ"?

"No," he said, "just 'Heavy Organ.'"

When David and Virgil returned from their summer vacation, Virgil began a meeting with an announcement: "Now, don't you kids start thinking that that this was David's idea! I decided that I'm not going to play a concert for kids at the Fillmore East. I'm going to play for them in Carnegie Hall!"

Marshall said, "If you want to attract a new audience for Bach by using a light show, you have to go where the kids are, Virgil. They're not comfortable at Carnegie Hall. They won't buy the tickets."

Arguments about money usually convinced Virgil quickly; but then he said, "I understand. But you can't call the concert 'Heavy Organ.' It has to be 'Virgil Fox Plays Bach.'"

"You know, the most successful talk show on television isn't called 'The Johnny Carson Show,'" Marshall said. "It's called 'The Tonight Show, starring Johnny Carson.' And that's true of all the most successful television shows, like 'I Love Lucy,' which was much more successful than 'The Lucille Ball Show,' which only lasted a few seasons."

Another argument Marshall used was that Heavy Organ was a "marketing vehicle." It was like a military tank. Even if it crashed and burned, you could still get out and climb aboard another vehicle. Virgil wouldn't be personally hurt if Heavy Organ didn't work.

Virgil thought a while. Then he said, "Okay, Kids, you win."

Working at the Fillmore East was an extraordinary experience. The outstanding, non-union stage crew of six people worked 14 hours and only cost $238! During a break for dinner, Virgil looked up at the marquee outside the theatre and declared, "I feel like I've finally come home!"

Decca recorded only the first of the two concerts Virgil played at the Fillmore East. I always regretted that the original Heavy Organ album (which became Virgil's best selling record!) was also his worst one, technically. Decca demanded that we not use the splendid Fillmore East sound system because it was monaural and they had planned to record in stereo. Virgil therefore turned up the Rodgers to distortion levels in order to provide enough sound to fill the 2,600 seat auditorium, which had terrible acoustics for music.

For the second concert some weeks later, the Fillmore sound system served excellently, and Virgil played beautifully.

The two Fillmore East concerts broke even, and we returned what was left to the original investors, who were thrilled to have been helpful. No one complained—except William F. Buckley Jr., who wrote:

> I got tickets [to the Fillmore East] on learning that Virgil Fox the organist would play Bach there tonight accompanied by a "light" expert. Lights are big this season. I had heard Fox a year before at Philharmonic Hall, marveled at his virtuosity, and appreciated his familiarity with Bach.
>
> We arrive, and there are hippies and non-hippies trying to get in, a sell-out. We are astonished by the crowd, only a minority of which is Woodstock Nation. The performance is god-awful, because Fox clearly wants to impress the kids by (a) the noise, and (b) his virtuosity. At one point during a prelude, I am tempted to rise solemnly, commandeer a shotgun, and advise Fox, preferably in imperious German, if only I could learn German in time to consummate the fantasy, that if he does not release the goddamn Vox Humana, which is ooing-ahing-eeing the music where Bach clearly intended something closer to a *bel canto*, I shall simply have to blow his head off. After the intermission, Fox introduces the "Passacaglia" at Wagnerian length, almost but not quite to the point of causing mutiny in the audience, whose stirrings become discernible after the fourth or fifth minute. The maestro then turns and snows them with his dexterity, which is undeniable, the problem being that it will be ten years before I can appreciate again the music he has played, so over-loud, so throbby, so plucky-wucky the *portamentos*, so Phil Spitalny the *cantandos*.

> We drive home. I speculate. How come it didn't hurt
> Fox more than it hurt us? And [a friend] as usual offers the
> only acceptable explanation, namely, that Fox is so much
> the evangelist, he must have figured that it was more
> important to fill the house with listeners who would hear
> Bach for the first time than worry about those who would
> resolve, like me, to have heard Fox for the last time.
>
> © *William F. Buckley Jr., 1971. Used with permission.*

The quote is from Bill Buckley's book called Cruising Speed, *which he sent to me as a result of some unrelated correspondence. Years later, Marshall and I invited Bill to serve on the board of a charity we ran, which he did for six years. For the past twelve years, we've remained good friends.*

Virgil Fox

I firmly believe that there's nothing wrong with the young people of the world at the present moment. It's the leadership that's totally lacking. Well, Bach can give leadership, and I can give 'em Bach!

My Bach is a red-blooded, gutsy Bach. His mind is universal, his heart is overwhelming, and the spirit that rides over the entire creativity of this enormous man is transcendental!

People need Bach and God, and there ain't one violinist or singer that can give the sweeping feeling an organist can. I play the King of Instruments!

My more conservative colleagues say I'm a showman, and I'm proud to be one! Communication is what an artist lives for—audiences on their feet screaming for more.

(Quotations from *Cue* now *New York Magazine* and *The New York Times*.)

Marshall Yaeger

I sat cringing in the audience during the opening moments of the first performance of Heavy Organ. I wanted to crawl under my seat whenever I felt Virgil was being particularly patronizing to the audience. Nevertheless, when it came time to write the program notes for the record album, I felt the truer story should reflect less Virgil's performance than the audience's reaction, which was the more astonishing. There was utter silence (out of kids!) except for the music, until the conclusion of each piece, when a mighty roar signified a new nation of born-again believers!

BACH LIVE AT FILLMORE EAST
VIRGIL FOX
HEAVY ORGAN

This record was made on the first day of December, 1970, when Virgil Fox brought the Rodgers Touring Organ to Bill Graham's Fillmore East, and with Joe's Lights produced an extravaganza that was a truly great occasion in the history of music.

Most of the spectators had never seen an organ concert. They sat in frozen wonder as the virtuoso performed mad digital feats. Beyond him, a spectacular, wide-screen light show blazed. At the end of every piece, the audience rose, movingly, in spontaneous ovation.

"Heavy Organ" amazed everyone. No one imagined that the hard-rock Fillmore audience would fill the theatre and make a non-swinging organist playing ancient music its new superstar.

It was an event whose time had come. For J.S. Bach is the master; and so is Virgil Fox. Fox plays Bach with all the composer's sense of drama, theatricality, humor, and humanity. And the Fillmore audience, as susceptible to reality as it is suspicious of pretense, followed Bach and Fox every inch of the way.

It was an evening with all the excitement of an inauguration. It was a truly new event: a tour de force that could not have been accomplished by any other solo instrument, nor by any ordinary musician.

In an era of highly touted non-events, this one was real and lasting.

© MCA Inc. 1971

Heavy Organ was to be the turning point of Virgil's late career. He adored young people; and he would now be able to reach a young audience that he could never have hoped to reach without the idea and superb execution that the Heavy Organ concept had provided.

Virgil had hit the big time in a new world of popular concerts; and he was overjoyed with his well-deserved success.

Virgil could now command fees that no organist ever had achieved in the concert world. Prior to Heavy Organ, an organist—even one of Virgil's caliber, if any had existed—would have to be content with being paid the same fee that would be paid to a second-rate cellist, or a young, unknown pianist or singer. Virgil had long before deserved enviable financial rewards and public recognition. At last, he would be able to enjoy them.

The famous English organist, E. Power Biggs, had sometimes overshadowed Virgil because of his regular broadcasts from Harvard's Busch Reisinger Museum, and because of his prolific recording career. That career was said to have been made possible because some of Biggs's associates pushed hard for him at Columbia Records. Biggs should be given great credit, however, for his innovative ideas as far as the musical material he recorded, and for making some of the organs he recorded even more famous. His recordings called attention to the "European sound" of certain famous historical organs in Europe. He also helped change the organ world's thinking about organ design, and started people thinking about "historical performance practices."

Virgil stated that he was about as interested in Biggs' approach to the organ as he was interested in "dried owl shit." He became

Signing Heavy Organ records

The members of Pablo Lights

increasingly vocal about the subject at his concerts, excoriating "the Baroque Boys" who wanted to relegate the organ to "a museum piece like an old Queen's comb in a glass case. These freaks hide their limitations behind their historical claims; and they call this music?"

Richard Torrence

Once, when my business partner Bill Perrotta was trying to get RCA to sign a contract with Virgil, he was meeting considerable resistance from the company until E. Power Biggs announced that he was going to play the big Wurlitzer organ at Radio City Music Hall. When The New York Times *asked Biggs what he thought of Virgil's Heavy Organ concert, Biggs said, "It depresses me."*

RCA's artists and repertoire director called Bill immediately to say, "When E. Power Biggs has to talk about Virgil to get publicity, RCA wants Virgil on its roster! Let's go to Radio City!"

We did, and the concert was awful. It was recorded by CBS Records but never released. (A four-microphone "chandelier"—to record quadraphonic sound—hung over the stage. At one point it was struck by a rising curtain and kept revolving around and around during the rest of the concert. Imagine what that sounded like!)

Virgil went on to make five great records for RCA during the mid-1970s.

The "Baroque Movement" disturbed Virgil greatly. Since he didn't have the time, talent, or inclination to write articles explicating his views and opinions, he chose the concert stage to rail against what he took to be a growing host of misguided theorists.

Richard Torrence had his own problems, because many people couldn't accept or understand why Virgil would stoop to play concerts on an electronic organ. Richard tried to preach that it was the music and the interpretation that mattered, not the instrument. Getting Virgil out of churches and into concert halls was clever, putting Virgil in a class by himself—which Virgil greatly relished. It also created venomous jealousy amongst his professional colleagues, and sometimes resulted in legitimate (but often prissy and vicious) criticisms, dismissals, and putdowns in some of the nation's more respected journals and newspapers. Some critics called Virgil a "cheap charlatan," and nothing but a theatrical "hustler-type salesman" for the organ and Bach. Virgil would fume with anger when he read these diatribes, although they seemed to pique the public interest even further. Virgil's concerts and audiences continued to increase in spite of the "puny maggots," as Virgil described his critics.

Virgil went out of his way to annoy these people in every way that he could: more lights, more smoke, more outlandish outfits, more rhinestones in the heels of his silk pumps, and even more sermonizing against the "bloodless performances and the historians who are nothing but barnacles on the ship of music!"

What I heard him say in private was even more colorful and graphic. "This movement has produced a number of gifted, proficient, and technically near perfect eunuchs who have embalming fluid flowing in their veins. They're completely and totally devoid of any kind of personality or ability to create a musical line. They're a bunch of little snots who sit and criticize everything and everybody. Why, they can't even play a simple hymn properly! What will become of our instrument? I pity any church stupid enough to hire them!"

Douglas Marshall is a concert organist, choral conductor, and teacher. He is also president and founder of Marshall Ogletree Associates, which represents Rodgers and Ruffatti organs in New England.

Douglas Marshall

I was privileged to study for nine years with Virgil Fox. My three lessons a week (beginning while I was still in high school) were either on the organ in his house or on the Æolian-Skinner organ at the Huntington Hartford Gallery of Modern Art in Manhattan where Virgil was Artist in Residence.

In 1972, when Virgil's relationship with the organ establishment was in a meltdown phase as his many peers and critics who had gotten aboard the "historic performance practice" bandwagon were out to get him, I decided to enter the American Guild of Organists National Playing Competition in Dallas.

Virgil wanted a chance to beat "those scavenger moss-backed nobodies" at their own game by having one of his students win the competition. Thus, he spent massive amounts of time coaching me. During these sessions, his remarkable ability to analyze and graphically express his thoughts continually amazed me. He was a man on a mission, determined to share everything and to make me persevere until I "owned" the music, and wasn't merely copying his style.

He knew exactly what I had to do to win—which was to play the pieces using all the stops, manual changes, and famous Fox phrasings that he would have used, but to leave out one essential "Fox" element (which I insisted I ought to use!), namely, the Swell pedal.

"Honey," he said to me, emphatically, "if you touch the Swell pedal in the Bach, you can't win!"

I didn't touch it, and I won the competition!

My problems didn't begin until I appeared before the entire convention to play the "Winner's Recital." I programmed and played as Virgil would have, using the Swell pedal during the "Prelude & 'Wedge' Fugue," and playing an orchestral rendition of "Nun komm, der Heiden Heiland" *on full strings with subs, supers, trems, and pizzicato pedal.*

The audience got rowdy, and there was almost no applause. Nevertheless, all the judges were gracious (except Clare Coci, who cornered me and told me plainly that I was not her choice).

When the magazine reviews came out, the only positive word in any of them was someone declaring my Vierne Sixth Symphony *"relentless." I heard rumors that the critics had collaborated to create as scathing a unanimous verdict as possible.*

Nevertheless, Virgil and I won the competition. He proved that his approach to the music was right. He beat them at their own game.

Marshall Yaeger

I wrote the following flyer copy for Virgil's concerts in 1968, before the Heavy Organ concerts began:

THE ORGAN

Born in Egypt two-thousand years ago; adopted by the Christian Church to fill the soaring Gothic space of stone cathedrals; a muted orchestra of pierced cylinders taught to chant in diverse voices by craftsmen of every nation in the Western World; Chief Celebrator of life, for a thousand years, Chief Mourner for the dead.

J. S. BACH

Made song and countersong for organ voices, his achievement equal in splendor to the great stone flowers of the Western World—the Roses of Cathedral windows; performed by five generations of musicians, who, over and over, set each shard of blue, of red, of white and green, painstakingly, worshipfully, anonymously, in place.

VIRGIL FOX

The greatest living interpreter of Bach's organ music; whose genius shot a burst of sun into the rose, poured color into each dark glass, and made the blue, a cobalt; red, carnelian; white, an opaline, and yellow, yellow diamond. To listen, one must look for colors.

One must go; for in a thousand years, how short a time there is between the rising and the setting of a sun!

Whom shall we admire more? Bach, or Bach's interpreter? The Rose, or the light behind it?

I got tired of reading musician's flyers that invariably began: "Dora Dumpling, born in Minneapolis, Minnesota on May 11, 1939, graduated from University High School in 1956...." and so on.

I was sure that any musician or manager who picked up Virgil's flyer and started to read, "Born in Egypt two-thousand years ago..." (overlooking the headline, "The Organ:"), would say, "Wha?"

The flyer for Virgil's Heavy Organ concerts used the same three paragraphs above and inserted the following before "One must go....":

PABLO LIGHTS
Prisms, lamps, and lenses swirl the Rose into the next dimension. This new man-made sun plunges through the terror and ecstasy of Bach, haloing the music's passion; enrapturing the mind and all its senses.

73. God Destroys Buildings Not Gracious to Music!

As Virgil's career continued to soar and flourish, so did mine. Richard had been after me to leave St. Mary's Church in order to devote more time to my Community Concerts, which were really taking off and required my being away from Wayne for longer periods of time. The church and Father Kier had been wonderful to me by letting me have an excellent assistant to take over for me when I was away. Father Kier always encouraged me to put my playing career ahead of my work at the church (which I still dearly loved). Richard and Father Kier finally talked me into leaving the church, and I reluctantly resigned from Saint Mary's shortly after Easter of 1970. This decision was difficult for me to make. Saint Mary's and its parishioners had been like a family to me, and the organ was dear to my heart. It was barely a month later when Reid and I had driven to Bryn Mawr to see a movie, that we were listening to the car radio on the way home, when an announcer came on to report a serious fire at a church on the Main Line. It was St. Mary's! I remember thinking it must have been St. Mary's, Ardmore; but then he said Wayne! Reid stepped on the accelerator, and in a short time, we could see the sky glowing red up ahead on the Lancaster Pike. As we approached our church, the flames were engulfing the entire building. I cried. Our exquisite organ would never survive such an inferno!

On the scene, I couldn't believe that Father Kier seemed to be enjoying the excitement of the fire engines and the onlookers! I realized that he had always wanted to redo certain parts of the church, and now would have his chance. I knew what he must have been thinking, and so I said, "You probably started the fire yourself!"

He roared with laughter. (It turned out that faulty wiring in the ceiling above the sacristy started the fire.) "Don't worry, Ted; we'll get another organ, and it'll be a Ruffatti! I guarantee it!"

He was actually devastated at the loss; but he shifted his eternally optimistic focus on the bright spots, and looked forward to a splendid new future for the church.

I promptly rescinded my resignation; but Father Kier would have none of it. "You continue with what you're doing. That's what God wants. We'll do okay, here; but we won't hesitate to call on you for

Ted Alan Worth in St. Mary's Episcopal Church, Wayne, Pennsylvania, after the fire

advice and help!" I remember playing the next Sunday services in the Parish Hall on a Rodgers organ the company had lent us. The services were jammed with bright faces eager to rebuild and make St. Mary's better in every way. I knew they would succeed, and that they'd get their new Ruffatti organ.

The insurance on the "old" Ruffatti had more than paid for the new one, although the new organ was fifteen ranks smaller. Father Kier used the difference in money to air-condition the church! He also had the organ and choir removed to the back of the church in a balcony that was specially built for that purpose. Virgil was so upset at the news of the organ's demise that he said he "felt heartsick. I've lost one of my ribs!" He had played two memorable concerts on it by that time. Of course, when we left the Philadelphia area there were many jokes about my having burned down the church to prevent anyone else from playing "my" organ!

I do confess to remarking, as I stood there watching the fire, "God destroys buildings that aren't gracious to beautiful music!"

Shortly after the unfortunate fire and my resignation from the church, Reid and I decided to move to New Jersey and take the other apartment in Virgil's carriage house, adjacent to Richard's and Marshall's, that had just been vacated. Virgil said he would have it decorated any way we wanted; and he was delighted to have us as tenants. Richard supervised the renovation of his next-door apartment, and it was perfect for us.

Richard needed help with WTM, Inc. and the Ruffatti business. Reid had proven himself highly organized running the St. Mary's Concert Series and Choral Society, and Richard decided that Reid was the person we needed in the business. Reid also helped Richard with the concert management, which had grown considerably in size and prestige. Richard had taken on another business partner by that time, named Bill Perrotta. Great things were therefore going on in "Torrence/Perrotta Management."

We had great fun living next door to each other. When Virgil was home—which wasn't too often—there were great musical evenings, feasts, and midnight invitations to join Virgil in the pool.

We didn't stay in Englewood for long, however. I had rented out the house in Wayne to tenants who used the place for boisterous parties and were constantly late paying the rent. After nearly a year of worrying about our little house, we felt we had to move back to Wayne to take care of the house (and remodel its entire interior). Reid resumed his work at the Cancer Research Institute. We had missed Wayne, Debbie duPont, and our friends there; and I felt I couldn't let my tenants continue to ruin my splendid little house. Virgil and Richard were upset at our decision, but we felt there was no alternative at the time.

74. Organ Arts

Virgil served on the committee that granted Fullbright Scholarships to deserving students who studied the organ. Although he was distressed at the "mere note pushing" of most applicants, he was impressed with one player, Anthony Newman, who was awarded one of the fellowships given out by the committee on which Virgil served.

Virgil served on that committee for two years, along with Alec Wyton and harpsichordist Albert Fuller. Virgil claimed they had a great time working together. He also claimed that he would tend to sit back and say nothing, which was uncharacteristic of him. Then, when the others had waxed eloquent about one of the tapes they had to listen to, Virgil would step in and steer the whole committee in the right direction (so he said). Actually, we heard from one of the committee members that Virgil truly was invaluable to the committee; and they had all formed a new level of respect for his knowledge and judgment.

In the early- to mid-1970s, the troubles between David and Richard seemed to flare up more frequently. David had no real job (other than errands and odd jobs that Virgil created for him) and a lot of time to complain to Virgil about Richard; the light show and its shortcomings; and the fact that Virgil was paying too much to Richard and the management, the Rodgers Company for the use of the organ, and the light show personnel. When Virgil was home, he and Richard would have minor rows over these subjects. When Richard would reason with him in person, Virgil would calm down; but when Virgil and David would go on the road again for weeks at a time, David would start in again arguing with Virgil in ways it was hard for Richard to deal with. By this time, Richard was not only running the sales and business affairs of Torrence/Perrotta Management, but he had also been hired (with Marshall Yaeger as the writer) to create advertisements for both the Rodgers Organ Company and Fratelli Ruffatti. On Richard's initiative, Rodgers began representing Ruffatti in the early 1970s on the premise (put forward by an organ builder named Jack Bethards in his dissertation on organ sales for a masters degree) that electronic organ dealers should offer potential customers the choice between pipes and electronics.

Rodgers recognized the enormous gifts that Marshall and Richard had to offer. Together they gave both companies the most brilliant advertising programs they ever enjoyed—before or since! This development didn't go down well with Virgil or David, who were both convinced that "Torrence" (by this time, it was no longer "Caméo"!) was making a fortune in the advertising world and wasn't tending to Virgil's business. Actually, Virgil was being better served than any other organist in history had ever been. He simply couldn't stand the idea that Richard wasn't at his disposal twenty-four hours a day, seven days a week. Virgil's attitude was distressing to Richard, who couldn't possibly have worked harder for Virgil or his career.

Eventually, and with David's prodding, Richard and Marshall devised a plan to help relieve the tension that David's inactivity produced. Why couldn't Virgil purchase the necessary equipment and truck and hire the necessary people to let David run the light show for the Heavy Organ concerts? As I always used to say, "Busy hands are happy hands!"

This idea, which appealed to both Virgil and David, is exactly what was done. David ran the light show right to the end of Virgil's career. This strategy relieved the strain between Richard and David; and Virgil was overjoyed that his David was finally a really productive and creative part of his life. It also served another purpose. It showed Virgil and David why things were "so expensive"—that no one connected with the show was becoming a millionaire at their expense. Peace reigned for a while.

David Lewis

Floyd Watson and I had gone to college together, and got the job driving the touring organ for Heavy Organ, which featured Virgil's friend David's "Revelation Lights" (which we used to refer to as "Revolting Lights") through Floyd's theatre organ teacher, Gaylord Carter. It all seemed so grand!

Floyd and I had seen the Pablo Light Show version of Heavy Organ at the Fox Theatre in San Diego, and were impressed by the images on the giant screen that seemed to fit the music. David's images (which we helped make as members of his "lumierist's" team) were more impressionistic, which is to say "lame."

Actually, our effects were more subtle than Pablo's were, and nicely suited to the music of J. S. Bach. One bitchy Boston critic (who described Virgil as "wearing a silver lamé tuxedo with a slightly ruffled shit"—[sic]) described our effects as "spermy" after a show at the Orpheum.

At the start of that first fall tour, the light show was a complete mess. The most memorable disaster occurred during a performance of a grand finale piece as Virgil raised his hand high in the air before the last crushing chord of the "Passacaglia and Fugue in C Minor."

Our "big" effect was to project a ten-foot tall picture of Bach's face above the organ. Floyd had warned David over a headset that the projector was seizing up; but David refused to turn it off. At the worst possible moment, Bach's image melted and ran down the screen!

Dear Virgil was so wonderful to me personally, especially whenever he and I were alone together. If Virgil didn't walk after practicing, he couldn't sleep. Sometimes I stayed awake long enough to walk with him in the wee hours of the mornings after a concert, after the hours of greeting an audience, the interminable baths (hot and cold), the long, late night meals, and the trip back to the hotels—often with a marvelous historical tour of whatever city we happened to be in. We usually got back by sunrise, then walked together in circles at the back of a Holiday Inn parking lot.

I adored him; and, like many others in his close circle, could never understand why he put up with David when he didn't have to. Virgil sometimes confided in me that he understood what we all had to suffer through, and he loved us for it.

I once got up the courage (after all, I was only a glorified "roadie") to tell him that there were people all over the country who would give anything to be his "partner in life," as he called it; who would be more truthful and honestly love him. He looked me straight in the eye and spoke very slowly and softly. "Chicken," he said, "I love my David; and I know that sometimes he doesn't say or do the right thing. But I'm a strange duck. I don't believe that anyone else would be willing to put up with me."

We never spoke of it again.

In defense of David, I have to say that he was mostly kind to us and sometimes fun (at least when we weren't getting ready for a show). We used to set everything up before he had time to get in the way. He had a lousy memory for musical themes, and so I sometimes had to sing the tune of the piece Virgil was about to play over a headset so David would know which lights to turn on.

I'll never forget the night Virgil said to me, "What would I ever do without you?" It seemed to make it all worthwhile. As many people discovered, Virgil had an uncanny way of saying the right thing when the chips were down. That big round face, the twinkling eyes, the deep low voice and the curved-up lip; the cape and bath towel; or, in later years, the crazy Amelia Earhart hat with the hound dog ears, just added to the overall image. You simply couldn't help but love him.

He also said to me once in a cruel and cold voice, "I'm trying very hard to like you," and I was crushed. Later, after that rather public blowup, he felt so bad that he turned off the organ and came out of the building to find me and apologize. He had been booked to play the giant five-manual Von Beckerath tracker organ in the Oratory in Montreal, and he was a nervous wreck. The top manual of the "museum piece" (or, as one newspaper put it, "tractor action organ") had about twenty-five stops playing on it, none of which coupled to any other manual. The key action was so heavy that it hurt Virgil's fingers. I could tell he was in pain, but he was still determined to use full organ.

In one of the most terrifying moments of my life, he asked me to play along on the top manual! (I could barely reach it without getting in his way.) At the end of the piece, Virgil took a huge bow at the railing. I felt included, and it was wonderful!

The summer of 1973 brought a change for Reid and me. While I had been on the West Coast for a tour, I spent some time in San Francisco visiting friends. While there, I learned from the local Rodgers Organ dealer—who operated out of the store that Clarence Leathurby had operated for many years—that he wanted to leave San Francisco and open up a dealership in Southern California. He thought I would be ideal as a dealer, and he suggested that I think it over. Nothing could have been further from my mind; but the idea of living in San Francisco again was appealing. Several of my friends at the Rodgers factory also thought my taking over the dealership and the store on Golden Gate Avenue was a great idea. After reasoning and pleading with Reid to run the store for me (his business acumen and organizational abilities and good sense were the keys to my even thinking of such a venture), he finally agreed. We bought out Phil Wickstrom, a Rodgers and Ruffatti dealer. On July 1, 1973, we became the Rodgers dealers for Northern California. We had a lot of fun redoing the showroom (Richard thought we ought to call it "Organ Boutique"), and we temporarily took a furnished apartment until we had settled ourselves properly. We decided not to sell or rent the property in Wayne yet, however. Of course, I continued my career and had more concerts than ever from CAMI's Community Concert series. We had a good staff of salespeople at the time, which allowed me to be away from the store for considerable periods. Virgil, Richard, Marshall, Bob Hebble, and Debbie duPont hated the idea of our being so far away; but all of them liked the idea of having a place to stay when they came to San Francisco. Reid's parents, who lived less than a mile from the carriage house in Wayne, looked after all details at the house so that we would have no worries on that score.

When we had the grand opening of "Organ Arts, Ltd.," our name for the store (suggested by Marshall), Virgil and David were present as were Richard and Marshall, Debbie duPont, Richard Purvis, and Andrew Crow; plus executives from the Rodgers Organ Company, and our dear friend and business associate, Francesco Ruffatti. Virgil was now convinced that I would make millions, but cautioned me at the time not to give up playing on the concert stage. "You never know what the future brings, Honey; but you can always use those mitts to make music and earn a good living."

Virgil loved the redone store; and he added a great deal to the opening by his mere presence. Of course, he knew nearly everyone, and had a great time entertaining at the party.

Richard Torrence

Apparently, within a few years, Ted's and Reid's store became sufficiently successful so that Ted was able to cancel his forthcoming season with Community Concerts. He claimed that playing 20 solo and Worth/Crow Duo concerts the following season would be more costly than staying in San Francisco "minding the store."

His decision made no sense to me until I realized that spending too much time on the road might damage his relationship with Reid—who was a young "hunk" compared to Ted, and who was living alone in the gayest of American cities while Ted was on the road four months out of the year.

Fortunately, Marshall and I had marketed another attraction called "Toccatas and Flourishes" for trumpeter Martin Berinbaum and organist Donald Dumler (who had just become the deputy

organist at New York's St. Patrick's Cathedral). After his first sea-
son, Donald decided against continuing to have a career on the
road; and so when Ted canceled his 20 concerts, I quickly replaced
Donald with Richard Morris, and convinced CAMI that Marty
and Richard would be an ideal replacement for Ted.

"Toccatas and Flourishes" became a sensational hit with the
Community Concert Series after we put the attraction together
with Bill Hennessy (who helped originate "the Divine Miss M" for
Bette Midler) to create humorous banter to go with a popular and
virtuosic program for organ and trumpet.

75. Leopold Stokowski

Also, during 1973, Carnegie Hall decided to install a custom built, five-manual Rodgers electronic organ in the revered concert hall. This development culminated several years' work between Richard Torrence and Julius Bloom, then executive director of Carnegie Hall. A year or so previous to this decision, Richard had asked me to play a demonstration on the Rodgers Black Beauty in Carnegie Hall for an audience of one person: Leopold Stokowski! I was thrilled to play for this great man. By now, he was a legend and surely my favorite conductor at the time—and Virgil's, too. I practiced as hard as I could, and had several works ready for the maestro to hear. This event would be an excellent opportunity for the Rodgers Company and me. Maybe he'd even invite me to be a soloist with the American Symphony Orchestra, which was based at Carnegie Hall.

Actually, Carnegie Hall had been given a large "tracker" instrument several years before. It was said that both Vladimir Horowitz and Leopold Stokowski had a great deal to do with stopping Carnegie from installing the tracker organ. It would have been necessary to extend the stage further into the audience at Carnegie; and neither of the artists wanted to risk what might result. Therefore, Carnegie called in Christopher Jaffe, a fine acoustician, who advised them that extending the stage and installing a tracker organ would "change the acoustics." Several acousticians claimed that a new installation might "improve" the acoustics; but—led by Julius Boom—the Board of Directors decided that they liked the acoustics the way they were; changing them was out of the question. As a former organist, well acquainted with E.M. Skinner's work, Stokowski wanted a well-rounded instrument to enhance literature written for organ and orchestra. He also looked forward to a modern organ that could supplement his many sumptuous arrangements. Clearly, the Germanic sound of a Dutch tracker instrument would not have been acceptable to his kind of musicianship.

Maestro Stokowski was then 89 years old! Richard arranged that he, Reid, and I would pick him up at his Fifth Avenue apartment and drive him to the hall. Reid drove my new red Cadillac convertible to the building, and we announced ourselves to the door attendant. In a few minutes, the great man emerged from the elevator. His great shock of white hair and unmistakable profile left no doubt as to who he was. He was most gracious, grabbing both Richard and me by the arms for support in the lobby of his building. Once in the car, I became thoroughly intimidated, and barely able to speak in his presence! He sat in the front seat, and Reid and Richard carried on nicely while I stared in awe. Stokowski asked what kind of car we were in. Reid answered, "A Cadillac." Then Stokowski "discovered" the name on the glove compartment, running one of his long, white fingers across the logo, and saying, "Cadiyyac; how nice!"

(Later, when one of us mentioned the famous Disney movie in which he appeared, he didn't seem to know what the speaker meant by "Fant-AY-zha." Finally, he seemed to get the reference, saying, "Oh, you mean "fan-ta-ZEE-ah"!)

We arrived at the hall. The maestro seated himself mid-way in the orchestra section of the house. The console was on the floor because it was too complicated to bring it onstage for the brief time of the demonstration. The speakers were placed on the stage.

"Who will play for me?" Stokowski asked. I stepped up to the console and turned it on, trying to remember what we decided should be the first piece. He announced imperiously, "Now I'm sure you play the organ magnificently, My Boy; but I'm not interested in you or any organ music!" I was devastated, crushed, angry, and confused; but I managed to control myself. "I want to hear the 32-foot stops. How many have we, and how can we control the volume of each? Play them each for me—slowly. Let the sound sink in; and show me what control you have over their volume."

I did so, one by one. Black Beauty had three 32s: two flues, and a big reed. You could control each one within the swell boxes (you could have them enclosed or unenclosed by the flip of a switch). Also, when you lifted off the tops of the stop jambs, you uncovered controls that greatly reduced or boosted the volume of all sections of the organ right from the console—which was helpful to anyone who had to play the instrument in halls of different sizes.

Fortunately, for us all, Black Beauty had the desired power and quality Stokowski was after. Certainly, the lowest notes shook the auditorium, which pleased the great man no end. He then came up to the console wanting to operate the master volume controls above the stop jambs himself! Then he asked to hear "all the diapasons alone," all the reeds alone, and the "Full Organ!" —which turned out to delight him. He also wanted to know if these wonderful new electronic instruments came any bigger than this three-manual instrument. "Can they build a five-manual organ?" he asked. We certainly thought so!

What I believed was really going through his mind was figuring out how he could augment the various orchestral scores for which he was so famous—whether Wagner, Mahler, Franck, Debussy, Moussorgsky, Tchaikovsky, or his own arrangements of Bach. We think he wanted to add 16-foot and 32-foot pedal lines and points to many of these works, really making the organ an integral part of the orchestra. Unfortunately, between this informal demonstration and Virgil's inauguration of the new five-manual instrument that was ultimately installed in Carnegie Hall, Stokowski died; and with him, his great vision of augmenting the orchestra.

"And now we go to eat!" Stokowski commanded. We drove him to a French *crêpe* restaurant near Lincoln Center. He said that he liked watching the Bretonne women in their native costumes and headdresses making crepes. It was clear, upon arriving at the restaurant, that he—like Virgil—knew the importance of a proper entrance. Everyone in the place knew that someone important had arrived. Several people came to our table to greet him, including Charles Wadsworth of the Lincoln Center Chamber Music Society. Reid and Richard had to make the conversation. I could do little but stare, which my friends kidded me endlessly about later. Normally, one can hardly get a word in edgewise when Richard and I are together; but not on that day!

After lunch, we drove the maestro back to his apartment, thus ending our three-hour encounter with one of the giants of the music world. The result was that Stokowski immediately wrote a letter to

Carnegie Hall recommending the purchase of a Rodgers organ for the auditorium. His signature took up nearly half a page, as I recall. It was this recommendation that got the attention for a new organ for Carnegie hall; and I'm grateful to have played a small part in that decision—even though I never got my "big chance" to play organ repertoire for Stokowski in Carnegie Hall!

Richard Torrence

When I instigated the demonstration by Ted Alan Worth of the Rodgers Touring Organ in Carnegie Hall for Leopold Stokowski, I asked the Rodgers Organ Company to pay $600 to move the organ into the hall. They refused, and I had to pay the bill myself.

At one point during the demonstration, Stokowski asked Ted to "play only the organo pleno *without the mixtures or the 32-foot stops."*

Ted obliged. Stokowski said, "No, I said, no 32-foot stops."

Ted said, "There are no 32-foot stops on, Maestro."

Stokowski said, "I hear a 32-foot open wood."

I knew what was happening, and so I piped up and said, "Maestro, that's the subway!"

Shortly after the demonstration, I received the letter to which Ted refers:

9 January 1970
Dear Friend

I doubt if Carnegie Hall would purchase an organ but, of course, we could try. Failing that we could try to find a person or a Foundation who would give an organ to Carnegie Hall. I will write today to Carnegie Hall suggesting they purchase and install a Rodgers Organ and let you know the result.

Greetings
LEOPOLD STOKOWSKI

76. The Carnegie Hall & Spivey Organs

Richard Torrence; Julius Bloom, Executive Director of Carnegie Hall; and Jim Walls, President of the Rodgers Organ Company finally met seriously about the prospect of installing an organ once again in Carnegie Hall. The original Kilgen had long since been removed. It had never been a success, having been installed in a most peculiar manner. It spoke through a "tone chute" installed a long distance away. Virgil said it had a 32-foot Bombarde that sounded like a "B29 coming in for a landing! But it was so slow to speak, you had to start playing it two or three measures before you wanted it to come on!"

The Flentrop tracker organ that had been donated to the hall was doomed after Julius Bloom made a brilliantly shrewd announcement responding to the discovery that the changes from installing the organ would affect the hall acoustically: "The installation of the mechanical organ in Carnegie Hall has been permanently delayed."

Those who wanted the organ, focused on the word "delayed." Those of us who didn't want a mechanical, "historical" organ, clung to the word "permanently." Everyone was happy for a while—especially us! It was after that announcement that Richard approached Julius and asked that Carnegie Hall consider installing a Rodgers organ.

Julius Bloom was determined that Virgil would have a hand in the tonal design of the new instrument. In return for Rodgers promising Virgil that they would build a duplicate instrument to replace Black Beauty, a large, five-manual specification was designed with a powerful amplification system and many speakers. Four 30-inch woofers were called for in the Pedal division to "move the room."

During the summer of 1974, the speakers were installed above the stage behind the high proscenium curtain; and the large pedal speakers were installed high in the stage house, where they developed a rich, beautiful sound. The amplifiers and generating equipment were located beneath the stage in four huge metal cabinets. The console, of course, could be moved anywhere on the stage. The solution was ideal, given the fact that there was no proper room for a large pipe organ in Carnegie Hall. Even the old chamber, high above the stage, had been turned into a boardroom; and the chute had been closed off.

No one could complain about tampering with the acoustics, because no part of the essential nature of the great hall had to be altered in order to accept the largest electronic organ ever built up to that time. On the evening of October 1, 1974, Virgil opened the new Rodgers Carnegie Hall organ in a solo concert before a packed house—and rave reviews!

Richard and Julius Bloom also designed an inaugural season that featured George Thalben-Ball (of the Temple Church, London), Pierre Cochereau (of Nôtre Dame in Paris), Claire Coci, and the brilliant young Richard Morris from Atlanta, who was also a student of Virgil's. It was a series that displayed not only the virtuosity of the

The Carnegie Hall inaugural organ concert (October 1, 1974)

players, but the versatility and endless possibilities of the new Rodgers organ. Marshall named the series "An Organic Continuum," for it included the Jacques Loussier Trio (a jazz group) and the Paul Winter Consort (of contemporary music) to emphasize the future of the organ as a concert instrument.

Richard had to fight against strong and entrenched forces to make this project a success. First, he had to persuade Julius Bloom and Carnegie Hall of the need for, and desirability of, an electronic organ. Then he had to persuade the Rodgers Organ Company to commit a quarter of a million dollars to develop and build such a large instrument. The plan that Richard, Virgil, and I actually promoted was for Rodgers to add Ruffatti pipes to the scheme, not only for their intrinsic musical value, but also to enhance the stage visually. The Ruffattis designed drawings for the project, but Julius feared that any alternation or addition to the back wall of the stage would evoke howls of criticism that would ruin the entire project. Richard pleaded tirelessly in favor of pipes being added to the Carnegie organ someday—at least 25 ranks of them! I believe that if these plans had been achieved, the instrument would have withstood any detractors.

William T. Armstrong, M.D. is a cardiologist in San Francisco. He was Virgil Fox's personal physician, as well as Ted Alan Worth's and Reid Betten's doctor and friend.

Dr. Armstrong

Alas, the Carnegie Hall Organ is no longer in Carnegie Hall! (But that's another story.)

After Virgil had played the opening concert on the huge five-manual Rodgers, for some reason the original "dogleg" bench for the organ was declared unsuitable, and it was returned to the factory. When Virgil heard about it, he called the factory and ordered them to "Send the bench to Bill Armstrong with his new Gemini Organ." Virgil later scrawled on the bottom of the footrest with a large felt pen: "Dearest Bill, This began with my concert on the stage of Carnegie Hall on October 1, 1974, and it now lives with you in California! Always my love and Best Wishes, Virgil Fox 9/21/75."

The bench is one of my prized possessions. Three years ago, when I contracted for a big four-manual instrument, the new console was built to match "Virgil's bench," not the other way around!

Richard and I and the Rodgers Organ Company, with the help of Allen Harrah (an Atlanta Rodgers and Ruffatti salesman at the time; much later to become the president of the Rodgers Organ Company!), had developed a combination organ of electronics and pipes; and the results were musically and visually remarkable.

The first of these instruments was built for Virgil's friend, Emilie Spivey of Atlanta. She had long wanted an organ in her magnificent home (on Lake Spivey near Atlanta); but after she heard the limited sound possibilities of the electronic instruments that Rodgers and its chief competitor, Allen Organs of Macungie, Pennsylvania were offering, she had abandoned all thoughts of an electronic organ for her home. A pipe organ would have been out of the question. When Allen Harrah met her, however, he made her an interesting offer.

"What if we added a Great Organ, consisting of principal and flute choruses, to a Rodgers organ? Would that interest you?" She was intrigued to such a degree that she bought the organ!

Allen Harrah ordered the pipes and a chest from Ruffatti. He also ordered Rodgers' newest three-manual electronic model. Initially, he purposely withheld the information from both companies that he intended to marry the two instruments. One other company had attempted to combine instruments many years before, but the results had been a huge failure. Allen Harrah, however, knew enough about both kinds of organs to be able to create a workable interface that allowed both electronically-produced and wind-produced sounds to blend. Furthermore, he came up with an ingenious design for the whole installation. He installed the console in a gazebo-like room that had been added to the drawing room. Previously, the room had featured a bay window view of Lake Spivey. The large drawing room itself had deep cabinets on the inner wall between the room and the entrance foyer. Into these cabinets went the speakers and the chest, on top of which was an attractive display of pipes. The dimensions of the rooms turned out to be perfect for a combination organ. The musical results caused a sensation!

When word got back to each of the two companies, Rodgers was apprehensive. Allen couldn't wait for Richard and me to hear his innovation—and by that time, he had already sold a second, larger combination instrument to a church north of Atlanta.

It was time to visit Emilie and see for ourselves. We were thrilled when we got down there and heard! Then James Walls, President of Rodgers, and Francesco Ruffatti gathered to see Emilie's organ as well. They, too, were deeply impressed. With some pushing from Richard, Allen, and me, the idea of creating a product that would be built by both companies became a reality. Emilie's instrument was named "Opus One" of this series; but technically, it wasn't a part of the series, for it was only a standard Rodgers instrument with pipes added. We carefully designed a new class of comprehensive instruments combining pipes and electronics before Rodgers announced its new line of combination organs.

Marshall wrote about the new product in monthly full-page advertisements in such publications as *The American Organist*. "The wonder of pipes and the magic of electronics" was how he called it. He also named the product "Gemini," after the sign of the Zodiac. The subtitle was: "The Twins. Princes of Instruments."

Richard Morris, who studied with Virgil Fox, later worked for his concert management, and eventually became a lead-

ing recital organist (teaming up with the trumpeter Martin Berinbaum, and later with organist Hector Olivera) on the Community Concert circuit.

Richard Morris

In the spring of 1972, while undergoing a theological "retread" process in a Trappist monastery, preparing to take up the priesthood, I met Emilie Spivey in her home. The "Opus I" Rodgers-Ruffatti combination organ was still being uncrated. She asked me to play (on her piano) a few parts of the Reubke "Sonata on the 94th Psalm," which I was then studying. (Much later I had the sad privilege of playing that piece at her funeral.) When I finished, she turned to Allen Harrah and said, "He must go and play for Virgil!" When I protested that my organ playing was hardly at the level of that great musician, she insisted. She even called Virgil herself and talked him into seeing me.

Some months later, I flew to New York for my first lesson at Virgil's residence in Englewood. It took place at the strange hour of 10 p.m. (I hadn't yet understood his preference for "vampire hours.")

I arrived in clerical collar, which was my practice in those days, and he immediately asked me, "Must I call you Father?" (I got the impression he wasn't particularly fond of Catholics.) I told him he could call me whatever he liked. He said, "Since I call everybody Honey, I think I'll call you 'Father Honey.'"

And so he did.

To my great relief, his comment after I played the first movement of the Bach "Trio Sonata in C" was, "Stunning! I haven't heard it played that fast or clean since Alexander Schreiner was 25! He hasn't played it since!"

We took a short break for a six-ounce bottle of Coke (for which he charged a dollar: "I can't just give these things away, you know!").

I had studied previously with some distinguished instructors, including Casadesus and Boulanger (refreshments free!); but I had never experienced such minute and generous attention to every detail regarding organ technique, registration, and interpretation. Nevertheless, he would invariably say, "This is the way I do it. If you want to do it another way, that's fine. Don't go out there and try to be me. Be yourself. That's what people want to hear!"

Prior to these lessons, it hadn't entered my mind to try to make a career as an organist. Virgil sensed my indecision, and we talked about it at great length. Finally, he came up with one of his incredibly phrased bits of advice. He put one hand on my shoulder, looked me straight in the eye, and said, "Take that religious collar off and play the organ the way you were born to!"

And so I did.

77. Virgil's Women Friends

There was never any question in Emilie's mind about who would inaugurate her new organ. Virgil had known Emilie for nearly thirty years. He had always said, "Honey, you've got to have an organ in this palace, just like Florence always had!" (Virgil's reference to Florence Candler was rubbing salt into a local wound.) "When you get one, I'll play the opening concert!"

When Emilie took Virgil up on his offer, David unfortunately coached him to demand his regular solo fee, which by that time had risen to $5,000. Emilie was crushed. It wasn't that she couldn't afford the fee, but she was disappointed that her dear friend Virgil would ask for any fee at all! Virgil (and David) had stayed with Walter and Emilie for days at a time whenever Virgil was in town. Having Virgil for a houseguest was no day at the beach! His sleeping and waking habits were abnormal, and he was as demanding about his food as if he had reserved a table at an expensive restaurant. Emilie's household help almost went into open rebellion, and Emilie had no skills when it came to the kitchen. Nevertheless, she and Walter cheerfully put up with all the inconvenience because Virgil was who he was, and because he never failed to entertain them. Emilie had also presented Virgil in concert many times, and had fought with the local Guild chapter to get Virgil on the program of the 1966 AGO National Convention in Atlanta. She wasn't fond of David, however, and when she realized that David was encouraging Virgil to demand a fee, she invited both of them to "stay home" for the organ dedication.

Virgil was hurt, and the incident began a short period of coolness between Virgil and Emilie. The upshot was that the honor fell to me. I was thrilled when Emilie asked me to play the two concerts she had scheduled to open the organ. She was willing to pay my fee; but because she had been so good to Richard, Reid, the Ruffattis, and me, I said that it would be an honor for me to play *gratis*. She paid all my expenses and treated me like a prince during the time I was preparing for the concerts. I also wanted to play for nothing so as not to upset Virgil even further.

Emilie's two concerts on the day of the inauguration of the organ took place in the afternoon and evening. She had invited all her musical, rich, and socially prominent friends from Atlanta and around the country. The day was splendid, and the food and decorations were superb! Virgil would have reveled in every moment of it, as did I; and it's too bad we both couldn't have had such fond memories of that day.

During the afternoon concert, one of the women sitting close to the console in the gazebo smiled at me several times. I was charmed by her smile, but even more, I couldn't help noticing the enormous diamond on one of her fingers. I later asked Emilie about this woman and the enormous "rock." Emilie identified her dear friend as Katherine Ryan. She said that the diamond cost more to insure than most diamonds would cost to purchase! (Katherine's grandfather, it seems, had invented the bottle cap!) A few months later, Katherine became the major donor of a new Ruffatti organ to be installed in the Roman Catholic Cathedral of Christ the King. (Sometimes it pays to play for nothing; or, as they say in church, "Give, and ye shall receive!" That lesson was one that Virgil never mastered. After David appeared on the scene, there was little hope he ever would.)

This discussion leads me to share some of my impressions of Virgil's relationships to people he knew who had considerable wealth. The subject beguiled him. Wealthy women of taste and culture, many of whom were eccentric, fascinated him the most, and he loved to tell stories about these women.

Rich women loved to tell stories about him, as well! One of the most memorable of these tales was revealed by the San Francisco doyenne, Irma Salz, who was Jewish. Upon being introduced to Virgil, she immediately realized how exotic Jews could be in the eyes of someone born in Princeton, Illinois. Apparently, in order to put Irma and her husband, Milton, at ease in the company of a Christian who didn't know many Jews, one of Virgil's first questions he put to her was, "Tell me; how many Jews *did* Hitler kill?"

"Six-million," shot back Milton.

(Fortunately, the relationship improved after that lowest of points. In fact, it became quite close, which was usually the case with Virgil.)

One of Virgil's closest relationships was with Mrs. John D. Archbold, whose husband had co-founded Standard Oil with John D. Rockefeller Sr. Archbold had amassed a fortune, which he left to his daughter Anne, who became a doyenne of Washington, D.C. society. Mrs. Archbold had met Virgil (when he was a sergeant in the Army Air Force) while he was stationed at Bolling Field with duties at Walter Reid Hospital. She was interested in the welfare of injured service members who were being rehabilitated at the hospital. Anne would regularly open her great house to these veterans, and she gave many parties for them. She always wanted entertainment at these functions, and so Virgil became an important part of these affairs. He would organize the many talented singers and instrumentalists to perform, often accompanying the singers on the piano, or leading "sing-a-longs" of popular tunes of the day on Mrs. Archbold's three-manual Æolian pipe organ in the music room.

Virgil and Anne became great friends. Mrs. Archbold invited Virgil to live in her house anytime he could manage to be away from the base. Virgil loved to say, "I slept between satin sheets in Annie Archbold's Palace the entire time I was in the service!" He was exaggerating slightly, to be sure; but Virgil loved the milieu because he could get to know so many of Mrs. Archbold's friends.

"Annie" Archbold invited Virgil year after year to her compound in Nassau, in the Bahamas, to enjoy the February sun, and to play a concert (for which she paid) each season in the Anglican Cathedral. Mrs. Archbold could be stingy, bold, and abrupt with her servants. One day, as Virgil tells it, she spied some dust on the top of her piano in the music room. She suddenly roared, "Donald! Polish the piano," as the poor servant flew about to find polish and dust cloth. She then began to beat him across the back with her sweater, roaring with laughter at the effect that this strange behavior had to have on young Sergeant Virgil Fox.

Annie was a direct person with a strong, loud voice to express her opinions. Virgil once asked her a question about how much money she really had (a question he was often known to pose almost immediately on meeting someone rich). Annie said, "How would I know? There's an office in New York filled with people that count it. Ask them!" Virgil roared with laughter, but he was still determined to find out the extent of her wealth. He never did, although Mrs. Archbold did leave him the $10,000 bequest when she passed away.

Virgil encountered many wealthy people when he became the organist of the Riverside Church. Mr. and Mrs. John D. Rockefeller Jr. were fond of him, and several times, he was invited to perform at their Tarrytown estate, "Pocantico Hills." The first Mrs. Rockefeller (Abby Aldrich Rockefeller) was particularly fond of him, and Virgil used to regale us with tales of his visits there. The second Mrs. Rockefeller (Martha Baird Rockefeller) was notably musical and appreciative of Virgil's helping her choose a new Steinway grand piano. ("Mr. Junior," as they called him, had asked Virgil to help his wife choose the piano at Steinway Hall). The second Mrs. Rockefeller never really warmed up to Virgil, however. She grew even less fond of him after the new organ at the Riverside Church was installed. It was far too loud and boisterous for her tastes. She preferred intimate Mozart and Schubert, whose music she liked to play in the solitude of her own music room.

Nan Erickson was the widow of the founder of the McCann Erickson advertising agency. Virgil visited her often in her Murray Hill house wherein her "million dollar Rembrandt" hung. (After she died, the Metropolitan Museum purchased the painting for *several* million dollars.)

Virgil also knew the widow of Gustav Mahler, who invited him (and once me) to share her Metropolitan Opera box, and to New York Philharmonic Concerts.

Robert Hebble

Almost every time I visit New York, I go to the Metropolitan Museum of Art to look at the famous painting by Rembrandt called "Aristotle Contemplating the Bust of Homer." It's like an old friend because it reminds me of the time when Virgil and I sat at Nan Erickson's Steinway piano, banging out "Tea for Two" right next to that famous painting.

When Mrs. Erickson died, the museum bought it from her estate for the highest price yet paid for a work of art: $5-million! Who knew?

78. HISS!

I shall mercifully omit the name of one of Virgil's dearest friends, the former wife of the scion of one of the richest families in the nation. This woman was quite beautiful, and she was a former singer who admired Virgil's genius greatly. She worked hard on behalf of an evangelical society, and she once invited Virgil (who dragged along Bob, Richard, Marshall, and me) to her country estate for what we thought was going to be a social party. As we were driving there, Virgil warned us not to ask for a cocktail, as this religious woman probably didn't believe in drinking—which was completely agreeable for our tea-totaling Virgil! When we arrived, the butler asked us what we would like for refreshments. Virgil glared in our direction, and so we all ordered iced tea. About five minutes later, one of the other guests arrived and, in a whiskey tenor, ordered a vodka stinger. Richard immediately switched to a gin and tonic, and the rest of us followed suit. We definitely needed a few drinks, because we had discovered that the larger party we were attending, which was being held out doors on the extensive property, was going to be a Christian youth "culture rally." Really!

Food was served to the privileged few, like us, who were invited into the house, and who had arrived before the other guests appeared for the outdoor party. After lunch, Virgil asked for some of the blueberries he had spied for dessert—but with sour cream rather than plain yogurt on them. Our host was quite proud of the blueberries, because they were prepared in a special way. First, they were frozen. Later, they were partially thawed for serving with the yogurt. Most of the blueberries seemed to have escaped the thaw, however, because when we bit down on them they were rock solid. Virgil said, "They're just like bullets! How the hell do we get out of this?" There was no escape.

Marshall, who hated plain yogurt and didn't want sour cream, figured out a solution. He walked into the kitchen and asked the butler for something different from yogurt or sour cream. He got vanilla ice cream! He gave back the blueberries and finished the ice cream in the kitchen, too embarrassed to return with his special dessert.

As the rest of us finished our "bullets," we noticed several teenage entertainers coming through the front door. Virgil described them as "pale faces"—pimply-faced youths devoid of style or make-up, carrying guitars and accordions.

We were herded out to the lawn area where the rally was to take place. At least 100 gold-colored chairs had been set up, and other guests were already sitting in them. Virgil and his guests were asked to sit with our host, which we knew spelled disaster; for all of us were prone to fits of hysterical laughter when stuck into absurd situations—which this one was guaranteed to be. (Virgil was always the worst in such predicaments!)

Rather than court disaster, we decided to separate. Richard, Marshall, and I found seats together, and Bob sat alone a few rows ahead of us. This arrangement was wise, because the Hebble-Worth combination could be lethal in such situations. We could disrupt everything by failing to control ourselves if something even remotely amusing occurred. We were certain that this program would provide ample opportunities for a complete and utter breakdown!

To make matters worse, the day seemed to be turning into one of those hot, humid, and stifling mid-summer evenings, in which there was no trace of a breeze. There began to appear, however, swarms of ravenous insects gathering forces. Virgil had been bitten once, already, and so he asked one of the servants for some bug repellent. The servant provided Virgil with what appeared to be an industrial size spray can of Raid that none of the rest of us would have touched. (It seemed to be more suitable for floors and corners than human skin!)

In front of us, once we were seated, was a makeshift stage with professional stage lighting. When every chair was filled (some with stunning people who looked quite prosperous—one of them was the famous bandleader, Lester Lanin), the "show" began.

The dreary parade of entertainers that followed was, to give the Devil his due, well intentioned. Mostly, it was youngsters giving the typical Christian conversion testimonial. These heartfelt episodes were followed by a grim program of sing-a-longs and solos played and sung by dull and untalented amateurs. The worst moment came when it was announced that all these cheery young folks had just returned from an evangelical tour of Europe, to which God had given them the opportunity to "bring culture to the Europeans." Shocking!

The affair dragged on and on. It seemed that every time some particularly jarring or offensive remark was uttered, or some hideously out-of-tune guitar and accordion duet was being performed, Virgil would use his bug bomb to punctuate the moment with a resounding HISS that none of the "chicks," wherever we were seated, could fail to notice.

I don't have to recount how many times we started to laugh, while tensing ourselves to regain control and not embarrass ourselves completely. The program got so bad that the bug bomb seemed to be going off continuously, all the more audible because of the stillness of the night. I'm sure that Virgil knew perfectly well the effect he was having on us. Apparently, it was sufficiently amusing to him to endure surrounding himself and those nearest him with asphyxiating gas!

Mercifully, there was an intermission—which was used to take up a collection! Baskets were passed, often filled with sizable checks. The baskets also contained blank checks, in case some of us forgot to bring our checkbooks with us. This system was definitely not like the one-dollar-per-person collection plate we were used to at church! I recall that one of the officers of Pepperidge Farm Bread had put in a large donation, which illustrates the quality of the crowd she had there.

I regret to admit that these people got no money out of us. Virgil raced into the house to avoid being in place when the plate arrived. When he came back, he wandered over to our section to make sure his aerosol bomb was making the right impression. His wicked smile revealed his delight in extracting at least a few memorable moments out of the gruesome affair.

After it ended, we paid our respects and thanks to our dear host (whom we all truly adored—she's one of the nicest of Virgil's friends I ever met!). The woman had obviously tried to make the best of a difficult and embarrassing situation. By that time, I think she'd guessed that she'd invited some of the wrong crowd.

We fled back to Virgil's Cadillac convertible with Lester Lanin, who had asked for a ride back with us, admitting he couldn't take any more.

Like Marshall, Lester Lanin was Jewish. These situations, and some others like it, have taught me that these kinds of proceedings don't sit well with most Jews. I consider myself a fervent Christian, but even I consider certain kinds of evangelism to be offensive whenever they assume that the rest of us (Episcopalians) who don't wear our Christian hearts on our sleeves are less sincere than the ones who proclaim their piety to anyone within earshot.

As for the Jews, let me just say in passing that when Virgil introduced Marshall to our hostess that evening, he immediately told her that Marshall was Jewish (for what purpose, I wondered: to make everyone feel even more uncomfortable?). Our host immediately remarked, "Well, some of our most fervent supporters are former Hebrews!"

Before we could leave the property, we had to pass through a gang of young people handing out religious literature. After Virgil accepted enough packets for all of us through the window, he floored the accelerator and raced down the road as fast as possible, leaving the window open long enough to throw out the literature (which included a tiny copy of the New Testament called "Good News for Modern Man," I'm sorry to report). He rushed toward the city, determined to make it to Rumplemeyer's before closing time.

We laughed almost all the way back. After the third serving of chocolate sauce at Rumplemeyer's, Virgil said, "How dare she trick us into going out there for a religious rally! What nerve!"

Marshall Yaeger

Virgil had, of course, made a fair amount of money from performing for church audiences, and I never witnessed him bite the hand that fed him by making disparaging remarks about Christian beliefs. I don't believe he took seriously any dogmas, however, because the beliefs he did espouse usually confirmed how much a sucker he was for any kind of woo-woo convictions—the more extreme the better.

"Red Blanket" (a Native American spirit that helped him find parking spaces) typified the kind of "true beliefs" of Virgil Fox during the time I knew him best. It was only one example of the mysticism, apparitions, spirits, witches, faith healers, and ghosts that wandered through the various "planes" ("earthly" and "spiritual") that Virgil believed human beings temporarily or permanently inhabit.

Virgil often quoted Harry Emerson Fosdick's remark that the only true "miracle" wasn't that we "surv-IVE" [death]; but that we "arr-IVE" [in the first place]. That quote was about as religious as he got.

Although that remark may indicate (not incorrectly) that I personally regard almost any kind of mysticism with skepticism—if not downright contempt—the fact is that for a period of time, while living in Virgil's house and sleeping across the hall from his bedroom, I began to see and hear strange goings-on while alone in our bedroom, usually in the morning. What appeared in occasional flashes was the impression of a silvery coffee can top flying from the left side of the room to the right, accompanied by the distinct sound of labored breathing.

I witnessed this apparition for several weeks with no insight into what it might be. Then, one evening, I mentioned it to Virgil and watched him turn pale.

"Someday I'll tell you what you saw!" he exclaimed.

For some reason, an explanation instantly occurred to me that seemed reasonable, and I shared it with him immediately.

"Did someone die in that room?" I asked.

"How did you know?"

"Was it Grace Weagly? Was she cremated?"

Virgil confirmed that my suspicions were true. Richard Weagly's mother had died of emphysema in that very room!

"And were her ashes put in a coffee can?" I continued. "And was the coffee can placed on a shelf on the wall of the bedroom?"

"Yeah!"

"And did she never receive a Christian burial?"

"How could you possibly know that Weagly never had a proper ceremony?"

I brought Virgil up to the bedroom and asked him if he could hear the heavy breathing (which might have been typical of someone dying of a lung disease) that was so evident to me.

Neither Virgil nor Richard Torrence (who accompanied us) could hear what I heard, even though I continued to hear it, even with two other people present! Then I realized that there are more things in heaven and earth, Horatio, than are dreamt of in your philosophy!

Of course I accepted the scientific fact that the whole business was completely in my head; but there it was; and I had to offer the best explanation I could—and better yet, one that my landlord, Virgil, would accept.

"I think she's sending us a message!"

Although I'm neither a Christian, nor a believer in any kind of hocus-pocus, I decided to hold a "Bell, Book, and Candle" ceremony to exorcise whatever was continuing to fly across the bedroom wall, especially on bright, sunny mornings, giving me the creeps. (I figured, it couldn't hurt!)

The ceremony was properly done (in my opinion, although I was the only witness), and was accompanied by some weird psychological portents. I let the Bible open randomly, and read some sections that seemed incredibly appropriate. Then I closed the book, rang a tinkly little dinner bell with which Virgil sometimes summoned his live-in servant to the dinner table, blew out an inch-long candle stub that had been stored for electrical blackouts, and left the room feeling there was something definitely in there, hovering around my back.

The flying coffee can lid's appearance continued for a time, but eventually diminished. Richard and I moved to the carriage house on Virgil's property leading to no further discourse with ghosts. Some years later, a certified (and rather famous) witch named Sybil Leek visited Virgil's house and confirmed that there was, indeed, a ghost still living between the walls of what had separated our bedroom from David's room.

I'm sure Sybil was wrong! I'm sure I settled the issue for Grace, and I'm pretty sure she currently rests in peace!

While practicing for a recital in London's Temple Church, where he was scheduled to play Franz Liszst's "Fantasy and Fugue on the Chorale, 'Ad nos, ad salutarem undam,'" Virgil noticed a strange movement out of the corner of his eye—or perhaps it was a gentle breeze that disturbed him several times. He was alone, and couldn't understand what was going on, when all of a sudden a voice said to him: "Move that passage along—hold back there—this is too slow—move ahead," and so forth.

Back in Philadelphia, Virgil swore to me that it was the spirit of Franz Liszt telling him how to interpret the work! I was skeptical, of course, but held my tongue (which could be understandably irreverent in those days—as well as these!).

However, when I left, Virgil asked me where I was off to. I simply said, "I'm meeting Brahms at the Allegro," referring to a local gay bar I had occasion to frequent.

"Oh, you!" he said.

David Lewis

There was a time when I had become interested in the "Spirit World," and I was "kinda good" at what they call automatic writ-

ing. When David and Virgil were having trouble at the castle, Virgil actually came to visit us in California and asked me to sit with them to contact the spirits, hoping to find out what to do. He appeared to get some useful information from the encounter, particularly the names of people to watch out for. Shortly thereafter, Virgil moved to Florida.

Gosh, maybe the whole thing was my fault!

---

79. The Hammond Castle

Virgil had approached both Emilie Spivey and Florence Candler for large sums of money several times. Usually, Virgil was raising money for an unreliable scheme. One such scheme was to "purchase" the Hammond Castle and Museum in Gloucester, Massachusetts. Jack Hammond, who was Virgil's dear friend (he had become rich by inventing guided missiles), died and left his estate and the Castle to the Roman Catholic Archdiocese of Boston. Virgil surmised that the Archdiocese didn't need or want a gigantic estate with horrendously expensive maintenance costs; and so he offered the Church a deal whereby he would live in the castle, run an annual concert series, and pay for the upkeep of the house for the rest of his life. This entire scheme would cost him about a quarter of a million dollars.

Of course, Virgil had recorded the organ of the Hammond Castle, which he adored, and probably coveted its 101 rooms; its ninety-foot high Great Hall that housed a huge pipe organ; its indoor pool with the façades of Tudor houses all around the pool; its drawbridge, Great Tower, and a fortune's worth of medieval treasures that included statues, furniture, tapestries, paintings, and precious artifacts.

We all thought Virgil was insane to assume such a responsibility, although we could imagine him running a museum while wandering through the cold Massachusetts premises like a deposed royal pretender. Richard Morris, who worked for Virgil's management at the time, composed a little ditty to the tune of "Pretty Baby":

> *Every queen must have her castle*
> *And now Virgil has one too*
> *Hammond Castle!*
> *Hammond Castle!*

There were a few drawbacks to the scheme, however. For one thing, the entire building leaked and needed a new roof. There were other significant malfunctions in the workings of the castle, of which the cost of repairs promised to be monumental. Then there was the cost of heating the premises!

Virgil would simply say, "Honeys, the concerts I'll give on that organ will bring in a fortune!"

It was true; the summer series always drew huge crowds. However, nothing happened the rest of the year. We pointed out this and other negative aspects to the scheme, not the least of which was the frigid winter. We knew how much Virgil loved sunshine and warm weather. Nothing could be further from that ideal than this dour edifice on Gloucester's "Hesperus Point" in the middle of winter, a long and difficult way from the Boston airport during inclement weather. None of these problems phased Virgil (or David, who was egging him on, I'm sure). He became more determined than ever to become a royal presence in his very own palace!

Virgil asked both Florence and Emilie for the quarter of a million dollars needed to assume the trusteeship of the castle and museum. Both turned him down politely. Privately, they both thought that he had finally "gone round the bend." Virgil could not be deterred, however, and continued to beg from almost every wealthy friend he knew for money, even the stingy Richard Simonton (who, it turned out, was privately trying to acquire the castle for himself!). In the end, it was Virgil's blessed and completely unselfish mother, Bird, who came to the rescue.

Bird had owned two farms in Illinois for years, although she resided in Pasadena, and later in Altadena, California. The farms were worth a great deal of money, and she supported herself from the rent of several tenant farmers that managed the properties. She finally agreed to lend Virgil the money he needed until, eventually, he sold and moved out of the Englewood mansion, using the profits to pay her back.

(Virgil had purchased the mansion for $68,000 and sold it for $238,000.)

From the beginning, the move to Gloucester generated one disaster after another. It seemed that every "improvement" he made angered either the archdiocese or the Gloucester Historical Society—whether these improvements entailed moving the organ console, or purchasing a second organ in order to enlarge the first

Virgil at the balcony console of the John Hays Hammond Museum

(reflecting his impossible dream to finally have an unparalleled large house organ), or redoing a suite for his private living quarters in his inimitable taste (which ranged from pink telephones to pink Cadillacs).

The revenues from the concert series were disappointing, despite the efforts of Virgil's 80+ mother, Bird, whom I vividly remember sweeping the walk, picking up cigarette butts after the crowds, and taking tickets; and some possibly libelous articles in the Gloucester papers about the "mad organist" and "his kind" of friends who had taken over their beloved museum in order to swarm like flies, throughout the property.

(Interestingly, it recently came out that E. Power Biggs was one of the major forces behind a vicious public relations campaign originating in Massachusetts to remove Virgil from his royal seat of power!)

The Hammond Castle misadventure mercifully ended none too soon—but unfortunately not soon enough to prevent Virgil from losing a great deal of money.

Floyd Watson

Several of the "roadies" and I were invited to the opening party at Virgil's Castle. At least we thought we had been invited, until Virgil told us that the "entrance fee" was fifty dollars each. "Hey, you invited me!" I complained.

"Well, Honey, everyone has to pay," Virgil said.

We reached a compromise. We could stay at the castle for nothing, but would have to pay for the food. Three of us went into town and bought a book each of restaurant checks. Every hors d'oeuvre we ate at the opening party we tallied up as accurately as we could. Virgil was furious, but finally said we could eat whatever we wanted. "No charge!"

David Lewis

Virgil's party was like stepping back in time, with an all-black dance band, which was out of character for Virgil, and everyone in tails and tuxes in that creepy old castle. They'd rented a bubble machine, maybe in homage to David's Revelation Lights, which was supposed to waft bubbles over a reflecting pool that Virgil and David had spent a fortune dredging out and restoring. The pool was at the end of the great hall, directly under the Cardinal's window—it was beautiful!

We were all pretty wasted (from champagne we had to sneak into the house in violation of Virgil's tea-totaling house rules). While trying to figure out how much soap to put in the hopper, we poured it all in.

It was amazing. Within minutes, the whole pool was covered several feet deep with an undulating mass of suds. No more wispy airborne bubbles! I remember using something just in time to stop the wall of foam from running down the stone steps into the great hall; but the rest of my memories of that wonderfully strange evening were blurred from that point on.

80. Skimming the Cream

During the latter part of his life, Virgil finally met one of the world's richest women, Mrs. Marjorie Merriweather Post. Mrs. Post was said to be "as deaf as a post," and so it was no mystery why she was so taken with Virgil. His loud, booming voice was more audible to her than any other. His artistry, engaging personality, and spontaneity, of course, also made him great fun to be with, and probably far more entertaining to her than most of the social guests she invited down to her Florida estate by the hundreds.

Andy Crow loved to tell tales of their visit to "Mar-a-Lago," Mrs. Post's Palm Beach "palace." (Donald Trump was a later owner.) Virgil had been invited by Mrs. Post to play a concert at Mar-a-Lago for one of her favorite charities, the Palm Beach Animal Rescue League (which is no doubt an essential charity in one of the richest neighborhoods in the world!). Virgil was to play in the "Pavilion" on the extensive property, which Mrs. Post erected for square dancing, which was one of her favorite pastimes. Andy tells of the wonderful treatment they received as guests. Virgil and Andy had separate guesthouses on the property. Every day they found a published schedule of events from which to choose. The mealtimes were listed for breakfast, lunch, and dinner; and they could choose whether to have lunch with the other guests (and sometimes Mrs. Post) or to have food brought to the guesthouse—much as would be done in a gracious hotel. Everything was free, of course, which delighted both Virgil and Andrew. There were even automobiles available for the guests. "Do you need a car?" Virgil loved to repeat. "Will you require a driver?"

The main house had 118 rooms. (The dining room had 27 different china patterns and at least 4,000 pieces of silver!) Virgil used to say that he never saw a leaf on the lawn because there was always a servant around to catch one as it fell!

Mrs. Post obviously liked Virgil. During many of the meals in the main dining room, she always seated him next to her. Then, when the Duke and Duchess of Windsor visited one day, she invited Virgil—and Virgil alone—to escort her to tea with the Windsors. Virgil had once exchanged pleasantries with them on a beach in the Riviera.

Richard Torrence

Virgil loved to tell the story about when he met the "Duck and Doochess." He was vacationing at a beach resort in the South of France when the famous couple came walking by. He happened to see the Duchess drop a rubber beach shoe, which he retrieved. When he caught up with them, he realized that paparazzi were taking photos of everyone. He spoke briefly to the couple and later recognized his photograph when it was published in a magazine. It shows the Windsors talking to Virgil. All it shows of Virgil is his right hand holding a rubber shoe.

After one of the evening feasts, she announced that there would be a square dance. Andy described a look of disbelief on Virgil's face as the guests began to move into place. "Imagine," he said to Andy in his stage whisper, "The richest woman in the world, surrounded by great art and the most famous people at her beck and call, and she wants to square dance!" Virgil, of course, swung into amused delight. Andy claims he entered the fun with great gusto.

It wasn't too long into his first visit to Mrs. Post's when Virgil "popped the question" he inevitably asked of all his rich friends, no matter how horrified our expressions became when he told us later. "Marjorie, if you needed to, exactly how much cash could you lay your hands on in the space of twenty-four earthly hours?"

Mrs. Post laughed, shrugging off the question graciously, saying, "I haven't the slightest idea!"

Virgil wouldn't give up, however. He broached the subject more than once, even telling her of his life-long wish to travel around the world with a moving pipe organ. She suggested he apply to her foundation for a grant. Richard and Marshall had often tried to explain that any rich person or foundation would probably consider his request if it would benefit more than one person (besides Virgil himself). Grants should aim toward an educational purpose, possibly involving emerging artists; or they should benefit the public through festivals and free concerts, which could help elevate the prestige of the organ and its artists. Virgil never understood such reasoning. His credo always was: "I stand alone." With such a narrow attitude, he was never able to secure the kind of charitable financial help he needed to realize his greatest dream.

None of his rich friends seemed overly offended by his forward questioning as to the vastness of their fortunes. (It's usually the case that rich people are flattered when given the opportunity to be asked to contribute!) Most of them probably blamed Virgil's childish questions on his eccentric genius. Certainly, his child-like delight with beauty and wealth contributed to his genius. Somerset Maugham quoted a Chinese proverb that credited all truly great gifted people with a child-like wonder that helps keep them youthful and creative lifelong. Virgil was certainly never bored, never boring, and always attracted to beautiful things, even of the smallest size. He was always ready to have fun, laugh, and entertain any audience, large or small, through music or entertaining repartee. Thus, he never damaged his relationships with his rich friends, even after making outrageous requests. These people genuinely loved and admired him, and they always forgave his child-like behavior.

He never got any significant amounts of money out of any of them; only, occasionally, a concert fee, accommodations, and meals. Only Annie Archbold remembered and left him money when she died. The moment he learned of his good fortune, he saluted heaven and said, "Thank you Annie. Have a good trip!"

Once, Florence Candler was visiting San Francisco on her way back to Atlanta from a trip to the Orient. Florence invited Richard, Marshall, and me to lunch at the St. Francis Hotel where she was staying. I'll never forget that lunch, because seated not ten feet from our table was one of my idols, the British actor Charles Laughton. I was fascinated by him and the group of attractive young men dining with him. Florence pounded the table and said, "Don't look at him— he's a bore!" I continued to look however. The conversation turned to Virgil and what he was up to. She then looked directly at Richard and said in her heavy Southern accent, "We all know dear Virgil! He skims the cream off the top."

I remember Florence telling a story about her boat trip to the Orient. She said that there was a nurse from Atlanta on the boat who tried to get friendly with her. At one point, the nurse said, "You must have a very elegant house!" Florence said she retorted, "There are only two things elegant about my house: the furnishings and *me!*"

(By that time Florence had sold the big Buckhead mansion, moving to elegant West Paces Ferry Road—but not into a grand house.)

Carlo Curley

When I left school, I headed for the bright lights of Atlanta, where I took a church job in a large Baptist Preaching Palace. After a while, I chanced to meet up with an elderly pillar of my congregation whose friendship, genuine affection, well-placed connections, substantial means, and unswerving generosity would alter my circumstances and overall direction forever.

Florence S. Candler was the widow of Asa Griggs Candler Jr., of the Atlanta Coca-Cola family and an ardent supporter of many artistic endeavors and institutions in the steamy South and beyond. Hers was very much "old money." She lived alone attended by a brace of devoted servants in a handsomely furnished residence in Atlanta's affluent Buckhead area, only minutes from the Governor's Mansion. This adorable chatelaine's affection for the organ was strong and well documented, as her previous home (a colossal mansion named "Briarcliff") had been enhanced by the presence of a 1925, four-manual Æolian organ of nearly ninety independent registers played not only by numerous Duo-Art player rolls, but by such illustrious figures as Bossi, Dupré, and Bonnet, to name but a few who had tickled her ivories and romped on her pedals with foreign abandon. The City Organist of Atlanta served as Organist to her household.

Through sheer luck flavored with a goodly portion of serendipity, and after I landed the church appointment and finally met Mrs. Candler, I was invited to consider her home my own. I was but a sweet-sixteen-year-old lad who urgently needed to be taken under wing by a sponsor. (She once quipped to a friend in her inimitable drawl that "Carlo doesn't live 'with' me. He lives 'in my house.'")

Whenever Virgil came to stay, and the occasions were plentiful, it was festival-time. Ours was a haven for him and his entourage. The magical late nights spent in darkened, mysterious churches; the wee-hour feasts accompanied by oodles of bawdy jokes, laughter and limericks; the piano duets and crazy sing-song sessions. Ah!

On one occasion, these memories-to-be were enhanced by driving up the steep driveway at Florence's to see the holly-bushes in front of the house covered in Virgil's hand-washed undergarments left to dry in the blazing sun. It seems that her staff had the day off, and the dryer was "too complex" for him to operate (this excuse intoned by a genuine virtuoso who could effortlessly conquer a six-manual flight-deck!). The lady of the house remained unfazed: "Virgil's an artist," she declared. "And we're here to make his life easier!" Fine. I would have been delighted if his personally cleansed knickers festooned every bush in sight.

While I'm certain that Virgil had at first been a little concerned, and possibly even a wee bit jealous of Florence's new and boisterous protégé, he was as kind and helpful as could be, never less than honest, and incredibly generous, consenting to hear me play at length, and taking me on board for lessons (or "sessions," as he called them, most of which were held in Englewood) as his hectic schedule allowed. My "honorary landlady" undertook to open her checkbook and cover all the charges such a relationship incurred.

Virgil Fox not only taught me to play the organ as I had never before dreamed possible, but to swim, to drive, to enjoy life to the fullest, to project *in everything with head held high; and perhaps, most importantly, to make my own way in the purist-laced organ scene in my own style, which I ever after attempted to do.*

There was only one "rich" woman in Virgil's life who came through for him time after time; and that was his beloved mother, Bird. Virgil had earned a lot of money in his life, but he spent it as fast as he took it in. Bird had helped with the purchase of homes in Teaneck and Englewood, New Jersey. She had endured the debacle with the Hammond Castle in Gloucester, and subsequently helped Virgil acquire the most beautiful of his homes, the Addison Mizner house, "Lagomar," in Palm Beach, Florida. She made it clear that these loans were against his inheritance, as she intended to divide her fortune evenly between Virgil and his brother Warren Fox, who had always lived in the shadow of his celebrated brother. The two brothers were on cordial terms (after what I heard was a difficult childhood together); but they were never close.

Virgil adored his "Mama," who was a driving force in his life. She was a strong, sensible woman, who was quiet and determined. She was very proud of Virgil's accomplishments, but she was well aware of his sometimes foolish behavior and expenditures. I can't believe she approved of Virgil's life style, or that she cared much for David (an opinion she declared to Richard on several occasions). She had forced Virgil's father, Miles, to go along with continuing Virgil's education in the United States and Europe. She had been there whenever Virgil was in need. Virgil recognized her devotion and adored her in return, often fawning over her in public to the point where it sometimes seemed insincere. It was not! On her part, she adored her gifted son, and was always an easy touch when he was in need or had some wild, new, impractical scheme.

Richard Torrence

> Virgil told me that when he decided he needed to study in Europe, he went to his "Mama." "Come here, Boy," she said.
>
> They went to the piano in the parlor. She opened the front of the instrument and took out a roll of bills. She asked how much it would cost.
>
> "Two thousands dollars, Mama."
>
> She peeled off the exact amount (it hardly made a dent in the roll) and said "Don't you tell Papa!"

---

81. The Royal V

After the October 1974 success of the new five-manual Rodgers organ in Carnegie Hall, Richard began to implore the powers that be at the Rodgers Organ Company to live up to their promise to replace Black Beauty, which had already traveled several million miles. After many moves, and jostling about on the road, it was showing signs of wire fatigue. This problem could easily have been remedied by a complete overhaul at the factory; but Richard hoped for an improved instrument, and Virgil had agreed with Rodgers that he would design a five-manual organ for Carnegie Hall if they provided a similar instrument for the road.

I'm reminded of the time in Englewood that Virgil's beautifully carved Æolian console had been refinished. It was hooked to various parts of several organs that he had acquired. Virgil looked at the three-manual console and said, "It's so beautiful but it's only three manuals. Maybe when I send it to Æolian-Skinner to have the keyboards rebuilt, I'll have them make it a four-manual." Richard was beside himself, because Virgil had just spent all his money on building the swimming pool, and many of his current bills had gone unpaid. Richard told Virgil that three manuals was quite enough, and that he couldn't afford another excessive luxury at the time.

"My concept of organ playing has nothing whatsoever to do with only three manuals!" was Virgil's immediate rejoinder; and he promptly ordered an extra manual for his home organ.

A five-manual touring organ the size of the Carnegie instrument was a tall order; but Richard pushed, and Rodgers finally agreed. Except for a few name changes in the specification, the touring instrument was an exact duplicate of the Carnegie Hall organ. Carnegie's console was a beautiful walnut finish. Virgil wanted a conventional concert black; "a Steinway look. And I want the console carpeted in royal purple."

Purple it became, which led to the name "The Royal Five." The Rodgers factory people were clever, and the silver leaf name under one of the manuals read "ROYAL V." Virgil loved that Royal "V"!

The factory invited me to play a preview concert for the local Portland, Oregon community that lived near the factory. The concert took place in the Hillsboro High School gymnasium, which had cathedral-like acoustics. The room was filled; and I can recall few organs, electronic or pipe, anywhere, that thrilled me more! It had intoxicatingly beautiful solo voices, and string stops of every variety. Virgil was not offended that I played the first concert on the new instrument, for he was to open it formally at the new outdoors Concord Pavilion across the Bay from San Francisco. As Reid and I were the San Francisco Rodgers dealers, it was up to "Organ Arts, Ltd." to see that the organ was properly installed and regulated. This important assignment delighted Virgil, as we had gained a reputation throughout the country for voicing fine-sounding instruments. Virgil and David stayed with Reid and me.

By this time, Richard Torrence had become "Vice President-Marketing" for Rodgers, and was actually sponsoring the concert through a local impresario (who had affected all of our lives), Charles Swisher. The Concord Pavilion is in a spectacular setting, high in the foothills of 3,800-ft. Mt. Diablo above Oakland. The large stage and shell are at the bottom of a hill, with seating sloping upwards and away from the stage. Lawn seating continues to slope even farther upwards, in the manner of a Greek amphitheater. The total seating capacity, with people on the lawns and hills, can accommodate as many as 12,500 people! The sound system was incredibly good, and had been designed by Christopher Jaffe, the world-renowned acoustician who had also advised the Rodgers Organ Company and Carnegie Hall on the earlier five-manual installation. We were therefore entirely pleased with the sound and impact that the Royal V made in that setting!

Virgil arrived several days before the concert with David. Virgil's mother arrived from Southern California, as well, for the opening. The first rehearsal took place after 9:00 p.m. Even in September, although the weather can be above 90 degrees during the day, it can be cool at night—especially when the wind is blowing, which it was. I remember Virgil's being quite taken with the whole setting, and immediately giving orders to the stage crew as to the lighting that he wished. This concert was to be a straight solo recital, not a Heavy Organ program with the light show. David, therefore, had little to do but complain, criticize, and generally antagonize Virgil—which didn't bode well for the event. The stage was literally filled with the speakers with which the Royal V traveled, including four 30-inch woofers for the Pedal division. Charles cleverly located these speakers under the mammoth stage, which had a resonance chamber that opened to the audience. His placement greatly increased their effectiveness. The whole organ was slightly enhanced by the Pavilion's own sound equipment, which included a fine reverberation system. At that time, no electronic organ had yet produced an effective (or even acceptable) reverb system. We were fortunate at Concord, therefore, as I had been fortunate in Hillsboro, for we had a cathedral-like ambience into which the organ "carried" the sound, with suitable power, invading the entire listening area and beyond.

I have no idea what had transpired that day; but when Virgil, David, and Bird arrived, Virgil was cranky and out of sorts. I really wished that he had been in a better mood for his first meeting with his new touring organ. We had all worked hard, and I believed that the people at Rodgers had outdone themselves. We were waiting for the usual Fox enthusiasm that I thought surely would come after he sampled a few of the organ's glorious sounds. He did not meet my expectations, however—at least on that first occasion. To make matters worse, Bird was uncomfortable because of the cold and the wind. We pulled out one of the large black wooden boxes in which the speakers were stored, and dropped her chair into it in order to shield her from the wind. The box was seven feet tall and made a little house in which to shelter her. It was odd and sad to see poor Bird, shivering in her black box to the left of the console. She was tired, and wanted to be anywhere but where she was; but Virgil insisted she stay put and endure the entire ordeal.

He started by improvising on the full choruses of each division. Bird held her ears. "It's too loud!" she cried.

Virgil replied with his "annoyance tone," "Ho! Ho! Ho! Honey, that's nowhere near the full organ!" He then proceeded to demonstrate what full organ sounded like, nearly deafening the poor dear woman. Out in the seats, the sound was thrilling; but on the stage, it must have been deafening. Virgil was used to such noise coming out of Black Beauty; but now there was a real quality to the sound, and not just a bludgeoning bombardment.

He then tried the new Solo reeds, including the razor-sharp post horns. "They sound like tin ash cans!" he roared; and, of course, Bird and David agreed (but for very different reasons!). I could easily have killed Virgil without delay; but I knew he was putting on an act and was just out of sorts. The hair on the back of his head was standing straight up like old gray wire (never a good sign!), and now was not the time for a confrontation. If the combined organs of the Riverside Church, Nôtre Dame, and Grace Cathedral had all been on that stage, side by side that evening, he would have found fault with them all!

Virgil didn't like anything that evening; nor did he stay long. Bird was running out of steam and was freezing; and David was not helping the situation with his ill-informed, "artistic" criticisms. Before we departed, Virgil said he wanted to come the next evening before he ordered any changes. "Change nothing Teddo. It'll fly!" We all went promptly into the city, to the Fairmont on Nob Hill, into the Brasserie, where Virgil could get "some sweets." Sugar could do wonders for his disposition, and things improved immediately. He finally admitted that he loved the console with its purple carpeted platform; and he was especially fond of the Royal "V" logo in silver leaf.

His second practice session was a great success. The evening was warmer, and he asked me to play the organ while he listened from several locations. Then he sat down at the console and began to tear into his programmed pieces. He said, "This is magnificent; a real triumph. What a sound!" Not one stop had been changed or altered, which made me feel much better, since I had been responsible for voicing the organ, first in the factory and later at the Hillsboro High School. He could hardly be pried from the console even at 3:30 a.m.

We were afraid the local sheriff might come because of the huge sound being carried into the homes of the thousands of people who lived not too far away.

Virgil's opening concert sold extremely well. It produced a loud, boisterous and enthusiastic throng—exactly what Virgil had come to expect from his Heavy Organ concerts. He began the Concord concert with his own stunning arrangement of "The Star Spangled Banner," which was followed, obviously, by the first of several standing ovations, much to his delight. (Virgil's methods of getting audiences used to standing up for him as early as possible were sometimes shameless!)

The rest of the program was as thrilling as the beginning. Both Virgil and the organ received screaming, stomping ovations and he played six encores! Virgil was deliriously happy with his conquest, and finally seemed to appreciate his splendid new organ. "Dearest boys," he said to Reid and me, "I can't thank you enough! This organ is the greatest! I'm so proud of it and you!"

I wanted to weep.

Charles F. Swisher is Vice-President of the Atlantic City Convention Hall Organ Society, Inc.

Charles F. Swisher

In 1971, I produced Virgil's first West Coast performance of Heavy Organ with Pablo's Lights in San Francisco's Winterland. The famous Decca recording of the concert captured the first time ever that an entire audience began to clap synchronously to Virgil's inimitable rendition of Bach's "Fugue à la Gigue."

Unfortunately, less than 2,000 people turned out, which was half what we had hoped for. I was about to lose my financial shirt when, immediately after the concert, Virgil's manager, Richard Torrence, told me that Virgil had decided to waive his $5,000 fee because (1) he realized how much money we had paid to provide the best possible sound experience for the audience, (2) because he knew the recording would be a winner, and (3) because he was so overwhelmed by the ambiance and response of the audience.

Later, in 1975, I was able to produce the world première of the Rodgers five-manual touring organ at the Concord Pavilion in Concord, California with Virgil. Twenty-four searchlights formed colored pyramids, halos, and rainbows over the Pavilion and Contra Costa hillside. About 3,000 people attended this unique event under the stars.

82. Hauling the Organs

The Royal V required a much larger truck to haul her enormous speakers, tone generators, and amplification systems. In fact, an 18-wheeler truck was required. The expense of hauling so much moving equipment had skyrocketed since Black Beauty had gone on the road nearly ten years earlier. At first, when Virgil, I, and the other organists who used Black Beauty began to play Community Concerts under Columbia Artists Management, the Rodgers Organ Company had graciously charged us nothing for the use of the organ at our concerts. (They weren't so generous with our management, however, charging Richard Torrence Management for every concert; and, for a period of time, almost driving it into bankruptcy!)

Needless to say, various fulltime road managers were required. The road manager drove the organ to each engagement, and supervised the moving in of the console and the setup of the speakers. He used the telephone quite a bit in order to coordinate the move to the next city. He also worked with the lighting and sound engineers in every hall, making sure they provided the various effects and accommodated the needs of every artist. When minor repairs were required, the road manager, who was trained as a technician, did his best. Sometimes we had to call the factory to send a specialist to help us out. More often than not, the road manager also provided the artists with a cheap taxi service to and from hotels, airports, and concert halls. Of course, he also had to supervise and oversee the maintenance of the truck and trailer. In my case, he also sold recordings in the lobbies during the intermissions and after the concerts. (David took over this position for Virgil's concerts.)

The Rodgers Organ Company now had not just one, but three touring organs on the road. The "Royal V" was the biggest. "American Beauty" and "Little Beauty" were the two three-manual Rodgers organs that Andy Crow and I used.

There was even a fourth touring organ, called the "convention organ," which was used for church conventions and for general rentals. This instrument was usually shipped by air rather than driven, and local dealers set it up.

All of these organs needed competent people to look after the problems of touring instruments—something for which there was little precedence at first, but for which several experts emerged in the decade-long experience. In fact, we were immensely fortunate to have great road managers! Among these heroic technicians, the first was the dearest, kindest, and most gifted person, who was great fun to boot! Andy Crow was one of the reasons that the touring organ program got off to such a good start (after Virgil's initial mess-up!), and developed into the enormous success it became. He adored Virgil, and was patient with his and David's excessive demands and criticism. He was even-tempered, and was devoted to the idea of bringing organ music to all parts of the country. We all owed an enormous debt of gratitude to Andy, who drove Black Beauty for hundreds of thousands of miles, acquiring in the process a problem with his middle ear that caused him intense episodes of vertigo. The disease was called "Ménières syndrome," which, in Andy's words, caused "the floor to become the ceiling," and made driving, playing the organ, and even walking hazardous at times. Andrew graduated from road manager to the stage himself when the "Duo" was conceived, and so we had to find a new road manager.

At one point, my dear brother-in-law, Jimmy Emmanuel, drove for Virgil. I was a little worried that Jimmy might not understand Virgil and be able to put up with his eccentricities, and so I sat him down for a little talk. I explained to him, as discreetly as possible, that I was gay, and so was Virgil. Jimmy just roared. "Did you think I didn't know?"

Virgil and Jimmy hit it off splendidly; and more than once, my beautiful sister, Christine, accompanied them on tours. Virgil adored them both, and treated them like his own son and daughter. We noticed that a lot more records and tapes were sold at the concerts when my sister sold them!

Jimmy was quite an attractive young man, and Virgil was concerned that some of the more "aggressive artistic types" around the concerts, and some others who were connected with various theatres and halls, would make a pass at him. Virgil would have none of that! "Jimmy, Honey! You be sure to tell me if any of those people try anything with you. I'll fix them!"

Jimmy just laughed. He obviously could take care of himself in any such situation. Jimmy and Chris loved how protective Virgil could be of any of his "chicks," and how true and genuine his love and protective nature were.

Other long-suffering and fine road managers and assistants included Christopher Morris, Ken Van Grunsven, Tom White, Bob Kendrick, Ron Kresky, and Chaz Dewesberry, followed by Virgil's great team of David (Jonathan) Lewis (whom Virgil sometimes called "Jonathan"—or Squeaky" because of his high tenor voice—and so as not to confuse anyone when Virgil summoned "the other David") and Floyd Watson.

Floyd Watson

When I first joined the Heavy Organ "team," I had really never been away from home. I was an impressionable 22-year old on the verge of meeting a god who was my idol, the greatest musician who ever lived!

When I came to the kitchen door for the first time, there was Virgil in a pair of baggy shorts and a tee shirt. Without any formal introduction, he grabbed my hand and led me into the living room. Merle Webster (who I guessed was his servant) had just finished hanging French drapes around an organ console. The drapes had just come back from the cleaners, and Virgil was there fiddling with a tape measure. He turned to me and said, "Floyd, Honey, these drapes, as you can see, are obviously shorter than when they left. I'm considering taking the cost of the drapes out of Merle's pay!"

Merle said, "Nothing comes out of nothing, Virgil."

That was my introduction to my great god, Virgil Fox!

Dinner was later that evening; and it included Virgil and David, six of their friends, and me. Virgil informed me that dinner would cost five dollars, and that my room for the evening would be an additional five dollars. These charges were due to "the high cost of running such an expensive household."

Well, I didn't have five cents, much less five dollars! I thought: I've come into the presence of a truly crazy person!

David Lewis

I had the same experience almost word for word on my first night in Englewood! Of course, staying at a motel would have cost us a lot more, and Merle's food was great. But at least at a Holiday

Inn we would have enjoyed a real bed and clean linen instead of a lumpy mattress perched on top of a pile of organ pipes in the attic.

During one of our visits, we once found Virgil on his hands and knees with his right hand plunged as far down into the toilet bowl as he could reach. He railed about our having flushed down some razor blades that plugged up the sewer system in the house. We stood there saying nothing and trying not to laugh. At long last, he produced a fist-full of ancient, rust-encrusted blades that had probably been down there for 40 years. "Ah ha!" he yelled, triumphantly, as if at last he'd found the proof of our poor upbringing.

We calmly explained that all the "roadies" who ever stayed in the house used electric shavers.

Needless to say, Richard Torrence Management coordinated all of us, booked the instruments, sold the attractions, created new ones, negotiated with Rodgers, placated everyone, and bore up stoically under frequent and unfair criticism! In the end, however, all of us knew that it was Richard, Marshall, and their staff who established and protected our careers. There was never any question about our love for them and for our supporters at Rodgers, first among whom were Rodgers Jenkins and Jim Walls.

Gradually, as expenses grew, so did our concert fees; and the Rodgers Organ Company asked us for a small fee at each concert to help defray the ever-mounting costs. At first, they assessed Virgil and me $300 per concert for the use of the organ, which seemed quite fair. One must remember, however, that the artist and not the presenter paid this fee. Therefore, the expense of hauling the organ was subject to commission charges, because Richard had to take his commission on the entire fee that he negotiated. Eventually, Richard worked a splendid deal with Columbia Artists Management. It was the only "co-management" deal that Columbia had at the time. CAMI managed no organists themselves, and Richard was the only concert management that was successful in establishing a thriving demand for organ concerts in CAMI's venues.

Most concert artists pay a 20% commission to their managers. In our case, we had to pay a 30% commission (half to Richard and half to Columbia). We were naturally disappointed that the expense of providing the organ could not be passed on to each presenter as it was for ordinary artists. (Normally each city or presenter would contract for a piano locally, for instance.) The fact that we offered the Rodgers Touring Organ in our contract was a major selling point, however, although it was becoming an increasingly expensive one for the artists.

Although this arrangement diminished our fees, we were all grateful for the concerts, the exposure for our instrument, and the good money the concerts brought in—for Richard continually succeeded in increasing our overall fees.

As the years went by, the organ fee grew to $500, then $600 per concert. By the time the Royal V went on the road, the organ fee had reached $1,000 per concert for that organ. Adding the 30% commission Virgil paid on that fee, the cost of touring with the Royal V was up to $1,300 per concert, which really began to sting.

Our fees from Community Concerts were paid directly to our management from the New York offices of Columbia Artists, minus their 15% commission on the total fee we received. Actually, Community Concerts received a considerably larger sum from their local organizations. That difference (or "differential," as they call it) went to pay for CAMI's expenses, personnel, and so forth. They had organized these audiences, after all; and in my case, provided me with 60 to 65 concerts per year that I would never have dreamed of getting.

Virgil, as his fee got higher, was booked for fewer and fewer concerts from Community; but he got more and more "straight" sales because of his new "star" status that resulted from Heavy Organ. Heavy Organ programs, and all of our concerts that were not Community Concerts, were managed entirely by Richard, who received the usual 20% commission.

When the organ fee went to $1,000 plus 30% commission, we all became concerned. Virgil was openly angry, spurred on by David's constant haranguing that both Richard and the Rodgers Organ Company were "making a fortune" off Virgil's name and talent. Virgil, deep in his heart, knew the truth; but David continually whittled away at him. On top of all of the bickering over the organ rental, the Royal V wasn't traveling well. There were always small mechanical things going wrong that David would magnify into much larger concerns than they needed to be. Such a behemoth was bound to have certain things go wrong from time to time.

When it first went on the road, the plan was that all the Royal V's electronic tone generating equipment (in giant, heavy and unwieldy, black cabinets) should be kept in the trailer of the 18-wheeler. Heavy-duty cables could then be run from the trailer to the stage, which would eliminate many difficult moving problems and considerably alleviate the wear and tear on the equipment. We decided that only the console, amplifiers, and speaker equipment should be moved from the trailer.

From the time of Virgil's first concert in Concord, this plan was not possible. The generator cabinets had to be brought onto the stage because the truck almost always had to be parked too far away to leave the cabinets in the truck. Therefore, the cabinets were constantly being moved from that time on, causing many unforeseen technical problems that only added fuel to the fire that David was trying to ignite.

David Lewis

The Rodgers Organ Company's Royal V had been a mess. We had all gone to Portland to act as consultants on the touring aspect of the new organ; but the company didn't follow one recommendation we made, and the organ only worked well for a single concert, as far as I can recall.

Every time we opened the back of the truck (which by then was a huge semi), handfuls of nuts and bolts fell out. Something was always not working.

83. A Day Late and a Dollar Short

Virgil learned that the Rodgers Organ Company was up for sale, and he was uneasy about who the next owners would be, and how long they would continue to subsidize keeping the Royal V on the road. He became increasingly dismayed when glitches occurred. David's endless prodding finally fired up Virgil into a minor rage, getting him to refuse to pay any fee at all for concerts where even the slightest thing went wrong. The current owners of Rodgers were dismayed as well at the ever-mounting costs of the Touring Organ Program. They made it quite clear to us that the fee we paid offset only the slightest part of the salaries and truck expenses they had to maintain year-around. Poor Richard got complaints from both ends: Virgil's constant accusations that he was being exploited and Rodgers' constant threat of reconsidering whether they should continue their expensive subsidies. I'm afraid I didn't help much either, as I recall complaining about paying so much for each engagement.

Richard bravely fought both factions for several years, and kept things running along as smoothly as he could. David was constantly urging Virgil to buy his own touring organ, rent his own truck and trailer, and hire his own drivers. If they paid the drivers "slave wages," David was convinced that Virgil would come out way ahead of the game. Virgil was intrigued, but Richard repeatedly convinced him that David's scheme made no financial sense. He managed to calm Virgil down temporarily, from time to time; but the subject came up continually; and, of course, the Royal V kept breaking down.

Richard Torrence

By May 1975, I had become director of marketing at Rodgers—soon to be made vice president. I moved to Portland for the last eight months of the year.

Theoretically, it was to my advantage as a concert manager to be an executive at Rodgers. I could manage and improve the touring organ program—and indeed, it was during that time that the Royal V was put on the road. Practically speaking, however, I became less related to the concert management as my business partner, Bill Perrotta, in New York, took over the day-to-day business of "Torrence/Perrotta Management." David used this opportunity to increase his influence over Virgil. (Bob Fry used to say, "He who controls the touring organ controls Virgil!")

Finally, after ten years working with Rodgers, I left and returned to New York to take over the management again. Marshall continued to handle the Rodgers advertising account, but that arrangement would also change as well.

With all the uncertainty over the future of the touring organ, I suggested that Virgil try out Carlo Curley's Allen touring organ at a church in Philadelphia. Carlo was very helpful—and so were the acoustics in the church.

Virgil began to call the Royal V the "Flying Dutchman," and to inquire about the current health of the retired Black Beauty.

"Why can't we fix her up again, and why can't I buy her and operate her myself?"

He told me that I could rent Black Beauty directly from him whenever he wasn't using her.

"Well, Honey, it will cost a fortune to run it, and you can help with the costs!"

Virgil even started planning to add multiple ranks of pipes to his old traveling companion, thus coming ever closer to his dream of taking real pipes on the road.

Virgil began to negotiate with Rodgers to purchase Black Beauty. The executives at the factory at that time were a little slow on the uptake, not knowing what to charge Virgil for a completely refurbished Black Beauty. It didn't help matters when one of the alternate drivers the factory had provided for the Royal V told Virgil that Black Beauty was completely worn out, would be impossible to fix, and would never be able to accept the pipes Virgil desperately wanted. This driver also told Virgil that the company was in such serious financial trouble that it might go bankrupt within six months, which really frightened our dear, gullible Virgil, who immediately called me to check out the story. I did my best to quell Virgil's fears, but some deadly seeds had already been deeply implanted.

I called my friends at Rodgers and told them they had better address the situation soon, as Virgil was preparing to go to their chief competitor, the Allen Organ Company, to see if he could get a better deal. I felt that Virgil's disloyalty to Rodgers was not imprudent, as his career had reached the point where he really needed a touring organ. Thus, the disappearance of the Rodgers Organ Company could severely threaten his future. No matter how much Richard and I tried to reassure him that the future wasn't that bleak, Virgil continued to be confused. David's poisoned tongue against everyone not under his or Virgil's control only exacerbated the confusion.

Finally, the Rodgers Organ Company was prepared to offer Virgil a completely refurbished Black Beauty—for the unheard of sum of one dollar! This amazing offer came during the summer of 1976, after nearly two years of intense discussions and wrangling back and forth between Richard, Virgil, David, the drivers, the Rodgers Organ Company, and some of the other artists—especially me. Above all, I wanted Rodgers to keep Virgil; but, as usual, they were true to the motto Richard often proposed for them: "A day late and a dollar short."

What happened was that one afternoon, Virgil telephoned me with the shocking news that he had made a substantial down payment—using his own money, which was practically unheard of for him!—on a custom four-manual organ to be built by the Allen Organ Company. I was stunned and dismayed, not because the Allen wasn't a fine organ (although I still believed that Rodgers made a finer instrument), but because I knew the touring organ program would never be the same. I immediately spoke to the head of Rodgers. That's when the company decided to offer Virgil a completely refurbished Black Beauty for the princely sum of a dollar. Virgil couldn't ignore the astonishing news, but he went on to say, "Well, it's about time! But who's going to repay me the thousands of dollars already paid Allen? That has to be part of the deal! Allen's certainly not going to give me back my money!"

I reported this conversation to my friends at Rodgers, and I suggested they pass the hat among their dealers to give Virgil what he demanded. I actually felt he deserved to be reimbursed after all the company had put him through. I also believed that Virgil, his reputation, his "aura," and his drawing power were commodities that Rodgers couldn't afford to lose. They were too involved with negotiating the sale of their company (to CBS Musical Instruments, it turned out) to pay attention to what was happening on the road; and they either didn't understand the magnitude of what their loss might represent, or they didn't care. As they saw it, they had met Virgil's clamorous demands and had accommodated him in every way they could for nearly eleven years. Perhaps they believed they'd had enough.

Perhaps they did have enough. Virgil soon began to tour with the Allen Organ, which he continued to do for the rest of his career.

---

84. The Circus Lady and Her Pet Snake

In my view, there was a deeper, more important reason for this change in touring instruments.

David obviously wanted to manage Virgil's career himself. He had always coveted this degree of control over his benefactor; but Virgil was at least sensible enough to realize that David lacked the intelligence, talent, taste, and personality to manage such a responsibility. He used to say things to us like, "Oh, Honey! The poor thing just doesn't understand!"

I don't believe that David had the education or the intelligence to understand how harmful he was to Virgil's career. Despite my strong feelings about the both of them, I have to hold Virgil, not David, ultimately responsible for most of the tragic things that happened to him during the last years of his life—the sad tale of which will occupy most of the rest of this book. I believe that everything began to go wrong with the demise of the Touring Organ Program, which David brought about by constantly manipulating and cajoling Virgil into purchasing an Allen organ.

Richard was becoming increasingly tired of Virgil's excessive demands. Virgil really required 24-hour service, seven days a week; and he always wanted Caméo personally, no matter how many competent people worked for Richard, to attend to every minor detail. In addition, the animosity between Richard and David had turned into severe detestation and loathing. Richard couldn't stand the sight of David, and could barely stand to be in the same room with him— especially after the move to Allen.

One day, after David had tastelessly recommended that Virgil should appear with him in a special Heavy Organ performance at Radio City Music Hall performing the Middelschulte *"Perpetuum Mobile"* for pedals alone, with the curtain raised only 20 inches so that only Virgil's feet could be observed by an audience of 5,000 sensation-seekers, Richard suggested what he took to be a perfect name for the Dynamic Duo: "I think their act should be called 'The Circus Lady and Her Pet Snake'!"

By this time, Virgil had moved to Palm Beach following the Hammond Castle debacle. Lagomar had been part of an even larger estate. The second floor contained a large, ornately carved music room. Virgil fell immediately in love with the magnificent space, and made plans to install a large residence organ there.

The house was less than a block from the Atlantic Ocean, which was one of the chief reasons he bought it. He loved to swim, and he thought this location would be ideal. He had considered moving to California to be near his mother and all of us; but San Francisco was often too cold for him; and Beverly Hills was too expensive for the kind of palace he had in mind. He liked Florida's warm climate, and the immense wealth and beauty of

Palm Beach. Above all, there was the warm ocean nearby in which to swim.

Virgil soon found out, however, that he could not go into the water whenever he pleased. There were schools of barracuda, sting rays, and jellyfish that threatened to hamper his aquatic activities. He often had to telephone the Palm Beach lifeguards to ask, "What's biting today?" He got so annoyed that he had another seventy-foot pool built right off the beautiful lanai room on the first level of the house—this time without the ridiculous enclosure and its moving-non-moving roof.

Although Virgil was delighted to move to Florida, managing him and his affairs became more complicated for Richard and his office staff. Virgil was now isolated and always susceptible to David's constant criticisms and complaints about the management—which further strained the close bond between Virgil and Richard. Richard was seriously considering other lines of work, for managing gifted but temperamental artists was hard and demanding, and the money wasn't great.

I believe that deep down, Virgil realized that Richard was managing him primarily because he loved him and deeply respected his great genius. Thus, Virgil never entertained any thought of changing his management. Why should he change when he had the best? Besides, Richard was part of the family—like one of his children, which remained the case in spite of all the arguments, misunderstandings, and out-and-out tirades on both of their parts. Richard remained firmly entrenched as Virgil's manager, Allen organ or not. In fact, Richard really didn't care which organ Virgil played, as long as Virgil continued to play successfully.

At last, it was announced, in late 1976, that CBS Musical Instruments (partially at Richard's instigation) had bought the Rodgers Organ Company. They had already purchased the Steinway Piano Company and several other musical instrument manufacturers. It was Big News in the industry when they decided to purchase Rodgers. We couldn't wait to tell Virgil. I wish I could have seen the look of dismay on his face when I told him over the telephone! He'd become fully convinced that Rodgers would not be in business much longer; and now the firm was part of the biggest company in the music business! Virgil also believed that CBS owned Columbia Records, for which he had recorded twenty years before. He would have dearly loved to sign another long-term contract with that company.

"Well, Honey, isn't that nice. At least you'll have an organ to sell."

The sarcasm fairly dripped from his voice. I could tell how much he regretted not being a little more patient, and not listening to so much vicious and inaccurate gossip. He never admitted it, however.

85. The Little Red Hen

As the summer of 1976 approached, Virgil would soon play what he thought was his last concert on the Royal V. Reid and I decided to produce a major organ festival in San Francisco featuring one of the fine pipe organs of the city along with the power and grandeur of the Royal V. Since, at that time, we were the Ruffatti representatives for the entire nation, we decided that St. Mary's Cathedral, with its grand four-manual Ruffatti, its architectural splendor, and a 2,500-seat capacity (that could accommodate an additional 2,500 standees!) would be the ideal place to hold such an event. Through my close friend Monsignor Robert Hayburn, then Archdiocesan Director of Music, and the then Cathedral Organist and Choir Director Ralph Hooper, we were able to negotiate a plan to use the Cathedral for a three-week festival.

The festival was to use what the French called *"son et lumiere"* (sound and light). I had had a wonderful experience with some lighting artists when I played a series of concerts for the Rainier Ale Company at Grace Cathedral. Charles Swisher, through Richard Torrence, arranged these events. The lighting artists were called "Crystal Rainbow," and I was highly impressed with their talent and dedication. They had turned Grace Cathedral at night into a magical space; and I felt confident that they would do the same at St. Mary's.

Charles F. Swisher

"Splendiferous Doings in Cathedral" was one of the headlines reporting the September 1971 sacred space concerts called "Amazing Grace." The San Francisco Examiner *called the atmosphere "sort of a great collective scene for lovers," while the* Oakland Tribune *admired "the splendiferous light show."*

For the occasion, the entire interior of the Gothic cathedral was illuminated with a vast array of theatrical lighting—from the clerestory windows above, down the stone columns, to the aisles below. Iridescent soap bubbles drifted from the ceiling, and incense burners were generously layered with frankincense and myrrh. Besides Ted playing the organ, popular recorded music interspersions included Judy Collins, the Beatles, Elton John, and Bob Dylan.

Crystal Rainbow didn't produce a light show such as Virgil used in his Heavy Organ concerts, which featured rear projections behind a huge screen. Virgil's "huge" screens would have looked like postage stamps from the back of St. Mary's—which rises almost 200 feet in the air! What we wanted was an environmental coloring of the vast space.

There aren't many stained glass windows in St. Mary's Cathedral. Rather, there are dramatic ribbons of stained glass that run up the huge tee-pee-like structure that rises above the cathedral floor. Most of the daytime lighting is natural (for example, one can view the entire city from all four walls on the pedestrian level). At night, except for the twinkling lights of the city, the huge coffered ceiling can be dreary and gray. The major lighting comes from a vast array of what look like searchlights centered in the distant ceiling. The effect is like a sports stadium: neither subtle nor flattering. I was confident that the Crystal Rainbow could transform this room into an enchanted palace at night.

We feared we might be taking a tremendous financial risk on a crazy scheme by producing this festival; but I remembered that the "Amazing Grace" cathedral concerts were sold-out financial successes, and I was determined that a great festival should highlight the King of Instruments. I was also certain that there's always a large audience for the organ, especially if you advertise properly.

Advertise! Advertise! Advertise!

That's what we did. We had great musical instruments, the Ruffatti four-manual instrument and the Rodgers Royal V (nearing retirement); and most importantly, we had a stable of artists who loved what they did, and who knew how to "turn on" an audience.

There was never any question as to who would open the festival. Virgil's popularity in the Bay Area was enormous. We knew with him as the headliner we couldn't lose. When I first approached him with the idea he was thrilled. I knew better than to ask him for a special fee for a "family member," although I knew he would, as always, use our apartment as his headquarters. Instead, I suggested that we might draw up a plan for the entire festival in which he might be one of the underwriters of the event, and thus partake in the profits. He thought I had a grand idea in suggesting that he become of one of the producers of the festival, especially since my offer entailed sharing some of the profits! However, when it came to risking even a thin dime on the affair, his answer was a resounding "No!"

The other artists scheduled to play were Joyce Jones, Diane Bish, Anthony Newman, Richard Purvis, and I. We planned a special concert as a tribute to San Francisco's own Richard Purvis. The concert featured many of his choral works performed by the San Francisco Symphony Chorus with brass, tympani, harps, and two organs. Purvis had retired from Grace Cathedral five or six years previously, and so I was certain that his concerts would be a great success.

One great advantage of our scheduling was that the festival took place over a relatively short period. Thus, the advertising (which was huge and expensive) served for all eight concerts. We decided that Virgil should give not one, but two concerts, with different repertoire for each recital. Virgil would now open the festival, and give his second concert in the middle of the festival (in case there was any flagging of interest or attendance). The Purvis tribute would close the event with great fanfare, both musical and promotional.

Our first step was to consult with a highly recommended, but then young and new, public relations firm, The Orsborne Group. Joan Orsborne, who devoted a great deal of time, talent, and energy to our project, was superb. We titled the festival "A Triumphant Blaze of Sound and Light," and advertised it as a "Festival of Organ Virtuosos and Illumination." We commissioned wonderfully colorful and artistic posters that were literally plastered all over town. There were newspaper, radio, and television ads on all the time. I doubt there were many Bay Area people who were unaware of the festival. Ticket sales began to mount, and we soon realized that we would be a success—largely because of Virgil's name. Our success pleased us no end.

The opening concert was Friday evening, September 10, 1976. Virgil's concert sold out all 2,500 seats. Thus we were unprepared for the throngs that lined up around the cathedral to buy tickets at the last minute, or to purchase whatever standing room might be left (we warned them to "bring your own pillow"). I was nervous about our first concert, since it conflicted with the great San Francisco tradition, Opening Night of the San Francisco Opera. I needn't have worried, since 5,500 people crammed into the cathedral on opening night.

The broadcast crews that normally televise the opening of the opera arrived at the cathedral to cover our event as well. As the audience poured in, two harpists accompanied the setting of the sun. The cathedral slowly began to be bathed in gorgeous light provided by the incomparable Crystal Rainbow. The four-manual console of the cathedral's Ruffatti organ and the Royal V's console were both moved into place on platforms so that the performers were visible from anywhere in the building.

When the announcer welcomed Virgil, and a pink spotlight hit his sequined jacket and diamond-studded shoes, the audience gave him a tremendous ovation. He went right to work on nearly one and a half hours of Bach.

The first section of each of Virgil's two programs was called "The Bach Gamut." These pieces were all the preludes and fugues from the 'A' tonality, straight through all the keys (another Marshall Yaeger invention, originally presented in a shorter program at Philharmonic Hall, Lincoln Center in New York).

The audience was composed of people from every age, class, musical taste, and lifestyle; but hordes of young people, which Virgil had captured as his fans from Heavy Organ concerts, dominated.

The whole audience sat silent and attentive, transfixed by Virgil's dynamic and musical approach to the transcendent counterpoint of Sebastian Bach. These "Bach Gamut" concerts were *tours de force*, and I never failed to marvel at Virgil's stamina and prodigious technique—and *memory!*—as he tossed off one after the other of the monumental preludes, toccatas, fantasies, and fugues with comparative ease, permeating them all with pure joy. The audience erupted with spontaneous praise after each of the mighty blockbusters.

During the intermission, I went back to see Virgil because he had asked me to change some general pistons for him during that time. "Honey, this audience is fabulous! You boys will make a fortune! Do you think we could reopen negotiations on my being a partner in this venture?"

I laughed and said I thought it was a little late for that, but we could think about it.

The second half of the program (the first half would have been a complete program for any other player!) included the "Scherzo" from the *Second Symphony* of Vierne, as well as his "Claire de Lune," and the monumental Franz Liszt "Fantasie and Fugue on '*Ad nos, ad salutarem undam.*'" This last piece elicited a full five-minute ovation and five encores! At the end of the concert, Virgil had tears in his eyes as he told me he had never been so thrilled, even at one of his own Philharmonic Hall concerts. He was electrified by the sound of both organs and the immense size of the audience—a size rarely encountered in an indoor space.

At dinner afterwards, Virgil again brought up the subject of becoming a belated partner in our venture. I was forced to recite the story of "The Little Red Hen." It seems that before she made plans to bake some bread, she had offered the three little pigs every opportunity to help her plow the ground, plant, water, harvest, and grind the wheat, help her knead the dough, and bake some delicious bread. Every time she asked them for help, their answer was an emphatic "No!"

Of course, they came running when they smelled the heavenly aroma of her freshly baked bread! She half-mockingly asked them who would help her to eat the bread.

"We will!" they cried.

Then it was the Little Red Hen's turn to say, "No!"

Virgil roared with laughter. I believe, however, that the moral of the story got through.

86. The Finger-Up-the-Ass Test

We had a great time with Virgil during his two-week stay with us. There were newspaper, television, and radio interviews galore; dinners at home (which he adored) and snacks and sweets before and after late night practice sessions. His mother came to San Francisco for the concerts, as did Hazel Gravel, his former soprano soloist from the Riverside Church and devoted close friend.

He coaxed Hazel into singing "Iris" and several striking oratorio and operatic solos for us during the practice sessions. Her enormous, thrilling voice filled St. Mary's Cathedral. I was sure he would ask her to sing at one of the concerts, but he didn't this time. (I think she was disappointed.)

During the period between his two concerts, two important but sad things occurred. Virgil got the news that his dear Aunt Etna had passed away at age 93, and he was very upset at the prospect of breaking the news to Bird. Both sisters had been extremely close all of their lives. Bird took the news well, however. After all, 93 was a long time to live; and Etna hadn't suffered at all—just passed away in her sleep.

Virgil gave his traditional salute, "Have a good trip, dear Etna," and that was that.

The other event was much more far-reaching for our dear, beloved comrade. Reid and I had a great friend, Dr. William T. Armstrong, who had been good and kind to us. He had a real appreciation for the organ and he loved its music. He played extremely well for someone who was unable to devote full time to practicing; and he had purchased a large three-manual Rodgers from us, augmented with seventeen ranks of real pipes that the Ruffattis had built.

The instrument turned out to be one of the most successful home organs I've ever heard (if I say so, myself, since I was partly responsible for its installation). His home, which was a Mediterranean style villa perched high on a hill, was a block from our apartment. The organ had a commanding presence in the gracious drawing room.

Bill had become Reid's and my personal physician. He had helped my mother, and was dear to her in her final illness. In addition, he was a fabulous cook and enjoyed entertaining. He was delighted to entertain anyone who loved the organ, and liked it even more if they could play. He had been a student of Richard Purvis, and later, coached a bit with me.

Because of our mutual interests, I always introduced Bill to the "visiting firemen" that came to town. Consequently, some of the most famous organists in the world played on his combination organ and were treated to the superb hospitality Bill always provided. I had introduced Virgil and David to Bill several years previously, and they became fast friends. Virgil loved to play the Rodgers-Ruffatti, and often practiced on it when he came to the Bay Area. We had to caution him, however, about loud practice after 10:00 p.m., as the organ was certainly audible a block away whenever its full resources were used. More than once, the police would arrive at night to silence an offender.

Virgil was so fond of Bill that he asked him to be his personal physician. He would have a complete physical nearly every year when he came to town. This year's physical was scheduled between the two concerts of the festival. It involved blood tests, an EKG, and a rousing run on a treadmill. Bill was a cardiologist; and for some reason, Virgil found this particular specialty gruesome, swearing he'd never go through such tests again unless he could be wired to an EKG machine while playing a vigorous piece, such as the Middelschulte "Perpetual Motion for Pedals Alone" after several encores!

Virgil announced that he had passed all his cardiovascular tests successfully, claiming to be as healthy as a horse.

Dr. Armstrong

Ted Worth first brought Virgil and David to dinner in my home in 1974, shortly after Ted had moved to San Francisco. Ted had told Virgil that my father (whom Virgil had never met) was gravely ill with cancer of the prostate and was staying with me while receiving treatment. When Virgil arrived, he immediately strode up the staircase to meet my father, not even glancing into the music room to greet the rest of the party. He sat beside Dad on the bed, visiting and comforting him for almost an hour. Later, Virgil often called to inquire about Dad's condition until Dad died. Later still, I became aware that Virgil's intimate knowledge of my father's clinical course with prostate cancer haunted him as he went through the same experience himself.

Ted Worth and I developed a close and loving relationship through the years. He often brought colorful and talented stars of the organ world to my home. After marvelous evenings of music and conversation, Ted would often "strongly recommend" that a visitor make an appointment for a cardiac checkup before leaving town. Virgil was no exception.

Ted was enamored of the treadmill exercise studies that I utilized to look for evidence of coronary heart disease. He was adamant that Virgil should get on "Bill's treadmill." Because of Virgil's nocturnal habits, he was never available for an appointment during normal office hours; and so I had to arrange for his exercise test in the back of our cardiac rehabilitation gymnasium after hours. I was terrified that this famous man might experience a cardiac arrest on the treadmill with only the two of us present, and without the usual support system available in the hospital's laboratories during office hours.

Nevertheless, everything went well from a medical/safety point of view. However, after I had pushed Virgil to "keep going, keep going!" until he achieved an adequate heart rate to make the stress test medically meaningful, he glowered at me and said, "Never again! If you want to see what happens to my heart during exercise, attach your machine to me while I'm playing the Middelschulte! But I will never get on that contraption again"!

Moreover, he never did!

The second concert was as successful as the first with even more people trying to jam their way into the cathedral. Not a single aisle was visible, just a sea of bodies in every direction. The fire marshal would not permit another soul to enter the building, and hundreds were turned away. Again, we were treated to an hour and a half of sublime Bach, and then staggering performances of the Franck *"Grande Pièce Symphonique,"* Debussy's *"Claire de Lune,"* and untold ovations. The throng simply wouldn't let him go. His final encore for each of the concerts calmed them down. It was Virgil's "goodnight song," a heavenly performance of Bach's "Air for the G-string."

I'm delighted to report that our Festival was a raging success! More than 30,000 people attended the eight concerts. Surely, Virgil's recitals were the major draws, as were Richard Purvis's. The Festival provided a great shot in the arm for the instrument. It proved to me how large the audience could be for the King of Instruments when players who love the instrument and who can impart their love and joy to an audience presented it in an exciting, imaginative way. Of course, no one presented the organ better than Virgil did.

I insisted that every artist speak to the audience. The ones we engaged usually did anyway. I also asked them to use both organs in their programs, which all of them were delighted to do. The Royal V sounded stupendous in the wonderful space. Also, both organs were used simultaneously in solo and accompanimental roles at the Purvis tribute, with Tom Hazleton and me taking turns on each instrument.

The "Richard Purvis Tribute" concert was a moving affair. More than once I detected a tear or two in Richard's eyes, and a slight faltering in his voice, which signaled to me that, despite his usually gruff exterior, the master was pleased and moved.

Of course, we offered Virgil tickets to the only other concert he could attend, which happened to be Joyce Jones's appearance. "Oh, Honey, I think we'll take Mama and Hazel out that night. They probably have heard enough organ this week," he said.

Nevertheless, lo and behold, who should be at the door buying tickets to Joyce's concert, but Virgil and his entire entourage? Fans and autograph-seekers besieged him, much to his delight. I thought this tribute to Joyce, whom he loved, was great; and very dear of him not only to support her, but also actually pay for tickets! It was so unlike him, I thought the old dear was finally beginning to soften.

On the way to get something to eat after Joyce's concert, however (for which Virgil insisted we all pay for ourselves), he took me aside and said, "Teddo! I expect you to reimburse me for the tickets. Why, I simply can't afford that kind of expense!"

I couldn't imagine that $35 was so terrible a hardship after earning $12,000 for the two concerts he played for us—not to mention his living with us for two weeks during his stay. He was still his old small-minded and truly niggardly self, and I happily repaid him. After all, we'd offered him as many tickets as he wanted to any of the concerts.

In a way, I was reassured. After all, what could we scream about if Virgil didn't always act true to form?

Virgil had gone through all his physical tests at Presbyterian Hospital, where Bill Armstrong practiced, and we assumed that everything was checked. We had been invited to Bill's house for dinner on one of the last nights that Virgil was in San Francisco. He had to get to Washington, D.C., where he was inaugurating the newly refurbished organ at National City Christian Church.

He was particularly fond of this organ, as he had practiced there while he was in the Army Air Force. He was also fond of the church's Music Director and Organist, Lawrence (Lonnie) Schreiber, who was a lifelong devoted friend and colleague. He was anxious to hear what they had added to this fine organ, although he would love to have stayed for my concert, the Purvis concert, and the rest of the festival. He also regretted missing the colorful and gifted Diane Bish's concert, for she was a new neighbor and friend in Florida.

Just before dinner was served, Bill reminded Virgil that there was one part of the examination that had been overlooked during Virgil's haste to get out of the hospital the previous week. "Really?" Virgil inquired, "And what is that?"

Bill replied, "The old finger-up-the-ass, Virgil; and we'll go upstairs right now and see about that. All men of your age should have that examination at least once a year."

Virgil turned beet red. "I guess I've been told!" Then, amid much jeering and laughter, he and Bill went upstairs to complete the examination. He returned with many more jokes over the situation; and the very pleasant evening ended with much laughter and fun and the usual glorious music-making on Bill's piano and organ.

Later that evening, when we got home, Virgil was preparing his nightly feast of ice cream. He had purchased no less than five half-gallons of his favorite flavors of a San Francisco brand called "Bud's" ice cream and spooned out portions from each. He informed us that Bill was concerned about his enlarged prostate, which had been normal the previous year. Bill made Virgil promise to see a specialist as soon as he got back to Florida after the Washington, D.C. concert. He cautioned Virgil to visit the specialist the minute he got home, and Virgil obviously took him seriously. Soon after he returned home in Palm Beach, Virgil went to the specialist. His prostate was indeed enlarged, and the doctor scheduled a biopsy. Virgil was naturally alarmed, but still relatively cheerful about the process.

Dr. Armstrong

Virgil was easy to entertain. All one needed to provide in the way of nourishment was southern fried chicken, cream gravy, mashed potatoes, chocolate cake with chocolate frosting and chocolate ice cream (only from "Bud's" ice creamery). "Bud's" had a small outlet in Noe Valley in those days. Virgil would ask me to drive him there late in the evening, just before they closed, where he would wait in the long line for hand packed ice cream. We would then go to "Just Desserts" where he would buy the chocolate cake with chocolate frosting. Returning home, he would stand in the kitchen with his fur coat and tam on, devouring his special goodies!

I gave Virgil a careful and complete physical every year. By "complete," a physician signifies that, in a man, the examination includes the prostate. Every year I checked all of Virgil. However, in 1976, when he came into my office for his exam, the office (which is set up for cardiology, not urology) lacked the necessary paraphernalia for a prostate exam. I told Virgil that I would get what-

ever was necessary and examine him in my home. The last night of this visit, I marched him upstairs for "the exam."

Surely, I'm wrong, I kept saying to myself! Yet, even to a heart doctor, there was no mistaking the bump I felt that hadn't been in him the previous year.

I pleaded with him to let me get the best urologist I could find in the Bay Area the next day. "No," he said; he simply had to leave. He promised to find his own specialist as soon as he got home and do whatever had to be done. I wasn't happy with his solution; for I knew that as a physician in San Francisco, I could do more for him as his advocate in my own city than he could do for himself in Florida.

However, after his tour, he called me to say that he had found a highly recommended expert, and that he would be undergoing surgery soon. He had cancer, but every test showed that it hadn't yet spread; and so there was real hope and expectation for a cure.

After the surgery, this expert told me, "If ever there was a cancer that was completely removed, this was the one!"

No further treatment was given to Virgil.

---

87. The Fox Touch

A week later, a seriously dejected, tearful Virgil called me with the news that his prostate was cancerous. He could barely say the word. He told me he felt completely unclean. He had never been sick a day in his life, had rarely drunk alcohol, abhorred cigarette smoke, and had always pampered himself. God knows he always got enough sleep!

I had never heard Virgil sound so depressed, or heard him sob like that. He told me he felt like walking out the door toward the ocean, wading in, and ending it all. I reasoned with him that prostate cancer was common; and since it was discovered at an early stage, he must do everything his doctors advised. I assured him that all would be well. I think I cheered him up a bit, for he knew everything I said was true. Later, David, Richard, Bob, and Bill Armstrong all told him the same.

Virgil swore all of us to complete secrecy about his condition. "You know the maggots and swine that hate me will have me disabled, unable to play, crippled, or God forbid, dead, if this news ever gets out!"

As usual, however, Virgil's important "secrets" became common knowledge, mainly because he himself could never keep his own big mouth shut! He had to share his secret with someone new, whom he immediately would swear to utter secrecy. He simply couldn't help himself. If you ever wanted private news to become public—quickly, tell Virgil!

Virgil said he had been referred to the finest doctor in the field to do his operation. He had been given two or three names of competent surgeons who could do it, but the one he went to first was the most highly recommended. Virgil was distressed to learn, however, that this doctor planned to do a radical procedure to remove all the surrounding lymph nodes, plus his testicles! Virgil simply couldn't condone that part of the plan. God knows why Virgil still needed testicles, but he seemed to believe that his "manliness" would be affected, that his deep voice would rise in pitch, and that his breasts might fill out.

The prognosis horrified him, and so he decided to get a second opinion from another doctor. This second doctor advised Virgil that a radical approach was unnecessary. When he assured Virgil of a complete recovery, Virgil decided to go with the second doctor.

During early December 1976, Virgil underwent surgery. Of course, he had all our prayers and good wishes. When he called me the day after his operation, he was in much better spirits. He said the first thing he asked the doctor as he was coming out of the anesthesia was, "Did you get it all?" The good doctor responded in the affirmative, and our dear Virgil was relieved. An enormous weight and fear was lifted from him.

His recuperation after he got home wasn't easy. I think he was often in pain. Virgil never liked taking painkillers. He called them "dope," and would bear a great deal of severe pain before taking any.

He also had a catheter in his penis, which annoyed him no end. He had to rest a great deal, and keeping Virgil Fox in bed was not an easy task. Of course, there was David, Mama, and a nurse to help him; but Virgil wanted to get up and walk. He always remembered that injured horses were supposed to walk. Nothing could dissuade him from this veterinary theory, and so he walked as much as he could, much to the dismay of those who were caring for him. As always, he was cranky, out of sorts, and demanding. He wanted to practice, go out Christmas shopping, or whatever. He had had the operation. It was a success. Why should he bother with any recuperation process? In retrospect, many of us believe that his incessant exercise lengthened the recuperation process. Although he didn't have an easy time of it, he forced himself to recover completely from the operation by using his well-known iron will.

Dr. Armstrong

Everyone who knew Virgil also knew how much he loved a leisurely hot tub bath and hated even the tiniest of drafts. At my hospital, every patient's room had a small shower. This scanty arrangement simply wouldn't do for Virgil! Therefore, during one of his hospitalizations, he roamed the halls until he found a real bathtub in a large room in another part of the hospital. He raided the laundry cart for armloads of towels, and he proceeded to cover the windows and any other sources of real or imagined drafts with towels. He then disappeared from his room for long, hot baths. His absence obviously caused considerable bewilderment among the doctors and nurses responsible for his care! Of course, housekeeping removed the towels as soon as they found them. Shortly thereafter, however, there appeared a large hand-printed notice in Virgil's new bathroom that stated that all towels were absolutely to remain in place, by order of (I must confess) Dr. Armstrong!

While I only knew Virgil a few years, he quickly became one of the most important and influential figures in my life. He was one of the kindest and most considerate people I've ever known. I will always be grateful to Ted Worth for bringing him to dinner that first night, so long ago.

The next time I saw Virgil was in early 1977. Reid and I had been in Palm Springs visiting our dear friend Debbie duPont, who a few years earlier had married a charming young man, Michael Hogan, whom she had met on one of her many visits to Honolulu. Richard had arranged for Virgil to make two recordings on the new five-manual Ruffatti organ built for Robert Schuller's Garden Grove Community Church, the original building on the campus of the now famous "Crystal Cathedral," which had not yet been built. (Richard and I had sold the organ to the church.) Virgil was to dedicate the instrument in April, and record on it in August. Virgil was taken with the brilliance and power of the new Ruffatti; and of course the Schullers—Arvella and Robert—were overjoyed to have Virgil record there. They were devoted fans and extremely fond of him; and Virgil always returned their affection.

The organist at that time was Richard Unfreid, who was also fond of Virgil and completely agreed with his "red-blooded" approach to the organ.

The resulting recording was unique because it was done, first of all, "direct-to-disc," which was the original "audiophile" system; secondly, it was recorded simultaneously on magnetic tape; and finally, it was recorded using the newest technology, digital tape.

For the direct-to disc, Virgil had to record complete "sides" of the record. (There could be no edits between pieces.) He had to make two complete LP's, which is a grueling task for any artist—especially one who had just recovered from a serious operation. In addition, almost all the works were "stem winders." For Virgil, the task was like playing four or five concerts per day, for several days. The label was a small and relatively new one, "Crystal Clear." Richard and a great recording engineer, Burt Whyte, had worked for an entire year to produce this innovative project.

Virgil was irritated by the fact that he was paid nothing up front for doing the recordings; and he would get no royalties until the sizable cost of making and producing them was recouped from sales. Richard had to cajole and reason with Virgil, and especially with the defiant David. Richard pointed out that things weren't the same in the recording industry as they had been in the old days with Columbia, RCA Victor, and Capitol.

I remember telephoning Richard from Palm Springs in August to see how things were going. He told me things were grim, and Virgil was on the warpath with everyone. The organ tuners, the recording people, and Richard were under fire constantly. Even David came under fire, as Virgil's demands became increasingly unreasonable.

Richard was pleased, however, with the artistic results. Virgil was extremely well prepared; and he, too, was pleased with the sound and the playing—even if the recording sessions had been the most grueling he'd ever been through, and the financial arrangements were not satisfactory.

Reid and I decided to make a short stop in Garden Grove to say hello, see how things were going, and lend any support we could before returning to San Francisco. To make matters more complicat-

Virgil with Arvella and Robert Schuller

ed, the organ had been dedicated the previous April before its final tonal finishing (churches are always jumping the gun!), so that it wasn't quite finished. Francesco Ruffatti himself was there, working feverishly to have everything ready for the recording sessions. I'm sure the organ blower was operating 24 hours a day, because the local organ tuners were constantly retuning the stops after Francesco finished every one of them!

Virgil was genuinely glad to see us. He looked good, although a little thinner and paler. I reasoned that the usual splendid pink glow to his skin had not yet returned.

He immediately started a tirade about the organ tuners, the grueling schedule, and the money—or lack thereof—which, of course, was always the root of all his grievances. Poor Richard had to bear the brunt of all of Virgil's carping, most of which he was powerless to remedy. Virgil wanted a different kind of recording contract, but Crystal Clear was the only company interested in recording the organ during this dreary period in the life of the classical recording industry. Richard felt that this recording might appeal to an entirely new group of people interested in the organ, namely the "audiophile freaks," whom he expected would go wild over the new recordings because of the pioneering techniques being used.

Actually, these recordings were the last commercial recordings Virgil ever made. David later made several recordings available for sale at Virgil's concerts; and the Virgil Fox Society brought out a 2-CD set entitled "Soli Deo Gloria" of Virgil's historic return to the Riverside Church in September, 1979. Although recorded in monaural mode, Bainbridge Records of Beverly Hills did a fine job of remastering and "stereo-izing" the tape for commercial release. The recording is essential listening for any fan of Virgil's. It documents a complete concert, from beginning to end, and fully demonstrates what Virgil could deliver to an audience: his monumental artistry, its intensity, and the delight he took in selling his beloved instrument and its marvelous repertoire to the general public.

The Crystal Clear albums came out first as two direct-to-disc LP's entitled "The Fox Touch" (Marshall's title), Volumes I & II. With no editing, and despite a slight slip here, or a slightly off-tempo there, these records, and the reviews for both Virgil and the new recording technique, were amazing tributes to Virgil's great artistry.

---

88. Honeydew Time

Virgil had canceled all his January and February concerts in 1977 to recuperate. When Virgil resumed his busy concert schedule in March 1977, things seemed to be going well. He was feeling like his normal self, and was relieved to be free of that dreadful word, cancer! In April of that year, he dedicated the five-manual, 117-rank Ruffatti organ for Garden Grove Community Church. Dr. Schuller's wife, Arvella, was a great fan of Virgil's, and an accomplished organist herself. Indeed, she had been Dr. Schuller's first organist on a small electronic instrument when he first opened the church at a drive-in theatre in the orange groves of Garden Grove, California.

When the Schullers opened the first church on the campus of what is now the Crystal Cathedral, they bought a modest three-manual Wicks that Virgil had also inaugurated. As time went on, and their TV ministry grew, Arvella felt that they needed a larger, more comprehensive instrument. She was devoted to the pipe organ and its literature. One never heard the words "It's too loud" come from that dear woman's lips! How wonderful to work for people like that!

It was during this stay in Garden Grove, when Virgil opened the new Ruffatti, that Dr. Schuller first asked Virgil to appear on his television show. The bond between the two men grew from then on into a close friendship.

There was a cute story about Virgil and Arvella. When Virgil arrived to practice for the inaugural concert, Arvella asked him how he was feeling. He replied, "About as well as you would if you'd had a catheter jammed up your penis for forty-nine days!" Arvella was taken aback, but she knew Virgil's humor quite well, and they both burst out in laughter.

Even then, I think Dr. Schuller shared his dream with Virgil of a great Cathedral rising on his property. The church's fame was growing so rapidly that the church simply had to have a larger worship space on the campus. However, there was no talk at that time of any monumental plans for the organ. I think most people probably intended to move the new Ruffatti to the new building; but I'm sure Arvella had dreams of what might be possible. I'm also sure that thoughts of a great instrument were crisscrossing Virgil's mind as well.

Virgil's career resumed its usual pace. However, the Heavy Organ bookings were not as numerous as they had been. Nevertheless, Virgil's solo fee continued to rise, which pleased both him and Richard.

Richard felt that Virgil should not have to work so hard at this stage of his career; but Richard also believed that he and Marshall should come up with a new idea to keep Virgil's career at its peak— to assure him of a lifelong place at the top of his profession. Unfortunately, the animosity between David and Richard grew, as David interfered more and more in Virgil's affairs—and the direction that Richard and Marshall wanted Virgil's career to take. It got so that that even Marshall could barely tolerate David's presence, and was beginning to dislike Virgil himself, who was increasingly unreasonable and difficult. Richard and Marshall often felt thwarted, and that they were sometimes not really helping Virgil, only going through the motions of doing the necessary daily tasks required. The management was certainly not able to keep any of the money it made from managing Virgil (there had to be too many people on staff), and so they suggested more than once that Virgil might consider changing managements.

This suggestion alarmed Virgil to no end; and he would always promise to improve and cooperate. "Why, not having you dear boys as my management is unthinkable! I won't have it!" A few weeks on the road with David's constant haranguing, and Virgil and Richard would start to bicker again. Eventually, Virgil would veto any new ideas "the boys" would suggest. It went back and forth in this way for a couple of years. Richard and Marshall hated being in that situation. For creative people such as they were, it was painful for them not to see Virgil grow into the stature they believed he truly deserved.

In the late fall of 1977, Virgil and David came to the West Coast on tour. They spent a few days with Reid and me. When Bill Armstrong saw him at one of his splendid dinners he gave for all of us, he was concerned that Virgil looked tired and drawn, and his color didn't seem right. Bill had talked to Virgil on the telephone about his condition since the operation, and he wanted to feel as positive as we had. He didn't want to interfere with Virgil's surgeons, but upon seeing Virgil, he felt something was wrong. Bill asked Virgil's permission to speak to his doctor in Florida and to examine the pathology reports. He promised to arrange for several doctors to look at them. Virgil said, "Of course, Honey; but he told me he'd gotten it all!"

When Bill examined the pathology reports he realized that Virgil's surgeon had removed one-half of a tumor but left the other half intact, which was now metastasizing. Indeed, they had not "gotten it all!"

After additional examinations at the hospital, it was obvious that Virgil still had cancer. The main fear was that the cancer had spread into the bones, which is what often happens when the disease goes untreated. Virgil had received no treatment for nearly a year, because he had assumed he was disease-free. He had trusted the doctor who recommended the less radical approach. He obviously picked the wrong person to trust.

Frederick Swann

Cancer of the prostate wasn't Virgil's first bout with the dread disease.

I remember back at Riverside in the early 1950s when, one Friday morning, doctors discovered a cancerous lump on Virgil's right hand between the thumb and index finger. They scheduled an operation for that very morning, at which point Virgil called me, almost hysterical, to warn me that two days later I would have to substitute for him for both the morning service and the afternoon oratorio (which was no less than Vaughan Williams "Dona Nobis Pacem"!). Even though I was terrified, I was too young to know how terrified I should have been!

We naturally feared that this dreadful news would depress Virgil, and diminish his spirit and zest for life. Oddly, it did not. He was determined to maintain the most positive, optimistic outlook on the situation; and he vowed he would "lick this damned disease!" From that time on, he engaged the services of the leading physicians and oncologists, most of them in San Francisco, to declare an all-out war on his condition.

The doctors adored him, appreciated his genius, and enjoyed his boisterous sense of humor. Virgil explained his situation to all of us fully in his simplistic way: that all the treatments boiled down to three choices: "You can cut it, burn it, or poison it!"

Virgil had already had surgery, albeit botched; and so chemotherapy was considered. Some doctors were concerned about the side effects, however. Virgil might be sick to his stomach constantly, and not be able to play concerts, which everyone knew was the main driving force of his life. Without the possibility of performing, Virgil would probably have deteriorated much more rapidly. Thus, his successful career was a true blessing at the end of it.

Considering all these factors, Virgil's doctors decided that his major therapy should be cobalt treatments. To their credit and relief, Virgil responded well to them. They were relatively painless; and the worst side-effect was the inconvenience of having to schedule them during his usual sleeping hours, which could otherwise go on well into the afternoons.

He was delighted with the results, and he began to look and feel like his old self, continuing his busy schedule. He enlisted the advice of nearly every doctor and friend he encountered without ever contradicting the treatment plans of his primary care physicians. The people who knew of his condition (and the number was growing proportionally to the solemn oaths of secrecy he extracted!) sent him articles on the subject. He read about new "cures" and encouraging treatments and drugs. The one that most intrigued him, for which he was most optimistic, was Interferon, which was still experimental and not yet available.

David was convinced that nutrition would play a primary role in his recovery, and so he purchased a giant juicing machine that they carried everywhere they went. David would prepare huge doses of carrot and other juices for Virgil to consume daily. During one of their visits to San Francisco, he went to a health food store to buy wheat grass juice, which was an emerald green concoction that certainly smelled like grass. Virgil dutifully drank it all.

I have to say that David was wonderful to Virgil. He catered to his every need. Apparently, Virgil's health crisis brought out the best in David; and it was touching to see him go to work to help his friend. One afternoon, just before Virgil got up, David was preparing some kind of beet juice and said, "I'll have to hurry because it's soon going to be honeydew time."

I asked him, "Do you put honeydew melons through the juicer?"

He said, "No, Ted. Virgil will soon be getting up and saying, 'Honey do this, Honey do that.' That's honey-do time!"

We laughed, because we both knew it was true.

89. A Very Nice Negress

Virgil had to spend several nights in San Francisco's Presbyterian Hospital before his cobalt treatments. These arrangements were more of an ordeal for the hospital staff than they were for Virgil. I remember one of the first times I saw him there (and we always visited him at least once a day when he stayed there), I read a note stuck on the door in his unmistakable handwriting forbidding anyone from disturbing him until after 12 o'clock noon! Everyone ignored his instruction, of course; but they kept the note attached for everyone's amusement.

I knew the hospital well, for my mother had spent a great deal of time there. She had passed away on the same floor as Virgil's room.

Bill Armstrong was a highly respected cardiologist on the staff of that hospital. Virgil was grateful for Bill's vigilance in every matter, saving him from redundant examinations and the endless visits by curious interns. Reid and I had special visiting privileges, and we usually saw Virgil after 10:00 p.m. We would bring him ice cream or sweets he always loved. There he'd be, propped up in bed reading, with his cape around his shoulders. He'd fly out of bed to greet us; and we would accompany this "madman" in his hospital smock that split down the back, with his red-lined cape on to cover his backside, to the nurse's station where there was a refrigerator. Virgil would push the entire store of medications aside, for he intended this refrigerator to store his private cache of ice cream! The nurses had gotten quite used to him, and most of them adored him. He called everyone by name, and he kept them in stitches with his irreverent quips and funny stories.

During one hospital stay, we advised Virgil to watch a television rerun of "The Joy of Bach," which was a program in which he had participated. He and the incomparable Rosalyn Tureck spoke about their respective approaches to performing the music of Bach. Their relationship began when he and Rosalyn were the attractions for what amounted to a cultural singles weekend on a posh Long Island Estate (called Harrison House) for an event called "Close Up On Bach." Marshall had dreamt up the idea, Richard made most of the arrangements for Harrison House, and nearly 150 people paid to attend.

Virgil was delighted to learn that "The Joy of Bach" was still being aired, and so he alerted the nurses and most of the other patients on the floor to watch it as well. We were all amused at the strong personalities and showy antics of these two virtuosos, and Virgil sometimes roared with laughter watching himself and Rosalyn trying to outdo each other.

"Listen to that!" he'd say. "What a lot of nerve she has! But she sure can play!"

During his frequent visits to San Francisco during the next few months, Virgil hoped to continue seeing as many of the people he adored as possible, and to visit the places he loved most on the West Coast. David told me that Virgil seemed to be revisiting his past everywhere he could all across the country as well as in Europe on his most recent jaunt. David believed that even though Virgil was confident in recovering completely from the cancer, he still didn't want to miss what could also have been his last opportunity to re-experience all the places, friends, and musical instruments that had delighted him the most throughout his colorful life.

In June 1977, Virgil and David traveled through San Francisco on their way to Virgil's first concerts in the Far East. Richard had arranged for him to perform a one-concert version of "The Bach Gamut" at the NHK Concert Hall in Tokyo, as well as the Jongen *Symphonie Concertante* with the NHK Orchestra.

Rosalyn Tureck and Virgil Fox at Harrison House (Herbert Hoover's summer White House) in Glen Cove, New York for "Close Up on Bach"

The NHK is Japan's largest television network, and obviously more dedicated to classical music than any U.S. network! Their concert hall has a large five-manual tracker organ built by the German company, Schuke. It has both a movable console, with electric action, and a tracker affair stuck somewhere underneath the pipes, where a performer using it would be hidden from the audience. (Poetic justice!) Obviously, Virgil chose the movable console.

If he had any concerns about whether the Japanese would be critical of him and his style of playing, he needn't have entertained them. Although these audiences were normally reserved, these people actually stomped and screamed! They had never imagined anyone could play the organ like Virgil played it; and they had almost never seen an organist use NHK's movable console–or play from memory!

Virgil was very taken with the Japanese, and he had a splendid time in their country. He told us, however, that the German console on which he played was laid out all wrong; and so he had requested (among other things) that the Great-to-Pedal 8-foot coupler be wired to a different toe stud. The organ's custodians were incredulous, saying that since the organ had been fabricated in Germany, it must therefore have been "correct." Virgil warned them that he wouldn't play a note until the console was standard according to his American requirements. Following this International Incident, they finally acquiesced. Once his huge success with the two concerts had established his authority, he looked forward to returning. The Japanese wanted him to play in other cities. Unfortunately, he never returned.

Virgil in Tokyo with the NHK Symphony

Shortly after he returned from Japan, he stayed with us in San Francisco to be "zapped," as he called the cobalt treatments. He was practicing at Bill Armstrong's house one evening, and Bill noticed that Virgil's hands seemed to be operating slightly differently from how they usually appeared when he played on the keyboards. Virgil saw nothing different, and swore his hands felt as comfortable as always. He said, "Well, Honey, you don't hear any mistakes, or notice too many split notes, do you?"

Nevertheless, Bill ordered X-rays taken of Virgil's hands. They revealed that several small fractures had begun to occur in Virgil's bones. We were horrified!

Bill also suggested that Virgil visit a prominent neurologist to see why his hands looked the way they did on the keyboards. It turned out there was a somewhat sizable tumor growing behind Virgil's ear that was pressing nerves that controlled motor neurons which, in turn, controlled Virgil's hand and finger dexterity. Virgil's primary physicians came together and recommended that Virgil have an immediate operation to remove the tumor. Back went our dear friend to Presbyterian Hospital, this time for a serious surgery.

Dr. Armstrong

When Virgil began to complain to me of bone pain, we realized that the cancer had spread widely. At this point, only palliative therapy (but no cure) was possible.

In July 1978, he called me while on tour to say that he was having trouble moving his left hand and fingers. The problem got so bad that he had to cancel several concerts. He flew to San Francisco where we discovered that his cancer had begun to involve his nerves. We began radiation treatments immediately, and his neurological problems abated over the next few weeks.

Virgil was brave, and tried to cover his concern with his usual fun self. He confessed to me, however, that he was terrified. When the surgery was scheduled, we were at the hospital one late afternoon and heard Virgil's tale of one of the nurses, "a very nice 'Negress,'" who came into the room to weigh him, followed by a scale the size of a Steinway piano! "I'll never know why they wouldn't let me step on an ordinary scale in the next room! Maybe they wanted to weigh my brain!"

(Once, when we stayed too long after visiting hours, another formidable nurse, who was just a tad grammatically-challenged, entered the hospital room with a warning: "You folks'd better scramble, or I'ze gonna give you all a *enema!*")

Shortly after entering the hospital this time, Virgil was told that the operation was canceled. The doctors had decided against it, and he was free to go home!

"Hurray, Teddo! Let's get the hell out of here!"

You never saw a person move so fast collecting his belongings, and making a beeline for the door! A great weight had been lifted from him. He hadn't wanted the operation, and now he felt liberated. We found out later that the surgery was so delicate and serious that had there been a single slip, Virgil might never have played again. Every one of Virgil's doctors agreed that the risk of such an outcome was unacceptable. They felt that performing was the best treatment available to him. However, they decided to treat the tumor with more cobalt treatments like the ones that Virgil had responded to so well previously. Virgil was concerned, however, that the number of "RADS" they were giving him was growing ever higher, and couldn't keep going up indefinitely–or so he believed. The treatments worked effectively, however. The tumor shrank quickly, much to everyone's relief.

Marshall Yaeger

I'm sorry to report that Ted Worth was almost as bigoted as Virgil, and used to drive me crazy with his racist remarks, which he, and several others mentioned in this book, often employed purposely to amuse themselves by risking offending me. These remarks weren't made out of cruelty or viciousness, but because the people making them thought it was really funny to see me squirm over, what to them, was an innocuous use of words like "Negress," for example, or "Jewess."

I could never understand how homosexuals (or African-Americans—such as Colin Powell, who, if a few skins had been tinged differently, or a few tables turned another way, would obviously have forced President Truman, in 1950, to continue segregating the Army!), or Jews (like my grandmother, who assumed that all Christians were drunkards and therefore always referred to gentiles with the same word, "schicker") could fail to understand that patronizing a group of people in order to be smart or funny (or worse, "moral"!)—isn't smart, funny, or moral! Other people, who consider themselves indisputably superior to homosexuals, African-Americans, or Jews, say equally cruel things about these minorities behind their backs. How, then, can otherwise fine and talented people who are members of minorities themselves (like Virgil Fox, Ted Alan Worth, or Colin Powell) fail to connect the dots? Bigotry is bigotry regardless of who practices it or what bloodstained or questionable flags are waved to excuse it.

I never heard Virgil use disparaging words about minorities until David came on the scene. Many of Virgil's friends were African-American, and I believe he was capable of adoring them as much as any of his white friends. David, on the other hand, got Virgil used to using the "N" word to refer to African-Americans and the "K" word to refer to Jews (although not around me). For Richard, it got pretty awful.

One hot summer, while Richard and I were still living on Virgil's estate, a race riot erupted in Englewood that seemed to ter-

rify the entire population. I recall standing in the driveway with Virgil and Richard while gangs of police cars raced up and down Palisade Avenue with full sirens blaring. Virgil turned to me and said, "Marshall! What do they want?"

I responded rudely. "What 'they' want, Virgil, is for you to stop calling them 'niggers'!"

He didn't like my answer one little bit; but I finally got to make my point.

Robert Fry

I first met Virgil Fox three days after I began working for Richard Torrence's management when I was commandeered to sit in Virgil's Cadillac during a business meeting in New York. The idea was that Virgil shouldn't have to pay for a parking lot. ("Oh, Bobby, I'm so sick of all this money changing hands!" he once said to me.)

All went well as we took off for Manhattan until Virgil realized, at the George Washington Bridge, that his toll book had expired. Gleefully, he ordered everyone to look out for a toll booth with a "colored girl" in attendance. He planned to divert the ticket-taker's attention from the expiration date by innocently asking (in his most charming and naïve manner) if this was the weekend for setting back the clocks.

Virgil was never subtle, especially when acting like a bigot; and he wasn't embarrassed in the least about his conviction that a black woman would be most likely to fall for his little scam—which, I'm embarrassed to say, went off without a hitch.

While the charmed attendant passed on his question to the next toll booth, Virgil helped her finish by tearing the ticket from the book himself ("Pull it, Honey!") then stepping on the gas—hard.

So Virgil saved himself a buck and a half, only to have his prejudice and stinginess fixed forever in what's likely to be a definitive biography.

Be warned!

90. I've Always Preferred My Organs Upright!

Virgil continued to be in contact with Dr. & Mrs. Schuller, who remained a great comfort to him throughout his ordeal. They certainly enriched his spiritual life; and their positive approach to every human problem gave Virgil the strength to carry on, possibly to conquer his affliction.

Meanwhile, they intelligently chose him to design their magnificent new organ for the Crystal Cathedral, a huge building, which the internationally renowned architect Philip Johnson was in the process of designing. This commission, and the thought of hearing and playing such an instrument, buoyed Virgil's spirits considerably, and refreshed his artistic sensibilities. The Schullers' plan was to move most of the five-manual Ruffatti from the old church (which was now called the Arboretum). They would leave the Antiphonal Organ—which was a complete instrument in itself, with its own two-manual console—in the balcony of the Arboretum so there would be an organ in that room for special assemblies.

A few years earlier, Dr. Schuller and Richard Unfreid, then Organist of the Garden Grove Community Church and its "Hour of Power," had intelligently taken advantage of a great opportunity. During one of the "re-do" experiments to improve the abysmal acoustics of New York City's Philharmonic Hall, the management had elected to throw out a marvelous baby instead of some tepid bath water. It chose to eliminate the fine four-manual, 98-rank Æolian-Skinner organ that Virgil, E. Power Biggs, and Catherine Crozier had dedicated in 1962. The management claimed that not only did they need the backstage space, but also the organ was harmful to the acoustics!

The organ world, which has most often been comprised of meek, fragmented, and divisive factions (that make up parts of my "worst world in the world") whimpered in its usual feeble way at this cultural disgrace. When Dr. Schuller made an offer to buy the beleaguered instrument, the hall accepted, and the deed was done! New York City's loss became a permanent gain for the Crystal Cathedral and for Southern California.

The Schullers stored the Lincoln Center instrument near the cathedral's campus until the church's overall design for the organ could be determined. Opinions were solicited from all over the country, but no clear consensus emerged on what to do with these two great instruments: whether to start again from scratch, or to choose a builder to finish the project.

Dr. Schuller placed Virgil in complete charge. Virgil decided that both organs should be combined as one, as they had similar specifications. He also recommended that the Ruffattis should be the ones to rebuild both instruments. His recommendation, of course, not only pleased me, but also obviously vindicated my artistic judgment (finally!) about the quality of the Ruffatti pipe organs, at least in the opinion of the greatest organist in the world!

Virgil recommended enlarging both instruments, which then totaled almost 200 ranks, by an additional 100 ranks, including one rank of full-length 64-foot pipes! The Ruffattis shuddered at this last request, fearing that the architect would never provide the space needed for such an enterprise for a single rank of organ pipes! Furthermore, the weight of such a rank when added to the 100 *additional* ranks that Virgil recommended would require an expensive and massive amount of structural support.

I told the Schullers to proceed with Virgil's plan. If it began to appear that the space and money were not going to be available, Virgil and the Schullers could always change the plan.

It didn't take long for Virgil's grandiose scheme to be diminished. Philip Johnson had completed almost all of his final plans for the cathedral (which called for a freestanding instrument). Virgil went to Dr. Schuller to ask for more space to be left for the organ, or for the architect to create new space. He was also troubled that Johnson had left too little space for the choir, which he believed should number well over 300 singers. Johnson's plans would have accommodated no more than 100.

Virgil's idea was that the church should have a large choir that would rival the Mormon Tabernacle. The builders explained that adding just the space to accommodate a larger organ, to say nothing of a choir three times the usual size, was going to cost millions of dollars. The Schullers firmly instructed Virgil that his design for the organ would have to fit within the space originally provided for the instrument. Everyone connected with the project was relieved when the Schullers finally put their foot down—especially the Ruffattis, who were frightened by the prospect of trying to install a 64-foot stop. Virgil continued to pressure as much as he could, but the current smaller design was already going to cause weight problems that would be expensive to confront.

For example, the builders had to bore into the foundation of the cathedral (for which the concrete had already been poured). The cost of the organ's twin three-story towers, and its central division housing the enormous Pedal division, was almost three-quarters of a million dollars! This development really bothered Virgil, who was still envisioning more divisions for the future. The Schullers calmed him down by pointing out that he would have to content himself with designing one of the ten largest organs in the world! He simply wasn't going to wind up with the largest.

Virgil accepted the new design with the certainty that the new organ would be one of the most beautiful and tonally powerful organs that he could imagine.

A marvelous and generous woman from Chicago and Palm Springs, Hazel Wright, donated money for this monumental instrument, making a one million-dollar gift to the cathedral for the new organ. When the final design of the stop specifications was almost complete, Piero Ruffatti (who does all the family firm's pipe configurations and case designs) immediately began to work on a visual layout that was spectacular. Besides an explosion of pipe-work for the front of the cathedral, there was a large rear Gallery organ, and divisions of exposed, horizontal trumpets high on each wing of the cathedral. These wing divisions were called the "Gospel" and the "Epistle" organs.

Philip Johnson was impressed by Piero's initial design. The two men worked well together in a spirit of collaboration. Piero tells a story about one of his final meetings in the architect's New York office. Virgil, David, Dr. and Mrs. Schuller, Piero, and Philip Johnson and his associates were all present to sign off on the final plans. Suddenly, one of Mr. Johnson's associates warned the group that Piero's design for attaching much of the new organ's façade to the framework of the new Cathedral would not pass the stringent California building codes pertaining to earthquakes. Both Mr. Johnson and Piero were dismayed. Piero had to begin immediately on a new design, which he quickly completed. The new design, which we see today, is certainly imposing, if not nearly as spectacular as Piero's original concept. At least the organ will never fall off the wall and injure anybody in an earthquake!

Despite Piero's brilliant first design, Phillip Johnson took exception to the look of the horizontal trumpets in the Epistle and Gospel divisions.

"Why, Phillip Honey, they'll be stunning," Virgil assured him. "All those shiny brass trumpets! It'll be a bevy of herald trumpets just like the Queen of England has!"

"Well, Virgil," Johnson said, "you may have a point. Personally, I've always preferred my organs upright."

Virgil howled at this remark. The two great men enjoyed working together, and the resulting trumpets were, of course, horizontal, as they should have been.

I recall an evening around our dining room table in San Francisco. Virgil had added some final touches to the console diagram, and had asked us all to sign our approvals to the disposition of the stops, coupler controls, manual and pedal pistons, expression shoes, and so on. He was delighted with what we assumed would turn out to be the largest drawknob console in the world. Most of the other "largest organs in the world" were controlled by consoles that had "tilting tablets," which Virgil believed could never approach the elegance or rich "feel" that drawknobs had. He agonized several times over the possibility of adding a sixth manual, which would had had to be slightly tilted in order to reach it properly; but he never liked inclined manuals of any kind. Therefore, he recommended only five. We all agreed.

I think this monumental instrument kept Virgil's indomitable spirit fueled. He dreamt of its tonal beauty. He wanted to incorporate into the new instrument some of his own valuable collection of what he considered "priceless" stops (he may have exaggerated their value a bit!), which he had collected from the instruments of E. M. Skinner and G. Donald Harrison. He had purchased the Æolian-Skinner organ from Old South Church, Boston—as well as the famous Harvard Chapel organ—so that he could have a proper instrument in his residence on which to practice. Many people in the profession had approached him from time to time to offer him this stop or that one from a fine organ that was being thrown away as outmoded and unfashionable in the name of the "tracker movement" that Virgil detested so much. Imagine throwing away beautiful examples of orchestral stops as though they were garbage!

"Well, kids, their loss is our gain!" he would say.

91. Caméo Quits!

The prospect of performing on this magnificent creation at its inaugural, playing concerts on it, recording on it, and possibly performing for Christmas and Easter services on worldwide television, intrigued Virgil greatly. It drove him ever onward, giving him faith and strength, despite the fact that his disease was spreading, and his treatments weren't entirely keeping up.

Virgil and David tried almost every cure or treatment anyone suggested. They investigated foreign medicines and consulted other medical institutions and specialists recommended by Virgil's many friends and admirers. We were constantly horrified by some of the quacks, kooks, and faith healers they consulted. "Well, Honey, what harm can it do?" said Virgil. "I'll naturally always do what my doctors say, but I want to consider anything that can conquer this damn thing!"

Virgil's professional career was moving forward as usual, despite a few infrequent cancellations for necessary medical treatments. There soon occurred a major change, however. Richard and Marshall were becoming stressed out in the concert management business, and more than a little tired of the constant bickering with Virgil and David. This bickering became expensive when David's litigious nature (he had actually considered suing a dry cleaning establishment for being late delivering a costume in which he intended to perform) led to a constant parade of legal exchanges in order to calculate commissions and expenses following almost every one of Virgil's engagements.

Several times, Richard had politely suggested that Virgil should please begin seriously to think about finding new management. Finally, the orders came out. This time Richard meant it. His management gave Virgil a year's notice to select another person or management firm for the future.

Richard Torrence

> By the spring of 1977, almost one-half of Virgil's performances (and almost every single Heavy Organ concert) required legal intervention and contractual renegotiations before Virgil would go on.

There seemed to be no end to the demoniacal tribulations that David and Virgil could cook up on the road. I finally decided to tell Virgil that I would do my best to help him find another management.

I remember the late night telephone call when I told him I had decided to take my company in a different business direction, and would no longer be working with individual artists. I promised to help him find the best management I could for him, and to make the yearlong transition as painless as possible for everyone.

Virgil was very upset. He accused me of wanting to get rid of him because he had cancer. In fact, he had told everyone that he'd been completely cured; and so I assumed that his argument was nothing more than an appeal for sympathy. If I'd known the truth, I would have waited it out and never suggested such a drastic change, despite my desperation to get away from the constant grief that Virgil and David were causing everyone else on a daily basis.

Virgil joined the roster of artists represented by Kolmar-Luth Management. Although his new managers were helpful and genuinely fond and proud of him, Virgil knew that things would never again be the same. I'm sure he felt abandoned and betrayed. He simply couldn't fathom why both Richard and Marshall would want to leave the concert management business! He was too self-centered to realize that classical concert managements are too labor-intensive (if they care at all about the careers of their artists) ever to do much better than break even financially. Observing Virgil's relations with his managers taught me how much concert artists like myself are so notoriously self-absorbed (we probably couldn't perform otherwise!) that we tend to feel that our God-given talents entitle us to absolute devotion, for which we need express only minimal appreciation. As Marshall often used to say, "Richard and I left the management field because the gratitude was simply too overwhelming!"

Richard had been warning Virgil for years, but it didn't matter. In many ways, Virgil brought about the sad end of his management relationship all by himself (although with massive help from David—but in the end, it was Virgil who was responsible). Whoever was to blame, we were all saddened by the termination of what had been a wildly successful collaboration.

In the final months of Richard's management of Virgil, there was a long overdue rapprochement between Virgil and the Riverside Church. Largely through the efforts of David, and Riverside's

Organist and Music Director Fredrick Swann, Virgil was invited to return to his beloved organ for a gala concert in May 1979. Fred had inherited the Director of Music position at Riverside after Richard Weagly retired. Virgil's departure from Riverside had been such a sore subject, that he didn't enter the doors of the church for fourteen years. Likewise, his relationship with Fred had cooled off after he left. To Fred's great credit, he pushed hard for this concert, doing some pretty fast talking and arm-twisting amongst the Music Committee, who showed little interest in seeing the likes of Virgil Fox again.

Frederick Swann

I almost lost my job helping Virgil get permission to return to Riverside for his final concert. After much polite pleading failed, I barged into a Board of Trustees meeting one night and "lost it."

It worked. Virgil came to play, and I remained at Riverside for several more years until I left to become Director of Music and Organist at the Crystal Cathedral. Robert Schuller has often mentioned that before Virgil died, he recommended me for the job to finish the organ "as I have planned it, and to play it as I would like it to be played."

Virgil had visited Fred and the church several months before his appearance to hear "his" organ, which he knew had undergone changes and improvements under Fred's direction. Virgil told me that he was mostly pleased with the refurbished instrument. The entire Gallery organ had become a proper instrument that could be played independently. When Virgil had opened the new organ, the Gallery division had used the old Hook & Hastings chests and some of its pipework, and was in many ways ineffective. Now there was a grand, new *en chamade* trumpet, the Trompette Majestatis, underneath a new, breathtaking statue called "Christ in Majesty" by Sir Jacob Epstein.

Virgil adored the trumpet, especially since it was a memorial gift to the organ from Tony Bufano, who for years had lovingly cared for and maintained the Riverside organ. Virgil, who had originally invited Tony to Riverside, was extremely fond and proud of his old friend who had done such good work for so many years. Virgil had also known Tony's mother, whom the trumpet celebrated; and he declared it a fitting memorial.

Virgil, although pleased with the "new" Riverside organ, told me, "Oh, Honey, it's still grand; but it's not the same! Wait until you hear the new 'honk' on the back wall that Tony gave in memory of his dear Mama! It's hair raising! You won't be able to keep your hands off it!"

When Virgil made the comment about the organ "not being the same," he wasn't being derisive. He was bound to be critical of any change to "his" organ made by anyone. I know, in his heart, he felt that the instrument had been improved in many ways. The console, which had had mechanical problems from the beginning, now worked perfectly. He said he felt that some of the soft stops had been altered, particularly an old Vox Humana in the Echo Organ. I reminded him that he had directed that the stop be moved just before he left the church, for the chest on which it sat had to be replaced. He had forgotten the truth, which would have explained the difference.

Frederick Swann

A few years after Virgil left the church, I obtained funds and permission to make changes in the organ, some of which Virgil had agreed should have been done years before. Unfortunately, some overly-zealous Fox fans assumed that any changes would "destroy a great monument to Virgil Fox." (Most of these critics had never heard the organ.)

When Virgil returned many years later to play his final recital, he asked me to improvise at length while he wandered all around the nave. I nervously awaited his reaction. When he returned to the console, he said, "Honey, it's not the same organ I left."

Then he smiled broadly and talked excitedly about what he had just heard, especially about the new major reeds at each end of the church. Afterwards, he had a thoroughly happy time preparing and performing a memorable recital.

Virgil wanted us present for the Riverside concert, as well as every close friend and admirer to come. The recital thus became a "Command Performance"—Virgil's command! Reid and I always regretted that other commitments kept us 3,000 miles away from this momentous occasion. Nevertheless, I heard that the audience was filled with famous people and old friends of Virgil's from all over the world (such as Van Cliburn) who came to honor his return to the Riverside Church.

Fred had problems, of course, getting Virgil to agree to a practice regimen that wouldn't alarm the neighbors who lived next door to certain sections of the Great Organ. There was to be absolutely no practice after 10:00 p.m.! In addition, all proceeds from ticket sales were supposed to benefit a cause agreed to by the Music Committee. (This "cause" was rumored to be for Virgil and David's benefit.)

By this time, Virgil and Richard Torrence rarely spoke. However, Virgil telephoned Caméo, inviting him to be his guest. He said that only one ticket was available (which meant that Marshall was not invited). I know that Virgil blamed Marshall quite a bit for Richard's having dropped him. Richard felt that Marshall had poured many years of his brilliance into Virgil's career, and he wasn't about to allow him to be slighted in such an awkward way.

Richard declined to attend, and I can understand why.

92. One Singular Sensation

The Riverside concert was an exhilarating experience for Virgil, and gave him renewed strength to begin what was to be his 53rd complete concert season, 1979-80.

Fortunately, the final concert at the Riverside Church was recorded through the efforts of Virgil's devoted friend, Marilyn Brennan, who had started the Virgil Fox Society. This concert, on his beloved organ at Riverside, is complete with Virgil's inimitable commentary. It includes encores and a closing hymn involving the entire audience. I was privileged to write the liner notes. Anyone interested in the instrument, and what great, musical organ playing is all about, cannot be without this remarkable documentation. Virgil didn't play his best concert ever. He was already quite ill at this time. However, the spirit, drive, musical line, and manual and pedal virtuosity are all there in abundance.

This season turned out to be busy. The devoted team of David Lewis and Floyd Watson, who adored Virgil and seemed to cater to his every whim, drove his Allen touring organ and light show equipment to the various engagements

Virgil and David continued to visit San Francisco many times during this final season, both for concerts on the West Coast, and for

(L. to R.) Van Cliburn, Bird Fox, Virgil Fox, and
Rildia Bee Cliburn (Van's mother) at the Riverside concert.

continued treatment for Virgil's prostate cancer condition, which was deteriorating, and for which he was still taking debilitating cobalt radiation treatments. They often stayed with us, providing rich and precious memories. We often went out for dinner together; but Virgil loved it most when I cooked. He loved it even more when Bill Armstrong cooked!

He especially enjoyed his walking tours of the city. Often, while we were walking around San Francisco, Virgil—swathed in one of his white mink coats, because he often complained of the cold—would stop to take in one of the breathtaking views. His face would radiate with joy. He would take deep breaths of fresh air and say, "Honeys, this is magnificent! How wonderful to be alive, here in this magic city; and, especially, to be with you two wonderful kids!" Other times he would just stare out of one of our windows (which, I must say, offered magnificent views from Delores Heights of the San Francisco Bay and its two famous bridges). Then he would look at me, and I would see tears streaming down his splendid and expressive face. I would put my arm around him and try to think of something positive to say—or even better something outrageous or funny—in order to elicit a loud, infectious laugh out of him, and change the mood. Then he would say, "Thanks, Teddy. I know I have to go on!"

These moments, although they're precious to me now to recall, were extremely hard for Reid and me to bear. Here was my old friend and idol, who never cried, who always knew exactly where he was going, and with a will of iron, now faltering, with an uncertain future, about to break into pieces. The idea of his emotional collapse was unimaginable to us; and yet, it was happening. Still, Virgil did his best not to despair. For the most part, he carried on with admirable courage.

Virgil loved the theatre, especially a good musical comedy. *A Chorus Line* was on every San Franciscan's lips at the time, and Virgil took us to see a marvelous matinee performance. Before dinner, Virgil took a short rest on our living room sofa. I was reading, and I noticed that he couldn't stop repeating the infectious rhythm and drive of the song "One Singular Sensation." I think he loved its vitality. I went back to reading. When I next looked over, I saw him resting peacefully with both of his beautiful, artistic hands crossed on his chest. I don't think I'd ever seen Virgil asleep before. I remembered him always as a hurricane of motion, or engaged in lively conversation.

As I think anyone might in my situation, I had the eerie sensation of seeing how he would look in his coffin, but only for a moment.

It was during this period that Virgil made a curious decision. He decided to adopt David as his son! He mainly wanted to make sure that David would have no problems inheriting the fortune he had planned to leave him in his will. Sometimes a relationship between an older and a younger man leading to an inheritance provided grounds for contesting a will; and Virgil didn't want members of his family to overturn his resolution to name David as his sole heir.

There was a major problem, however: homosexuals adopting each other is against the law in the State of Florida (and only Florida!). Thus, Virgil and David had to pretend to be residents of California in order for Virgil to adopt David in California. In so

Virgil's white mink coat (late 1970s)

doing, Virgil perjured himself, and thus canceled the legal force of the adoption—a problem that would surface later when the family did, in fact, contest Virgil's will.

(What happened was that Virgil's brother, Warren, counter-sued David in response to David's suing him, and tying up Bird's estate after both she and Virgil had died. David claimed, by some mysterious logic, that he was Bird's legal grandson because of Virgil's having adopting him. Thus, he felt he was entitled to one-half of Bird's multi-million dollar estate!)

One evening, as Bill Armstrong was serving dessert to us in his house, Virgil posed an odd question to us. "Suppose a person were to give power of attorney to a friend. Would that entitle the friend to write checks on that person's account until there was no more money left? Or could there be a limit to how much the friend could draw?

"Maybe half?" Virgil went on. "How can you do it legally? Is it possible?"

All of us were bewildered and embarrassed, as poor David was sitting right there amongst us! Virgil was obviously worried that if he gave David power of attorney, all the money might disappear. We suggested that one needed to choose a person one could absolutely trust before giving anyone such power. I asked Virgil, "Are you referring to David?"

"Oh, Honey don't be silly, certainly not!" Virgil said.

He wasn't being truthful, however; for it turned out that Virgil was beginning to have trouble signing his name with the unique flourish he always used. He was also concerned that he might create a disaster unnecessarily by enabling David to sign checks for him simply as a matter of convenience.

---

93. Burying a Hatchet

It was during this visit to San Francisco that I decided to try to bring Virgil and his old friend, partner, collaborator, and lover, Richard Weagly, together "to bury any old hatchets." They hadn't seen or spoken to each another in fifteen years. Richard was living in semi-retirement in Southern California. He had been Director of Music at La Jolla's Bishop School, and served as the music director and organist of a large Roman Catholic church in San Diego. Some years earlier, he had married an old friend and ardent admirer, Anna Brandt, whom we had all known and loved from the old days at Riverside. Anna was the librarian for the Riverside Church Choir, and so she obviously understood the entire situation.

I had seen and spoken to Richard and Anna several times in the previous years. In fact, Weagly had purchased a large Rodgers organ from me for his church in San Diego! He insisted that I give the dedication concert on this new organ; and that opportunity brought him, Anna, and me together for many delightful times.

He would often reminisce over lunches and dinners, sometimes with tears in his eyes (Richard was always highly emotional), talking about his relationship with "our Virgil"—which all who knew about it agreed had been a stormy, but certainly creative and important, association.

Weagly would talk on and on about Virgil's great gifts as an organist, about his genius and how much he loved, cared for, and missed him. He would follow these panegyrics with tirades against his former soul mate: his selfish, inconsiderate, and outrageous behavior, and his never paying attention to his great teachers— Wilhelm Middelschulte, Louis Robert, and Marcel Dupré. He said Virgil often flagrantly did just the opposite of what these men instructed him to do. He always had to be the center of attention. Then Richard would reopen his never-ending wound, "that creature!" meaning David.

There always seemed to be a love-hate relationship between the two men. Richard was, however, very concerned and saddened over the decline in Virgil's health. Several times he broke down crying, hoping to see Virgil once more before one of them went "on to glory."

I had told Virgil that I had seen Weagly several times in San Diego; and Virgil seemed genuinely interested in how he was, whether he was aging well, and so forth. I told Virgil that Richard had grown quite stout, but still had his striking mane of silvery white hair and sapphire blue eyes. I finally said that Richard wanted to see him again, and that I thought if I invited him to San Francisco he would probably be happy to come. After all, I said, Weagly had come when I invited him to visit with David McK. Williams several years before. David McK. was then living in a comfortable retirement home in St. Paul's Towers in Oakland. We often invited him for lunch or to attend a concert. He was always a delight, and deftly "held court" at these affairs. Why not? He was a true aristocrat; and he never forgot it. He attended almost every concert of the festival at St. Mary's Cathedral, and his presence had delighted Virgil. Richard Weagly revered David, and so he was happy to come up north and spend a day with him.

Virgil said, "Well, of course he'd come up for David McK. Williams. He'd never come up here for me! I know that devil too well!"

"Wrong!" I replied. "He's on his way here this very minute!"

Of course, I had cleared the meeting with David, who had been the main reason for the two dear friends and lovers breaking up. David agreed that a reunion at this point was a good idea. He was actually gracious about the whole affair.

"I don't believe it!" cried Virgil.

"You'd better believe it," I said, "because we're leaving here this minute to pick him up at the airport and bring him here to you!"

"My God, how wonderful! I'd better go and make myself look presentable. Aren't you kids sweet to make this happen!"

Reid and I went to the airport to pick up Richard Weagly. He was in rare form and anxious to see Virgil again. When we walked into the apartment, he and Virgil embraced warmly—with tears, of course. We decided to leave them alone for a few hours before dinner. We were sure they both felt awkward, having not seen each other for fifteen years, or even spoken on the telephone.

Virgil's only comment to me about the meeting, just as we were leaving for dinner, was that they both had a wonderful time together, and that there were no cross words. He thought that Richard looked quite well, except that he had grown so "large." Virgil was moved and grateful to have had the opportunity to see and talk to his old friend and collaborator one more time. Richard, on his part, was appalled at Virgil's appearance and color; but he tried his best to fight back the tears. Seeing dear Virgil in his weakened state was hard for him to bear.

Virgil wanted us all to go to dinner at one of his favorite seafood restaurants, "Scotts," in the Marina. It was an early dinner, as Weagly wanted to get back to San Diego that evening. Although it was a warm day in San Francisco, Virgil wore one of his two white mink coats with what looked like a matching pillbox hat. He looked absurd, but we had all grown used to seeing him in weird get-ups. Weagly was appalled; but for once, he made no comment. The rest of

Virgil's ensemble was pure Palm Beach. He wore a fuschia silk shirt, white trousers, pink hose, and white shoes—all beneath the full-length white mink coat and matching hat!

I remember the restaurant being crowded, and so we had to wait in line for a quite some time. Virgil, as usual, held court, laughing and telling stories in his stentorian voice. People couldn't fail to notice us being entertained by our famous friend—which he always enjoyed. He had obviously lost none of his flamboyance or joy in being with people and drawing attention to himself.

As we were led to our table, Virgil went first. Some young people who had been in line behind us began to laugh and joke about "the mad queen in the fur coat." (Who could blame them?) Weagly turned on them, tears in his eyes, and said, "That is one of the greatest musicians in the world! He's dying of cancer, and you dare to laugh?" I dragged Richard away from the astonished kids. I was so proud of Weagly, defending Virgil the way he did. I wished he'd done it more often, and sooner. The two men might still have been together!

(Richard Weagly died June 4, 1989.)

---

94. Casa Lagomar

The last time Virgil was on the West Coast was for a tour that took him both to Northern and Southern California. He was scheduled to play in the large auditorium at Marin Civic Center, the unique group of public buildings designed by Frank Lloyd Wright. Whenever he visited San Francisco, he saw his primary physicians, and usually continued his series of cobalt treatments. Virgil and David stayed with us. It presented a peculiar situation for Reid and me because he would play his new Allen organ for the first time in San Francisco—where we were the Rodgers dealers! Actually, I was most interested in how the electronic organ would sound.

Virgil was afraid that too few people would hear about the concert. For example, he wasn't sure that any advance advertising had been done. He had telephoned the presenters, only to hear that ticket sales were poor, which was unheard of for Virgil's concerts. "Kids, you see how they think that just by mentioning my name, there'll be a full house automatically. Why, there'd be an overflow crowd if they just let everyone know I was coming! They have to pay for advertising in newspapers and on radio and TV! What are they thinking of? Honeys! Couldn't you help them out and tell them what to do? You remember the throngs that were here in San Francisco at those fabulous concerts at St. Mary's Cathedral! Can't you guys help?"

This occasion was one of the few times in our lives when we had to refuse to help. It was too late in the game to do much, for the concert was less than a week away. I think it was actually a benefit concert for a small church in Marin County that had dreamed of making a lot of money on the affair in order to pay for a new organ for their sanctuary. (It would be an Allen, of course.) The affair was obviously poorly managed. The night of the event, there were no more than 350 people in an auditorium that seated 2,000!

All the fine and wonderful doctors, nurses, and people who had tended to Virgil throughout his illness and during numerous hospital stays were in the audience. Andy Crow had traveled down from Olympia, Washington to be there too. Virgil was in his usual splendid style, pretending that the hall was completely jammed, and giving of himself to the fullest—as he always did. The only odd thing I noticed occurred during one of his first speeches. His voice broke, and he asked for a glass of water. After a few sips, he was fine, and he played like a demon through a blockbuster program of one monumental work after another. During the intermission, we overheard his doctors expressing astonishment at how Virgil could play at all, considering his condition. Maybe they didn't know our Virgil, and the drive and determination that was so much a part of him.

Virgil actually played stunningly that evening, revealing almost nothing of his condition. He seemed to come alive when he saw the spotlight; and the audience he adored welcomed him warmly. He seemed to put new meaning into his regular speech to his audiences: "If you'll come across, I'll come across!"

He surely did that night, as did they. I should have suspected, although I did not, that this concert would be the last time I would ever hear my beloved friend perform.

Charles F. Swisher

I last heard and spoke with Virgil Fox at a concert in the Marin Civic Auditorium on April 8, 1980—his last in California. His olive skin and quiet attitude gave things away. "Adorn Thyself, O My Soul," "My Soul Doth Magnify The Lord," "Abide With Us Lord Jesus," and "We Thank Thee, God" on the program were quiet reminders to us of what was to come.

The inevitable late night meal took place at the Brasserie in the Fairmont Hotel around midnight. Virgil was in rare form! He had played well, and we were howling over some joke, when he suddenly turned serious and said to me, "Honey, you have been so effusive about my playing. What did you think of my new organ?"

I let a very long pause go by. I looked around, I hesitated, and then I said, "Well, it has a nice Harp!"

Virgil erupted with laughter. "I guess I've been told! But really, what did you think?"

I felt the organ was not bad, but it certainly lacked the power that Virgil always required from an organ. "It had no thrill, nor any magic soft; and the Pedal division sounded weak, sort of like a rubber band," I said. There was forced laughter, for he knew exactly what I meant—and he knew it was true. He immediately changed the subject.

The Allen organ, today, has improved in all those areas; but my lifelong loyalty has always been to Rodgers. The Allen organ was the first credible electronic instrument; but with the Rodgers Touring Organ Program and the involvement of all of the artists, Rodgers surged ahead in its reputation (although never in sales). Still, both organs were "the best of the breed" at that time.

During the summer of 1980, Virgil's health continued to deteriorate. I spoke regularly with him. Although he never complained, he sounded fatigued and unlike his usual self. We had two major installations of Ruffatti organs going on during that period: one in Chattanooga, Tennessee; and the other one, a large five-manual instrument in Orlando, Florida. Virgil had often invited Reid and me to visit his handsome home and spend some time with him in Palm Beach. In June, Reid and I were finally able to accept his invitation. When we arrived, Virgil was in St. Joseph's Hospital for radiation treatments, and he had to spend the night there. David was a gracious host. He assured us that Virgil would return the next afternoon.

The house was grand, with large, spacious rooms and a beautiful music room on the second floor that was walled with linen-fold paneling. I'm sure the main reason Virgil bought the house was that he envisioned a grand organ at one end of the paneled room. This room had been a dining room in the original, much larger house, which was now detached from the main house. Virgil's new home was airy and light; and his colorful furnishings fit right into the tropical environment. The pool and gardens were great! It was the nicest house that Virgil ever owned!

When Virgil arrived home late the next afternoon, Reid and I were shocked by his physical appearance. In just a few months, he had deteriorated considerably. He seemed thin and frail; his color was bad; and it was hard for him to walk. We tried desperately to fight back tears and keep from breaking down. Virgil's spirit, however, was still alive; and the enthusiasm in his greeting saved the situation.

"Oh, Honeys! At last, you're here, and I can entertain you as you've entertained us so often. What do you think of this palace?"

With that, he embraced us and kissed us warmly, so happy to have friends around him, as always. He went into the house, but not up to his bedroom suite on the second floor, as he could no longer negotiate the staircase. He went into a downstairs guest suite (which would be his until the end) to rest. Just before sunset, he called Reid and me to his side. He said he wanted to get dressed and walk with us so we could see his splendid beach and ocean, which were only a few hundred feet away. We could hardly believe he had the strength to accompany us, but, as usual, there was no stopping him.

"I've waited a long time to show you two kids my ocean and beach; and I'll be the one to show it to you and no one else! It may be slow going, but we'll get there!"

With Reid on one side, and me on the other, we hobbled along the path to the ocean, where his purchase of Casa Lagomar had brought with it a small bit of oceanfront. It felt like I had been given a precious privilege to be able to support a man that I loved so much. He had always been our support and leader. He had always walked briskly in a determined way, and always taken every possible shortcut. He had always pointed to an objective and said, as he pushed or drove us where he wanted to take us, "The shortest line between two points is the fastest way!"

On this day, Virgil was relying heavily on us. He was frail and stooped—a dear soul who had always made a point to stand erect (with a characteristic deep breath that went with it). He now resembled his dear mama, Bird, who was in her 90s!

"I feel like an old crippled lady, Kids," he said. "But I know I'll get better!"

We joked and laughed all the way to the beach, which took us nearly half an hour—to walk half a block. When we got there, we sat down to rest and enjoy the sunset. "I wonder what's biting today, Kids?" he laughed.

We had a joyous time with him for about an hour. The way back to the house provided a spiritually private moment. I don't ever think I ever felt closer to this dear and magnificent soul. Although the experience was heart-breaking, it was strangely uplifting to witness the strength and beauty of a spirit such as Virgil's!

We spent several more days with Virgil and David, who were superb hosts. We visited most of Virgil's favorite restaurants and haunts. As usual, we window-shopped on Palm Beach's fabled Worth Avenue—as we had done years before in New York and Paris—after the stores had closed. We ended the evenings with huge helpings of ice cream and chocolate sauce, seated outside his favorite ice cream parlor in the balmy Florida evening. Virgil was annoyed that there were so few people around. None of the "swells" were in residence, as the summer was ending, and the "Season" hadn't yet begun.

He regaled us with tales of conversations with many of the super-rich, glamorous jet-setters he'd met. "Honeys, I wish they were here so you could see them! You'd love it! In a month or so, the streets'll be jammed. It's totally different then."

He told us about his friend and neighbor, "The Queen of the Hammond Organ," Ethel Smith, a boisterous woman whom he enjoyed immensely and who had been very kind to him.

95. Measuring the Coffin

Bob Hebble had also moved to Florida after purchasing a lovely Spanish-style house in West Palm Beach, a short drive from Virgil's. As always, Bob's new home was stunningly appointed and filled with antiques. He had two magnificent Steinways, a fine Rodgers organ, and an ever-growing collection of mostly impressionistic paintings. For years, Bob had helped Richard, Marshall,

Reid, and me to collect paintings. Several times, he had made gifts to us of fine paintings, some of which were done by his mother, who took up painting when she was in her 70s.

Virgil loved Bob's house and furnishings and was very proud of his success as a composer of organ and choral music. By that time, Bob's original organ works and arrangements were in great demand. Nearly all had been published.

For several months, Bob met with Virgil at either one of their houses to collaborate further, as they had for years, on making annotated, careful arrangements of all the organ literature that had helped make Virgil famous. We organists owe them both a great deal for all their painstaking efforts. Several volumes of these works are available.

In November 1980, Virgil was to inaugurate the new five-manual Ruffatti at St. Paul's Lutheran Church, high atop St. Paul's Lutheran Towers in downtown Orlando. Reid and I had sold the organ two years earlier.

Reid and I had to get back to Orlando where the voicing of the new Ruffatti organ was progressing nicely. Francesco Ruffatti had arrived there to supervise the finishing of the reed stops. Reid soon had to return to San Francisco. I stayed on to assist in the finishing of the organ however I could. I telephoned Virgil nearly every night, and he sounded as if he felt stronger. When the brilliant *en chamade* trumpet was finished, I called Virgil and played it for him over the telephone. He was delighted with the sound, even long distance, and wanted to hear the full organ.

"Hit it, Kid!"

The organ sounded splendid to us both, because the organist sat literally in the midst of 85 very telling ranks in that church. Virgil screamed joyfully, "Oh, I can't wait to get at that beauty! Oh, Honey, I'm really looking forward to playing that concert!"

By this time, rumors of Virgil's condition were rampant all over the country. People who had booked him for concerts that season were getting worried, wondering if he could fulfill his engagements. Among them were the Reverend Ernest Pretsch and Keith Bailey, the Pastor and Organist of St. Paul Lutheran Towers in Orlando. We heard the following week that Virgil was in the hospital again for more treatments. Francesco was anxious to see him, and so Keith Bailey drove Francesco and me to Palm Beach for a few days' visit in early September. We arrived at St. Joseph's Hospital, a place Virgil hated. He used to say, "That's the place old people go to die!"

Virgil seemed in good spirits, and I felt he looked better than he had when we last saw him, several weeks before. The large, private room was gently lighted, with special lights on the bouquets of flowers and plants that had been sent from many well wishers. "Welcome to Podesta Baldocchi," said Virgil, referring to the famous San Francisco flower shop he loved to visit. He was overjoyed to see Francesco, and delighted to meet Keith. This visit to the hospital was to correct a growth in his leg that made walking difficult. "I had some trouble with my leg, Cesco; but these old pins will work fine in a day or two, so they tell me."

I could imagine what was going through Keith's mind. Here was Virgil, nearly crippled, and scheduled to open the new Orlando organ in less than a month—for a $12,500 fee! Virgil was in good spirits, laughing, joking, and obviously glad to have company. Francesco, however, looked terrible.

Virgil wanted news of the progress on the huge organ he had designed for the Crystal Cathedral, which the Ruffattis were now building at their factory in Padua. He wanted to know all about Cesco's father, his brother Piero, and their families, whom Virgil knew and loved. He and Francesco were talking fast and furious when Cesco turned to me, his complexion an awful shade of green. He grabbed me and ran from the room, about to be sick.

Quite sick, and quite soon.

I brought him to the nearest restroom just in time, and waited outside until his drama was finished. He emerged nearly in tears, saying that he couldn't bear to see a man he revered so much in so weakened a condition. He always knew Virgil to be strong, agile, and vigorous. How well I shared his feelings! When we arrived back, Virgil was concerned, for he understood why Cesco got so sick. Virgil was touched, although Cesco feigned a feeble excuse about an allergy to hospitals.

David arrived with some friends who were visiting from Kitchener, Ontario. Virgil loved the company; but at one point, he called me over to the bed and whispered, "You see that man over there with David? He's measuring me for my coffin! He's an undertaker you know."

I almost fell off the bed laughing. Virgil broke up too; but it turned out later that he might have been more insightful than he realized. He knew, after all, that David had worked for a month in an undertaking parlor while still living in Canada.

Dr. Purcell, one of the resident physicians, entered the room. Virgil liked him especially because of his name, which he explained brought to mind the famous "Trumpet Tune" by Henry Purcell. Dr. Purcell and all the doctors and nurses looked forward to looking in on Virgil, as he was always fun and full of the devil. Dr. Purcell asked how Virgil how the staff was treating him, and how the food tasted. Without a moment's hesitation, Virgil replied, "Just fine, Honey. The food tastes like shit. But what have they *done* to it?"

After we stopped laughing, we all took our leave. Virgil needed to rest, and visiting hours had long since ended.

Virgil improved quickly and was about to leave the hospital when David, Virgil's dear friend Robert Schuller, and I came to visit him. This visit obviously did a lot for Virgil's morale, and he was flattered and pleased. After the visit, Dr. Schuller and his television producer and David and I had lunch at a small café. The experience was like sharing a meal with Virgil, for nearly everyone in the restaurant knew who Dr. Schuller was and wanted to greet him. He was gracious and kind to everyone who stopped by the table.

Dr. Schuller was concerned that Virgil's condition was deteriorating, and he asked us all to pray for his recovery—as he was doing. It was during that lunch that Dr. Schuller said to me, "Ted, I want you to know that Virgil said to me that if anything should prevent him from overseeing the new organ for the Crystal Cathedral, you're the only person he'd trust to take charge. I'm counting on you."

I assured him that I would be honored to help him in any way. I believed that Virgil was going to recover, however, partly because I knew how much he cared to hear and play the monumental instrument he had helped create.

96. There Always Were Three

I stayed a few more days in Palm Beach, while Cesco returned to Orlando with Keith. Virgil went home the next day, but had to return for radiation and other treatments every couple of days. We visited him every day, and had some grand times over ice cream and other treats; but we couldn't help noticing how easily he tired.

Bob came over to visit Virgil, who was obviously happy to see him. He always loved it when the two of us were together. We often joked about calling ourselves "the Sisters Death and Night" after two characters mentioned in Ralph Vaughan Williams' *Dona Nobis Pacem*. Suddenly Virgil stared off into the distance. He muttered something mysterious, almost incoherent: "But there always were *three*."

I think both Bob and I guessed that Virgil was referring to the "three chicks": to Bob, Richard Torrence, and me. We had always been his "first-born."

Then he said, "Why hasn't Caméo called or come down to visit me?"

I said, "Richard probably thinks you're angry with him, and he doesn't want to upset you."

"Mad at him! Why, Honey, he's the dearest, sweetest child, and I miss him!"

I said I would tell Richard.

The final night I was in Palm Beach, I was alone with Virgil, seated near his bed. David had implored me to do everything I could to lift Virgil's spirits and try to make him laugh. David was exhausted

"There always were three," Richard Torrence, Robert Hebble, Ted Alan Worth at Emily Spivey's house, Rodgers/Ruffatti Opus One pipe division in background (1973)

with taking care of all the needs and demands of a dying man, and he couldn't seem to make Virgil laugh any more.

Virgil was weak and pale when he grasped my hand and asked me to pray for him. He claimed that he believed he would definitely get well again, but he had too little patience for all the bed rest and the convalescence.

"I have to get ready. The preacher's coming," he said.

I said, "Who's that?"

"The faith healer."

"What faith healer?"

I was horrified! Virgil started his infectious, devilish laugh. "Oh, Honey, David wants me to see him. He's been here before."

"What does he do?" I asked.

Still having fun, Virgil told me how the preacher prayed over him, then held his hand over Virgil's stomach until Virgil admitted he could "feel heat" as the preacher extracted the cancer from his body.

"Oh! My God, of all people to allow such goings on!" I exclaimed.

"I know, Honey; but it satisfies David. At this point, I'll try anything! Anybody at this stage would try anything!" he said, through faint laughter. I then asked him "How much?"

He roared with laughter! "Fifty dollars—each time!"

"Who pays?" I demanded to know.

"Who do you think?" he said. "You devil!"

Then he got more serious, saying, "I love you so much! You'll always be *Numero Uno* with me!"

With that, and with much kissing and hugging, I said my final good-bye to my idol.

I had to leave early the next morning to return to Orlando. As I came downstairs with my luggage, I looked to my right through the banister columns and saw Virgil. He was barely awake. David was administering medication. Virgil was undressed, and his head was bowed. My poor, dear friend looked so helpless and frail, it broke my heart. I wanted so much to rush in and take him in my arms; but I knew he wouldn't want any of his chicks—or anyone except David—to see him so vulnerable and worn out.

I stood there a while longer. It seemed like the peaceful end of Bach's *St. Matthew Passion*.

"*Ruhe sanfte, sanfte ruh.*"

Rest softly. Rest well.

I prayed for God's help to relieve his suffering. I didn't realize it, or want to realize it; but that brutal, tender memory would remain the last image I had of Virgil Fox alive.

I returned to Orlando for a few more days, then had to get back to San Francisco. I telephoned Virgil daily, and he seemed to be in good spirits. Bob continued to visit him almost every evening, as Virgil was keen on continuing their work on the collaborative project of his arrangements of the repertoire for which he was so famous. No matter how weak he was, the work seemed to breathe renewed energy into his tired body.

Virgil was also trying to practice as much as he could. As sick as he was, he was determined to fulfill his obligations for the coming season. One of the first concert bookings was to be an appearance with the Dallas Symphony where he was to play the Saint-Saëns *Organ Symphony* and the Poulenc *Organ Concerto*.

I was concerned. How in the world could this poor, dear, frail man—whom I last saw living in his own guest room because he could no longer negotiate stairs—be able to walk onto a stage and captivate an audience in the special way he did?

Bob had told me over the telephone that he saw Virgil literally crawl to the organ to try to renegotiate the thorny passages of the Poulenc *Organ Concerto*, which he hadn't played in a long time. Bob said that Virgil would often get lost, that he couldn't hear all the pitches, and that his poor fingers wouldn't work properly.

None of these problems deterred him, however. He was completely convinced that he could, and would, appear, as always!

---

97. Going Home to Die

Virgil was driven by another motivating factor, as always. He needed the money! He thought he needed it desperately. He'd spoken to me about what would happen if he couldn't go on tour, and if he couldn't meet his obligations for his extraordinary medical expenses. He therefore wanted me to offer his "priceless" collection of organ stops (mostly some miscellaneous ranks of E. M. Skinner organs that he had in storage in Florida) to Dr. Schuller and the Crystal Cathedral for $50,000.

Ted Alan Worth, Robert Hebble at the Denver A.G.O. National Convention (1998)

I was interested in helping him because the stops, as he described them, sounded like just what we needed for the organ being assembled in Southern California and Italy. Dr. Schuller agreed to Virgil's proposal, and he bought most of the collection for the church. He was happy that his financial contributions would help his dear friend.

Some of the best of these ranks were subsequently installed in the Crystal Cathedral organ. Others were rejected as inferior, incomplete, or damaged. Virgil continued to practice as best he could while continuing his treatments at the hospital. At one point, I was told that certain blood transfusions he was receiving were having a beneficial effect on him, and had given him a new burst of strength and energy.

David Lewis

For the last year or more, Virgil was in great pain, particularly in his middle back. Either David or Shirley Burt would administer morphine shots; but since they made him forget the music, and since he usually flat-out refused to use music, he always refused the shots if he was going to practice or perform.

(Shirley Burt was both Virgil's and his mother's nurse and friend. I'm convinced that she is responsible for keeping Virgil going and for keeping David from having a serious nervous breakdown. She was wonderful, and a refreshing source of reason in our crazy world.)

We found that it relieved some of the pain if we stood behind Virgil and gently pressed on his back. We took turns doing this for hours while he rehearsed. He would take a break every now and then and go lay down on a stack of packing blankets we had made up for him behind the curtains where the stagehands couldn't see him.

Miraculously, performing before an audience released Virgil from the pain. He was transformed, it seemed, by "mind over matter." When the concerts were over, he came down fast. There were no longer any long encores or social encounters.

Once back at the hotel, after a bath and a good shot of morphine, he'd be ready to go. I recall some hysterical dinners while he was in this state. He had no problem remembering all his favorite limericks and bawdy songs. He was like the old Virgil; but it was hard for us to keep smiling. David aptly described it as "Watching a giant bleed to death, drop by drop."

David was wonderful, and as kind to everyone as possible during these last years. He truly seemed to love and adore Virgil. It took me many years to recognize his greater qualities, but they were certainly there whenever it really mattered. Those of us who spent time with the two of them witnessed it repeatedly. Whatever David had done to or taken from Virgil and his career didn't matter any more. He was there to hold our dear Virgil's hand and be with him when he died. All the rest of us got to go back home and try to put the horror of it out of our minds.

About a week before the engagement with the Dallas Symphony, Virgil said he was feeling like his old self and "raring to go!" Wisely, he and David had arranged for the brilliant organist, Ladd Thomas, to come to Dallas as an "understudy, just in case" who could fill in for him at a moment's notice should Virgil's strength flag or he not be able to carry on.

Ladd knew the Poulenc well. Virgil asked me whether I would be willing to substitute if the need arose. It had been so many years since I'd played the piece, and I was understandably uneasy about playing an Allen organ, that I felt it would have been awkward (to say the least!) as well as difficult for me because of the emotional stress I would be under worrying about Virgil's health.

I heard that everything went well at the rehearsals; and the conductor, Eduardo Mata, was pleased with Virgil's tempos and interpretation. He was aware of Virgil's condition, and he was apparently in awe of his determination and artistry.

Virgil was supposed to play two performances. The first one went well. David Lewis stood behind him the whole time, turning pages, and helping with the organ. He gave an almost mystical account of his experience about the concert on a radio program produced in Provo, Utah, devoted to Virgil's life that left me in tears. How Virgil must have hated having to play with music displayed on a rack! He obviously couldn't trust his memory any longer.

David Lewis

The last concert in Dallas, with Eduardo Mata and the Dallas Symphony, was an event. It took place at 8:15 p.m. on Friday, September 26, 1980. Virgil had been practicing at home in Florida with Bob Hebble playing the orchestra parts on the piano. Bob told us that Virgil couldn't play for more than a few minutes at a time. He assumed that an actual concert would be impossible. Virgil, however, insisted. He was determined to start that last season, and to get the ten grand.

When I picked him up at the airport, I was shocked at what I saw. There was the world's greatest organist, and my greatest friend, being wheeled out in a chair looking white and very sick. I thought to myself, "There's no way!"

They told me that Ladd Thomas was there as a stand-in organist, just in case. Ladd and his wife, Cherry Rhodes, loved Virgil; and Ladd's mother had recently died of cancer, so he was prepared and sympathetic.

Somehow, Virgil got through the rehearsal with the orchestra. He finally had to use music, and I had to turn pages. Two things were obvious: he was completely deaf in his left ear; and his fingers, hands, and arms were so weak and sore from bone cancer that he couldn't reach the top rows of the drawknobs. I therefore had to interpret the balance of the organ and orchestra for him and do much of the registration.

The concert went quite well. There were a few missed notes, but not too many. Virgil's playing was as fast and as thrilling as ever. The first half was the Poulenc Organ Concerto and the second half was the Saint-Saëns Organ Symphony. Virgil did all of his usual doublings, playing his non-written pedal scales and all.

I felt something remarkable in the air. Virgil couldn't possibly play this music—he could barely sit on the bench; and yet he did it. I felt the presence of guardian angels supporting him, and I wasn't the only one who had that distinct impression. As the last note sounded, I disappeared behind the console so that Virgil would be alone to receive the ovation. I saw the whole cello section of the orchestra looking like they'd just seen a ghost. The first-chair cellist said to me, "Did you feel it? Did you feel it? I've never felt anything like that before in my life!"

I honestly believe that angels helped our beloved Virgil play this last concert just so that he could take his final bow! It was as if God himself were weeping, saying to Virgil, "Well done, you good and faithful servant!"

The saddest words I ever heard came the next night when the concert was to be repeated. Ladd refused to get into his tuxedo, while Virgil was fully dressed and in the bathroom just before he had to go on. At last, a small, devastated voice came from inside the bathroom. Virgil simply said, "I can't do it." Ladd would have to change and go on in his place.

After the concert, packing up the organ in the truck for the last time, ending my own marvelous career as Virgil's driver, I went up to Virgil's room in the hotel to find him propped up in bed, looking yellowish gray and with huge eyes. He smiled and held my hand saying, "Oh, Chicken, how was it? Was there any color?"

I assured him that he would have been proud of Ladd. Next day, Shirley flew back to Palm Beach with Virgil and told us that during the flight it became obvious to her that Virgil had a large tumor behind his eyes.

Virgil had hosts of friends and fans in Texas, many of whom had come to the Dallas concerts. For example, Rubin Johnson and James Johnston came from Austin. Virgil and David had been guests in their impressive homes many times. Rubin was CEO and President of one of Austin's most prestigious banks, and Jimmy was Vice President. They had flown to Dallas that day in their private jet to be at the concert and see Virgil. Many times during the previous years, they had been helpful to him, taking him to every possible cancer specialist and treatment center they could find. After the concert, they offered to take Virgil any place he wanted to go in their jet. Virgil couldn't decide where to go. He thought he might like to visit us in San Francisco, where Bill Armstrong and his physician friends had cared for him so well. He did, however, truly love his home in Florida—although he dreaded going home "to die" in St. Joseph's Hospital.

David felt they had to go back to Palm Beach, and he convinced Virgil that it would be the wisest decision. Therefore, Rubin and James took Virgil and David back to Florida.

When he arrived back home, Virgil's condition rapidly declined. The effects of the beneficial blood transfusion had worn off, and he became more frail and exhausted than ever. He wasn't eating properly, and he was losing weight. Poor David was nearly hysterical with worry, and exhausted trying to care for him.

Richard Torrence called Virgil, and they reunited over the telephone after more than a year of not speaking. Richard promised to come down to Florida within the week and Virgil insisted he stay with him and David. Richard said it would be too much trouble for David, and explained that he had already arranged with Bob to stay at his home in West Palm Beach.

"The bathrooms are too small!" Virgil insisted. "Stay with us!"

Within a short time, Virgil returned to the dreaded hospital. He almost never complained about pain or discomfort, and he was always reluctant to take painkillers. Now, when he really needed them, the doctors apparently were too cautious about giving him morphine to ease the pain. They knew they had a famous patient at the hospital, and I believe they were afraid to give Virgil enough painkillers to make him comfortable lest they be accused of making a high-profile celebrity drug-dependent.

We all found the situation intolerable. The idea of Virgil's suffering was especially unbearable to those of us who loved him dearly. I understand that during the last few days of his life, he suffered terribly, going in and out of a coma. To make matters worse, the hospital prevented David from being with him full-time in his room, claiming that he wasn't a blood relative! David told me about Virgil crying out in pain, and speaking incoherently in French as if he had been in Paris.

We were appalled at this kind of treatment, and we arranged for Bill Armstrong to fly to Florida in order to demand that Virgil be released from the hospital. Bill would then care for him at home, giving him whatever pain relief he needed, assisted by Shirley Burt.

This plan was well underway when on an early Saturday morning, October 25, 1980, Virgil died.

The greatest light of the organ world we had ever known had gone out of our lives. I got the news from Bob Hebble and Bill Armstrong almost simultaneously. I was devastated. I wasn't surprised that Virgil had passed away—we all knew his death was imminent. I was grieved that he had suffered so greatly. I was sickened that he was unable to escape from the hospital that he so dreaded. I gave him the same splendid salute that he had given his Aunt Etna and his dear friend Anne Archbold years before: "Have a wonderful trip, dear Virgil!"

Richard Morris

I learned of Virgil's death just before a concert in Charleston, West Virginia. Bob Kendrick, also a former "driver/slave" for Virgil broke the news to me. To my surprise, since I was never part of Virgil's "family," I broke down crying. It was as if I had lost my father. In a professional sense, I suppose I had.

Bob consoled me with a remark that Virgil once made about me that I've cherished ever since. "That Morris boy!" he said. "He smokes, he drinks, and he's a Catholic! But after I'm gone, he may be the only one left."

I'm not sure exactly what Virgil meant; but I've been trying to live up to those expectations ever since.

Robert Hebble

In 1979, I bought a house in Florida about a mile from Virgil's house in Palm Beach. I moved in ten months before he died.

Virgil kept up a bit of a concert schedule, but most of the time he was either at home or in Good Samaritan Hospital in West Palm Beach. He would invite me over every single evening that he wasn't out of town to talk about music, and we decided it might be a good idea to document the actual performance practices for some of the various works that made Virgil famous.

When I would get to the hospital, Virgil was sometimes in such great pain he could hardly raise his head. He would say, "Oh, Bobby, I don't think I can do this tonight, I just feel so awful!"

I had my tape recorder and some music paper and scores, and I'd ask him a few questions about future organ transcriptions or arrangements we might write. I'd say something like, "I'll leave in a minute; but before I go, could you just tell me, in this piece, where do the Swell reeds come on?"

Immediately, Virgil would rise up, pull over a small table, prop the music on the table, dangle his feet, and for the next several hours, begin to play the Riverside Church organ in his mind. He'd play the metal table, and he'd dictate to me: "Hit 'Swell One', open the Choir box half way," and so on, while I furiously copied down whatever he said.

Shortly after, his doctors told me, with a single voice, "Virgil's in such great pain that the morphine doesn't help him any more. The only time he's pain-free is when you talk to him about the music!"

Of all my reasons to be grateful to Virgil for his contributions to my life, I thank God for being able to help in that way.

Over the course of those ten months, every week the time diminished a little more that Virgil could work with me. Toward the very end, we could work only for fifteen or twenty minutes. David always saw to it that we weren't disturbed, and served whatever refreshments were appropriate, understanding how important the work was to Virgil. One night Virgil called to tell me what time to come over, and suddenly said, "Bobby, you've really helped me focus my mind on music, and you've never even mentioned the disease I have— you'll never know how much it means to me and how grateful I am!"

I couldn't stop the tears at that point.

A week to the day before he died, I invited Virgil and David to have dinner with my mother, my friend Ed Krynicki (who later played at Virgil's funeral), and me. Virgil pushed some food around on his plate, then went to lie down until the rest of us finished.

We all went into the music room, and he climbed onto the organ bench and tried to play the first two measures of the "Adagio Cantabile" from Symphony IV of Widor. They were as simple as could be, but he couldn't get the keys down. He didn't have the strength. It was the last time he sat at an organ.

He looked at me sadly and quoted the "sixth Word" spoken by Christ upon the Cross: "It is finished." Then he turned to get off the bench, saying, "Okay, you take it and see what you can do with it."

Those were the exact words he'd used 30 years before, when he asked me for the first time to improvise on the Riverside organ.

When he left my house, he could barely walk to the car. He was about to get in when he turned to Edward Krynicki and said, "Always remember that the space between the notes is as important as the notes themselves!"

I'm sure Ed never forgot the lesson.

Virgil died the following Saturday while David cradled his head, gently speaking in his ear, "Virgil, you've said these words to audiences your whole life. Now, you listen to them:

Come, sweet death.
Come, blessed rest.
Take my hand and gently lead me on."

Virgil turned his head a bit—I'd like to think toward a more glorious organ than he had ever heard. Then he died.

The first half of my life, really, was Virgil Fox. I still think of him all the time. It's an honor to be asked to contribute to this written legacy.

I love you, Virgil. I'm doing the best I can.

Good night.

---

98. The Last Kiss

The news spread everywhere immediately; and for the next few days, telephones rang throughout the world. David called us several times from Florida to discuss his plans for a private funeral service that would take place in a few days at Virgil's house in Palm Beach. There would be a second, more public funeral service celebrating Virgil's life on Sunday afternoon, November 9th, at the Crystal Cathedral in Garden Grove, California.

Virgil's closest friends came from all over the country to Florida during the next few days. Bill Armstrong, Shirley Burt, David Lewis, and Floyd Watson arrived with me from California. Many of Virgil's close friends from Texas arrived. Roberta Bailey Johnson, Virgil's former manager, flew in from Boston. A contingency from Washington, D.C. led by Virgil's dear friend Lonnie Schreiber from National City Christian Church was there. James Dale came from the United States Naval Academy in Annapolis.

Unfortunately, Richard Torrence, who was Virgil's beloved friend and greatest career collaborator, didn't make it to Florida in time to see Virgil alive. On the day he was to fly down, Virgil was already slipping in and out of a coma; and so Richard postponed his trip until after David called him to notify him of Virgil's death. He then flew down for the funeral.

Virgil's mother was not told of Virgil's passing at first. She was in her 90s and was becoming feeble-minded (she barely spoke any longer). It was thought that she might never need to know. Eventually, she was told.

Every guestroom in Virgil's house was filled, and several had to be shared with two or three people. Marilyn Brennan and Virgil's old New Jersey friend, Alice Mathieson, assisted with the meals, acting as major domo for David, who held up well under the circumstances. Richard and I chose to stay with Bob.

I went over to Virgil's house the evening I arrived. David greeted me warmly. He was dressed entirely in black. After an embrace, he took me by the hand and led me up the stairs to the music room. "Teddy dear, you'll be the first of the 'family' to see him. The undertaker's done a beautiful job!"

We rounded the corner to the entrance of a lovely wood-paneled room, and my heart nearly stopped. The air was overpoweringly sweet. The smell of flowers was almost oppressive. Organ music played. It was one of Virgil's recordings! At that moment, it was the "Sicilienne" from the Duruflé *Suite, Opus 5.* The room was dimly lighted except for a single large candle (which looked like a paschal candle).

There was Virgil in an open casket! The sight of him took my breath away. Of all people who hated open caskets, Virgil had been the most vociferous! He had an absolute horror of the practice, always saying, "They'd better not have an open casket for me!"

I was of course disturbed by this violation of Virgil's clear wishes, but I said nothing. There he was, looking peaceful (though heavily made-up), his superb pair of talented hands crossing his body— and clasping a red rose!

Another sight that jarred me was a ring on his fourth finger. Virgil had never worn rings or jewelry of any kind, except for a handsome wristwatch and expensive studs and cuff links that he wore for his concerts. I remembered that he owned a ring; but whenever he wore it, he would take if off before a performance, saying, "It's gilding the lily! Rings aren't appropriate on the hands of a musician."

Virgil sometimes wore some diamond and sapphire formal jewelry, which had been given to him by Florence Candler, and had belonged to her late husband. Of course, there were also the rhinestones on his shoes and jackets when he played his Heavy Organ concerts. Other than those exceptions, I never saw Virgil wear any kind of jewelry in his civilian dress (which was quite flamboyant enough!) in the 30 years that I knew him.

David and I were alone with Virgil's body, when David suggested that I should feel free to kiss Virgil. Although the suggestion horrified me, I was willing to touch one of his hands. The experience wasn't at all unpleasant. David, however, was apparently moved to kiss and embrace Virgil's body. I'm sure the sentiment was genuine, but I was nevertheless appalled. The entire scene was completely bizarre, as far as I was concerned. Shortly afterwards, several people came into the room to view the body, among them, dear Richard—who was as appalled as I, but at least had been spared "the last kiss"!

David Lewis

Preparations for the first, private, funeral were most interesting. David had set up candelabras around the most beautiful teakwood casket you can imagine. Ted Worth kept muttering, "Virgil would hate this!" Virgil had often said that viewings were barbaric, and he would not have one! He said, "I don't want people poking around at me!"

It was creepy. Every morning for a week, David would invite us all to go upstairs and see his "father." A longtime mortician friend of David's was sleeping in the room next to Virgil's body for constant "touchups." Things actually got really funny, and we all felt that Virgil would appreciate the preposterousness of it all. Just before the actual service, we all stood round for a last peek at the corpse when Ted, in a loud stage whisper announced, "Look at the nose! She's rotting!"

99. Come, Sweet Death

The private funeral service took place on a sunny, hot afternoon at Virgil's Casa Lagomar on October 28, 1980. The music room was completely filled. Virgil had previously agreed with David that Richard, Bob, and I, the three "chicks," were to be given positions of honor on a front row sofa, where we were to witness the peculiar but strangely dignified service that was to follow. I say "peculiar," because it was a combination of the standard Christian burial service and some additions from the Rosecrucian Society, of which David claimed to be a member, and about which I was understandably unfamiliar. The officiating clergyman was a Roman Catholic priest of whom Virgil had been fond, the Reverend Father Walter Hartnett, who had also been very attentive to Virgil. Although Bob's partner, Edward Krynicki, had the unenviable job of playing the organ for some of the service on Virgil's tiny, rented, self-contained Rodgers organ, he did a beautiful job. Other preludial music was provided by Virgil himself! (on recordings).

David delivered a thoughtful eulogy, and gave an opportunity for anyone present to tell stories about how Virgil's genius and friendship had touched their lives. This portion of the service was inspiring and touching. There was a single hymn, which was Virgil's favorite, "O God, Our Help in Ages Past." I'm sure Virgil wouldn't have appreciated our "congregational singing." It was weak, as too many of us simply weren't up to singing that afternoon. For example, Richard was completely dissolved in tears, unable to make a sound.

Following the service, there were suitable refreshments. We reminisced around the house, gardens, and pool that our departed friend loved. I remember standing with Richard near the entrance to the house with several other friends when we spied a car that was covered by a tarpaulin on the side of the driveway. It was Virgil's old 1963 white Cadillac Eldorado convertible that had been recently rebuilt. He had driven it until the original engine almost fell out! We recalled our wonderful times in that car. We laughed, and remarked that probably no one else could ever drive a Cadillac in quite the way Virgil did.

David Lewis

I had the fun of driving Virgil's 1963 white Cadillac Eldorado Convertible as part of the move from the Hammond Castle to Palm Beach. What an experience! Nothing worked; but to Virgil, it was a treasure.

The hood, which seemed miles long, opened in three places due to the New Jersey rust. The windows stayed permanently up, the top had seized up, and the heater was stuck on. The return spring on the accelerator was missing, so I had to drive the entire way with one foot on top of the gas pedal and the other foot under it so I could slow down.

The car still moved at the only speed that Virgil ever drove, which was too fast. I think it got about eight miles to the gallon, and we were just beginning the gas crisis.

During the next few days, David consulted us all by telephone about his plans for a public funeral service to be held at the Crystal Cathedral on Sunday afternoon, November 9, 1980 with Dr. Robert Schuller officiating. David's plans were elaborate and included a twenty-four hour period when the public would be allowed to view Virgil lying "in state" in his open casket. We were all appalled by the thought of another open-casket ceremony. How would Virgil look in another week?

Thankfully, the tight schedule of services and other functions permitted no more than a five-hour "viewing" before the service. We were also told that the funeral director (the same friend of David's from Canada that Virgil was sure was measuring him for a casket in the hospital room) took one look at Virgil after his trip to California, and demanded that the casket be closed permanently! He was actually an agreeable man, and a great fan of Virgil's. Finally, Virgil's wishes were to be honored!

David asked me to play for the service, and I was honored. I felt, however, that Richard Unfreid, the cathedral organist, should participate. He was accustomed to working with Don Fontana, conductor of the cathedral choir; and so he accompanied the singers in their selections. I also thought Bob should participate. Therefore, after the postlude, Bob played a splendid improvisation.

Before I could get to the West Coast for the funeral, I was scheduled to replace Virgil at the opening concert on the new Ruffatti organ at St. Paul's Lutheran Towers in Orlando. Virgil just missed his date there, which was the weekend after his death. Richard accompanied me to Orlando for the practice sessions, but had to leave before the concert. Bob came up for the concert, and helped me at the console, as I needed the support.

The concert was memorable: the church was packed. The organ was glorious!

I played like a pig.

I recall finally making it to the last piece—quickly, because I had stopped dead in several of the pieces that went before and just let them be. Bob finally leaned over and whispered, "Either you finish one of these pieces, or I will!"

I got through the last one, but I certainly wasn't applauded back for encores!

It was the worst concert I ever gave. The whole situation overwhelmed me; the great loss was finally beginning to sink in. I flew out of Orlando immediately after the concert for Los Angeles.

The Crystal Cathedral organ wasn't scheduled to arrive yet. The Philip Johnson cathedral had opened only six weeks before Virgil died, and so he never saw its completion. I asked the Rodgers Organ Company to lend Virgil's wonderful touring organ (the Royal V) to the cathedral for the two years between the cathedral's opening until the completion of Virgil's "dream organ." We therefore used the Royal V for the service. It was a fitting memorial, and it sounded marvelous in the spacious acoustics. Those of us who worried about what the tremendous expanse of glass walls would do to the sound were relieved.

The twin towers to house the front portion of the new organ were already in place. They resembled a pair of three-story apartment complexes! In order to cover the open towers (and hide the speakers in them), large, green bamboo panels were set into the towers.

The afternoon of November 9, 1980 was sunny and warm. The sounds of Virgil's artistry filled the cathedral as his recordings played while hundreds of people came up to Virgil's coffin to pay their last respects. David had asked Andy Crow to drape the coffin with Virgil's cape. The famous rhinestone studded silk concert shoes were on top of the casket, along with a framed portrait of Virgil. Sometime during the service, the picture fell off the casket and the glass broke. Richard Torrence and I considered this unexpected touch to be poetic justice for what was, for us, an unacceptably tacky treatment for the top of a casket.

Just before the service began, I played the "Prélude" to Duruflé's *Suite, Opus 5*. The opening hymn was one of Virgil's favorites, "The Church's One Foundation." The Crystal Cathedral Choir then sang Brahms's "How Lovely Is Thy Dwelling Place" and Bach's "Sheep May Safely Graze." (Virgil used to remind us always to play the piece at a butcher's funeral!) There was a greeting and a reading of scriptures by Dr. Schuller. The lovely hymn, "Savior Again To Thy Dear Name We Raise," with descant by David McK. Williams, was sung. A dear friend of Virgil and David flew in from Phoenix to give a beautiful rendering of Gounod's "O Divine Redeemer" in a magnificent tenor voice. Then David gave what should have been a heartfelt and touching eulogy. It started off fine, but went on and on until it began to get maudlin. I seem to recall that David dedicated his future life on Earth to Christ that day, and pledged to take full responsibility for completing the organ on behalf of the Crystal Cathedral spiritual community!

I then had to play Virgil's ingenious arrangement of Bach's "Come, Sweet Death," which was not an easy task for me! I could barely see the stops for the tears welling up in my eyes. I kept telling myself that this work was neither sad nor mournful, but a magnificent testament to the Resurrection. Indeed, I meant the piece to be a joyous celebration of Virgil's transition to eternal life in Paradise!

The silence resounded as the final C-sharp minor chord tapered to a whisper. I was afraid to look up to see the cathedral awash in tears, but Dr. Schuller shrewdly brought us all back with a meditation delivered in his uniquely sonorous voice.

"Well, Honey," he began, causing the audience to erupt in laughter that released the tension. He went on to explain how Virgil called all of his friends "Honey" (probably even the Duke of Windsor!). He told about his and Arvella's long association with Virgil. He spoke of the new organ, how much it meant to Virgil, and how much it would mean to them. His speech was as positive and refreshing as any I've ever heard, and he managed to inspire us all!

After the final hymn (Virgil's favorite, "O God, Our Help in Ages Past") and a benediction by Dr. Schuller, the pallbearers took their places on either side of the casket. The pallbearers were Virgil's two main physicians in California, Bill Armstrong and Dr. Paul LaVoie; his friends from Texas, James Armstrong, James Johnston, Rubin Johnson, and Adolph Kremel; his close California friends, Reid Betten and Gene Burt; and his dear, loyal road managers, David Lewis and Floyd Watson.

These men carried the casket down the main aisle of the Cathedral as I played Mulet's "Thou Art the Rock." Then Bob took over and played an extraordinary improvisation. As they approached the main door, where the hearse was waiting, David Lewis (amidst tears) shouted "Bravo!" and Bill Armstrong cried out "Go, Virgil!" reminding us all of the boisterous cheer at the first Fillmore East Heavy Organ concert. I realized that here was the last, fulminating moment I would witness in a coast-to-coast string of funeral services comprising what we lovingly called Virgil's "Final Tour."

Outside, as the hearse moved slowly away, everyone applauded—for the last time.

Louise B. Clary

I remember being with Virgil at the Peabody while he worked out his arrangement of "Come, Sweet Death." I sat on the bench beside him while tears flowed down his cheeks because the music moved him so deeply. He said, "I want to go to heaven with that tune!"

I'm glad to learn that Ted's "Come, Sweet Death" was probably the musical peak of his final sendoff at the Crystal Cathedral.

For 20 years, I worried they might not have realized what the piece meant to him!

---

100. Les Voix Celestes

After the service, there was more socializing and reminiscing. Many of the stories were superb, and the laughter and camaraderie lasted until late in the evening. It was an ideal time to see old friends, and to become acquainted with many people whom we knew only peripherally. David was somewhat disappointed that the cathedral wasn't filled to capacity. He spoke harshly to the Schullers, because he was convinced that the least they could do for the privilege of burying Virgil would have been to take a full-page ad in the Los Angeles Times, advertising the service.

David was still uncertain where he should finally place Virgil's ashes after the body was cremated. Virgil had read an article about cremation many years before. It stated that the process was done in extremely high temperatures; and that while the flames were consuming the body, there were often great bursts of colored light. This idea appealed to him greatly, and it was therefore the way in which he wanted his remains to be disposed.

We all thought, with the Schullers' approval, that Virgil's ashes should be placed somewhere near the great new cathedral organ. Someone suggested that a tasteful marker, such as a bronze likeness of Virgil, could be placed in the case as a fitting permanent memorial.

David hated the idea. He insisted that a large statue should be erected on the cathedral grounds, similar to the memorial to Johann Sebastian Bach in front of the Thomaskirche in Leipzig! Who would pay for such an absurdity? David insisted that the Schullers should raise the money. He made no offer to contribute to the cause, although he was about to come into a healthy inheritance from Virgil's estate.

The truth of the matter was that David wasn't thinking clearly at that time; and he tended always to have delusions of grandeur whenever it came to Virgil. The Schullers had been generous and accommodating in making the cathedral available. They did everything possible to please David, and to give their beloved friend a wonderful, inspiring, and dignified service. No one could have asked more of them, or of the attentive and sensitive cathedral staff. David was acting in an unreasonable and selfish manner to people who had been good and kind to him. I'm sure their relationship did not go well following that painful period.

Several other memorial services and celebrations of Virgil's life took place in cities from San Francisco to New York. Some were sponsored by the American Guild of Organist chapters, whose members certainly sensed the magnitude of their loss. The last great memorial service was fittingly given at the Riverside Church. It was led by Fred Swann. I'm told that it was a memorable and rich experience (it included a performance of Bob Hebble's "*Haec Dies Resurgam*"), and that it was well attended by Virgil's friends and fans. Virgil, of course, had long since been cremated, and David allowed his ashes to be displayed in an urn that was present at the service.

David couldn't decide where Virgil's remains should finally come to rest. He was annoyed with the Schullers, of course. He considered the Riverside Church to be unworthy of the honor. He apparently concocted a scheme to bring the ashes to Paris to sprinkle a portion around the statue of César Franck in the lovely park in front the Church of Ste. Clothilde. He also told people he wanted a portion of the ashes to be mingled with his own when he passed away and was cremated. He always had strange ideas, and many of his friends thought he behaved almost ghoulishly about the ashes, which he often carried around with him.

I saw and heard little of David after Virgil died. We saw a portfolio of his photographs, which he hired someone to take. He told us he intended to make his fortune as a male model. Richard Torrence was almost convulsed with laughter when he saw these photos and heard about David's intentions.

"Good luck! He'll need it," was all Richard could say.

Virgil left David the whole of his estate. We surmised that Virgil's property in Florida, when it could be sold, would net David about $750,000. Meanwhile, David immediately disposed of Virgil's Allen touring organ, selling it through Marilyn Brennan to a church in the

New York area. He also put the house in Palm Beach on the market almost immediately.

David kindly intended to give several of us meaningful gifts from Virgil's possessions as mementos. He gave Bill Armstrong a splendid diamond and sapphire ring that David had ordered made out of one of Virgil's cuff links that had been the gift of Florence Candler. He gave me a lovely gold ring in which was set the pearl from a stickpin that Virgil sometimes wore in his tuxedo shirt. He gave Bob a Florentine stone fountain (which was broken!) from Virgil's garden, and a collection of Holiday Inn towels that were among the hotel laundry that Virgil used to steal while traveling around the country. (One of these towels was the actual bath mat on which Virgil used to sit to practice. I suppose David considered that this piece of bathroom paraphernalia had mystical properties, since Virgil had sat on it while creating music.)

David gave Richard Torrence a valuable book about Addison Mizner, the Florida architect and designer of Virgil's home. David also asked us if there were any items in the house that we particularly admired. Most of us remembered one or two items that we would have particularly treasured. For example, I always loved the oil painting Virgil had of a French organ case. Called *"Les Voix Celestes,"* it was painted in shades of blue, purple, and fuschia—very impressionistic. It wasn't a valuable work, or even a very good one; but I always loved it. Bob and Richard also made a few similar minor requests. We felt it was fairest for David to retain all of the benefits of Virgil's estate, and so we offered to buy these sentimental items.

For some reason, David sold, stored, or disposed of everything that Virgil ever owned; and he never granted any of our requests.

—San Francisco, 1992

Postlude

Marshall Yaeger

Bird Fox died at 97, only a few months after her son.

David lost his "grandson" claim against her estate, but he kept all of the money and possessions that Virgil owned during his life.

David moved to Canada, got married, and opened a bed-and-breakfast that failed after a few years. According to some, it seems that he gambled a lot of Virgil's money on hopelessly quixotic lawsuits—the most frivolous of which was to sue NASA for mental anguish after the Challenger spaceship blew up.

David went bankrupt and lost everything. He renounced his past ("I want nothing to do with Virgil Fox or any of that past life!") and simply walked away from the house where he had stored all of Virgil's remaining treasures and detritus. Members of the Virgil Fox Society (which by that time had become a strong and tightly knit organization under Marilyn Brennan's leadership) rescued many of the items for posterity.

As for Virgil's ashes, the story concludes not unlike the tale of Moses, who died before his people reached the Promised Land. According to the Old Testament, "only God knoweth of his sepulchre unto this day."

Richard Torrence

I realize that although Virgil is the subject, and Ted the narrator, of this book, some people may consider the protagonist and the antagonist of the story to be David and me. In a sense, we both fought for Virgil's artistic "soul." In the end, David won.

However, as I said to David at the funeral at Virgil's house in Palm Beach, "I think that Virgil made the right choice. You stayed with him the whole course. In the end, he needed a 'mate' more than he needed a manager."

I was speaking then of the private Virgil, whom I knew so well. Taking the larger view of one of the most remarkable musicians of his time (whom I also knew so well), I regret that too many people were offended by a showman when they should have been dazzled by a genius. I think we were well on the way to changing the world's impression. David clearly thwarted us.

All stories end. After Ted and Reid closed Organ Arts in San Francisco, they continued to represent Ruffatti as Worth Betten Associates until Ted died. The Ruffattis were always as loyal to Ted as Ted had been to them—and as Virgil had been to me. (Virgil could certainly have changed managers many times after the phenomenal success of Heavy Organ.)

In his final decade, Ted played many concerts for Rodgers, consulting often with them about organ design and voicing. Eventually, he even supervised the voicing of Ruffatti organs. The Albert Schweitzer Memorial Organ in Spivey Hall, Jonesboro, Georgia (given by Emilie Spivey) is a superb example of Ruffatti's craft and Ted's ears.

Marshall and I spent the 1980s in the special events field in New York, using many of the lessons we'd learned from managing Ted and Virgil. We became the heads of a charity, then professional fundraisers. In the 1990s, our corporation, Circles International (the nominal publisher of this book), became a business consultant to the government of St. Petersburg, Russia, where I lived for seven years as the only American to work closely with Mayor Anatoly Sobchak and his First Deputy Mayor, Vladimir Putin.

In the mid 1990s, Reid was diagnosed with cancer of the stomach. Shortly afterward, Ted was diagnosed with cancer of the bile duct. Reid died in Ted's arms in a San Francisco hospital that Ted's Uncle, Dr. Ludwig Emge (one of Ted's earliest musical influences), helped create.

Bob Hebble and I were privileged to spend some of Ted's last days with him. On October 25, 1998 (which was 18 years to the day after Virgil died), Ted, Bobby, and I agreed to complete the book that Ted had started. Two days after Christmas, Ted died on his sofa in the arms of his brother and sister.

Virgil once told me that he and Richard Weagly had been together for as many years as Christ had lived (33). Ted and Reid were together 30 years, and would have stayed together far longer if they had lived. For many of those years, Reid's parents seemed distant toward the relationship. Ted feared they may have felt that he had robbed them of their child. However, in May 1999, Reid's parents and siblings arranged for Ted's Memorial Service and burial at Valley Forge, near the town where Ted and Reid first moved in together. In death, both their graves were only steps apart. By the time he died, Ted had become one of the most beloved members of Reid's family.

This book, and all the contributions in it by all the writers, most of whom Ted suggested, is a memorial not just to Virgil Fox, but more properly to Ted Alan Worth, who, next to Marshall, was my dearest friend.

With a statue purchased in Italy on the roof of the solarium in Englewood

Virgil Keel Fox

May 3, 1912. . . . . He is born in Princeton, Illinois.

1926 . . . . He makes his concert debut at Withrow High School in Cincinnati before an audience of 2,500.

1926-1929. . . . . . He studies in Chicago with Wilhelm Middelschulte, who was then Organist of the Chicago Symphony.

1929. . . . . He is selected unanimously by the National Federation of Music Clubs as winner of its Biennial Contest in Boston— the first organist to win this honor.

1930. . . . . He graduates Salutatorian from Princeton Township High School.

1931. . . . . He becomes the first organist to win a full scholarship to the Peabody Conservatory in Baltimore, where he studies with Louis Robert. During the school year, he plays five recitals from memory and performs with the school's symphony orchestra.

May 1932 . . . . . He receives the "Artist Diploma"—Peabody's highest award. He has the distinction of being the fourteenth organist, and the first one-year student ever, to receive the award. He is also the first student ever to receive the "Church Organist's Certificate" at the same time. He also receives the Harold Randolph Award ($100) for having the highest examination grades.

Fall 1932 . . . . He goes to Paris for a year to study with Marcel Dupré at St. Sulpice (where he also took lessons from Joseph Bonnet, for which he got into trouble with Dupré).

Apr 26, 1933. . . . He makes his European debut at London's Kingway Hall before an audience of 1,100.

Fall 1933 . . . . . . He makes his New York debut at the Wanamaker Store's 118-rank organ, and joins the management of Bernard Laberge, a major organ impresario.

Jan 1934 . . . . . . He makes his first American concert tour. The Episcopal church on Capitol Square in Madison, Wisconsin declines to book him for a fee of $50!

May 1, 1934 . . . . He is appointed Organist of St. Mark's Lutheran Church (where he plays a four-manual E.M. Skinner with an Echo division) in Hanover, Pennsylvania. Richard Weagly is appointed choir director.

1935 . . . . He is appointed Organist at Brown Memorial Presbyterian Church in Baltimore, which also has a four-manual E.M. Skinner organ. Richard Weagly follows as choir director.

May 8, 1936 . . . . . He becomes the first organist to play a paid-admission concert at Carnegie Hall, New York. He is presented by his first concert management, Bernard R. Laberge Mgt., Inc.

May, 1936 . . . . . . He is appointed head of the organ department at the Peabody Conservatory.

Aug/Sep 1938 . . . He plays in Great Britain at King's College Chapel, Cambridge; Lincoln Minster; Durham Cathedral; and in Germany at the Thomaskirche, Leipzig (Bach's church— where he becomes the first American organist ever to perform publicly there); Marienkirche, Lübeck (Buxtehude's church); and Dom zu Berlin. An admiring reviewer in the *Leipziger Tageszeitung* writes, "He reveals the innermost secrets of the art of Bach."

Summer 1939 . . . He plays "Come, Sweet Death" at the AGO National Convention in the Wanamaker store, Philadelphia.

1941 . . . . His arrangement of "Come, Sweet Death" is published by H.W. Gray.

1942 . . . . He enlists in the Army Air Force and takes a leave of absence from Brown Memorial Church and the Peabody Conservatory. He enters as a Private and is promoted to Staff Sergeant. While stationed at Bolling Field, he plays three recitals and five services weekly. Eleanor Roosevelt attends. He has to nod to her after each piece so that she can check off her program and know where he is. She explains to him that she is totally unmusical! He plays three times at the White House on the ornate Steinway piano.

Apr 29, 1945 . . . . . Staff Sergeant Fox plays a recital at Cadet Chapel, West Point, New York, on a 206-rank organ.

1946 . . . . After having played more than 600 concerts while on duty, he is discharged from the Army Air Force.

1946 . . . . He accepts the position of Organist of the Riverside Church, New York, with Richard Weagly as choir director.

Feb 1946 . . . . He plays 44 major works (in three concerts) from memory at the Library of Congress under the auspices of the Elizabeth Sprague Coolidge Foundation.

1948 . . . . The Riverside Church acquires a new five-manual Æolian-Skinner console for the Hook and Hastings organ.

Jul 1949 . . . . He meets Albert Schweitzer in New York.

Sep 1950 . . . . . . He plays in England at the Cathedral Church of Christ, Canterbury; and in Paris at the Salle Pleyel.

1952 . . . . He is voted "America's Most Popular Organist" by 17,000 subscribers of *Choral and Organ Guide*.

Aug 1952 . . . . . . He plays in England at the Cathedral Church of Christ, Canterbury.

1953 . . . . He is chosen by the State Department to represent the United States at the First International Conference on Sacred Music, in Bern, Switzerland.

Jul 1, 1954 . . . . . . He plays for the first time with the Boston Pops Orchestra, Arthur Fiedler conducting, at Boston Symphony Hall.

Mar 25, 1955 . . . . He gives a solo dedicatory recital on the new organ at the Riverside Church.

Mar 31, 1955 . . . He gives an orchestral dedicatory recital at the Riverside Church with the New York Philharmonic, Dimitri Mitropoulis conducting. The program includes Bach's *Concerto in D Minor* and Joseph Jongen's *Symphonie Concertante*.

Dec 1955 . . . . He plays for the AGO Midwinter Conclave at the Wanamaker Store, Philadelphia.

Jun 1956 . . . . He plays the Guild Service for the AGO National Convention at Riverside Church: American première of Ralph Vaughan Williams' *Dona Nobis Pacem* with the Riverside Choir, Richard Weagly conductor; American première of Maurice Duruflé's *Suite, Opus 5*. He plays "Roll Out the Barrel" on the Paramount Theatre Wurlitzer during a late night theatre organ concert.

1957 . . . . He shares with Frederick Swann the title and duties of Organist of The Riverside Church, New York.

Sep/Oct 1959 . . . . He plays in Europe at the American Church in Paris, St.

Matthäuskirche (Munich), St. George's Hall (Liverpool), Colston Hall (Bristol), the Royal Air Force Church of St. Clement Danes, and Birmingham Town Hall.

May/Jun 1960 ... He and Frederick Swann dedicate the Austin organ in Christ Chapel, Riverside Church, New York.

He records six albums for Capitol Records.

Jun 1960 .... He plays the Jongen *Symphonie Concertante* for organ and orchestra with the Detroit Symphony at Ford Auditorium during the AGO National Convention.

Jun 1961 .... He records Joseph Jongen's *Symphonie Concertante* with George Prêtre and the Paris Opera Orchestra at the Palais de Chaillot in Paris.

Sep 1961 .... He plays in England at St. Mary Abbots, Kensington, and at Birmingham Town Hall.

1961-1962 .... He is presented in several all-Bach concerts at Riverside, organized at his request by E. Paul Fitz Gerald. He decides that playing all-Bach recitals should be a main theme of his career from this point on.

Jun 1962 .... He hires Richard Torrence as his secretary and personal representative.

Jun 1962 .... He plays at Richard Simonton's home for a private concert during the National Convention of the AGO in Los Angeles, California.

Dec 15, 1962 .... With Catherine Crozier and E. Power Biggs, he dedicates the new Æolian-Skinner organ in Philharmonic Hall at Lincoln Center for the Performing Arts, New York.

Jan 7, 1963 ...... He performs the first solo organ recital at Philharmonic Hall (and later that month makes the first recording on the new organ for Command Records).

Apr 1963 .... He informs Roberta Bailey that, effective in June, Richard Torrence will be his concert manager.

Jun 1963 .... He becomes (and often insists on being called) "Dr. Fox" after being awarded an honorary degree from Bucknell University in Lewisburg, Pennsylvania. He claims that the honorific helps him get better service from hotels and airlines.

Fall 1963 . . . . He records an all-Bach album for Command (his first was for RCA Victor in the 1950s, also at Riverside).

Sep/Oct 1963 . . . . He plays in England at Bolton Parish Church and Birmingham Town Hall.

1964 . . . . He records on the Wanamaker organ in Philadelphia in the spring; records the organ at Royal Albert Hall in London for Readers Digest Records in the fall; and records "The Christmas Album" for Command at St. Paul the Apostle, New York.

1964 . . . . He receives the "Distinguished Alumni Award" from the Peabody Conservatory in Baltimore.

Jun 1964 . . . . He plays a morning concert at the Wanamaker Store during the AGO National Convention in Philadelphia, and celebrates the release of his Wanamaker Command album.

Sep 1964 . . . . He begins his "sabbatical" from the Riverside Church.

1965 . . . . He makes two final records for Command, both at Boston Symphony Hall.

Jun 1965 . . . . He resigns from the Riverside Church.

Jun 1966 . . . . He plays at "The Temple," Atlanta, Georgia, for the AGO National Convention.

Spring 1967 . . . . . He plays his first recital on the Rodgers Touring Organ ("Black Beauty") in St. Petersburg, Florida.

Apr 23, 1967 . . . . He plays a Philharmonic Hall recital (Mendelssohn, Duruflé).

Dec 24, 1967 . . . . He performs on the "Ed Sullivan Show."

1968 . . . . He hires Alix Williamson to publicize his career at the urging of Richard Torrence and Marshall Yaeger. Williamson requires that he perform a four-concert series in New York that she can publicize.

1969 . . . . He records an album of hymns on the Rodgers Touring Organ for Kapp Records ("Songs of Inspiration").

Oct 21, 1969 . . . . . He performs "The Bach Gamut" on the first of the Fanfare for Organ series at Philharmonic Hall.

Nov 25, 1969 . . . . . He performs "The Gallic Greats" on the second of the series.

Jan 18, 1970 . . . . . He performs "La Belle Époch" on the third of the series.

Feb 24, 1970. . . . . . He performs "The Contemporary Concerto" on the fourth of the series with the Symphony of the New World (Joseph Jongen *Symphonie Concertante,* Jan Hanus *Concerto for Organ, Strings, and Tympani,* and the Francis Poulenc *Concerto for Organ, Strings, and Tympani).*

Dec 1, 1970 . . . . . . He performs the first "Heavy Organ" concert with Joe's Lights at the Fillmore East, New York, recorded by Decca Records, a Division of MCA Inc.

Dec 14, 1970 . . . . . He performs the second Heavy Organ concert at the Fillmore East.

Apr 27, 1971 . . . . He dedicates the four-manual Saville #100 (172 equivalent ranks; the largest electronic organ at that time) in the Auditorium Theatre, Chicago, Illinois with chamber orchestra, Victor Allessandro conducting.

1971-1974 . . . . . . His four Heavy Organ "live" recordings are listed among *Billboard* Magazine's best-selling classical albums during most of this period.

Summer 1971. . . . He begins his first national Heavy Organ tour with Pablo Lights, playing in Washington, D.C. at Constitution Hall, and as far West as the University of Wisconsin in Madison.

Oct 14, 1971 . . . . . He plays his first West Coast performance of Heavy Organ with Pablo's Lights at Winterland, San Francisco. Decca records the concert.

Summer 1972 . . . . He tours Heavy Organ with concerts at Wolf Trap Farm Park in Washington, D.C. and at Temple University Music Festival, Philadelphia, Pennsylvania.

Oct 14, 1972. . . . . . He plays his final Heavy Organ concert with Pablo Lights in Beckman Auditorium at the California Institute of Technology, Pasadena.

Oct 17, 1972 . . . . . He plays his first Heavy Organ concert with Revelation Lights at San Diego College.

Nov 9, 1972 . . . . . He appears on the "Mike Douglas Show" to promote an album of wedding music for Decca Records.

Dec 20, 1972 . . . . . He plays Heavy Organ in Carnegie Hall, recorded by RCA.

*Stage seating section added for the
sold-out concert at Kennedy Center (1973)*

May 2, 1973. . . . . He appears again on the "Mike Douglas Show."

Jun 15, 1973. . . . . . He plays "Tea for Two" with Liberace on the "Mike Douglas Show."

Summer 1973 . . . . He tours Heavy Organ with concerts at Wolf Trap Farm Park in Washington, D.C. and at the Meadowbrook Festival near Detroit, Michigan. According to Wolf Trap Farm Park (seating capacity 6,000), the two largest "draws" in the facility's history are Heavy Organ with Virgil Fox and the popular duo-piano team, Ferrante and Teicher.

Oct 5, 1973 . . . . . He plays for the first time (as a "Founding Artist") at Kennedy Center in Washington, D.C. Martin Feinstein, head of Kennedy Center, calls two weeks before to schedule an after-concert party for Virgil, expressing surprise that the concert is already sold out! As a Founding Artist, he gets his name chiseled in a white marble wall of the Kennedy Center (and, according to Richard Torrence, "gets chiseled out of a fee!").

Dec 1973 . . . . He records a second Heavy Organ concert in Carnegie Hall, also released by RCA. Audience sings "Adeste Fideles."

Jan 7, 1974 . . . . . . Heavy Organ receives a positive review in *Time* Magazine.